FAMILIES OF VIRTUE

ERIN M. CLINE

FAMILIES OF VIRTUE

Confucian and Western Views
on Childhood Development

Columbia University Press / New York

Columbia University Press

Publishers Since 1893

New York   Chichester, West Sussex

cup.columbia.edu

Copyright © 2015 Columbia University Press

Library of Congress Cataloging-in-Publication Data

Cline, Erin M.

Families of virtue : Confucian and Western views on
childhood development / Erin M. Cline.

pages cm

Includes bibliographical references and index.

ISBN 978-0-231-17154-0 (cloth) —
ISBN 978-0-231-17155-7 (pbk.)
ISBN 978-0-231-53904-3 (ebook)

1. Confucian ethics. 2. Moral development—China—Philosophy.
3. Parent and child—China—Philosophy. 4. Filial piety—China—Philosophy.
5. Philosophy, Confucian. I. Title.

BJ1289.3.C55 2015

170.83'0951—dc23

2014023674

Cover design: Mary Ann Smith

Cover image: © Masterfile

For my parents, who provided the warmth of three spring seasons to my tender blade of grass,

For my husband, Michael—the yin *to my* yang *and the* yang *to my* yin, *and for our children, Patrick and Bridget, who have surely taught me more than I could ever hope to teach them*

CONTENTS

ACKNOWLEDGMENTS

GRATEFULLY ACKNOWLEDGE the help of many colleagues and friends in the writing of this book. I am especially grateful to those who read and commented on the entire manuscript, including three reviewers for Columbia University Press. I owe a special debt of gratitude to P. J. Ivanhoe for encouraging me to write this book in the first place and for reading and commenting on numerous drafts. In addition to his indispensable feedback at every stage of the project, I am grateful for the friendship of P. J. and his wife, Hong, and for their inspiring model of loving, supportive parenting. I also owe special thanks to Bryan Van Norden, who offered detailed comments and suggestions on the manuscript, which resulted in a much stronger book. I am also grateful for his encouragement and for the excellent model of careful scholarship that his work has provided over the years. I am also particularly grateful to Michael Puett, whom I admire in more ways that I can enumerate here and whose suggestions and encouragement were immensely helpful.

I presented material from this book in many different forums over the years, and I am grateful to audiences at the conference on Confucian and Liberal Perspectives on Family, State, and Civil Society at the City University of Hong Kong, the Oregon Humanities Center, and the annual meetings of the American Philosophical Association and the American Academy of Religion for helpful comments and questions, which influenced this work. I also want to thank those who read parts of the manuscript and/or offered helpful feedback on the various philosophical, textual, and historical issues connected with this project, including Eric Hutton, Mark Unno, Pauline Lee, Leigh Jenco, Justin Tiwald, Hagop Sarkissian, and Chenyang Li.

I am grateful for the generous support of Georgetown University, the Oregon Humanities Center, and the University of Oregon for grants and fellowships that provided the time and the resources essential to the completion of this project. I am particularly thankful to the Theology Department at Georgetown University and my wonderful department chair, Chrisopher Steck, S.J., for providing the support that made this book possible. I am fortunate to have a truly wonderful group of colleagues and friends at Georgetown who support and encourage me in numerous ways. While I cannot mention all of them here, I am particularly grateful to Jonathan Ray and Daniel Madigan, S.J., for their interest in this project and for their encouragement. I also want to thank Kevin O'Brien, S.J., for kindling in me a devotion to the Ignatian tradition and for patient, astute, and generous guidance and encouragement in all things. I am truly grateful to my friends in the Society of Jesus for showing me meaning and beauty in another kind of family.

I want to express my appreciation to the entire editorial team at Columbia University Press. I am particularly grateful to Wendy Lochner, my editor, for her advice and encouragement and to Christine Dunbar for her invaluable assistance.

Most importantly, I am grateful to my family for showing me the meaning of all the things I write about in this book. My parents, my brother, Kelly, and his wife, Jamie, and their children have been a constant source of support and love. My husband, Michael—my perfect complement in all endeavors—read every draft and provided invaluable feedback and encouragement and helped me find the right publisher. He also cared for our children for many hours while I worked on this book. Our children, Patrick and Bridget, inspired me with firsthand experiences of many of the things I write about in these pages and most of all with their spontaneous outpourings of love and affection.

INTRODUCTION

THERE IS CONSIDERABLE evidence that parent–child relationships during infancy and early childhood serve a unique and irreplaceable role in moral development. This has been borne out in experiments showing that the capacity for lively expressions of joy or anger in six-month-old infants depends upon their attachment to supportive, responsive parents during the early weeks and months of life, as well as in controlled studies revealing that children whose parents are supportive and responsive in the earliest period of life exhibit an increased capacity for sympathy as preschoolers. Despite such evidence, philosophers have given little attention to the role of the family in moral cultivation during these formative years. This book examines the reasoning on this question by a range of philosophers and scientists—from ancient Chinese philosophers, to Aristotle and Locke, to contemporary care ethicists and attachment theorists—and argues for the importance of understanding the unique and irreplaceable role of parent–child relationships in early moral development, not only for contemporary ethics and political philosophy, but for our attempts to address contemporary moral problems through the crafting of public policy.

Historically, while the views of many thinkers on these issues fall short of compelling, distinctive and fascinating theories and ideas concerning the specific nature of parent–child relationships during infancy and early childhood and their role in moral development are found in the work of some of the most influential ancient Chinese philosophers, specifically those associated with the Confucian tradition. They argue that the general ethical sensibilities we begin to develop during infancy and early childhood are the basis for nearly every virtue and that parent–child relationships are the primary context within which this early moral cultivation occurs. They describe how and why parent–child relationships provide a foundation for our moral development, and they further contend that early childhood development within the family is not simply a private or purely ethical matter; it has a direct and observable impact on the quality of a society and thus deserves the attention of political philosophers and policy makers.

These Confucian views have a number of features that differ from views put forth in the history of Western philosophy. This is apparent in the sustained attention Confucian philosophers give to the role of parent–child relationships in moral development, which contrasts with thinkers such as Aristotle and Locke, who, although they note the importance of the family, dedicate little space to this topic relative to other topics and do not offer detailed accounts of why and in what ways parent–child relationships are important for such development. The Confucian views stand in even greater contrast to those of philosophers such as Plato and Rousseau, who argue that the role of parents in children's education ought to be severely limited. The views of early Confucian philosophers also stand out for their recognition of the critical nature of the earliest years of children's lives; even Locke, who acknowledges that childhood moral education is important and that the role of parents is vital, does not argue for the unique and irreplaceable importance of infancy and early childhood.

More recently, contemporary care ethicists such as Sara Ruddick and Nel Noddings have given sustained attention to the ethical significance of parent–child relationships, but they differ in a number of important ways from the early Confucians. In addition to focusing most centrally on the positions, experiences, and insights of mothers, care ethicists argue that caring in at least some ways takes precedence over other practices, virtues, and capacities. The early Confucian philosophers I examine focus on a broad range of virtues and practices that are a part of moral education and cultivation, with an emphasis on the complementary roles of both parents as well as siblings in that process. Early Confucian philosophers also add a new dimension to our appreciation of the parent–child relationship in their contention that the prenatal period and the earliest stages of infancy are developmentally important in ways that can influence a child's character—an opinion that is not only absent from the work of care ethicists but also at odds with some of their views.

The writings of ancient Chinese philosophers on these matters merit our attention not just because they offer fresh philosophical insights into the role of the family in moral development—we have good reasons to think they *were right* about a number of the ideas for which they argued. This work puts these early Confucian views into conversation not only with the work of contemporary philosophers, but with the best empirical work on early childhood in the social sciences. An extensive body of research in the social sciences—including the work of attachment theorists and human ecologists, as well as impressive longitudinal studies that track the impact of supportive, responsive parent–child relationships from the earliest weeks of life through adulthood—supports and can help us to further develop some of the central tenets of ancient Confucian views concerning parent–child relationships; such work renews and strengthens ancient Chinese philosophy for our own times, demonstrating that many of the views of Confucian philosophers are defensible and worth developing in a contemporary setting.

In addition to extending and augmenting discussions of the family and moral development in contemporary ethics and political philosophy, the philosophical insights arising from these early Chinese views can be applied in ways that promote positive social change as well as policy change. Confucian philosophers maintain that the prenatal period, infancy, and early childhood represent a unique and irreplaceable opportunity for moral cultivation, and they offer rich and detailed accounts of the specific role that each of these stages has. There are a number of reasons that ethicists, political philosophers, and policy makers as well as scholars of Chinese thought should be interested in these accounts. An awareness of how Confucian thinkers viewed these early stages of development augments our understanding of how various virtues and moral capacities are instilled, helping us to understand precisely when the process of moral cultivation begins and how it works. Additionally, early Confucian views and the empirical evidence concerning the unique nature of parent–child relationships during the earliest stages of our development together offer a variety of key insights into the proper role of the family in a society and suggest some specific ways in which we might reconsider our policies as well as our social practices and attitudes toward the family, especially around such issues as mandated paid parental leave, breast-feeding, and marriage.[1] Because early Confucian accounts of moral cultivation and parent–child relationships during the prenatal period, infancy, and early childhood align in a number of key areas with the empirical evidence we now have concerning these stages of development, they serve as proof that Confucian philosophy can be a distinctive and valuable resource for contemporary philosophers, both theoretically (in the fields of ethics and political philosophy) and also practically (in showing how philosophical work can make a genuine contribution to our society).

I have chosen to focus on Confucian accounts for a number of reasons. As I argue, early Confucian sources offer rich and detailed accounts of moral cultivation during the early stages of human development, but no one has yet offered a full-length study of this aspect of Confucian ethics.[2] I contend that there are a number of reasons that ethicists, scholars of Chinese thought, and policy makers should be interested in these accounts. While understanding my aims, however, readers should not lose sight of my disciplinary orientation as a philosopher: unlike scholars in virtually all other disciplines in the humanities, who regard studying works and traditions from other cultures as important, philosophers have been slow to acknowledge the importance of studying non-Western philosophical traditions.[3] Early Confucian views of parent–child relationships, early childhood, and moral cultivation provide a clear illustration of some of the ways in which Confucian philosophy is a distinctive and valuable resource for philosophers as well as others. In focusing on early childhood, however, it is not my intention to minimize the importance of other stages of development; indeed, even though I focus primarily on early childhood, for the reasons described earlier, I will discuss textual evidence concerning the later stages of children's moral development and moral cultivation during adulthood as well. Readers should take this as a reminder of the emphasis Confucian thinkers placed on attending to the entire course of our development. Even though they maintained that the earliest years of our lives play a unique role in our moral development, Confucian thinkers argued for the special importance of parent–child relationships and moral cultivation throughout the entire course of our lives.

It is important to clarify that my central argument is not that we can or should take early Confucian views off the shelf, adopting these ancient views and practices wholesale. I argue that although several features of early Confucian views have constructive value, a number of them need to be further developed, refined, or amended. My argument here is not unlike discussions about the contemporary value of Aristotle's ethics; while several features of Aristotle's view are an excellent resource for contemporary ethics, a number of other aspects need further exploration.[4] Accordingly, I am interested not only in describing and analyzing the views of early Confucian philosophers, but also in deploying them in a contemporary constructive project. Confucian views are valuable for us because they are rooted in another culture and as a result have the unique potential to highlight some of our own unexamined cultural assumptions. This is one of the very best potential outcomes of the more global world in which we live: we have a unique opportunity to learn from other cultures, including the philosophical traditions that underpin and inform them.

In recent years, as there has been increasing interest in Chinese philosophy, philosophers have continued to ask an important question: What are the distinctive contributions that Chinese philosophy can make to our understanding of philosophical issues? There are at least two important matters to address separately, although they are related: First, what is distinctive or different about views found in Chinese philosophy when compared with Western philosophy? Second, what kinds of contributions can Chinese philosophy make to contemporary philosophy? The issue, then, is whether studying Chinese philosophy is constructively valuable and not simply a purely descriptive task or a matter of studying history—be it intellectual history or the history of philosophy. In my view, the question of what is distinctive about the views of Chinese philosophers is best addressed not by lumping them together as a whole and searching for commonalities between different thinkers and traditions but by studying individual Chinese thinkers and the various aspects of each thinker's views. Only after doing this kind of careful work can we fully recognize and appreciate some of the commonalities within the traditions, movements, and periods that constitute Chinese philosophy. After all, if philosophers in another culture were encountering Western philosophy for the first time, and they asked us what is distinctive about Western philosophy, even though we might be able to highlight some broad, defining themes in Western philosophy that were not defining themes in the other culture's philosophical traditions, we would be best able to answer the question by talking about specific philosophers and their views. Certain features of Aristotle's account of the virtues might be distinctive when compared with ethical views in another philosophical tradition, but others might not. What is distinctive about Aristotle's ethics would probably not be the same as what is distinctive about Kant's ethics. So the distinctiveness question can ultimately only be answered by selecting individual thinkers and views in one tradition and comparing them with thinkers and views in another tradition, after which some broad themes may or may not emerge.

However, the question of contribution is another matter: one might successfully show that a view is distinctive but fail to prove that it makes a contribution. We can see that this is true simply by looking at the history of Western philosophy: some views are indeed distinctive but do not help us to sort out any important questions in contemporary philosophy. There are many different ways in which a view might be distinctive, and many ways in which a view might make a contribution. Being distinctive seems in some way to be a prerequisite for making a contribution—if a view is an exact duplicate of another, it would be hard to see how it might contribute something novel. But given the backdrop of cultural and historical differences, views from different traditions are extremely likely to vary from one another in some ways. Indeed, when most philosophers ask about distinctiveness, they are really asking whether a view is distinctive in a philosophically significant way: Is it different enough to be able to make a contribution to our understanding of a given matter? There are, of course, many different kinds of contributions in which philosophers are interested. A view might help us to understand something more fully—something that interests almost all philosophers. A view might also help us to promote positive changes— something that appeals to philosophers who are interested in ethical claims that reflect and inform actual practice. As I indicated previously, in this work I will argue that early Chinese views of parent–child relationships, early childhood, and moral cultivation can make contributions in both of these areas.

Just as there has been increased interest in Chinese philosophy in recent years, there has been a growing focus on the family, owing especially to the work of feminist philosophers. This interest is not confined to the discipline of philosophy, wherein such analysis has primarily been driven by efforts to bring women's experiences and perspectives to bear on philosophical issues. In the sciences, for instance, interest in the role of the family stems in part from the increasing recognition that brain development is most rapid during the first three years of life, and that parent–child relationships are the most important part of a child's early experiences. An extensive body of empirical evidence has shown that these early years have a unique potential and are an especially opportune time to intervene in order to improve children's lives in a variety of areas. This recognition has garnered attention in the area of public policy, leading to greater pressure on policy makers to fund early childhood intervention programs that focus on the first three years of life and that target the early experience within families.

In this book, my aim is to engage with the work that has been done across these disciplines and for the first time to bring the Chinese tradition to bear on this set of issues.

OVERVIEW

The book proceeds in three parts. The first addresses the following question: What did early Chinese philosophers think about parent–child relationships, early childhood, and moral cultivation? Chapter 1 introduces the close relationship between moral cultivation, the family, and the task of creating and maintaining a good society as it is presented in the best-known early Confucian texts: the *Analects*, the *Mengzi*, and the *Xunzi*. I argue that these texts not only emphasize the central importance of moral cultivation, the unique role of parent–child relationships, and the importance of filial piety, but also the clear and direct relationship between the family and a good society. This first chapter presents textual evidence for views that are familiar to most specialists in early Chinese philosophy, but my discussion of these views is essential for one of the larger arguments of this work: that early Confucian views of the relationship between the family, moral cultivation, and politics are distinctive when compared with views on these matters throughout the history of Western philosophy. The views I discuss in chapter 2 will be new to most specialists in early Chinese philosophy, because although the strong emphasis on filial piety in classical Confucian texts has been widely acknowledged and discussed, there has been little attention focused on what these texts have to say about moral cultivation during the earliest years of a child's life. I argue that the *Analects*, the *Mengzi*, and the *Xunzi* each present neglected insights on early moral cultivation, even though the topic was certainly not the main focus of these works. I then examine several other early Confucian sources that offer more detailed accounts of the view that the earliest years of a child's life represent a unique opportunity for moral cultivation. I argue that these works clearly and explicitly present the view that the earliest years of a child's life are a unique and irreplaceable opportunity for moral cultivation and that parent–child relationships are the most important aspect of this process.

The second part of the book speaks to the following question: How are early Confucian views of parent–child relationships, early childhood, and moral cultivation distinctive when compared with views in the history of Western philosophy? Chapters 3 and 4 compare the early Confucian views discussed in the first part of the book with views on the family and moral cultivation in the history of Western philosophy and argue that Confucian views on these matters are distinctive in a number of ways. In chapter 3, I discuss the views of various thinkers in the history of Western philosophy from Plato and Aristotle to Locke, Rousseau, and Dewey. Chapter 4 examines discussions of parent–child relationships in the work of feminist ethicists, with a focus on the work of Sara Ruddick, Nel Noddings, and Virginia Held. In both chapters I highlight the ways in which the Confucian views outlined in the first part of the book differ from the views of Western philosophers, including the fact that the general ethical sensibilities we develop early in childhood are, for early Confucian philosophers, the basis for nearly every virtue, and that the early experiences within families have a direct bearing on the quality of a society and thus are central not just to ethics but to political philosophy and public policy as well. In addition to the distinctive claims Confucian philosophers make about the family, I argue that the Confucian tradition also brings a unique, poignant, and powerful set of stories, anecdotes, approaches, and practices to reinforce and encourage an ethical understanding of the family and its role in moral development.[5]

Yet even if, as I argue, the Confucian tradition offers a distinctive perspective on these matters, why do Confucian views of the relationship between parent–child relationships, early childhood, and moral cultivation warrant serious consideration, and what can they contribute to our understanding of these areas? The third and final part of the book is dedicated to answering these questions. In chapter 5, I argue that there is substantial empirical evidence to support a number of early Confucian claims about the role of parent–child relationships in human moral development, the unique importance of the earliest months and years of a child's life, the nature and possibility of moral self-cultivation, and the task of creating and sustaining a good society. I discuss lines of evidence from attachment theory, human ecology theory, and early childhood intervention programs, and relate them to the Confucian views I have discussed. Chapter 6 argues there are productive, helpful resources in Confucianism for helping us to rethink the role of parent–child relationships in a good society and that Confucian philosophy can serve as an important and distinctive resource not just for ethicists and political philosophers but for policy makers as well. I outline a number of specific areas in which Confucian views can augment and support our efforts to promote social change as well as policy reform.

At a practical level, social change is incredibly difficult to bring about, for it involves not just policy change, but also changing citizens' ways of thinking and acting. I argue that the humanities—including the work of philosophers—can be of considerable assistance here. We need citizens to reconsider their views on how important the earliest years of a child's life are and to recognize the dramatic and tangible ways in which the right kinds of parental caregiving during these early stages of development can shape the entire course of a person's life. The kinds of stories, anecdotes, approaches, and practices discussed in the texts of early Confucianism can make an important contribution to this process. Because our views and practices are heavily shaped by culture, I argue that we ought to make use of resources in both the sciences and the humanities in order to bring about change that encompasses not only our public policies but the views and practices within individual families as well. I argue that Confucian thought can serve as a new, important, and highly unique resource in this process, and that this study represents an example of how work in the humanities can be combined with work in the sciences in complementary and mutually enhancing ways to promote tangible societal change. As a result, this chapter helps to show not only why we need Chinese philosophy but why we need philosophy, the humanities, and the academy more generally—for very practical reasons.

Throughout this work, I will aim not only to describe and argue for the view that Confucian thought can serve as a distinctive and helpful resource in these ways but to situate myself within the Confucian tradition and draw upon traditional Confucian resources as I pursue this task. Accordingly, this book represents, in its own distinctive way, a contemporary, constructive Confucian account of the issues I discuss.

"EARLY" CHINA AND MORAL CULTIVATION

Before proceeding any further, I want to address briefly two important terminological issues in my work. First, in referring to "early Confucian views," I include texts associated with the pre-Qin period (the period prior to 221 B.C.E.) as well as the Han dynasty (206 B.C.E.–220 C.E.).

Although scholars of Chinese thought typically separate the Han from earlier periods in Chinese history, and many scholars of early China uncritically privilege and seem to prefer earlier texts over Han texts, all of these are early by Confucian standards, and I will present evidence for the contention that there is considerable continuity between the views of early childhood moral cultivation presented in the Han texts and the earlier texts that I examine. My approach here is partly inspired by the Confucian tradition: Confucians throughout history have regarded the large and wide-ranging collection of sources that are a part of the Confucian tradition as just that—part of a coherent whole. It is important to take account of the diversity within the Confucian tradition and the different periods during which different texts came together, and, as readers will notice, I attend to both of these tasks throughout this work. At the same time, with the constructive aims of this work in mind, I argue that we should draw upon different early Confucian sources and regard them as a constructive resource for us today, because together they bring a rich set of views and approaches concerning parent–child relationships and early childhood moral cultivation (e.g., defensible views of filial piety, accounts of prenatal cultivation, inspiring stories of parents who balanced gentle nurturance with discipline).

Additionally, one of my aims is to emphasize the fact that Confucian thinkers advanced views very early in their history that were not put forth in Western philosophy until only very recently, and this fact highlights some of the truly distinctive features of Confucian philosophy. Although I will note the likely dates of the texts I discuss, I will not address text-critical issues in this work, because the controversies concerning the precise dating of particular texts and passages are not relevant to my aims in this work, which are to show that texts from remarkably early periods in the Confucian tradition express an appreciation for the unique connections between parent–child relationships, early childhood, and moral cultivation, and to argue that these views have constructive value for us today. The questions of precisely how early these texts are and who composed them are not issues that in any way affect my arguments in this work, because my central concern is with the ideas found in the texts I discuss.

The second terminological issue is that I will refer throughout this work to childhood "moral cultivation" instead of childhood "moral education," because the former more accurately captures certain features of early Confucian views of infancy and early childhood—namely the fact that during these early stages one is not just instructing or teaching children explicitly about virtue but actually beginning the process of developing and nurturing their moral sensibilities and capacities through a variety of methods and approaches. "Moral cultivation" also highlights the continuity between Confucian accounts of moral development during infancy and childhood and Confucian accounts of moral self-cultivation (meaning "the cultivation of the self"). Discussions of this process in the Confucian tradition, as we shall see, include the activities and approaches of parents during the earliest stages of their children's development and the approaches and activities we engage in when we work intentionally to improve ourselves.

FAMILIES OF VIRTUE

I

WHAT DID EARLY CONFUCIAN PHILOSOPHERS
THINK ABOUT PARENT–CHILD RELATIONSHIPS,
EARLY CHILDHOOD, AND MORAL CULTIVATION?

1

MORAL CULTIVATION, FILIAL PIETY, AND THE GOOD SOCIETY IN CLASSICAL CONFUCIAN PHILOSOPHY

Treat your elders as elders, and extend it to the elders of others. Treat your young ones as young ones, and extend it to the young ones of others; then you can turn the whole world in the palm of your hand.

—MENGZI 1A7

B EGINNING VERY EARLY in the Confucian tradition, Confucian philosophers argued for the primacy of parent–child relationships in human moral development and the nature and possibility of moral self-cultivation.[1] They also argued that the key to a flourishing society lies most fundamentally in these two areas. As Philip J. Ivanhoe puts it, "Confucians believe that one cannot successfully pursue the ethical life outside of fulfilling certain familial and social obligations. One cannot develop a moral sense without knowing what it is to love and be loved within a human family, and one cannot love and care for one's family without a deep and abiding concern for the society in which one lives" (2000a:22). This chapter describes Confucian moral cultivation, including the special role of filial piety and family relationships, and its role in creating and sustaining a good society, as put forth in the *Analects*, the *Mengzi*,[2] and the *Xunzi*.[3]

In grouping these three thinkers together and examining their views as representative of "early Confucianism," I am not claiming that their views represent a single, uniform, ethical theory. Indeed, one of my goals in this chapter is to show the very different ways in which these thinkers understand the ultimate ground for moral claims, seen most clearly in their views of human nature. These differences represent some of the reasons Kongzi,

Mengzi, and Xunzi each have unique insights to offer regarding the relationship between the family, moral education, and political philosophy. As will become apparent, although I do not see these thinkers as representatives of the same view, I do see them as belonging to the same family of ethical views. As Bryan W. Van Norden argues, the good life for these thinkers involves participation in communal ritual activities, aesthetic appreciation, intellectual activities (but always with an ultimately practical aim), caring for and benefiting others (with greater concern for and obligations to those bound to one by special relations such as kinship and friendship), and the joy that comes from virtuous activity (even in the face of adversity) but also appropriate sadness at loss (2007:116–117).[4]

Confucian views are strongly focused on the good of groups such as families, communities, and societies, and less concerned with—though by no means neglectful of—the welfare of individuals. Confucian philosophers developed a shared account of the virtues that reflects this focus, and we turn our attention first to the way in which these virtues help to constitute the Confucian Way in the thought of Kongzi.

KONGZI

Filial piety and brotherly respect—are these not the roots of humaneness?

ANALECTS 1.2

Anyone with even a passing familiarity with the Confucian *Analects* knows that moral cultivation and filial piety are important themes in that text.[5] But how, precisely, do early Confucian thinkers like Kongzi understand these concepts? What does moral cultivation involve, and what is its aim? Kongzi's account of moral cultivation emerges as a response to the instability, suffering, and unrest in his society. As a potential remedy to what he viewed as primarily a moral malady, Kongzi argued that people should return to the way of life embodied in the earlier part of the Zhou dynasty, which was a time of peace, harmony, and stability. Maintaining that the key to political stability lies not in the governmental policies or laws of the Zhou but in Zhou *culture*—particularly in the virtues and moral and religious practices prized during the Zhou—Kongzi insists in the *Analects* that the solution he offers is not new. Rather, he claims to be a transmitter of Zhou culture and not an innovator of some new ideal or value system (7.1).[6]

In 3.14 Kongzi says, "The Zhou surveyed the two dynasties that went before, its ways are refined and elegant. I follow the Zhou." Here, the image of the Zhou dynasty surveying or taking stock of the Xia and Shang dynasties helps to show that for Kongzi, Zhou culture incorporated the best aspects of the cultures that preceded it, which reaffirms the view that this way of life has been tested and proven in actual human experience. He sees the Zhou as a culmination of wisdom, and a clear expression of what the world looks like when people follow what he calls the Way. Kongzi sees himself as advocating a return to a way of life—including a program of moral cultivation—of which we can be certain; for him, we do not have to speculate about this solution to social and political problems because it has already been shown to engender a society that is not only stable but harmonious and flourishing. These latter qualities are important, for although Kongzi sought social order and stability, he sought them only as necessary but not sufficient parts of a good society. On such a view, it is better for a state to be good and fail than simply to endure. Additionally, while Kongzi maintains that humane laws and policies are important, he does not think the problems in his society can be resolved primarily through legal and policy reform. Rather, the solution requires leading people to reflect on and reshape their values and priorities—including their attitudes, beliefs, and practices.

For Kongzi, the Way (*Dao* 道) of the former kings and sages resembles a well-trodden path defined by a particular set of virtues, certain kinds of roles and relationships with others, and cultural practices such as rites or rituals (*li* 禮). In many ways, moral cultivation represents the heart of the Way, because following it is largely defined by the task of actively and continuously cultivating those virtues, relationships, and practices. But these are not separate tasks; the cultural practices that are a part of the Way are one of the primary means by which one cultivates the virtues and nurtures the relationships that are central features of a good life. The "rites" are a set of traditional moral and religious practices, including what we would call rituals, social customs, rules of etiquette, and sacrificial offerings, which together constitute a unified code of conduct. These rites specify much of the content of Zhou culture in terms of the patterns of behavior that govern interactions between members of families, communities, and society as a whole. While acting in accordance with the rites does not guarantee a harmonious outcome, the rites are a necessary feature of a harmonious society: "What ritual values most is harmony. The Way of the former kings was truly admirable in this respect. But if in matters great and small one proceeds in this manner, the results may not always be satisfactory. You may understand the ideal of harmony and work for it, but if you do not employ ritual to regulate the proceedings, things will not go well" (*Analects* 1.12).

To be sure, one important function of ritual is that it helps to guard against an overly narrow focus on achieving ends such as harmony. More generally, the rites enable the kind of moral cultivation that helps to define the Way, because following them helps individuals to behave in ways that promote values like harmony and that both reflect and cultivate the right sorts of attitudes and feelings toward others.[7] The rites encourage and often require us to think more about others, which can shape our character in critical ways, even when the ritual being followed appears to be a "minor" matter of etiquette. For example, addressing and greeting an older family member or teacher in the proper manner is not only an expression of respect and appreciation for them (something that usually contributes to more harmonious interactions), it also reminds us of our relationship with that person, the things she or he has done for us, and the ways in which she or he is a role model for us; all of this can shape our character in subtle ways by contributing to the cultivation of virtues like reciprocity and humility.[8]

When a person follows the rites properly, she not only makes certain gestures and behaves in certain ways but reflects on the reasons for doing so. In *Analects* 10.25, we are told that Kongzi acted in accordance with the rites by bowing down from his carriage when he passed someone dressed for a funeral, even when the mourner was a lowly peddler. This behavior not only expresses concern for others regardless of their position in society but prompts us to reflect on the ways in which we are bound to others by common human experiences, thereby cultivating a deeper sense of concern for others.[9] Accordingly, it is not surprising that the virtue of ritual propriety associated with mastery of the rites is an expression of excellence in character.

The path of moral self-cultivation is the key to realizing a harmonious, flourishing society for Kongzi, because it is the only way in which a person is able to claim the virtues, roles, and practices that define the Way. In 8.7 we are told that for those who devote their lives to the path of Confucian moral self-cultivation, "the burden is heavy and the Way is long. They take up humaneness as their burden—is it not heavy? Their way ends only with death—is it not long?"[10] The ideals that an individual works toward on this path are visible in a number of important ideas and discussions, but in the *Analects* the goal of self-cultivation is made especially clear in Kongzi's conception of humaneness (*Ren* 仁) and his description of the cultivated person (*junzi* 君子), which typically designate the highest ideals to which those following the Way aspire. In the *Analects*, "humaneness" refers to the most virtuous state of character, designating the accumulation and complete mastery of all of the Confucian virtues.[11] *Analects* 6.22 stresses that humaneness is only achieved through a rigorous commitment to the forms of moral cultivation that help to define the Way: "Humaneness means tending to the difficulties first and leaving benefits for later—this can be called humaneness." *Junzi* is Kongzi's term for the most highly cultivated person. While this term was originally used to refer to "the son of a lord," indicating individuals born into noble families, in the *Analects* it designates ethical achievement; being a *junzi* is the achievement of those who are most highly cultivated and who serve as moral exemplars. The cultivated person embodies the full range of Confucian virtues, including filial piety, trustworthiness, courage, and wisdom. According to Kongzi, though, despite having attained the heights of moral achievement, the cultivated person continues to exhibit an unwavering devotion to the path of self-cultivation.

Where does this path begin? According to the *Analects*, it initiates within the context of the family, where the right kinds of relationships with family members—especially parents—begin to nurture, develop, and shape the capacity to feel and act in ways that reflect the virtues and values of the Way. In the next chapter, we will examine precisely what the *Analects* and other early Confucian texts have to say about the early moral education of children and youth, but for now I want to focus on Kongzi's general account of moral cultivation within the family—and particularly the special role of filial piety.[12] *Analects* 1.2 formulates the view that our feelings, attitudes, and actions toward our parents and elder siblings play a foundational role in our moral development: "A person who is filial to his parents and respectful of his elder brother is rarely the kind of person who is inclined to go against his superiors, and there has never been a case of one who is disinclined to go against his superiors stirring up rebellion. The cultivated person applies himself to the root. 'Once the root is established, the Way will flourish.' Filial piety and brotherly respect—are these not the roots of humaneness?"[13] The quotation from the *Book of Odes* in this passage indicates a connection between the cultivation of filial piety (as the "root" of a person's moral character) and the ability to follow the Way throughout one's life. Filial piety and brotherly respect make it possible and perhaps even likely for an individual to develop the other virtues and moral sensibilities that are a part of the Way. Accordingly, among the virtues that are a part of the Way, those that are unique to the family have a privileged place, because, the text maintains, other virtues and moral capacities stem from the feelings and capacities a person develops in response to parents and older siblings. As Ivanhoe points out, "The strongest feelings are originally and forever those within the family. The virtues of 'filial piety' and 'respect for an elder brother' are the source from which one draws in extending and developing such feelings for others and are the most profound examples of the type of concern that characterizes those who are [humane]" (2002a:3).

Although cultures throughout the world value filial behavior, Chinese culture stands out for the amount of attention paid to and the unique importance claimed for filial piety. From very early on, entire texts were devoted to this topic. The *Classic of Filial Piety* states that filial piety "is the root of virtue. Teaching and learning arise from it." This text further contends that the affection for one's parents that grounds this virtue develops during childhood.[14] In order to understand fully why the early Confucians placed such emphasis on filial piety, we must understand something about their religious beliefs, specifically the widespread belief in ancestral spirits in ancient China. Michael Puett describes early China as "a haunted world. Ghosts were pervasive and dangerous, and the living regularly performed sacrifices in an attempt to control or mollify the dead" (2011:225).[15] Zhou culture, like the Shang, devoted a great deal of time and energy to communicating with various kinds of spirits, which were viewed as more powerful and ethereal members of this world. Of these various spirits, those of dead humans had a special place. Early Chinese beliefs held that certain souls and energies left the body when a person died and that this could be dangerous for the living: "Some of the demonic forces—which would then simply be called ghosts (*gui* 鬼)—would tend to haunt the living. Harboring jealousies and resentments, they would be drawn to where they once lived and would send down disasters and misfortunes on their living family members" (Puett 2011:226).

Puett writes that the desire to prevent these dangers gave rise to rituals and sacrifices designed to remove the souls and energies to places where they could be "controlled, contained, and transformed into forces that would at least cause less harm to the living and potentially even be beneficial to them." Some rituals, performed for the souls that would have floated away after the death of the body, included offerings placed with the body in the tomb to keep the souls in the tomb and prevent them from becoming ghosts who would harm living people. Other rituals were performed for the spirits, in order to transform them into ancestors who might work on behalf of their living descendants (Puett 2011:226). These rituals were also designed to domesticate other kinds of spirits, since ancestors were made more pliable by sacrifices and could thus be called upon for assistance with other spirits. Yet as Puett points out, the rituals did not always work: "Ghosts would still haunt the living, and spirits would still send down harm and misfortune upon the living as well. Thus, the rituals were a never-ending attempt to keep the ghosts and spirits at bay. And for brief periods of time, such rituals might even be successful—but usually not for very long" (Puett 2011:227).

To elicit a favorable response from the spirits, sacrificial offerings of food and drink needed to be appropriate in size and quantity and accompanied by prayers for assistance and thanksgiving, music, and often dance; they also had to be presented with the proper attitudes of piety, devotion, and gratitude.[16] So, a favorable response from the spirits required sacrificers to cultivate themselves. Because making sacrifices to one's ancestral spirits in a reverential and filial manner was viewed as critically important—not just for individual families but for entire communities affected by those spirits—having and raising children who would continue to make sacrifices to their ancestral spirits came to be viewed as a religious and moral obligation. Indeed, as we shall see in the following section, Mengzi claims that the failure to have children is the most unfilial of actions (*Mengzi* 4A26). Over time, Confucians came to have a variety of reasons for viewing filial piety as important, but the religious origins of their view help to explain why they placed such a strong emphasis on this virtue in particular.[17]

In the *Analects*, one of several reasons ancestral sacrifices are considered important is that they serve an ethical function: when performed properly, they help people to cultivate virtues such as filial piety, which are a central feature of a good life. This is not an insignificant point, for it shows that relationships with ancestral spirits were not viewed as radically disconnected from relationships with other humans. Kongzi is explicit about this in *Analects* 11.12, when Zilu asks how one should serve the ghosts and spirits: "The Master said, When you don't yet know how to serve human beings, how can you serve the spirits?"[18] Kongzi suggests we cannot serve the spirits properly or in a way that is meaningful until we have learned to properly serve humans.[19] In 3.11 Kongzi suggests again that an understanding of ancestral sacrifices has important ties to a human's understanding of the world, perhaps suggesting that it is an important part of governing: "Someone asked about the meaning of the ancestral sacrifice. The Master said, I don't know. Someone who knew its meaning would understand all the affairs of the world as if they were displayed right here—and he pointed to his palm."

Returning to the subject of filial piety in the *Analects*, it is helpful to have a sense of the reasons *why* filial piety is regarded as a virtue that one cultivates if one is dedicated to the Way. Filial piety is "a cultivated disposition to attend to the needs and desires of one's parents and to work to satisfy and please them," and it includes a deep sense of gratitude, reverence, and love for one's parents.[20] Early Confucians offered multiple justifications for filial piety as a virtue, including the view that children owe their parents gratitude for bringing them into being. One expression of this view in early Confucianism is the claim that children are a physical extension of their parents; this was thought to establish an overriding debt and grounded the obligation not to harm one's physical body—a view seen clearly in the first chapter of the *Classic of Filial Piety*: "One's body, hair, and skin are received from one's father and mother. Not to injure or harm these is the beginning of filial piety."[21] Yet the analogy with borrowing seems inappropriate in the case of parent–child relationships, because children did not exist when the debt purportedly was incurred. Although one might argue that children "still owe their parents some kind of obligation as an expression of gratitude for being brought into existence," Ivanhoe argues that upon further consideration, such appeals are not at all evident or straightforward. In order for any action to be a legitimate source of gratitude, it must not only be in the actual interest of the recipient but must also be done out of an attitude of caring *for her or him*. Given these criteria, it is at least problematic to claim that children in general owe their parents a debt of gratitude for being brought into existence (2007:300).

Not only is it not evident that mere existence itself is a good, but most children are not created *for the child's own good* (whatever that might mean); some are born as a result of their parents' own pursuit of sensual gratification, others because their parents believe their own lives will be enriched, and others because their parents believe they have a religious duty to procreate.[22] Early Confucians, as we have already seen, did believe that having children was a religious duty.

While such reasons are not well founded and do not offer compelling reasons for us to cultivate and value the virtue of filial piety today, Confucian views of filial piety and parent–child relationships do offer some persuasive justifications for it—especially with the understanding that filial piety is an appropriate response to good parental care. The earliest source to advance such a view is the *Book of Odes*:

> Oh father, you begot me!
> Oh mother, you nourished me!
> You supported and nurtured me,
> You raised me, and provided for me,
> You looked after me and sheltered me,
> In your comings and goings,
> You [always] bore me in your arms.
> The kindness I would repay,
> Is boundless as the Heavens![23]

As Ivanhoe points out, "The main point of this passage is to express the broad range of goods and the overarching attention and care that good parents provide for their children. More importantly, it conveys the love that motivates such parents to care for their children and the natural gratitude, reverence, and love that such attention tends to generate in those who receive it" (2007:303).

The following poem by Meng Jiao (751–814) offers further evidence of this view in the Confucian tradition:

> Thread, in the hands of a loving mother,
> Becomes the coat to be worn by her wandering son.
> As the time draws near for his departure, she stitches it tightly,
> Fearing that he may be slow to return.
> Who would claim that a tender blade of grass,
> Could ever repay the warmth of three Spring Seasons?[24]

Ivanhoe argues, "The true basis for filial piety is the sense of gratitude, reverence, and love that children naturally feel when they are nurtured, supported, and cared for by people who do so out of loving concern for the child's well-being" (2007:299). Later in this work, I will further discuss this argument and build upon it in relation to the fundamental importance of Confucian views concerning the role of parents in early childhood moral cultivation, but for now I want to highlight the fact that Ivanhoe's argument directly concerns the relationship between filial piety and early cultivation:

> Parents play a remarkably important role in influencing and shaping the early development of their children. If they regularly care for their children for the children's own good, they contribute in profound and enduring ways to the future character, attitudes, sensibilities, and inclinations of these young people. It is absolutely essential for the view described here that these goods, which serve as the basis of filial piety, be given out of love for and for the good of the child. They are expressions of love, not an investment made with an eye on future returns. (2007:304)

One important feature of filial piety is the extent to which it includes a deeply felt sense of reverence, gratitude, and love for one's parents. This aspect of filial piety is seen clearly in the *Analects*, where being a filial daughter or son has as much to do with one's feelings and attitudes as it does with one's actions. *Analects* 2.7 says, "Ziyou asked about filial devotion. The Master said, Nowadays it's taken to mean just seeing that one's parents get enough to eat. But we do that much for dogs and horses as well. If there is no reverence, how is it any different?" This passage distinguishes between performing one's filial duties in the same way that one would perform any other duties or chores and having an emotional attitude of respectfulness or reverence that accompanies one's conduct.[25] In 2.8 Kongzi points out, "The difficult part is the facial expression. As for young people taking on the heavy work when there's something to be done, or older people going first when there's wine and food—can this be called filial devotion?" Here again, Kongzi indicates that there is a difference between simply fulfilling one's duties as a younger person, including giving elders precedence, and having the virtue of filial piety. Watson notes that this passage may refer to watching the faces of one's parents to see how they are reacting or keeping the proper expression on one's own face (2007:21n2). Facial expression or demeanor is an outward manifestation of inner reflections and feelings.

Managing both one's own feelings and one's sensitivity to the feelings of others, including the sense of respectfulness mentioned in 2.7, is what Kongzi recognizes as the challenging aspect of being filial. Many people can go through the motions, but filial piety requires an individual to behave in such a way that a spirit of deep-seated respect or reverence for her parents and elders is a part of her demeanor. Although obedience and respect for one's parents' wishes are a part of filial piety, Kongzi makes clear that filial piety does not involve automatic compliance. In 4.18 he says that remonstrance with one's parents is a part of being filial: "In serving your father and mother, you may gently admonish them. But if you see they have no intention of listening to you, then be respectful as before and do not disobey them. You might feel distressed but should never feel resentful." The disposition cultivated in the context of one's relationship with one's parents serves as a basis for interacting with others. One learns about patience and good judgment and what real respect requires in a relationship.

It is important to note that *Analects* 1.2, which specifies that filial piety and brotherly respect are the "roots" of humaneness, also says that an individual who is filial does not stir up a rebellion. This passage is one of several that make an explicit connection between filial piety in the family and stability at the political level, suggesting filial piety constitutes the roots of political order. In 2.21, quoting from the *Book of Documents*, Kongzi says, "Filial, only be filial, a friend to elder and younger brothers—this contributes to government." He goes on to remark, "To do this is in fact to take part in government. Why must I be 'in government?'" In this passage Kongzi maintains that being filial is a form of political service and not simply a form of service within the family. Instead of a bifurcation between the political and the family, we find a continuum. The government cannot on its own create a stable and harmonious society; these things must be cultivated within the context of the family, where we learn to think and feel for others in certain ways. The family serves as a model for the ideal state. As we shall see throughout this work, the view that the family and parent–child relationships in particular have clear and direct relationships to political matters is a distinctive feature of Confucian ideas concerning the family.

The emphasis placed on feelings and attitudes as well as actions in the account of filial piety in the *Analects* is also a distinctive feature of the other virtues that help to constitute the Way. As we have seen, the rites are an integral part of the Way, and in 3.26 Kongzi remarks on the emotional attitudes and demeanor that are a part of the virtue of ritual propriety: "Standing above others but without magnanimity, carrying out rites but without reverence, conducting funeral proceedings but without grief—how can I bear to view such as these?" Further, when Kongzi is asked about the roots of ritual, he responds, "A big question indeed! In rites in general, rather than extravagance, better frugality. In funeral rites, rather than thoroughness, better real grief" (3.4). Here Kongzi indicates that the "roots," or what is most basic, in ritual include the feelings that inform and motivate the rites and that partly constitute the virtue of ritual propriety. We should be reminded here of Kongzi's remarks about filial piety being the "root" of humaneness. Both of these passages can be seen as evidence that Kongzi sees certain kinds of emotional sensibilities as lying at the root or foundation of the virtues. In other words, our moral development begins in some important sense with certain kinds of emotional experiences, and this is where virtues such as filial piety and ritual propriety initially begin to develop. As we shall see in the next chapter, parents do much to nurture the development of these feelings in children and to shape the dispositions to which they give rise.

Analects 15.10 compares moral cultivation to a craft and maintains that to become good at one's craft, one must seek out others who are virtuous: "A craftsman who wants to do his job well must first sharpen his tools. Whatever country you are in, be of service to the high officials who are worthy and become friends with the men of station who are humane." Kongzi repeatedly emphasizes the importance of "looking to those who possess the Way in order to be set straight by them" (1.14).[26] In the *Analects*, humans are thought to have a natural tendency to gravitate toward and be influenced by those who are virtuous, a view that is related to traditional Chinese understandings of Virtue or moral power (*de* 德) that preceded Kongzi.[27] In 13.4 Kongzi says that if there are leaders who love ritual propriety, rightness, and trustworthiness, "Then the people from the four lands adjacent, bearing their little children strapped to their backs, will gather around."[28] On this view, we are drawn to virtuous leaders and have a strong tendency to respond in kind to their virtue. The idea that the virtue of particular individuals can have a transformative effect on society is especially apparent in discussions of the cultivated person: "If the cultivated person treats those close to him with generosity, the common people will be moved to humaneness. If he does not forget his old associates, the common people will shun cold-heartedness" (8.2).

* * *

These passages help to show that although the Confucian tradition heavily emphasizes the priority of familial relationships in moral development and human flourishing, Kongzi maintains there is a close relationship between the flourishing of individual families and the quality of the state. Kongzi says in *Analects* 1.6, "A young person should be filial when at home and when going out, respectful of his elders. Conscientious and trustworthy, he should care widely for the multitudes but have affection for those who are humane."[29] Having the proper feelings toward others is an essential part of moral development, and the cultivation of moral feelings in the context of filial relationships naturally leads to their extension in wider settings. On this view, individuals who cultivate filial piety and respect in their relationships with their parents and elders are also likely to develop a strong sense of accountability to and responsibility for other members of society. In the *Analects*, moral cultivation helps to explain how we come to have certain attitudes toward others, attitudes that emerge through the development of a set of virtues. These virtues are all ultimately rooted in the family, for the virtue most closely tied to healthy parent–child relationships in the Confucian view—filial piety—provides the foundation for Confucian moral cultivation.

Having seen the close relationship between moral cultivation, filial piety, and political thought in the *Analects*, we turn in the next section to Mengzi's account, which goes a step further by examining specifically how and why people develop different virtues and moral capacities, and the origins of these virtues and capacities in human nature.

MENGZI

*Because his parents were not in accord with him, he felt like a poor man
who has nowhere to turn.*

———————

MENGZI 5A1

The late fourth-century B.C.E. philosopher Mengzi shared Kongzi's view
that filial piety and self-cultivation are critical to the task of creating and
maintaining a good society, and he sought to develop an account of human
nature that would help support Kongzi's view.[30] Indeed, Mengzi was the
first Confucian thinker to explicitly discuss the relationship between human
nature and self-cultivation, maintaining that self-cultivation is a process of
developing our original inclinations toward goodness.[31] His writings on this
subject sparked the first major debate about human nature in the Confucian tradition when Xunzi, whose view we will examine in the next section
of this chapter, argued against Mengzi's account. While both Mengzi and
Xunzi saw themselves as interpreting and defending Kongzi's view, their
competing accounts of human nature each serve as a new foundation on
which to ground Kongzi's view.

In working to appreciate Mengzi's general account of moral cultivation
and the special role of the family in his account, it is helpful to understand
from the outset how Mengzi understands his own task as a philosopher.
When asked by one of his students why he enjoys engaging in disputation,
Mengzi denies that he does so and describes the problems in his society and
the ways in which it has degenerated since the time of the Zhou. He points
to his rival philosophers, the Mohists and Yangists, and says that if their
Ways are not discarded,

and the Way of Kongzi is not made evident, then evil doctrines will dupe
the people, and obstruct benevolence and righteousness. If benevolence
and righteousness are obstructed, that leads animals to devour people. I
am afraid that people will begin to devour one another! Because I fear

this, I preserve the Way of the former sages, fend off Yang and Mo, and get rid of specious words, so that evil doctrines will be unable to arise. If they arise in one's heart, they are harmful in one's activities. If they arise in one's activities, they are harmful in governing. When sages arise again, they will certainly not differ with what I have said. . . . I, too, desire to rectify people's hearts, to bring an end to evil doctrines, to fend off bad conduct, to get rid of specious words, so as to carry on the work of these three sages. How could I be fond of disputation? I simply cannot do otherwise. (*Mengzi* 3B9)

Mengzi's account of human nature is designed to show how the problems of his society can be remedied, and in offering his views Mengzi explains how people may advance themselves along the Way. According to Mengzi, all human beings are born with four observable, active moral senses, or "sprouts" (*duan* 端), that are already in their initial stages of development. He uses the metaphor of sprouts to express and enhance this idea by describing how these four moral senses, if properly nourished and protected from harm, eventually grow into the virtues of benevolence, righteousness, propriety, and wisdom (*Mengzi* 2A6, 4A27, 6A6). He says in 4B11, "The great person does not think beforehand of his words that they may be sincere, nor of his actions that they may be resolute;—he simply [speaks and does] what is right."[32] In this passage Mengzi makes clear that cultivated persons no longer struggle to conduct themselves virtuously, for they have developed such virtues as sincerity to the point that they possess a stable disposition to behave in certain ways.[33]

Mengzi refers to the initial moral senses we all possess as "hearts," or feelings:

The feeling of compassion is the sprout of benevolence. The feeling of disdain is the sprout of righteousness. The feeling of deference is the sprout of propriety. The feeling of approval and disapproval is the sprout of wisdom. People having these four sprouts is like their having four limbs. To have these four sprouts, yet to claim that one is incapable (of virtue), is to steal from oneself. . . . In general, having these four sprouts within oneself, if one knows to fill them all out, it will be like a fire starting up, a spring breaking through! (*Mengzi* 2A6)[34]

Mengzi's choice of a metaphor here is telling: "Like sprouts, our moral sense is a *visible and active*, not *hidden or latent*, part of the self."[35] In order for Mengzi's program of self-cultivation to work, people must already possess an active and visible moral capacity that can be developed.

In support of the claim that all humans have moral sprouts, Mengzi offers examples of how our moral tendencies are observable and active in our responses in various kinds of situations: "Suppose someone suddenly saw a child about to fall into a well: everyone in such a situation would have a feeling of alarm and compassion—not because one sought to get in good with the child's parents, not because one wanted fame among one's neighbors and friends, and not because one would dislike the sound of the child's cries" (*Mengzi* 2A6).

Mengzi argues that these natural moral capacities are rooted in the heart-mind (*xin* 心), which contains cognitive and affective faculties, including the four moral sprouts and volitional abilities. He variously refers to our natural moral tendencies together as the "child's heart-mind" (赤子之心), the "innate heart-mind" (良心), and the "fundamental heart-mind" (本心).[36] Because the moral sprouts reside in the heart-mind, humans use their moral sense when they think and reflect: "The function of the heart-mind is to reflect. When it reflects, it gets things right; if it does not reflect, it cannot get things right" (*Mengzi* 6A15).[37] Mengzi maintains that reflecting on good conduct produces a special feeling of joy that reinforces our moral sense and gives us moral courage. If we delight in our moral sprouts, "then they grow. If they grow, then how can they be stopped? If they cannot be stopped, then one does not notice one's feet dancing to them, one's hands swaying to them" (*Mengzi* 4A27).

On this view, all human beings are the same in having an active, visible moral sense, and those who use it "follow their greater part."[38] Mengzi further expounds on this claim with the parable of the barley sprouts: "The soil is the same and the time of planting is also the same. They grow rapidly, and by the time of summer solstice they have all ripened. Although there are some differences, these are due to the richness of the soil, and to unevenness in the rain and in human effort" (*Mengzi* 6A7). Mengzi emphasizes that everyone starts out with moral sprouts, and while some aspects of the sprouts' environment are the same, others are different. In the parable of Ox Mountain, we learn that although the trees on the mountain were once beautiful, they were not protected from a variety of harms. Similarly, moral sprouts need a safe and nourishing environment in order to flourish. In the case of Ox Mountain, "there were sprouts and shoots growing there. But oxen and sheep then came and grazed on them. Hence, it was as if it were barren" (*Mengzi* 6A8). For Mengzi, the animals on Ox Mountain are a metaphor for the variety of harmful influences people sometimes encounter. In 6A9, he says, "Even though it may be the easiest growing thing in the world, if it gets one day of warmth and ten days of frost, there has never been anything that is capable of growing. It is seldom that I have an audience with the king, and when I withdraw, those who 'freeze' him come. What can I do with the sprouts that are there?" Here Mengzi expresses dismay at the negative influence other people have on the king despite his own efforts to awaken the king's natural moral tendencies. While Mengzi's advice and examples are like sun and warmth nurturing buds or sprouts, the bad influences of others are like a stretch of cold weather that devastates the sprouts. In the parable of the man from Song, Mengzi also expands this metaphor, describing a man who tugged on his shoots of grain in an effort to make them grow more quickly and inadvertently uprooted them. Here Mengzi indicates that humans must neither neglect their moral sense nor try to force it to grow. These passages show clearly that Mengzi does not think humans are born with fully developed moral capacities; rather, they are born with an inclination toward goodness. Mengzi stresses that we can see these moral capacities in action simply by observing human behavior. But although one's moral "sprouts" are visible and active right from the start, they are in need of considerable encouragement and growth for the individual to develop into a moral person.

For Mengzi, then, the task of moral cultivation requires the nurturing of natural moral tendencies. It is not a matter of instilling something new or reshaping a person fundamentally, and he makes this clear in his debate with Gaozi, who claims that instilling the virtues of benevolence and righteousness in people is like carving cups and bowls from a willow tree. Mengzi responds critically to Gaozi's contention that human nature resembles a willow tree: "Can you make it into cups and bowls by following the nature of the willow tree? You can only make it into cups and bowls by violating and robbing the willow tree. If you must violate and rob the willow tree in order to make it into cups and bowls, must you also violate and rob people in order to make them benevolent and righteous?" (*Mengzi* 6A1). For Mengzi, humans *already* have good tendencies that can be extended in order to develop virtues like benevolence and righteousness, and so it makes little sense and can actually be harmful to people when moral cultivation proceeds as though this moral potential does not exist. This is why he repeatedly talks about those who have failed to cultivate the virtues as having "lost" their hearts—their natural moral capacities—while those who are virtuous are those who have not lost their hearts (6A11, 6A10). He also discusses "nourishing the greater part" of oneself (6A14, 6A15), and in 4B14 he says that the cultivated person makes advances in learning by "getting hold of it in himself. Having got hold of it in himself, he abides in it calmly and firmly. Abiding in it calmly and firmly, he deeply relies upon it."[39] Mengzi emphasizes that one's natural moral tendencies are not enough in themselves but must be nurtured and cultivated: "The five domesticated grains are the finest of seeds. But if they are not mature, they are not as good as wild plants. Similarly, benevolence depends on reaching maturity" (*Mengzi* 6A19).

In addition to the idea that our moral cultivation depends upon the nurturance and encouragement that others provide when we are young—something that will be the central focus of the next chapter—moral cultivation, in Mengzi's view, also requires us to look within and take hold of our own natural moral sensibilities, gradually increasing our recognition of and reliance upon them. Cultivated people differ from others because they preserve and develop their natural moral sensibilities, and when they display the virtues that grow from these sensibilities, others tend to respond in kind: "The benevolent person cares for others. The person of propriety shows respect to others. Those who care for others are generally cared for by them. Those who respect others are generally respected by them" (*Mengzi* 4B28).[40] This passage helps to show how Mengzi believes society can be transformed, and his account is in line with Kongzi's account of Virtue, or moral power (*de* 德).

Mengzi describes the virtue of benevolence as "the quiet home in which humans should dwell" (*Mengzi* 2A7).[41] Such a claim, for Mengzi, indicates that the sprout of benevolence is part of our nature and thus we are "at home," or fulfilling our most natural inclinations, when we are benevolent, but it also highlights the connection between being virtuous and the importance of the home in which we are raised and in which our moral sprouts are first nurtured. For Mengzi, as for Kongzi, family relationships play the most critical role in moral development, and he is even more explicit than the *Analects* in his assertion that these relationships must be properly cultivated in all settings in order for a society to flourish: "If one is careful about providing instruction in the village schools, emphasizing the righteousness of filial piety and fraternal respect, those whose hair has turned gray will not carry loads on the roadways" (*Mengzi* 1A3; cf. 1A7). This passage draws a direct connection between the cultivation of filial piety and fraternal respect and the elderly being properly cared for—something that is the responsibility of families.

For Mengzi, political problems often originate when people do not understand and cultivate proper relationships within the family. This issue also motivates Mengzi's claim that honoring one's parents is the most important thing a filial child can do: "In being a filial son, nothing is greater than honoring one's parents. In honoring one's parents, nothing is greater than caring for them with the world" (*Mengzi* 5A4).[42] Here Mengzi ties filial responsibilities to political responsibilities, seeing them as mutually supportive. He discusses the connection between the cultivation of good family relationships and the good of the rest of society in a number of places: "Treat your elders as elders, and extend it to the elders of others; treat your young ones as young ones, and extend it to the young ones of others, and you can turn the whole world in the palm of your hand. . . . Hence, if one extends one's kindness, it will be sufficient to care for all within the Four Seas" (*Mengzi* 1A7). For Mengzi, a flourishing society depends upon the capacity of its members to *feel for* one another and to act on those feelings, and this is why he spends so much time elaborating the relationship between an individual's feelings for her family and her feelings for others. For Mengzi, those feelings already lie within us, in the form of our natural moral feelings: "The Way lies in what is near, but people seek it in what is distant; one's task lies in what is easy, but people seek it in what is difficult. If everyone would treat their parents as parents and their elders as elders, the world would be at peace" (*Mengzi* 4A11). Mengzi reinforces this point in 7A15, where he specifies just how early our natural moral tendencies are visible within the context of family relationships: "Among babes in arms there are none that do not know to love their parents. When they grow older, there is none that do not know to revere their elder brothers. Treating one's parents as parents is benevolence. Respecting one's elders is righteousness. There is nothing else to do but extend these to the world."

Throughout this account Mengzi refers to the imagery of sprouts growing and extending their shoots and branches, which helps to show how his theory of human nature is integrated with his view of the relationship between the family, moral cultivation, and the task of creating and maintaining a good society. Mengzi says, "Who does not serve someone? Serving one's parents is the root of all service. Who does not preserve something? Preserving one's self is the root of all preservation" (*Mengzi* 4A19). In 5A1, Mengzi makes clear that our feelings for our parents represent not just our initial natural moral feelings; if these feelings develop into the virtue of filial piety, they always remain strong:

> When people are young, they have affection for their parents. When they come to understand taking pleasure in beauty, then they have affection for those who are young and beautiful. When they have a wife and children, then they have affection for their wife and children. When they take office, then they have affection for their rulers. . . . But people of great filiality, to the end of their lives, have affection for their parents.

For Mengzi, there is a natural connection between affection and care for one's family and the capacity to care for others, evidenced in his claim that cultivated persons "treat their kin as kin, and then are benevolent toward the people" (*Mengzi* 7A45). The three things that cultivated people take joy in, Mengzi says, are first,

> that their father and mother are both alive and their siblings have no difficulties. Their second joy is that looking up they are not disgraced before Heaven, and looking down they are not ashamed before humans. Their third joy is getting the assistance of and cultivating the brave and talented people of the world. (*Mengzi* 7A20)[43]

Interestingly, Mengzi concludes this passage by noting that cultivated people do not take joy in being rulers, an indication that they are interested not in power but in teaching and nourishing people. In this passage we see the triangulation of the cultivated person's central concerns: first, filial piety and fraternal respect; second, being attentive to moral self-cultivation, including constant attentiveness to and examination of oneself; and third, contributing to the betterment of other members of society. Here we see the connections Mengzi draws between commitment to the family, to the task of self-cultivation, and to other members of society. These three areas are tightly bound together.

In 7A14 he also affirms the relationship between moral cultivation and political concerns: "Good regulations do not win over the people as well as good instruction. People are in awe of good regulations, but they love good instruction. Good regulations will get material resources from the people, but good instruction will win over the hearts of the people." For Mengzi, winning over the people's hearts means working to help their natural moral sensibilities develop and flourish. In 7A21, Mengzi goes on to say that although the cultivated person has political concerns, including the desire for a large territory and population, these are not the things in which he rejoices. Rather, he revels in "the benevolence, righteousness, propriety, and wisdom that are based in his heart as his nature. These are clearly manifest in his life and demeanor. They fill his torso and extend through his four limbs. Though he says nothing, his four limbs express them" (*Mengzi* 7A21).[44]

In terms of moral responsibilities, in Mengzi's view, the ruler's role resembles that of a parent. One aspect of this analogy is the powerful example the ruler provides for people in relation to moral cultivation, but it also concerns the political policies a ruler institutes and the way he governs. According to Mengzi, the sole purpose of rulers and states is to bring about the welfare of their people. He further maintains that until people's basic needs have been met, the task of moral cultivation cannot become a reality.

> For this reason, an enlightened ruler must regulate the people's livelihood to ensure that it is sufficient, on the one hand, to serve their fathers and mothers, and on the other hand, to nurture their wives and children. In good years, they are always full. In years of famine, they escape death. Only then do they rush toward the good, and thus the people follow the ruler easily. (*Mengzi* 1A7)

Without the people's basic needs provided for, Mengzi asks, "How could they have leisure for cultivating ritual and righteousness?" It is significant that Mengzi associates people's basic needs with their responsibilities in the context of the family: serving one's parents and nurturing one's wife and children are the primary needs that must be met. Mengzi also draws upon the family as a model for the various ways in which good rulers provide for their people's protection. In 1A4 Mengzi says, "Animals devour people, and people are appalled even when animals eat others of their kind. Now, one who governs is the people's parent. But in what respect is one a parent to the people if one leads animals to devour them?" Mengzi is well aware of the extraordinary power a ruler has over the people, similar to the power parents have over their children, but in both cases it should be unthinkable to act against the best interests of those for whom one is responsible.

The metaphor of parenting is a powerful tool for communicating Mengzi's view of political leadership, as well as his vision of a good society: "When one delights in the people's delights, the people will also delight in one's delights. When one worries about the people's worries, the people will also worry about one's worries" (*Mengzi* 1B4). These remarks underscore the integral role of moral psychology in Mengzi's account of human nature and moral cultivation, as well as in his political philosophy. It also becomes clear in passages such as this one that Mengzi envisions a society whose members exhibit a sense of sympathetic understanding and reciprocity (*shu* 恕). In 4A9, he says that past rulers lost the world

> because they lost the people. Losing the people is due to losing their hearts. There is a Way for getting the world: if you get the people, you will then get the world. There is a Way for getting the people: if you get their hearts, you will then get the people. There is a Way for getting their hearts: that which you desire, share with them in accumulating, and that which you dislike, do not inflict on them. People turn toward benevolence like water flowing downward or animals running toward the wilds.[45]

The references to acquiring people's hearts is connected to Mengzi's concern with developing incipient virtuous inclinations, and his reference to water flowing downward recalls his debate about human nature with Gaozi in 6A2. While Gaozi insists that human nature is neutral—like water that flows east or west depending upon how it is dammed—Mengzi points out that although water does not distinguish between east and west, it clearly distinguishes between up and down: "There is no human who does not tend toward goodness. There is no water that does not tend downward" (*Mengzi* 6A2). Mengzi's remarks in 4A9 also draw upon the attractive power of a ruler's Virtue.[46]

In 2A1 Mengzi says that if, in troubled times, a ruler puts into practice a benevolent government, nothing can prevent his becoming sovereign. He goes on to quote Kongzi, saying, "The flowing progress of virtue is more rapid than the transmission of [royal] orders by stages and couriers" (*Mengzi* 2A1).[47] Mengzi's reference to "the flowing progress of *de*" (德之流行) helps to illustrate his idea of how virtue comes to characterize an entire society. It is clear that Mengzi not only believes that the ideal of a benevolent government can be achieved through the cultivation of virtues like filial piety, but also that having a benevolent government ensures the survival and growth of these values in his society and in surrounding societies as well. In 2A5 Mengzi says that if a ruler has fair policies and carries them out through such things as giving honor to people with talent and virtue, employing these people, and not taxing goods in the marketplace when he levies rent on the shops, "then the people of neighboring states will welcome [him] like a father or mother. To lead sons and younger brothers to attack a father and mother is something that has never succeeded since the birth of humans."[48]

In 1B5 King Xuan of Qi asks Mengzi what a true royal government is, and Mengzi replies with a description of King Wen's government:

> Guilt for crime did not extend to the criminals' wives. The old without wives were called "widowers," the old without husbands were called "widows," the old without children were "bereft," the young without fathers were "orphans." These four were the poorest among the people and had none to bring their cares to. King Wen, in applying benevolent government, put these four first.

What is especially significant here is Mengzi's assertion that members of society who have been marginalized by the death of a spouse, the death of parents, or the inability to have children—individuals who might not be accommodated within a family-based ethical and political vision for society—ought to be made the first objects of the king's regard. The reason King Wen makes these groups the first objects of his regard is that he recognizes these individuals have suffered losses unlike any other. Mengzi stresses that King Wen not only *provides* for widowers, widows, the childless, and orphans, but makes them the *first* objects of his regard, which is consistent with the Confucian view that the family has a highly unique role in creating a good society. It is to be expected that Mengzi would highlight King Wen's concern for the childless, because of the religious views that motivate the obligation to have children and subsequent descendants. But Mengzi takes a wider view of the goods associated with the family by noting that King Wen includes orphans, who suffer the misfortune of not having parents to nurture their early moral development, and widows and widowers, who suffer the misfortune of not having a spouse with whom to share the burdens, joys, and challenges of life. Those without families ought to be a leader's top priority when it comes to providing for people, for, in Mengzi's view, the greatest disadvantage one could suffer in a society is to be without a family.[49]

Of the specific examples of filial piety and governing that Mengzi considers, Sage-King Shun is among the most well known. In a number of places, including 7A35, Mengzi praises Shun's filial piety, writing that if Shun's father had murdered someone, Shun "would have secretly carried him on his back and fled, to live in the coastland, happy to the end of his days, joyfully forgetting the world." Much like *Analects* 13.18, in which Kongzi expresses his disapproval of a son who immediately reports his father to the authorities after learning that his father stole a sheep, this passage does not necessarily undermine the importance of having a sense of justice or of one's obligations as a member of society (or in Shun's case, as the ruler).[50] Rather, it shows that according to Kongzi and Mengzi, obligations to one's parents take precedence over almost any other. At least in some circumstances, they viewed it as wrong to report one's father to the authorities. Both Kongzi and Mengzi make it clear that the virtues and moral sensibilities that enable us to become good members of a society are the natural outgrowth of our relationships with our families. When Mengzi says, "Treating one's parents as parents is benevolence. Revering one's elders is righteousness. There is nothing else to do but extend these to the world" (*Mengzi* 7A15), he indicates that our natural affection and respect for our parents and elders constitute the primary core of mature moral sensibilities. It is not surprising, then, that filial obligations are consistently seen as central in the *Mengzi*.

It is also important to pay close attention to Shun's actions in this passage and to contextualize them. First of all, in the scenario Mengzi describes, Shun abdicates the throne, which could be interpreted as an indication of his recognition that his actions, in taking his father into his care and fleeing the state, make him ineligible to serve as king. It certainly shows that he is unwilling to abuse his power: he does not simply pardon his father and continue to rule. Additionally, in taking his father to a remote area and remaining with him there, Shun protects the people from being harmed by his father. His actions, then, do not excuse his father's wrongdoing, as they would, for example, if he simply turned his father loose. Instead, on Mengzi's account, Shun essentially puts his father under permanent house arrest and serves as his jailor.[51] In these respects, he balances his filial and state duties. Regardless of whether we approve of this balance, Shun's actions do not show a disregard for his responsibilities to other members of society.

The *Mengzi*, though, offers a rather extensive background story concerning the events that transpired in Shun's relationship with his father; this can help us understand the significance of this widely cited scenario. Shun is not an ordinary individual, nor is his relationship with his parents remotely normal. Mengzi indicates that Shun was hated by his parents and by his elder brother, who attempted to murder him multiple times (5A2), but Shun only responded with love and affection for them (5A3, 5A4), and his way was "simply that of filial piety and fraternal respect" (6B2). Shun did not blindly follow along with traditional filial obligations in all cases, though. In 5A2 we learn that Shun did not inform his parents when he was to be married, because they would have prevented his marriage: "If he had informed his parents, then he would have had to abandon the greatest of human roles, which would have led to enmity with his father and mother."

In 4A26 Mengzi discusses why it was acceptable for Shun to deviate from the traditional practice of a child informing his parents about his plans to marry: "Among the three unfilial things, to have no posterity is the worst. Shun's taking a wife without informing his parents was in order to avoid having no posterity. Cultivated persons regard it as if he had informed them."[52] In both of these passages, Mengzi indicates that fulfilling the traditional obligation of a son in Shun's case—by notifying his parents of his marriage—would have resulted in a loss of filial piety in the long term, because it would have forced him to "abandon the greatest of human roles" and commit the most unfilial act: not having children. These remarks are especially significant, because they exhibit a concern not simply with performing the right action or bringing about good results in the immediate future; rather, filial piety sometimes means acting in ways that are only appreciated with the fullness of time. Shun seems to have had an especially keen sense of this with respect to his situation. Throughout the *Mengzi*, Shun is praised for having "fathomed the Way of serving one's parents" (4A28), and we are told that in the end his father was moved by his son's example and reformed his ways (5A4).

The fact that Shun is a moral exemplar despite having a terrible family situation might lead one to conclude that Mengzi thinks we have sufficient natural resources to become good even in the absence of a nurturing family environment. However, this would seem to be inconsistent with Mengzi's view as it is seen in many of the passages examined in this chapter. One possible explanation is that Shun's family life was closer to normal during his early years, but a traumatic event prompted a dramatic change in his relationship with his parents and elder brother. It must also be remembered that Shun is one of the sages, who were men of extraordinarily strong natural moral capacities. In Mengzi's view, Shun may have simply been born with greater moral strength than the rest of us; we might say that he started out with stronger, more fully developed moral sprouts than most people and as a result was able to endure a terrible environment without it destroying his potential or stunting his moral growth. In 1A7 Mengzi says that such individuals are the exception rather than the rule: "Only a superior individual can have a constant heart while lacking a constant means of support. Most people will not be able to maintain a constant heart if they lack a constant means of support."[53] In 5A5 Mengzi offers what could be viewed as a religious explanation for Shun's special capacities, writing that Heaven chose Shun and gave him the throne, "revealing its Mandate through actions and affairs."[54] Mengzi also says that Heaven prepares people for great service with great hardship (6B15), which seems to apply readily to Shun's case.

However, despite Shun's extraordinary moral capacity and his special religious mission, Mengzi still maintains that Shun was "the same as other people" (4B32). For Mengzi, we all have natural moral tendencies that set us on the path of virtue, and as a result of these tendencies and their remarkable potential, we all have the capacity to become sages. Although Shun was exceptional in many ways, he was still deeply hurt by his parents' rejection of him, which is a profoundly human response. In 5A1 Mengzi considers the question of why Shun would sometimes go out into the fields, crying and weeping. He writes that Shun was greatly pained that his parents did not love him, and explains,

> Of the scholars of the kingdom there were multitudes who flocked to him. The sovereign designed that [Shun] should superintend the kingdom along with him, and then transfer it to him entirely. But because his parents were not in accord with him, he felt like a poor man who has nowhere to turn to. To be delighted in by all the scholars of the kingdom, is what men desire, but it was not sufficient to remove his sorrow. (*Mengzi* 5A1)[55]

This passage highlights Shun's story as a poignant example of the critical role of parent–child relationships throughout a person's life, something central to Mengzi's account of how a good society is created and sustained.

XUNZI

It is the environment that is critical!

XUNZI 12/118/1

Although Xunzi and Mengzi agree on many aspects of moral self-cultivation, Xunzi does not believe that humans are initially inclined toward goodness. For Xunzi, humans are morally blind at birth, influenced only by their physical desires, which lead them to destruction and harm. Accordingly, humans must be stamped with the shape of morality, and their desires channeled and redirected to accord with the Way. There are important differences between Mengzi's "developmental model" of moral self-cultivation, evident in Mengzi's claim that we can cultivate the moral "sprouts" we are born with, and Xunzi's "re-formation model," which is expressed in the metaphors he uses. Like warped boards that are re-formed with steam and pressure to fit the Confucian design, humans are capable of moral cultivation—although it is a long and difficult process.[56] Xunzi writes, "Through steaming and bending, you can make wood straight as an ink-line into a wheel. And after its curve conforms to the compass, even when parched under the sun it will not become straight again, because the steaming and bending have made it a certain way" (*Xunzi* 1/1/3–4:1).[57]

Xunzi maintains that rituals and social obligations "are produced from the deliberate effort of the sage; they are not produced from people's nature. Thus, when the potter mixes up clay and makes vessels, the vessels are produced from the deliberate efforts of the craftsman; they are not produced from people's nature" (*Xunzi* 23/114/8–9:250). These aspects of Xunzi's view help to explain why he places such great emphasis on the role of a person's environment in the sort of person she becomes, and he uses a range of natural metaphors to express and develop his account.

> The root of the *lan huai* plant is sweet-smelling angelica, but if you soak it in foul water then the cultivated person will not draw near it, and the common people will not wear it. This happens not because the original material is not fragrant, but rather because of what it is soaked in. Therefore, the cultivated person is sure to select carefully the village where he dwells, and he is sure to associate with well-bred men when he travels. This is how he avoids corruption and draws near to what is correct (*Xunzi* 1/1/20–1/2/1:2–3).[58]

As we have seen, Xunzi rejects the view that humans are guided by an innate moral sense. Instead, as he maintains in this passage, they tend to take on the character of their environments. This makes the role of teachers and role models critical: "If you do not concur with your teacher and the proper model but instead like to use your own judgment, then this is like relying on a blind person to distinguish colors, or like relying on a deaf person to distinguish sounds" (*Xunzi* 2/8/3–4:14). For Xunzi, we simply begin with no sense of morality, which is akin to being unable to see or hear, and the analogy he draws with seeing and hearing helps to show that he conceives of moral cultivation as the process of acquiring moral sensibilities. Through a long and arduous process of self-cultivation, we are capable of acquiring moral capacities and the ability to judge situations properly, but the extent to which we acquire these capacities is a matter of the quality of the moral education we receive from teachers and role models as well as the effort and persistence of our study.

Given Xunzi's view of human nature, it is not surprising that he emphasizes how difficult it is to bring about behavioral change. He maintains that moral cultivation is a long-term process, and he returns to the metaphor of carving wood, metal, and stone to express and develop this view: "If you start carving and give up, you will not be able to break even rotten wood, but if you start carving and do not give up, then you can engrave even metal and stone" (*Xunzi* 1/2/11:4). He asks where learning begins and ends, arguing that "if you truly accumulate effort for a long time, then you will advance. Learning proceeds until death and only then does it stop. And so, the order of learning has a stopping point, but its purpose cannot be given up for even a moment. To pursue it is to be human, to give it up is to be a beast" (*Xunzi* 1/3/7–9:5). The last line of this passage is significant, because it shows that Xunzi sees us as developing capacities that define humanity when we develop moral capacities. Yet we can see how Mengzi and Xunzi mean very different things when they say that humans have the capacity for morality. For Xunzi, this capacity only becomes visible after a great deal of training and hard work, while for Mengzi, it is visible and active from the start, needing only the proper environment and cultivation to grow.

We have seen that for both Kongzi and Mengzi, natural feelings of affection and love within the family provide the foundation for the development of a person's moral character. Xunzi maintains that humans innately care for their own kin; of living things that have awareness, "none fails to love its own kind." Xunzi goes on to say that "none has greater awareness than humans, and so humans' feelings for their parents know no limit until the day they die" (*Xunzi* 19/96/10–13:213).[59] Because these feelings "know no limit," Xunzi contends that such feelings can lead to vicious action, just like other aspects of our uncultivated state. As Van Norden puts it, on a Xunzian view, "My innate love of my own kin might lead me to thoughtlessly and selfishly harm others to benefit my own parents or children" (Van Norden

2007:47). So according to Xunzi, the innate concern we have for our kin needs to be re-formed in order to reflect the virtue of filial piety.[60] Xunzi, then, is quite unlike Kongzi and Mengzi in his view, for he does not see the natural feelings humans have within families as something to be extended or developed. Rather, like our physical desires, filial love is unruly and dangerous and needs to be tamed and domesticated in order to serve moral ends.[61] We might even infer from his remarks that Xunzi is concerned that filial love might undermine political and social institutions through nepotism.

Xunzi describes a thoroughgoing transformation of one's person as the result of moral cultivation. He writes, "The learning of the cultivated person enters through his ears, fastens to his heart, spreads through his four limbs, and manifests itself in his actions. His slightest word, his most subtle movement, all can serve as a model for others" (*Xunzi* 1/3/14–15:5).[62] In passages such as this one, we see that Xunzi is concerned with transforming not simply behavior, but character: "Thus the learning of the cultivated person is used to improve his own person" (*Xunzi* 1/3/17:5-6).[63] Without the proper teachers and role models, Xunzi says, people will follow along with their nature and see things solely in terms of benefit to themselves.

It is noteworthy that for Xunzi, cultivated persons do not seek their own material interests, because this disposition is in direct contrast to our nature. As we have seen, Xunzi believes that human beings innately—before moral cultivation—seek the fulfillment of their own physical desires. On Xunzi's view, then, humans are natural egoists, and the task of moral cultivation and education is to move them from egoism to a moral point of view. To be sure, the form Xunzi describes is not normative egoism, or the view that humans *ought* to seek what they perceive to be their own benefit or gain, but a kind of descriptive psychological egoism, or the view that humans *do* seek what they perceive to be their own benefit or gain. Obviously Xunzi is referring to a particular form of descriptive egoism: his type only concerns humans in their natural state, before moral cultivation, and this state is not, nor should it be, permanent. His descriptive egoism is also confined to seeking the fulfillment of physical desires, as opposed to other kinds of personal benefits or gains. In his description of the cultivated person, though, we can see clearly that Xunzi believes people can depart from this natural form of egoism through the acquisition of other-regarding desires and moral sensibilities.

In a number of places, Xunzi makes clear that his concern is not confined to moral self-cultivation, but includes the task of creating and sustaining a good society. He maintains that these two areas are very closely related: "Now how about the way of the former kings and the ordering influence of *ren* [benevolence] and *yi* [righteousness], and how these make for communal life, mutual support, mutual adornment, and mutual security?" (*Xunzi* 4/15/20:28). Xunzi writes that even brothers would fight with one another over property if they followed their nature. "However, let them be transformed by the proper form and order contained in ritual and *yi* [righteousness]. If so, then they would even give it over to their countrymen" (*Xunzi* 23/114/17–18:251). It is through moral cultivation that people are transformed in such a way that they might be generous to other members of society and make sacrifices not simply for their own gain but for others in need.

Xunzi maintains that when political leaders have cultivated the virtues, they have tremendous motivational power and influence over the people. Xunzi seems to share aspects of Kongzi's and Mengzi's view that virtuous leaders have the power to attract and influence others. However, an important difference is that for Xunzi, people *already* must be following the path of self-cultivation in order to be influenced by a ruler in this way. According to his account of human nature and self-cultivation, we only begin to recognize the value of moral exemplars and traditions *after* we have successfully begun the learning process. It is important to keep this aspect of Xunzi's view in mind when considering his remarks on the virtuous ruler: "practicing loyalty, trustworthiness, and evenhandedness is more persuasive than offering them rewards and prizes; and making sure first to correct what lies within oneself and only then slowly reprimand what lies with others is more awe-inspiring than threatening them with penalties and punishments" (*Xunzi* 10/46/15–16:92). If Xunzi has the power of a ruler's *de* in mind when he maintains that a virtuous ruler more effectively motivates people to work toward a harmonious society than incentives or punishments, then he must be describing the ruler's influence on members of society who are already following the Way. So if Xunzi does share an understanding of moral power with Kongzi and Mengzi, it would seem to be a weaker (and perhaps more plausible) view, because on Xunzi's account of human nature, the presence of someone with this kind of virtue would be insufficient to move people to take up the task of self-cultivation, although it might play an inspirational role for those who are already engaged in this endeavor. This, as we shall see in the next chapter, makes the early influence of parents and other family members even more critically important in setting a person on the path of moral cultivation, in Xunzi's account.

That is not to say, however, that Xunzi does not value the role of laws and policies in good society. To the contrary, Xunzi articulates a much more robust appreciation for the role of laws and policies in a good society than either Kongzi or Mengzi. He maintains that an exemplary ruler not only cultivates benevolence and the standards of righteousness, but also works to rectify the legal code (*Xunzi* 9/41/5). "The punishments and laws he sets out for state and clan are all laws in accordance with *yi* [righteousness]. Those things which the ruler is extremely vigorous in leading his various ministers to turn their heads to are all *yi* intentions" (*Xunzi* 11/49/18:99). Xunzi maintains that there is an absolute obligation on the part of the government to provide for the people:

> Universally keeping watch over the people, universally caring for them, universally ordering them, so that even when the year's harvest is ruined by drought or flood they will not face the disasters of freezing or starving—these are the works of sagely lords and their worthy prime ministers. (*Xunzi* 10/44/17–18:88)

What is the relationship in the *Xunzi* between the family and these types of societal concerns? The *Analects* and the *Mengzi* both describe cases in which there was an apparent tension between filial piety and uprightness according to the law, between loyalty to one's parents and loyalty to the laws of the state. Xunzi addresses this issue as well, noting first that "to be filial upon entering and to be a good younger brother upon going out is lesser conduct. To be compliant to one's superiors and devoted to one's inferiors is middle conduct. To follow the Way and not one's lord, to follow *yi* [righteousness] and not one's father is the greatest conduct" (*Xunzi* 29/141/19–20:325). Xunzi might appear at first to be saying just the opposite of what Kongzi and Mengzi seem to say, namely that filial piety and loyalty to parents should *not* take precedence over other obligations.

We must read further to understand Xunzi's point. He goes on to discuss cases in which a filial son should not follow orders, including, first, when following orders would endanger his parents, but not following orders would make them safe, and, second, when following orders would disgrace his parents, but not following orders would bring them honor.[64] "If one understands the proper purposes of following and not following orders, and if one can be reverent, respectful, loyal, trustworthy, scrupulous, and honest so as to carry these out vigilantly, then this can be called the greatest filial piety" (*Xunzi* 29/142/2–3:325).[65] Xunzi clearly recognizes that there are exceptional cases in which we will be required to do something out of the ordinary and in violation of the orders or laws we would normally follow. In such cases, it would be wrong for us—and out of line with the Way— to adhere to the usual standard for conduct. It is important to recognize, though, that for Xunzi these are exceptional cases. Once we examine everything Xunzi has to say in this passage, we can appreciate his point when he says that fulfilling filial duties to parents and elder siblings is "lesser conduct," while following the Way in actions outside the family is the greatest conduct, for it requires more of us in terms of our moral capacities. These capacities are not disconnected from the virtue of filial piety, however, and filial piety will continue to play an important role in our ability to act as we should, whether that means "following the Way and not one's lord" or "following righteousness and not one's father." We see that Xunzi's picture here seems to be in line with the *Analects*' claim that filial piety is the root of other moral capacities and virtues and grows when we extend our moral sensibilities not just to our families but within our immediate communities and then to other members of society.

Throughout the *Xunzi*, the importance of attending to family relationships and roles is presented as centrally important, as is the deference and respect for elders cultivated within the context of filial piety. When the cultivated person meets a fellow villager, "he enacts the *yi* [standard of righteousness] of an elder or junior. When he encounters his seniors, then he enacts the *yi* of a son or younger brother. . . . When he encounters those who are lowly or who are young, then he enacts the *yi* of being guiding and tolerant. There are none for whom he does not feel concern. There are none for whom he does not show respect" (*Xunzi* 6/23/15–16:44). A part of the cultivated person's Way stems from the capacity to extend to others his demeanor toward his own parents and elder siblings. The ability to understand and respond appropriately to the needs of older members of a community and of society in general is augmented by the understanding of the sort of care a son or daughter would want aging parents to receive. In addition to providing care to the disabled, Xunzi maintains that governmental policies should take into account the special needs of orphans, widows, widowers, and elderly members of society who do not have children—advice reminiscent of the *Mengzi*.[66] These groups, as I noted in relation to Mengzi's discussion, have in common the loss of spouses, children, or parents, and Xunzi, like Mengzi, clearly recognizes that these losses are especially harmful to a person's well-being. Yet alongside his emphasis on the role of laws and policies, Xunzi maintains that the role of cultivated persons in a good society is irreplaceable: "With the cultivated person present, even if the rules are sketchy, they are enough to be comprehensive. Without the cultivated person, even if the rules are complete, one will fail to apply them in the right order" (*Xunzi* 12/57/5–6:117).[67] In light of Xunzi's account of human nature and his assertion that the right kind of political leader and the proper society can help transform a person's character, it should not surprise us that he concludes book 23 with the resounding declaration, "It is the environment that is critical! It is the environment that is critical!" (*Xunzi* 12/118/1).[68]

* * *

In this chapter, we have examined the strong emphasis the early Confucians placed on moral cultivation and their view that the family has a special role in this process and their assertion that moral cultivation helps to create a good society. These writers maintain that genuine, far-reaching change in a society is possible when we recognize that parent–child relationships generally and filial piety in particular provide the foundation for a person's moral development. In the next chapter, we examine what the early Confucians have to say about the role of environment during the earliest years of a child's development. As we shall see, a number of early Confucian sources provide considerable detail on the specific and observable ways in which the quality of the relationships between parents and children during infancy and childhood directly affects a society.

2

INFANTS, CHILDREN, AND EARLY CONFUCIAN MORAL CULTIVATION

The matters of choosing attendants and early instruction are most urgent. Now, if the crown prince receives a good education and his attendants are correct, then he will be correct. If he is correct, then the people of the world will be settled. . . . This is the task for our time.

—BAOFU, 15

ALTHOUGH SCHOLARS HAVE given considerable attention to the virtue of filial piety and the centrality of family relationships in the early Confucian tradition, there has been little investigation of early Confucian views of parent–child relationships during childhood or the moral cultivation of children.[1] In this chapter I explore what early Confucian thinkers have to say about moral cultivation during childhood, especially in the earliest years of a child's life but also including discussions of youth. I will focus on three primary questions: First, to what extent is childhood moral cultivation an important part of the views of Kongzi, Mengzi, and Xunzi? Second, are the early years of a child's life viewed as a unique and irreplaceable opportunity for moral cultivation in early Confucianism? Within the context of this question, I explore how early Confucians understood the roles of parents and caregivers, as well as rites and filial piety, in childhood moral cultivation. Third and finally, I discuss the question of how childhood moral cultivation is related to the task of creating a good society in early Confucianism.

CHILDREN AND YOUTH IN EARLY CONFUCIANISM

In *Virtue Ethics and Consequentialism in Early Chinese Philosophy*, Bryan W. Van Norden writes that unlike Plato, Aristotle, and Zhu Xi, who have "much to say about the education of the youth," the early Confucians "say little on this topic" (2007:50). He notes, "This may reflect the belief that early childhood was not an important time for ethical conditioning," but adds that Joel Kupperman has "suggested several alternative explanations for why Kongzi seems to have ignored this topic" (2007:50n102). Indeed, Kupperman points out that the *Analects* says relatively little that explicitly concerns the ethical importance of early upbringing, which is a marked contrast to the extensive discussions of the more advanced stages of ethical development in the text (Kupperman 1999:37). Kupperman suggests three possible reasons for this omission. First, "teachers and writers, including philosophers, often do not say what does not need to be said: what it can be assumed that virtually everyone in the audience already knows." Kupperman implies that early Chinese thinkers *did* regard the early upbringing of children as ethically important—so important, in fact, that it did not need to be emphasized. He writes that early upbringing may not have been problematic in Kongzi's China, as it was in Aristotle's Greece, and as a result there was not a pressing need to address the topic; this view is supported at least in part by the fact that Kongzi was indeed addressing issues he viewed as problems in his society. However, among the problems Kongzi articulates in the *Analects* is a lack of filial piety— seen, for example, in his statement "Nowadays [filial piety] is taken to mean just seeing that one's parents get enough to eat. But we do that much for dogs or horses as well" (*Analects* 2.7). These issues do not seem to be entirely disconnected from the matter of moral cultivation during childhood and youth, since young people were expected to fulfill various kinds of filial duties in relation to their parents in Kongzi's time.[2]

The second possible reason Kupperman offers for the lack of attention to early upbringing in the *Analects* is that Kongzi's students "were no longer small children when they arrived, and it would be natural for him to have much more to say about the stage of their ethical development in which he had a major role than about much earlier stages." This explanation is more promising, and it takes into account the fact that different texts have different intended audiences, as did the teachings of which they are records. For instance, Xunzi, whose audience was primarily composed of lords of state, their ministers, and people aspiring to be ministers, spent much of his time addressing topics related to governance. As we shall see in this chapter, a variety of texts in the Confucian tradition do address the early upbringing of children, but a number of these are geared toward particular audiences—including mothers who are raising children and rulers who need to understand the connection between the early upbringing of children and the work of creating and sustaining a good society. The third explanation Kupperman offers is that Kongzi may have regarded this sphere of education as the province of the family and thus "best left to the judgment of parents" (Kupperman 1999:37). This explanation, like the first one he offers, is less compelling; as we shall see in this chapter and have already explored to some extent in the previous chapter, the early Confucians—including Kongzi—consistently maintained that family and society are integrally connected. A number of early Confucian thinkers further argued that early childhood moral cultivation is a matter that directly pertains to a good society, and this is why they offered arguments to rulers on the subject. For this reason, it is not quite accurate to say they viewed it as a private matter.

Van Norden maintains that Kongzi is not the only early Confucian thinker who leaves these matters largely untouched. He says that Mengzi, too, fails to discuss the education of children at any length, again noting the contrast with ancient Greek philosophers and also mentioning modern psychological literature on this topic: "It is interesting that there is a paucity of discussion of childhood education and conditioning in the *Mengzi*. Childhood experience is stressed as a crucial factor in character formation by both Plato and Aristotle, as well as by modern developmental psychologists of various persuasions" (Van Norden 2007:229). Van Norden acknowledges David Wong's argument that there are Confucian texts "that suggest the importance of childhood nurturing in the family for ethical development. However, Mengzi himself does not seem to stress the importance of childhood itself as a unique, irreplaceable opportunity for ensuring the growth and continued existence of our sprouts."[3] He adds that Mengzi "seems more interested in the influence of environment on adults than he does in its influence on children" (Van Norden 2007:229).

In what follows I examine what Kongzi and Mengzi, as well as Xunzi, have to say about the topic of the moral education and cultivation of children and youth. I argue that although moral cultivation during childhood is certainly not the main focus of these texts, there are a number of passages demonstrating the writers' assumption that the matter is important.

THE ANALECTS

Perhaps the most obvious passage from the *Analects* to make clear the importance of early moral cultivation is 1.2:

> A person who is filial to his parents and respectful of his elder brother is rarely the kind of person who is inclined to go against his superiors, and there has never been a case of one who is disinclined to go against his superiors stirring up rebellion. The cultivated person applies himself to the root. "Once the root is established, the Way will flourish." Filial piety and brotherly respect—are these not the roots of humaneness?[4]

The recognition of the absolute importance of filial piety and its role as the foundation of ethical sense is perhaps the clearest indicator of how important the early Confucians considered childhood education to be. This passage refers to establishing the "roots" from which humaneness grows. As we saw in the previous chapter, humaneness is a quality possessed by those who have mastered the full range of Confucian virtues. This allows us to appreciate the full force of the claim: filial piety and brotherly respect are the roots of the other virtues; they provide the foundation for the entire course of a person's moral development. One of the main points of *Analects* 1.2 is that the problems seen in adulthood—such as the tendency to defy one's superiors or stir up a rebellion—have their deepest origins in family relationships. While the passage does not specify when we begin to cultivate filial piety and brotherly respect, it is important to attend to the developmental metaphors expressed in the claim that the *roots* need to be established in order for the Way to *grow and flourish*. The development of roots is part of the earliest stage of a plant's growth, and as roots continue to grow, they also enable the rest of the plant to grow and flourish. These developmental metaphors suggest that the development of filial piety and respect for elders begins during the earliest stages of an individual's moral education. Given how early our relationships with our parents and elder siblings begin, it seems reasonable to assume that these virtues are initially cultivated during childhood.[5]

There are other passages in the *Analects* that give us some indication of how Kongzi views childhood education. *Analects* 7.29 recounts the following story:

> The people of Hu Village were difficult to talk to [about the Way]. Therefore, when a young boy from the village came for an interview with the Master, the disciples hesitated to let him in. The Master said, "In allowing him to enter, my concern was with what brought him here, not with what he did after he left. What was so wrong about that? If a person purifies himself to enter, I accept his purification—but I do not expect guarantees about what he will do once he leaves."[6]

In this case, Kongzi is receiving an uncapped youth for an interview, and the boy has learned and followed correctly the proper purification rituals, which shows he has undergone a notable degree of moral education. Capping traditionally occurred at age nineteen, so we can assume that the boy is a teenager or younger.[7]

In considering what this passage may tell us about Kongzi's views on children's moral cultivation, we might infer that Kongzi sees the boy because he thinks a young person will be more malleable and open to instruction than the other people in this village, who are difficult to approach. Indeed, some commentators understand this passage as an indication of Kongzi's optimism about the possibility for change; if this interpretation is correct, then Kongzi might be drawn to the child's sincerity and perhaps also his unique potential as compared with the adults in his village. It is at least plausible that Kongzi would be impressed with the boy's understanding of and appreciation for the rites; this reverence, combined with his young age, is an indicator of his potential. We might also view this passage in relation to *Analects* 9.23, where Kongzi says, "Respect those younger than yourself [後生可畏]. How do you know that the coming generation may not prove as good as our present one? But if a person lives to forty or fifty and hasn't been heard of, then he's no longer worthy of respect." In this passage, Kongzi affirms the potential of the young, as compared with those who are older, suggesting that at a certain point in a person's life, change is unlikely and that person's character can be reliably inferred. This, of course, implies that personal change is more likely earlier in life. This passage offers further evidence of the importance of the moral education of the young.

In *Analects* 19.12 we find another relevant passage. Here, Kongzi's student, Ziyou, says, "Among the disciples of Zixia, the younger ones are competent at sprinkling and sweeping, receiving and responding to guests, advancing and retiring.[8] But these are minor affairs. Question them on the fundamentals, and they have no answer. How can that be?" Upon hearing this, Zixia says, "Ah—Ziyou is mistaken. In the Way of the cultivated person, what is to be taught first, what can be put aside until later? It's like the case of plants or trees, which require different types of handling. But the Way of the cultivated person—how can it be handled correctly? And who understands it from beginning to end?—only the sage can do that!" Although this passage does not refer to young children, it does concern older youths. Edward Slingerland notes that here we find Ziyou

criticizing Zixia for making his younger disciples practice minor ritual tasks instead of teaching them about the "important" issues, but what he fails to understand is that only someone who starts at the beginning of the Way of the *junzi* can truly walk to its end. This means that the teacher must distinguish between the "grass" (the younger students at the beginning of the path) and the "trees" (the more mature students capable of advanced work), and target his instruction accordingly—forcing students to learn things of which they are not yet capable leads only to exhaustion. (Slingerland 2003:225)

Slingerland quotes from Bao Xian's commentary on the passage: "Zixia's point is that those who are taught the Way too early will inevitably be the first to grow tired, and therefore he starts his disciples off with minor tasks, and only later instructs them in great matters" (Slingerland 2003:225).

This passage thus emphasizes the importance of age-appropriate moral cultivation as well as the value of tasks that may appear insignificant but in fact have an important impact on development of moral character. It also confirms the view expressed in *Analects* 1.2: one grows up to follow the Way only if the proper "roots" are established, "starting at the beginning and working through to the end." The beginning stages, as 1.2 tells us, include the cultivation of filial piety and respect for elders, as well as the mastery of tasks like sprinkling and sweeping the floors or receiving and responding to guests, as 19.12 states. While 1.2 specifies the virtues one must cultivate early in life in order to follow the Way, 19.12 gives us a sense of the specific activities that can contribute to the development of these and other virtues and moral sensibilities in the young. Here the *Analects* resists a sharp separation between the moral cultivation of children and youth and the everyday activities of life. Moral cultivation does not occur in a classroom or consist primarily of formal lessons but is continually integrated into the activities and interactions that are a part of a child's daily life. We see, then, that both the theoretical dimensions of this process (i.e., descriptions of the virtues and moral sensibilities children must develop) and the practical or applied dimensions of it (i.e., specific activities that shape a child's character) are discussed in the text.

Analects 18.7 tells of an encounter Kongzi's disciple Zilu had with a scholar-recluse, perhaps a proto-Daoist, who seems to reject certain aspects of traditional society and culture by living in seclusion and avoiding an official position. This person nevertheless presents his two sons to Zilu in the proper manner when he invites Zilu into his home. Zilu later notes the contrast between these behaviors: "You understand that the etiquette between elder and younger cannot be set aside. How, then, can the right relations between ruler and subject be set aside?" Zilu is puzzled by the contrast between the scholar-recluse's observation of proper relations between elders and juniors and his disinterest in an official position. This passage highlights the importance of relations between elders and juniors and in particular the proper introduction of one's children to guests in Kongzi's time; it also indicates that customs regarding the proper upbringing of children were observed even by people who intentionally rejected other traditional practices. This shows that child-rearing practices were widely agreed upon and valued, even in the midst of political disagreement. It also helps to make clear that for Kongzi and his students, the Confucian Way constituted a comprehensive way of life. Zilu has difficulty making sense of how the scholar-recluse could accept certain standards for the relationships between children and their elders while rejecting those concerning his relationship to the ruler; this confusion arises from the fact that the customs regarding the proper upbringing of children were important to Kongzi's followers and were, for them, an integral part of the Confucian Way. Like the other passages we have examined, this passage shows that the *Analects* affirms the importance of the moral cultivation of the young.

There is very little in the *Analects* specifically concerning parents' roles in the moral cultivation of their children during childhood and youth, but one passage remarks on Kongzi's relationship with his son. In *Analects* 16.13, Chen Gang (Ziqin) asks Kongzi's son Boyu whether he has received any special instructions as a son:

> No, replied Boyu. But once, when my father was standing by himself and I hurried across the courtyard, he said, Have you studied the *Odes*? Not yet, I replied. He said, If you don't study the *Odes*, you won't know how to speak properly! So after that I studied the *Odes*. Another day, when he was standing by himself and I hurried across the courtyard, he said, Have you studied the rites? Not yet, I replied. He said, If you don't study the rites, you won't have any basis to stand on. So after that I studied the rites. He gave me these two pieces of instruction. Afterward Chen Gang, delighted, said, I asked for one question and learned three things. I learned about the *Odes*, I learned about the rites, and I learned that the cultivated person maintains a certain distance in relations with his son.

It is tempting for contemporary interpreters to focus on the last line of this passage and to read it in light of our own values and practices. From this perspective, 16.13 seems to present the picture of a cold and alienating father–son relationship. This may be how we would judge the relationship, but is it how someone from Kongzi's culture and time would view it? The commentarial tradition is a helpful resource here. The Song commentator Sima Guang writes, "To 'keep at a distance' refers not to being cold or alienating, but rather to being timely in the way one allows one's son to approach, and always receiving him with ritual propriety. The point is simply that father and son do not consort with one another day and night in an indecently familiar manner."[9]

Other passages in the *Analects* that refer to "distancing" support Sima Guang's reading. In 6.22, Fan Chi asks about wisdom, and Kongzi says, "Work to lead the people toward what is right. Respect the ghosts and spirits but keep them at a distance—this can be called wisdom." What does "respect the ghosts and spirits but keep them at a distance" mean? Just as some contemporary interpreters are inclined to give 16.13 a negative connotation, a number of contemporary interpreters have suggested that in 6.22 Kongzi distances himself from traditional religious beliefs and practices.[10] However, this reading would conflict with passages in the *Analects* that describe Kongzi's observance of traditional sacrificial practices (e.g., 10.8), and it also fails to explain why keeping the spirits at a distance should be given more interpretive weight than respecting the spirits. Slingerland points out that "'respecting the ghosts and spirits while keeping them at a distance' is understood by most [commentators] as fulfilling one's sacrificial duties sincerely and in accordance with ritual (3.12), without trying to flatter the spirits or curry favor with them (2.24)" (Slingerland 2003:60). As Michael Puett argues, in 6.22 Kongzi is "not claiming that spirits do not exist. Indeed, he explicitly called on people to be reverent toward them" (Puett 2002:97).

There is significant evidence to support the view that "distancing" (*yuan* 遠) in both 6.22 and 16.13 refers to maintaining appropriate filial distance according to the dictates of ritual. At a general level, a father maintains distance from his son by remembering his role as teacher, guide, and disciplinarian. At a specific level, he follows ritually appropriate conduct. This view takes seriously the power differential between parents and children; good parents do not try to create the illusion that this distance does not exist by behaving as their child's friend. Likewise, children acknowledge this distance by showing their parents respect and following their guidance. Similarly, one keeps spirits at a distance in order to show them respect, a practice that is also advisable on Kongzi's view, because he disapproves of attempts to curry the favor of the spirits in order to further one's own selfish ends. The patterns of conduct that include keeping an appropriate distance as an expression of respect are codified in the rites.

Now, there are multiple reasons why Kongzi's conduct toward his son might strike us as unappealing. First of all, when we speak of "keeping someone at a distance," it is not a favorable expression with regard to any relationship, let alone one with children. Indeed, unlike the Confucians, we rarely use that phrase to describe appropriate conduct in relationships. Additionally, these patterns of conduct obviously do not conform to contemporary liberal Western views of parent–child relationships, which encourage more affection, closeness, and outward displays of emotion by children and parents alike. Similarly, many evangelical Protestant Christians today encourage viewing one's relationship with God in an open light, wherein one does not maintain "distance" from God in a spirit of reverence or respect but rather cultivates an affectionate friendship with God, especially in the person of Jesus. There is an important parallel here, and it serves as a reminder that the relationship between parents and children was in some ways akin to a religious relationship in ancient China.

Taking into account the religious context of early China—in which filial piety was a part of ritual propriety in sacrificing to ancestral spirits and in which one had filial obligations to the dead and the living alike— can help us make better sense of these kinds of passages in the *Analects*. I would argue that the most plausible reading of the passage does not see it as valorizing fathers who are cold, neglectful, and alienated from their sons, but rather as a description of appropriate filial distance. We have good reasons to judge harshly the lack of paternal involvement—including the lack of closeness between fathers and sons—in ancient China and throughout most of human history, including our own culture until very recently. But we should distinguish that normative task from the task of describing and understanding the overall aims and intentions of Confucian practices historically. It is also important to avoid assuming that a given practice or phrase means the same thing in ancient China that it means to us; "keeping one's son at a distance" meant something different in ancient China than it would mean for parents today. Additionally, we may find that there are aspects of the Confucian view that we agree with, even if we do not agree with their application of those views in specific practices.

MENGZI

The *Mengzi*, too, contains a number of passages that refer to the younger members of society and their moral education and cultivation. The first of the "five relationships" mentioned in *Mengzi* 3A4.8 is that of parent and child, and Mengzi claims that "the relation of father and children is one of love [親]." A couple of things are especially noteworthy here. First, Mengzi refers to "children" or "sons" (子), and we do not have any reason to think this is an exclusive reference to adult parent–child relationships. On the contrary, as we shall see, Mengzi says explicitly that infants naturally respond to their parents with love. Second, this passage describes the *character* of proper parent–child relationships, and in commenting on the fact that this relation should be characterized by love, Mengzi exhibits an awareness that children are critically shaped by the kind of relationship they have with their parents. In this passage, Mengzi also offers *instruction* on the character of the most fundamental human relationships by describing the features that should define these relationships above all else. This is important, because it shows this passage can at least plausibly be interpreted as relating to the moral cultivation of children.

On such an interpretation, this passage helps us to see that for Mengzi, moral cultivation does not simply consist of learning the rites or mastering filial duties; moral cultivation occurs partly as a result of the feelings that parents and children have for one another. The child's character is critically shaped not only by the things her parents teach her, but also by the relationship that develops in the course of their daily interactions, including especially the love and affection that define this relation. Such a view is consistent with Mengzi's discussion of human nature, as well as his account of the important role that family and community relationships play in the process of moral cultivation.

Mengzi makes other references to very young children and the way they are shaped by loving relationships with their parents. *Mengzi* 7A15 says, "Among babes in arms [孩提之童] there is none that does not know to love its parents. When they grow older [及其長也], there is none that does not know to respect its elder brother. Treating one's parents as parents is benevolence. Respecting one's elders is righteousness. There is nothing else to do but to extend these to the world." In this passage Mengzi indicates that moral cultivation consists of *extending* both the natural responses of infants to their parents and, as they grow, the natural sense of respect they have for their older siblings. More importantly, Mengzi claims that extending these fundamental moral impulses constitutes the primary core of mature moral sensibilities such as benevolence. This passage shows very clearly, then, the importance of early moral education for Mengzi; mature moral sensibilities are not viewed by him as developing in a separate (and later) stage from humans' earliest moral impulses. On the contrary, the core of our mature moral sensibilities is first seen within the context of the family, in the moral impulses we initially exhibit in relation to our parents and siblings.

Once again, we see that for Mengzi early childhood moral education is largely defined by the way we are shaped by our relationships with our parents and siblings, and he ties this claim to his theory of human nature, telling us that these relationships grow out of our natural tendencies. Mengzi begins in this passage by discussing infants, and it is reasonable to infer that he thinks the process of moral development begins in early childhood. He does not suggest that our natural moral tendencies remain static for several years before the process of cultivation begins; indeed, if Mengzi held such a position, one would expect him to discuss it, especially because such a view stands in tension with his agricultural metaphors for the development of our incipient moral inclinations. Sprouts are dynamic and active, growing steadily from the start; after sprouts are planted, "they grow rapidly" (6A7)—this suggests that moral development begins during the earliest stages of a child's life.

Mengzi also discusses the moral education of young adults. In 6A7 he says, "In years of plenty, most young men [子弟] are gentle; in years of poverty, most young men are cruel. It is not that the potential that Heaven confers on them varies like this. They are like this because of that by which their hearts are sunk and drowned." Here Mengzi describes the critical role of a young man's environment in shaping his character and nurturing or harming his natural moral inclinations. We should note that in this passage, Mengzi explicitly refers to *young men* who are *already* either gentle or cruel due to the way that their environment has affected them. According to this passage, the process of moral development—specifically the cultivation or destruction of inherent moral tendencies—has already occurred in young men. Clearly Mengzi is not discussing moral cultivation during adulthood; among other things, he is stressing just how early in life the process of moral development begins and how quickly our natural moral tendencies can visibly flourish or be damaged beyond repair. Such a view is consistent with what we have seen thus far in Mengzi's writings.

In some places Mengzi provides more detailed advice regarding the earlier stages of moral education and cultivation. In 7A24 he emphasizes the importance of students' completing lessons in the proper order, which resonates with what we saw in the *Analects*, when it was mentioned that students should master minor skills before proceeding to more challenging subjects. Mengzi also specifies the importance of an individual having teachers other than his parents. When asked why the cultivated person does not teach his son, Mengzi replies,

> In order to instruct, you must correct what someone else does. If the correction does not work, one must follow it up with reprimands. If one follows it up with reprimands, then it will hurt the feelings of the son, who will say, "My father instructs me by correcting me. But my father is not always correct himself." Then the father and son will hurt the feelings of each other. (*Mengzi* 4A18)

Mengzi says that this situation leads parents and children to become estranged from one another. He is aware that care should be taken to avoid straining or damaging parent–child relationships unnecessarily, and he understands that it is important for children to learn to cultivate healthy relationships with adults other than their parents. An additional dimension of this passage is Mengzi's emphasis on the importance of children learning to take criticism from others, which is essential for self-cultivation. These are significant insights; children do benefit from opportunities to interact with and learn from adults other than their parents, and as he points out, children are often less likely to challenge other, less familiar adults in the ways they challenge their own parents. The tendency of children—even very young children—to challenge or "push the envelope" with their own parents stems partly from their confidence in the parent–child relationship and their comfort level and familiarity with their parents.

There are many other passages in which Mengzi emphasizes the critical role that a person's moral surroundings and influences—like other aspects of her environment—play in her development. *Mengzi* 7A36 recounts a situation in which, after observing the king's son, Mengzi remarks, "People's surroundings affect their *qi* like nourishment affects their bodies. Great indeed is the influence of a person's surroundings. Are we not all someone's child?" He then adds, "The house, the carriage, horses and attire of the prince are mostly the same as other people, yet the prince is different. This is because of the surroundings. How much more if one were to dwell in the wide house of the world."[11] Here Mengzi distinguishes between moral education and bodily nourishment or material comfort, noting that he observes a difference in the prince's moral character that is due to his moral surroundings as opposed to his wealth and privilege. With the remark "Are we not all someone's child?," Mengzi reminds us that our parents profoundly shape our character and play the most critical role in defining our surroundings—which includes not just having our physical needs met but the moral education we receive. Indeed, the last phrase, "to dwell in the wide house of the world," is a metaphor for having excellence of character, and Mengzi elaborates on this metaphor in 3B2:

> To dwell in the wide house of the world, to stand in the correct seat of
> the world, and to walk in the great path of the world; when he obtains his
> desire *for office*, to practice his principles for the good of the people; and

when that desire is disappointed, to practice them alone; to be above the power of riches and honours to make dissipated, of poverty and mean condition to make swerve from principle, and of power and force to make bend—these characteristics constitute the great man.[12]

We can see in this passage that Mengzi is concerned not only with moral cultivation but with the influence that a morally cultivated ruler can have on a society. In 4A20 Mengzi says, "If a ruler is benevolent, no one will fail to be benevolent. If a ruler is righteous, no one will fail to be righteous. If a ruler is correct, no one will fail to be correct. As soon as one makes the ruler correct, the state will be settled." Here we see again the close connection between moral cultivation and political philosophy in early Confucian thought. Most importantly, all of these passages help to show that Mengzi affirms the importance of early childhood moral cultivation, even if he does not provide a systematic account of what early childhood moral cultivation involves.

XUNZI

Given that both Kongzi and Mengzi discuss the importance of early moral cultivation, it is unsurprising that Xunzi addresses the topic as well. All three of these thinkers are self-cultivationists and thus share an interest in moral development. Just as Mengzi's agricultural metaphors suggest the importance he places on early moral cultivation, certain features of Xunzi's discussion suggest the importance of early cultivation in his thought. In book 2, Xunzi says:

If he is scrupulous, honest, properly compliant, and a good younger brother, then he can be called a good youth [善少]. If he has in addition to these a love of learning, amenability, and a keen mind, then he will have talents equal to those to whom none are superior, and he may use them to become a true cultivated person. If he is lazy and cowardly, if he is shameless and cares only for food and drink, then he can be called a bad youth [惡少]. If he has in addition to these a fierce disobedience and a dangerous, villainous lack of respect for his elder brothers, then he can be called an inauspicious youth [詳少], and he may even fall so far as to suffer capital punishment. (*Xunzi* 2/8/7–9:14-15)[13]

We can be reasonably certain that those Xunzi calls "youths" (少) in this passage would have undergone considerable moral education and cultivation by this time in their lives, because Xunzi does not think it is possible for an individual to be diligent, obedient, and respectful of elders without considerable cultivation and re-formation of character. Since he maintains here that there are indeed "good youths"—who exhibit considerable moral cultivation even though they are still young—Xunzi must view the early moral education of children as both important and quite rigorous. Xunzi's references to "good youths" and "bad youths" employ the same language he uses to describe the character of human nature: while humans only become good (善) through extensive cultivation, our natural, uncultivated state is bad (惡). The last line of the passage further suggests that a person who has not undergone significant moral cultivation by the time he is a "youth" has little or no hope for rehabilitation, for Xunzi suggests that such a one may suffer death as punishment. In considering Xunzi's assertion that these youths are "inauspicious," it may be helpful to recall the claim made in *Analects* 1.2 that young people who cultivate filial piety are not those who stir up rebellions. In contrast, Xunzi's "inauspicious" youths engage in activities (including villainous disrespectfulness to elders) that suggest their future is unsalvageable. This passage indicates that Xunzi thinks children's moral cultivation is absolutely critical at the earliest stages, for if young children are not properly cultivated, there is little hope of reforming their character as youths.

Additional passages in the *Xunzi* make it clear that the young must be engaged in study early on to succeed on the path of self-cultivation. In these passages, the *Xunzi* offers quotations from Kongzi, an indication that in Xunzi's time, Kongzi was seen as emphasizing early moral education: "Not being able to devote one's strength to learning when one is young, and so having nothing to teach others when one is old—this I consider shameful" (*Xunzi* 28/140/11:322). This passage emphasizes the connection between diligence and discipline in learning as a child and the ability to make a contribution to society as an adult. In a related passage, Kongzi is quoted as saying that the cultivated person reflects on the fact that if he is young and yet does not study, then when he becomes older he will have no abilities. "This is why the cultivated person, when he is young, reflects on being older, and so he studies" (*Xunzi* 30/144/22–23).[14] This passage again highlights Xunzi's view that the path of moral self-cultivation begins early. Those who will become cultivated people foresee and reflect on the consequences of their actions when they are young, understanding that their lives when they are grown will be affected by their present choices. Additionally, from an early age they understand and abide by the distinctions between ages and the corresponding age-appropriate roles, such as studying and instructing.

Indeed, in a number of places, Xunzi discusses the appropriate order for "elders" (長) and "youth" (幼 or 少), and these passages help to show that Xunzi thinks the moral cultivation of the young is important. He refers to how the ancient kings established appropriate differences (差) between the old and young (*Xunzi* 4/17/1), and how they adorned the old and young accordingly to make clear the distinctions between them (12/60/5). "To divide the intimate from the more distant, to give proper ordering to elders and the young—this is the way of the former kings" (24/119/12:260). He considers the differences between the old and young alongside those of lord and minister, superior and inferior, and the noble and the lowly (11/54/12), and notes that the cultivated person is careful to observe all of these distinctions (19/90/10). Xunzi notes that there are principles or patterns (*li* 理) that must be followed in relationships between the old and the young (22/110/14), and he also associates the proper order for the old and young with the standards of righteousness. According to Xunzi, if among lord and minister, superior and inferior, the noble and the lowly, and the old and the young, everyone behaves according to the standards of righteousness, then everyone in the world will desire to do the same (16/76/18). "When social distinctions and the standards of righteousness are kept clear," Xunzi says, then a ruler is cherished by the people "like a father and mother" (16/75/13–14).[15] Xunzi also highlights the problem of being "young and yet unwilling to serve one's elders" (5/18/7) and says that when people follow their unlimited desires, which are a part of their unrefined nature as humans, "the young insult their elders," among other calamities (10/42/18).

These passages concerning the appropriate order for the old and the young are interesting to consider in light of Xunzi's claim, "The children of the Han, Yue, Yi, and Mo peoples all cry with the same sound at birth, but when grown they have different customs, because teaching makes them thus" (*Xunzi* 1/1/8:1). Xunzi is clearly aware that children stand in need of moral cultivation from birth and are shaped dramatically by that process. When Xunzi decries the young insulting their elders or being unwilling to serve them, it is clear that he thinks they should have already learned to show proper respect for their elders. Xunzi does not say that the youth simply have yet to undergo this process of moral cultivation, or that they are just too young to understand the distinctions between the old and the young. Instead, he gives multiple examples of the proper order for the old and the young being observed by *both* the old and the young. These passages do not explicitly describe the process of instructing and cultivating young adults, but because Xunzi does not believe people naturally behave in the proper ways, the idea that moral cultivation of the young is being practiced is implicit.[16]

EARLY CONFUCIAN VIEWS ON THE UNIQUE ROLE OF EARLY CHILDHOOD

The question of whether there is an appreciation in early Confucianism for the unique role of childhood—especially its earliest period—in the process of moral cultivation is particularly important. For even though there are references to children and youth and their cultivation in classical Confucian texts, this does not necessarily mean that the earliest stages of development were recognized by early Confucians as having *unique and irreplaceable* importance in a person's moral formation. It is not simply the *ease* of cultivation that is in question here; rather, the possibilities of certain forms and aspects of cultivation are themselves at stake. One who defends the unique and irreplaceable role of early childhood moral education might contend that it is possible for adults to mitigate and manage many of the problems that stem from not having had certain learning experiences as a child, while still maintaining that those experiences can never be replaced and that, as a result, the process through which an adult might address these problems, as well as the outcome of that attempt, will differ in significant ways from the how the matter is approached by someone who did encounter these lessons in early childhood.

In examining early Confucian views on this question, I highlight passages from the *Book of Odes*, which dates between 1000 and 600 B.C.E.; the *Book of Rites* (*Liji* 禮記), a comprehensive account of the rites that were codified during the Warring States period (403–221 B.C.E.) and early Han dynasty, as compiled in the Han dynasty (206 B.C.E.–220 C.E.); and the late fourth-century B.C.E. text *Discourse on the States* (*Guoyu* 國語). I also include passages from two additional Han works, *Collected Biographies of Women* (*Lienuzhuan* 列女傳) and *Protecting and Tutoring* (*Baofu* 保俯), which I argue shed significant light on early Confucian views of moral cultivation in childhood. As in the previous chapter, by referring to these texts and thinkers as representative of "early Confucianism," I am not suggesting they represent a single, uniform ethical view. Rather, I argue that their understandings of moral cultivation in childhood, like many other aspects of their accounts, help to show that they subscribe to the same family of ethical views.

THE BOOK OF RITES

The *Book of Rites* serves as one of our most important resources regarding the rituals that helped define early Confucian culture. Like other ritual texts, such as the *Book of Etiquette and Ritual* (*Yili* 儀禮) or the ritual text(s) on which book 10 of the *Analects* is based, it consists of ritual injunctions and anecdotes, offering specific details concerning the performance of rites that are central to texts like the *Analects* and the *Xunzi*. Early Confucian ritual texts cover tremendously diverse terrain, including the wide range of experiences that were a part of life in ancient China and the specific practices that imbued those experiences with meaning for the early Confucians. Among the ceremonies detailed in the *Book of Rites* are some of the specific practices that were a part of raising children. Chapter 10—entitled "Inner Pattern" or "The Pattern of the Family" (*Neize* 內則) because it concerns the rites governing family conduct inside the home—offers explicit and detailed instructions about the moral cultivation of children. It expounds on the Confucian rites pertaining to childbirth and to the earliest days, months, and years of a child's life, including the education of and expectations placed upon children as they grow. It even specifies various ages and their respective educational goals.

As in much of the *Book of Rites*, the practices described concerning the birth of a child are those adhered to by the rulers of states and their families. The text specifies the following concerning the first caregiver of an infant son (the crown prince): "A special apartment was prepared in the palace for the child, and from all the concubines and other likely individuals there was sought one distinguished for her generosity of mind, her gentle kindness, her mild integrity, her respectful bearing, her carefulness and freedom from talkativeness, who should be appointed the boy's teacher" (*Liji* 10:472–473).[17] It is remarkable that this passage explicitly states that the boy's first teacher was a woman. Teachers were highly esteemed, and although she was a teacher of the inner chambers (as Dorothy Ko has noted), this is nevertheless noteworthy. A number of additional things are of interest. First, the teacher is to be chosen for her moral virtues (as opposed to her experience, physical attributes, educational background, or intellectual abilities), which indicates a concern with the moral influence she will have on the child and the moral education for which she will be responsible. In addition and more importantly, the text specifies that the teacher should be chosen when the child is still a newborn, before the traditional shaving of the child's hair at three months old and before the naming ceremony. This indicates a concern with the moral influence the teacher will have even during the first weeks of the child's life. Finally, it is significant that this practice is followed for an heir to the ruler of a state, as it shows a particular concern with the upbringing of a moral ruler from the earliest months of his life. As we saw in the previous chapter, the early Confucians believed good rulers had an extraordinary influence on the people, as a result of their virtue. This passage indicates that rulers' virtue can be cultivated from the very beginning of their lives, and that this process occurs partly through virtuous caregivers.

The *Book of Rites*, as we will see, is not the only early Confucian text that evidences the belief that caregivers have a direct moral influence over children while they are still infants.

PROTECTING AND TUTORING

The early Han dynasty text by the classical scholar, philosopher, and poet Jia Yi (200–168 B.C.E.) entitled *Protecting and Tutoring*, from chapter 48 of the *History of the Han*, provides even greater detail on the concern with moral cultivation in early childhood. Jia Yi starts off by asking why the ancient rulers of the Three Dynasties had "the durability that comes from possessing the Way, whereas the Qin suffered the setback of suddenly losing it?" He goes on to write, "The kings of ancient times, from the moment the crown prince was born, consistently raised him according to proper ritual forms," and examples of these rituals are specified (*Baofu*, 11).[18] This passage affirms the importance of the rites in childhood moral cultivation, and in addition, the moral cultivation of the ruler's heir, starting from the time he is an infant, is offered as the explanation for the moral and political success of these dynasties. To be clear: the future ruler's moral cultivation during early childhood is not *one* of the explanations the text gives for his later political success, but *the* explanation. Jia Yi singles out the practice of raising the crown prince according to proper ritual forms *from the moment he was born* as the critical factor in the rulers' demonstration of "the durability that comes from possessing the Way." This claim clearly indicates the belief that from birth, infants can be morally cultivated, and the fact that this early cultivation—and not just moral cultivation throughout one's life—is seen as the reason for the rulers' virtue and success helps to show that Jia Yi sees early childhood as a unique and irreplaceable opportunity for moral cultivation.

The text goes on to give specific biographies illustrating this process: "In ancient times, when King Cheng was young and in swaddling clothes [at the start of the Zhou dynasty]. . . . Protecting entailed guarding his person, tutoring entailed assisting him in virtue and righteousness, and teaching entailed guiding him in his educational training" (*Baofu*, 12). As a result of this early instruction, "Even when the crown prince was a small boy, he had some discrimination," as his tutors and teachers "firmly made clear to him filial piety, benevolence, ritual propriety, and righteousness, and so guided him in his practice. They banished the depraved, and did not let him see evil actions. So in all cases they chose upright officials, those who cared for their parents and siblings, those of broad learning, and those with mastery of the techniques of the Way to defend and assist the crown prince." These individuals lived with the prince and were his constant caregivers, and as a result, "from the moment the prince was born, he only saw correct affairs, only listened to correct words, and only traveled the correct ways. Those who were to the crown prince's left and right, those behind and in front of him, each one was a correct person."

The text concludes that "since he was accustomed to living alongside correct people, he could not but be correct himself, much like those who are born and grow up in Qi cannot but speak the language of Qi" (*Baofu*, 12). This line is reminiscent of claims in both the *Mengzi* and the *Xunzi*. As we have seen, Xunzi claims that "the children of the Han, Yue, Yi, and Mo peoples all cry with the same sound at birth, but when grown they have different customs, because teaching makes them be this way." In 3B6 Mengzi makes a similar claim, relating language acquisition to moral cultivation even more explicitly:

> Do you wish for your king to become good? Let me explain how. Suppose there were a Chief Counselor of Chu who wished for his son to learn to speak the dialect of Qi. Would he direct people from Qi to teach him, or would he direct people from Chu to teach him? . . . If one person from Qi teaches him, but a multitude of people from Chu distract him, even if he strives every day to understand the Qi dialect, he cannot succeed. But if you pick him up and plant him in the midst of a neighborhood in Qi, after a few years, even if he strives every day to understand the Chu dialect, he cannot succeed. Now, you say that your fellow minister

Xue Juzhou is a good noble. Suppose you direct him to live in the king's residence. If those in the king's residence old and young, common and distinguished, are all like Xue Juzhou, with whom will the king do what is not good? If those in the king's residence, old and young, common and distinguished, all oppose Xue Juzhou, with whom will the king do what is good?

All of these passages emphasize the importance of one's environment for moral cultivation and invoke an analogy with language acquisition. This is not insignificant, for here the early Confucians are exhibiting their awareness that childhood represents a distinctive opportunity for both moral cultivation and language acquisition. This, of course, is something we now know to be accurate. It is much more difficult to acquire a second language the older one gets, and the evidence for this even shows that if we do not rehearse certain phonemes at critical ages, we largely lose the ability to make such sounds correctly. In addition, if one is not taught *any* human language in youth, it becomes hard to be proficient in any. So there are complex, parallel courses of development occurring here.[19]

Jia also offers rationales for why early childhood represents such a unique opportunity for moral cultivation, writing that "the quality of the crown prince is determined by early instruction and the selection of the prince's attendants. Now, if one begins the crown prince's instruction before his mind is overflowing, then changes are easy to complete" (*Baofu*, 15). Here Jia indicates that learning is easier for the child before his mind is "overflowing" with other ideas, information, and experiences. The detailed analysis Jia offers is especially striking. In *Representations of Childhood and Youth in Early China*, Anne Kinney writes that "Chinese thinkers of the Han dynasty (206 B.C.–A.D. 220) were the first to focus extensively on childhood in philosophical discussions, in history writing, and in educational theory" (Kinney 2004:9). Kinney argues that the work of Xunzi influenced Han thinkers who wrote about childhood, something that is especially apparent in discussions that go beyond the imperial household to encompass children in all households. This interest in the Han was an outgrowth of the widespread acceptance of Xunzi's (fl. 298–238 B.C.) theory that children came into the world with a host of potentialities that require development through instruction. Idealistic Confucians of the Former Han took the theory a step further, arguing that once education was made available to all, the population at large would be led into an era of peace and high civilization. (Kinney 2004:10)

Here we can see how deeply classical Confucian understandings of human nature influenced subsequent accounts of moral cultivation, which were seen as the key to a flourishing society. Mark Csikszentmihalyi points out that the Confucian emphasis on moral education and cultivation grew over time: "Many Han writings on self-cultivation practice differed from their Warring States precursors in emphasizing education over speculation about the original content of human nature" (Csikszentmihalyi 2006:1). Although the category of human nature remained important, "for many writers the crux of the discussion shifted from nature to nurture, and specifically to the critical role of education and teaching in shaping moral behavior and training a good ruler." As Csikszentmihalyi indicates, during the Han dynasty the focus of many of the most influential philosophers shifted from theory to practice. What this seems to imply is that they largely accepted certain theoretical assumptions and turned to the task of implementing them, rather than continuing to debate the theories that underlay their practices. As we shall see later in this work, this marks an interesting point of difference between it and the history of Western philosophy.

DISCOURSE ON THE STATES AND "PRENATAL CULTIVATION"

As Kinney observes, "The search for the stage at which an individual began to establish habitually good or bad behavior naturally led thinkers further and further back into childhood as the appropriate starting point for moral education" (Kinney 2004:9). But Kinney also notes that claims about the need for moral education to begin in early childhood are made much earlier than the Han. The earliest reference to a program of princely education that is focused on early childhood is found in the late fourth-century B.C.E. text

Discourse on the States. Indeed, what is especially intriguing about this text is not only its early date and the fact that it emphasizes early childhood moral cultivation, but also that it appears to be the earliest Confucian text to claim that moral cultivation begins during the prenatal period with "prenatal cultivation" (*tai jiao* 胎教).[20] As we shall see in this section, other Confucian thinkers developed the understanding of this practice quite extensively.

In *Discourse on the States* we find a conversation about developing an heir's virtue through a tutor's instruction that in many ways resembles what we have been examining in the work of Jia Yi. *Discourse*, though, goes on to say that King Wen's virtue "resulted not only from formal instruction, but also from the spiritual purity and equanimity of the king's mother during her child's development in utero and her exemplary behavior throughout his early childhood" (*Guoyu* 1988:386–387).[21] The *Book of Odes* also celebrates King Wen's mother, Tai Ren, stating that she "acted only with virtue" and was both reverent and loving (*Shijing*, mao 236, 240; Legge 1970b). The *Odes* also notes that she became pregnant and bore King Wen and goes on to describe what an outstanding ruler he was (*Shijing*, mao 236). *Collected Biographies of Women* offers the most detailed account of Tai Ren's character, describing her as "upright, sincere, decorous, and engaged solely in virtuous conduct." Most importantly, like *Discourse*, *Collected Biographies* specifies that when Tai Ren was pregnant, she practiced prenatal cultivation: "When she was with child, her eyes beheld no evil sights, her ears heard no perverse sounds, and her mouth uttered no careless words. She was able to teach her child in the womb [能以胎教]." The text goes on to explain that in ancient times, a pregnant woman practiced prenatal cultivation in a variety of ways:

> She would not eat food with odd flavors; if the food was cut awry, she would not eat it; if the mat was not placed straight, she would not sit on it. She did not let her eyes gaze on lewd sights or let her ears listen to depraved sounds. At night she ordered blind musicians to chant the *Odes*. She spoke only of proper things. In this way she gave birth to children of correct physical form who excelled others in talent and virtue. Thus, during pregnancy, one must always be cautious about [external] stimuli. If one is stimulated by something good, then [the child] will be good. If

one is stimulated by something evil, then [the child] will be evil. People's resemblance to various things at birth is in every case due to the mother's being stimulated by external things, so that in form and voice they come to resemble these things. (*Lienuzhuan* 1.6:7)[22]

What is striking about the story of King Wen's mother is that it emphasizes the role that her behavior during pregnancy played in the sort of person he became. Accordingly, it introduces the view that moral cultivation begins not at birth, but during pregnancy. Prenatal cultivation was aimed at influencing the moral development of children at the earliest possible stage. Pregnant mothers are advised to carefully monitor all they see, eat, hear, and say, and to be sure their deportment is ritually correct. Kinney writes that these instructions were generally based on the principle of "simulative transformation" (*xiaohua* 肖化), according to which the things that affect the pregnant mother simultaneously affect the fetus (Kinney 1995:27).

We have already encountered the idea that young children are affected by, and more specifically that they come to resemble, the things to which they are exposed. For example, Jia Yi's claim that the crown prince "only saw correct affairs, only listened to correct words, and only traveled the correct ways" is an instance of this type of view. The claims we find regarding King Wen's mother in *Discourse on the States* and *Collected Biographies* take this idea a step further back and apply it to pregnancy. In the *Collected Biographies*, Liu Xiang explains that if a pregnant woman is moved (*gan* 感) or affected by good things, it will impact her child positively, and the same basic principle was believed to hold for bad things.

According to Kinney, by the Han we find clear evidence of the "widespread circulation and acceptance of theories on the moral instruction of small children," including the cultivation of fetuses, with three of the most prominent Confucians of the early Han—Jia Yi, Dong Zhongshu, and Liu Xiang—all advocating beginning moral cultivation as soon as possible (Kinney 2004:11).[23] Both Jia and Liu also addressed prenatal cultivation, and Kinney writes that these educational theories "gradually gained acceptance as the influence of Confucianism came to eclipse all contending schools of thought in the Han court" (2004:11). The body of literature on this subject continued to grow. Manuals instructing women on "nurturing the fetus" (養胎), found in the Mawangdui manuscripts from the early second century B.C.E., offer month-by-month instructions concerning the development and nurturance of the fetus, with prohibitions and recommendations regarding the pregnant mother's foods, activities, sights, sounds, and emotions (Wilms 2005:276).[24] Sabine Wilms writes that these instructions were clearly aimed at producing offspring who were not just physically healthy but also had sound emotional and moral characteristics. Although the Mawangdui manuscripts and a number of later texts on this topic focus more on physical transformation, Wilms emphasizes that this literature was

> not only intended for concrete therapeutic purposes, but had larger social, cosmological, and philosophical ramifications. The texts . . . combine strands of philosophical and religious accounts of cosmogenesis and fetal development with literary traditions of medicinal therapy in pregnancy and childbirth and of behavioral and dietary taboos for the mother during pregnancy. (Wilms 2005:278)

So, the interest in the cultivation of good moral character continued to appear alongside developing concerns with physical health in texts outlining the proper nurturance and cultivation of the fetus.

Although some of the claims early Confucian texts make about the impact on a fetus of the mother's experiences and surroundings might strike us as implausible or overly simplistic today—such as the idea that if the mother is affected by good things, the child will be good, and if she is affected by evil things, the child will be evil—there are some aspects of this view that we should endeavor to appreciate. For example, although we know that a fetus is not affected by the muffled sounds she hears in the same way that a young child can understand and be influenced by the things she hears, it is true that the health of a fetus can be impacted if its mother is under stress, and thus indirectly influenced by the people and things that are a part of the mother's environment during a pregnancy, including what she hears and sees. Even more importantly, we know that people who listen to certain kinds of music or view certain kinds of scenes feel more or less relaxed, confident, and uplifted. These influences can have a wide range of effects. A person who is optimistic, energized, and happy is more likely to think about and do things that will benefit her child at any stage of development, both during pregnancy and after.

Once the child is born, the example the parents provide, and even such things as their facial expressions, influences him in a variety of ways. Parents' actions and decisions are guided by their mind-set, which is partly a function of their environment. Additionally, of course, we know it is true that as soon as a pregnancy begins the expectant mother should modify her health-related habits in order to best prepare for her child; the child's development and behavior after birth are often impacted dramatically by expectant parents' decisions on this count. So the general idea that parental responsibilities begin during the prenatal period—responsibilities that can significantly change the sort of person a child will become and which we may thus reasonably call "moral responsibilities"—is something we know to be accurate today, although our reasons are primarily based on scientific evidence.[25] We also understand that it is not a matter of a simple causal connection, as the early Confucians argued. There are connections, but they are not simple and usually are not so direct.

It *is* the case, though, that there are clear and direct links between pregnancy and self-cultivation in mothers. As we shall see later in this work, expectant mothers who reflect on the ways in which their environment can affect their unborn child are more likely to engage in self-cultivation precisely because they believe their child will benefit, and they are also more likely than others to *succeed* in changing certain attitudes and behaviors.[26] The process of prenatal cultivation, then, is not something that benefits only the developing child; it can also contribute in important ways to the ongoing process of moral cultivation in the mother. This is particularly important for a society that recognizes the connection between the family and creating a good society, for there must be support not only for the earliest stages of moral cultivation in children but also for the ongoing process of moral cultivation in adults, and the prenatal period represents a unique opportunity for moral cultivation in parents. Although the early Confucians who advocated prenatal cultivation may not have been aware of this fact, it is certainly in keeping with their interest in and emphasis on the process of moral cultivation, as well as moral psychology and the relationship between those two.

COLLECTED BIOGRAPHIES OF WOMEN

The attention given to prenatal cultivation in early Confucian texts highlights the experience of pregnancy—an experience belonging uniquely to women. Stories such as that of King Wen's mother also affirm the unique role of women in their children's upbringing after pregnancy. Indeed, *Collected Biographies of Women*, compiled by Liu Xiang (ca. 79–8 B.C.E.), is not only the first extant Chinese work that is focused solely on women, but the first work of this kind anywhere in the world. It tells us much about the critical role mothers were thought to have in early childhood education.[27] The text features 125 biographies of women from early China, specifically detailing these women's virtues and vices. The oldest stories describe the lives of women who purportedly lived in the eighth century B.C.E., while the most recent stories concern women in the Han; there are many stories set in the periods in between.

Since these biographies detail the wide-ranging roles and relationships that shape women's experiences throughout the course of their lives, the text is a significant source of information about early Confucian views of women's roles in the moral cultivation of their children. Kinney writes that the text is particularly enlightening with respect to early Confucian accounts of moral education, because it sets forth "in more than a few scattered comments methods for moral training in early childhood," while also affirming the transformative role of mothers in the moral education of their children (Kinney 2004:20–21). As we shall see, especially noteworthy aspects of *Collected Biographies* include its account of the relationship that develops between mothers and their children during pregnancy and throughout a child's life, its description of the methods used by mothers in the moral cultivation of their children, and its endorsement of the view that the early years of a child's life are a unique and critical time for moral cultivation. Like Jia Yi, "Liu Xiang recognized that moral development was a slow and gradual process, and that it was far easier to transform the malleable nature of the child before bad habits and behavior had become ingrained" (Kinney 2004:25).

The first chapter, "Biographies on the Deportment of Mothers," features a number of important remarks about the process of moral cultivation in young children, and Lisa Raphals points out that this chapter "clearly takes early childhood as the beginning of moral development and explicitly recognizes the importance of women" (Raphals 1998:22). This chapter had an enduring influence on the Confucian tradition. Raphals notes that it "was widely quoted in later periods for its examples of mothers' efficacious education of their sons; in particular, Zhu Xi (1130–1200) made extensive use of it in his *Instructions for Learning* (*Xiao xue*), including the emphasis on prenatal instruction" (22). One example of the clear emphasis on the moral cultivation of children is seen in the story of Xie, who grew up to become the minister of instruction during sage-king Shun's reign as well as the father of Cheng Tang, the founder of the Shang dynasty. We are told that as Xie grew up, his mother, Jian Di, "taught him about moral principles and the various degrees of precedence in human relationships. Xie, by nature, was intelligent and benevolent. He was able to cultivate her teachings and thus finally established his reputation" (*Lienuzhuan* 1.3:4). His mother "esteemed benevolence and exerted herself reverently. . . . She taught according to the correct principle of things, extended mercy, and possessed virtue. That Xie served as aide to the ruler was no doubt due to his mother's efforts" (*Lienuzhuan* 1.3:5). Here the text straightforwardly outlines the qualities of Xie's mother and how she taught her son according to the rites and the order of relationships, exhibiting benevolence and kindness while also maintaining a firm hand. The qualities of an exemplary mother and caregiver are made clear in the text's description of her. Additionally, Xie's success is attributed to his mother's efforts to give him a good moral education, similar to the way in which Jia Yi attributes the success of the Three Dynasties to the care and moral cultivation the crown princes received as infants. The important difference, of course, is that Xie's *mother* is credited for his early moral cultivation and upbringing.

In some cases, *Collected Biographies* even specifies that a child's mother alone deserves the credit for cultivating her son's excellence of character. The biography of Tu Shan, wife of sage-king Yu, the reputed founder of the Xia dynasty, is an example. The text tells us that Tu Shan raised her son Qi alone while her husband was taming the floodwaters: "Alone, Tushan taught with great insight and thereby brought about Qi's education. When Qi grew up, transformed by her virtue and following her teachings, he established his renown" (*Lienuzhuan* 1.4:5).[28] The text emphasizes, "Yu went forth to divide the land. While Qi wept and wailed, alone, his mother ordered their affairs, she taught him about goodness until finally he succeeded his father" (*Lienuzhuan* 1.4:5–6). Here again we find the early Confucian conception of Virtue, or moral power (*de* 德), at work, as the text notes that Qi was transformed by his mother's virtue; it was not only her teaching but her virtue that brought about her son's early moral cultivation.

The biography of King Wu's mother, known by the honorific title Wen Mu 文母, notes that she "was benevolent and understood the Way." She "taught her ten sons so that from the time they were small until they were grown, they never laid eyes upon evil or perversion" (*Lienuzhuan* 1.6:7). This passage is particularly interesting for a couple of reasons. First, it emphasizes that she prevented her sons' exposure to harmful influences, which is a consistent concern in early Confucian texts that discuss early moral cultivation, as we have seen. Second, the text specifies that she protected and instructed her sons from the beginning of their lives until they were adults, noting the temporal aspect of moral cultivation and the need for it to continue over the entire course of a child's development. This is something Liu Xiang emphasizes in *Collected Biographies*. Kinney writes that although we find a number of common ideas and phrases concerning moral education in the text, including "to teach and transform" (*jiaohua* 教化), and "to transform and instruct" (*huaxun* 化訓), the idea of "gradual transformation" (*jianhua* 漸化) is particularly distinctive, as Liu Xiang was the first thinker to explicitly relate this idea to the moral cultivation of children (Kinney 2004:22–23). "Gradual transformation" is the notion that virtuous character develops through a slow and steady, step-by-step process of moral cultivation, and in *Collected Biographies* this idea is evident in the way that the values and behaviors of families are gradually instilled in children. We have already seen this idea at work in Wen Mu's constant instruction of her sons.

Kinney notes that gradual transformation is also emphasized in the story of Mengzi's mother, whom Liu Xiang praises for understanding "how children are gradually imbued with the values and behaviors of those around them" (Kinney 2004:23).

The story of Mengzi's mother and her remarkable dedication to her son during his childhood is the most widely known story in the text. Indeed, it is recalled in a traditional saying that serves as a reminder of the importance of parents making sacrifices for their children's well-being and that is well known in both Chinese and Japanese: "Mengzi's mother moved three times [孟母三遷]." It is worth noting that although this particular story about Mengzi's mother is perhaps the most widely known, there are multiple stories in *Collected Biographies* that recount her moral instruction and influence on Mengzi both as a child and as an adult. We can easily appreciate, then, not only from this story but also from the fact that there are stories about the influence of Mengzi's mother throughout his life, why Liu Xiang praises her understanding of the gradual process of moral cultivation.

> Mengzi's mother lived near a graveyard. During Mengzi's youth, he enjoyed playing among the tombs, romping about and pretending to prepare the ground for burials. Mother Meng said, "This is not the place to raise my son." She therefore moved away and settled beside the marketplace. But there he liked to play at displaying and selling wares like a merchant. Again Mother Meng said, "This is not the place to raise my son," and once more left, settling beside a school. There, however, he played at setting out sacrificial vessels, bowing, yielding, entering, and withdrawing. His mother said, "This, indeed, is where I can raise my son!," and settled there. When Mengzi grew up, he studied the Six Arts, and finally became known as a great classicist. A cultivated person would say, "Mother Meng was good at gradual transformation" (*Lienuzhuan* 1.11:18).[29]

Without question, passages such as this one affirm the transformative influence that virtuous mothers were believed to have on their children through moral cultivation. It is also significant that Mengzi's mother is a widow; her story appears to be the first story recorded in human history about how a single mother raised her children. The quotation from the *Book of Odes* that closes the passage is used to emphasize what accomplished individuals were given that enabled them to become such admirable people, and in *Collected Biographies* we repeatedly see that the scholars and sages of early Confucianism, renowned for their virtues, were provided a nurturing environment in which they were encouraged to develop as moral people right from the start. Mengzi's mother does not simply throw up her hands and say to herself that these early years are not really what matters and hope that things will improve by the time Mengzi is ready for moral cultivation. On the contrary, she understands that his moral cultivation has already begun and that it will continue throughout his childhood and youth, and even when he is a young man.[30] Stories such as this help to confirm what we have seen evidence of in a range of early Confucian texts: the authors believed the earliest years of a child's life represent an extremely important opportunity for moral cultivation, and parents must be vigilant about all of the influences that are a part of a child's environment, because of the unique nature of these early years.

Collected Biographies gives us a firmer sense of the kinds of things that were a part of a child's early moral education, including the instilling of two virtues that were particularly important: ritual propriety and filial piety. The *Book of Rites* makes it clear that children were to be educated in following the rites at a young age. Some of the rites applied specifically to children, and the text specifies the ages at which children were expected to master them. This means that in early Confucianism, the rites shaped a person's character from a very young age. For example, the *Book of Rites* specifies that "at the age of seven, boys and girls did not occupy the same mat nor eat together; at eight, when going out or coming in at a gate or door, and going to their mats to eat and drink, they were required to follow their elder:—the teaching of yielding to others was now begun" (*Liji* 10.33:478). The latter rite is clearly tied to teaching filial piety to young children, which helps to show that filial piety was not something that was cultivated only in older children or young adults. At thirteen, the text specifies, boys "learned music, and to repeat the odes, and to dance the *shao* 勺 (of the duke of Zhou). When a full-grown lad, he danced the *xiang* 象 (of king Wu)" (*Liji* 10.34:478). Here we find a distinction drawn between dances learned when one is younger as opposed to full-grown, which again shows that the rites were a part of a child's moral cultivation throughout her or his years.

After being capped at nineteen, a boy "first learned the (different classes of) ceremonies, and might wear furs and silk. He danced the *da xia* 大夏 (of Yu), and attended sedulously to filial and fraternal duties. He might become very learned, but did not teach others;—(his object being still) to receive and not give out" (*Liji* 10.34:478). This passage shows that capping did not represent the completion of a person's moral education, because boys at this age did not teach others; learning was still considered their primary task. However, we are told that boys at this age "attended sedulously to filial and fraternal duties," indicating they were well educated and practiced in fulfilling their filial and fraternal duties by this point in their lives and were thus expected to fulfill them with great seriousness. In order for boys to have mastered their filial duties to this extent by age nineteen, filial piety is something that must have been a part of children's program of moral cultivation from quite a young age. It is significant that deference and filial piety were valued in boys and girls, for this helps to show that filial piety serves as a critical part of the foundation for a person's moral development, regardless of gender.

Although girls and boys were educated in gender-specific activities, the experiences and training of girls, unlike in many other ancient cultures, was not excluded from classical texts. The *Book of Rites* specifies that at age ten, girls learned the arts of

> pleasing speech and manners, to be docile and obedient, to handle the hempen fibres, to deal with the cocoons, to weave silks and form fillets, to learn (all) woman's work, how to furnish garments, to watch the sacrifices, to supply the liquors and sauces, to fill the various stands and dishes with pickles and brine, and to assist in setting forth the appurtenances for the ceremonies. (*Liji* 10.36:479)

Although girls' education consisted largely of instruction in domestic activities, which marks an obvious similarity with most other traditional cultures, the fact that these activities were recognized as important enough to merit inclusion in the *Book of Rites* represents a significant difference from most other ancient cultures. It is also worth noting that the text specifies that the proper age for women to marry in early China was twenty or twenty-three (*Liji* 10.37), as opposed to the childhood marriage practices of later China and much of the world—practices that have contributed to the oppression of women. The older ages specified in the text help to show (among other things) that women were seen as moral agents fully capable of cultivation and that the early Confucians thought they ought to receive an education before they married; indeed, these ages suggest that women's moral education and cultivation—including their knowledge of the rites— as well as their domestic skills, were all quite advanced by the time they married.[31] Since we have already seen the important role that women had in the moral cultivation of their children in early China, we can further appreciate the need for women to receive a proper education.

While the focus of this work is Confucian accounts from the Han and earlier, Zhu Xi has a great deal to say about childhood education that is explicit and interesting, and his views can augment our understanding of the concrete things involved in Confucian childhood education. In antiquity, Zhu Xi tells us, at age eight boys entered a school for lesser learning, where "they were instructed in matters such as ritual, music, archery, charioteering, calligraphy, and mathematics, as well as in matters of filial piety, fraternal respect, loyalty, and fidelity."[32] The lesser learning of the ancients, he says, "fostered truthfulness and inner mental attentiveness in young children. Their germs of goodness would thus become manifest. Still, they were unable to infer from lesser learning the affairs of greater learning, so they entered the school for greater learning" at age fifteen. Zhu Xi stresses, though, that children's education began much earlier: "From the time they entered the school for lesser learning, the ancients were already personally familiar with many matters" (Gardner 1990:89). He goes on to report that "in antiquity young children were taught as soon as they could talk and eat. What they studied included cleaning and sweeping and polite conversation. Thus when they grew up, they could easily discuss matters" (Gardner 1990:94).

* * *

In the final section of this chapter, I discuss early Confucian accounts of the roles of mothers and fathers and the analogy between parenting and political leadership, according to which a good ruler is understood as "the father and mother of the people." If one is interested in the moral development of children and the way in which moral education is understood within a given cultural or philosophical perspective, an exploration of the roles of parents and caregivers is a good place to begin. A child's earliest experiences are those involving her primary caregivers, usually her parents, and as a result we can learn a great deal about how the moral cultivation of children was viewed from accounts of what good parents and primary caregivers were like. As we have seen, although the *Analects*, *Mengzi*, and *Xunzi* express general views concerning the nature of these relationships and the way in which they affect children, these texts do not offer much detail concerning the kind of impact the day-to-day interactions of children and their parents or caregivers might have on a child's moral character. Several other early Confucian texts address these matters, however, detailing the moral education children should receive and the reasons children need to be instructed and cultivated in certain ways at early ages.

"THE FATHER AND MOTHER OF THE PEOPLE"

In order to contextualize early Confucian views concerning the roles of mothers and fathers, and how husbands and wives worked—both independently and in ways that were complementary—to promote the moral cultivation of their children, it is helpful to examine the presentation of traditional gender roles in these texts.

Early Confucians outline distinct social roles for men and women; these expectations, along with the rituals governing them, imposed significant limitations upon both men and women, but for women the restrictions were especially severe. Whereas at least some men had access to political power through positions in government and opportunities to become students of teachers such as Kongzi, *no* women had these opportunities. Women were expected to obey their husbands (in addition to their parents), but no early Confucian texts suggest that men should obey their wives.[33] Nevertheless, it is important not to confuse later Chinese ideas and practices with those of early China; as I have emphasized throughout this chapter, the women in many of the stories and anecdotes from this period are confident and effective agents, celebrated for the remarkable influence they had on their husbands, sons, and daughters-in-law, and on their society as well.[34] Many of these women were educated about the rites and recognized for their intellectual and moral virtues.[35] These aspects of their stories represent a deep and important contrast to the abuses of women that were legitimated by late Ming–Qing neo-Confucianism, yet it remains the case that many aspects of early Confucian views and practices limited women's potential and placed them at a disadvantage.

I want to be especially clear about this, because I aim to highlight some central features of early Confucian views of mothers and fathers that enabled and contributed in positive ways to the moral cultivation of children, but I do not want to minimize the harmful features of these views or suggest that any of these conceptions of family roles and relationships—male or female—ought to be recovered or embraced. In later chapters, I will discuss some of the ways in which particular aspects of these views might be applied constructively in a contemporary setting, but, as I will argue, feminist views must inform such efforts.

* * *

It is difficult to present a clear picture of early Confucian views concerning the roles of mothers and fathers without first discussing marriage and the roles of husbands and wives in that partnership. Early Confucian texts tend to view these roles as closely related, but marriage is particularly foundational for parent–child relationships, as the following passage from the *Book of Rites* suggests:

> The respect, the caution, the importance, the attention to secure correctness in all details, and then (the pledge of) mutual affection—these were the great points in the marriage ceremony, and served to establish the

distinction to be observed between man and woman, and the righteousness to be maintained between husband and wife. From the distinction between man and woman came the righteousness between husband and wife. From that righteousness came the affection between father and son; and from that affection, the rectitude between ruler and minister. Whence it is said, "The ceremony of marriage is the root of the other ceremonial observances." (*Liji* 41.3)[36]

One feature of early Confucian views of the roles of husbands and wives that this passage highlights is the importance of having and knowing one's own distinctive role, and the importance of the rites governing those matters. As Lisa Raphals points out, the *Book of Rites* "distinguished men and women ritually by prescribing identical or analogous but distinct activities for each. As Patricia Ebrey puts it, 'Men and women should do different things, or the same things differently'" (Raphals 1998:215). The text states, "The observances of propriety commence with a careful attention to the relations between husband and wife," and it specifies that ritual propriety requires, at least to some degree, separate spaces for husbands and wives; for instance: "Males and females did not use the same stand or rack for their clothes. The wife did not presume to hang up anything on the pegs or stand of her husband; nor to put anything in his boxes or satchels" (*Liji* 10.2).[37] Additionally, "The men should not speak of what belongs to the inside (of the house), nor the women of what belongs to the outside" (*Liji* 10.1).[38] The latter passage makes reference to the "inside" (*nei* 內) and "outside" (*wai* 外), a distinction that informed many early Chinese discussions of men and women and that was used in a variety of different ways in early Chinese texts. The terms sometimes refer to the inner life and outward behavior of an individual or to the activities and affairs internal or external to families and states. Very often, *nei* refers to the actions and events within the "inner" family realm, in relation to the actions and events in the "outer" (*wai*) public arenas of our lives. As Raphals argues, in these cases *nei* and *wai* refer to "two distinct modes of 'inner' and 'outer' activity, and only secondarily to actual physical locations" (Raphals 1998:213). Now, the *Book of Rites* does not necessarily present a historically accurate picture of how women actually lived or what the actual practices were. In the Han, for instance, there was probably not such a strict physical separation between men's and women's spaces, nor were women confined to the "inner" home.[39] In this work, though, my aim is not to present a historical account of how early Chinese families actually cultivated their children or to present evidence concerning the accuracy of early Confucian historical claims, but rather to present an argument concerning early Confucian normative views on these matters.

While the rituals described in the passages cited limit men and women in ways that rightly strike us as overly restrictive and unappealing, one redeeming feature of such practices is that they can help prevent petty arguments and tensions that stem from husbands and wives not having adequate space to themselves—which would have been a more pressing concern in ancient China, where households included multiple generations of one family. Such practices also ensure that men and women will be able to make distinctive contributions, and they seem designed to prevent couples from ignorantly criticizing each other's contributions, thus promoting a kind of respect and certainly promoting harmony. While modern Westerners do not have fully analogous practices, it is customary for us to have separate chests of drawers, sides of the closet, and sets of chores for which we are responsible, all of which function (when properly honored) to promote a more harmonious relationship between spouses. Such practices, when they involve an equitable division of labor, can have the added benefit of ensuring that one spouse does not carry an undue share of the work.

Now, a contemporary critic might point out that instead of specifying rituals that confine husbands and wives to separate tasks, it would be better to have them participate in the same tasks at least to some extent, so that they can gain a firsthand appreciation for one another's contributions. There is certainly merit to this view, but even in a contemporary setting, it is not always possible, for practical reasons, for both members of a couple to take part in all tasks, and one insight we might take from Confucian ritual practices concerning husbands and wives is that they ought to refrain from criticizing one another's efforts in areas in which they do not contribute. According to early Confucian views, there are important connections between this dimension of marriage and the relationships between parents and children, and this is at least in part because the rites partly specify how husbands and wives can work together in complementary ways for the good of their children. One of the truly distinctive features of early Confucianism is the degree to which the tradition makes the norms governing everyday social relations, customs, and practices *explicit*, as opposed to leaving them mostly implicit, as happens in many other traditions and cultures.

The idea that the roles of husbands and wives ought to be complementary is linked in a number of early Chinese texts to correlate pairs of *yin* and *yang*, but as Raphals argues, prior to the third century B.C.E., "*yin–yang* polarities are mostly cyclic and relatively nonhierarchical. Overall, *yin* and *yang* are not used in analogy with earlier heaven–earth or gender-based polarities" (Raphals 1998:142).[40] In the second and third centuries B.C.E., analogies between *yin* and *yang* and male and female were used loosely, but "they did not disparage the female at the expense of the male, and, indeed, in some cases, explicitly preferred the female mode" (142). In these views we see a constructive view of complementarity that came to inform Confucian views of marriage; as Raphals writes, a number of these texts "present a complementary polarity between two modes of action that accomplish different things and are useful in different ways" (Raphals 1998:156). However, in the first century B.C.E., the analogy between *yin* and *yang* and male and female "became a common aspect of *yin–yang* language as part of the gender hierarchy embedded in Han correlative cosmology," seen most notably in Dong Zhongshu's *Luxuriant Gems of the Spring and Autumn* (*Chunqiu Fanlu* 春秋繁露) (Raphals 1998:142).[41] The *yin–yang* chapters of this work combine a preference for *yang* with an explicit disparagement of *yin*, as seen for example in chapter 43, entitled "The Exaltation of *Yang* and the Abasement of *Yin*." Csikzentmihalyi points out that in this work, "*yin* and *yang* are neither equal and complementary, nor opposite and of radically different value"; Dong Zhongshu argues that the relationship of hierarchy and interdependence between *yang* and *yin* is the normative standard for the relationship between husband and wife (Csikzentmihalyi 2003:163). Dong writes,

> Complementary means that there necessarily is a top and a bottom, a left and a right, a front and a back, an exterior and an interior. . . . *Yin* is *yang*'s complement, a wife is a husband's complement, a son is a father's complement, and a subject is a ruler's complement. Everything in the world has a complement, and each instance of complementarity has *yin* and *yang*. *Yin* is connected with *yang* as *yang* is connected with *yin*; a husband is connected with a wife as a wife is connected with a husband. (*Chunqiu Fanlu* 53)[42]

As Csikzentmihalyi puts it, "What this means is that although society needs the achievements that *yang* is responsible for, *yang* require the presence of *yin*, so in a real sense any achievement is a result of the interdependence between the two" (2003:163).

Dong Zhongshu's account of complementarity and interdependence is limited in unfortunate ways by its strict association of husbands with *yang* and wives with *yin*, as well as the privileging of *yang* over *yin*, and, as Raphals notes, this view came to dominate the Confucian tradition "to such an extent that earlier *yin–yang* gender analogies are all but ignored" (Raphals 1998:168). An amended view of complementary spousal roles that would be more readily applicable to contemporary understandings of spousal relationships might draw upon those earlier Chinese sources that describe *yin* and *yang* as complementary but only loosely associate them with male and female spheres of activity and do not privilege *yang* over *yin*. Additionally, such an updated view might work to apply Confucian views to these earlier understandings of complementarity by emphasizing that each individual, male or female, has many aspects and character traits that might, to varying degrees and in different ways, express qualities associated with *yin* and *yang*. This means that spouses can contribute in distinctive and complementary ways to their shared goals. For instance, married couples might work to arrange their lives—including the division of labor inside and outside the home, as well as parenting responsibilities—in ways that draw upon each individual's strengths, so that the roles of one spouse complement those of the other. At the same time, in order to be faithful to Confucian self-cultivationist sensibilities, spouses could take on tasks that further cultivate their virtues and capacities, as well as their sensitivity to and appreciation for each other. Such an approach would be faithful to the emphasis on complementarity that is central to early Confucian views of marriage, while rejecting the sexism that defines Dong Zhongshu's understanding of *yin–yang* gender analogies.[43]

Although Dong Zhongshu's account appears in the Han, a number of earlier stories and anecdotes present information about the ways in which husbands and wives operated together in order to fulfill their roles as parents. As we saw earlier in this chapter, the *Book of Odes* notes the exemplary character of King Wen's mother, Tai Ren, and the text specifically states that she, "with" her husband (King Wen's father), "acted only with Virtue (*de* 德)" (*Shijing*, mao 236). This line stresses the way that her Virtue, or moral power, contributed to the success of her husband and how they together, as parents, contributed to the virtue of their son. The *Book of Odes* also states that Tai Ren was loving toward her mother-in-law and that her daughter-in-law (King Wen's wife) "inherited her excellent reputation" and as a result of following in Tai Ren's footsteps was able to bear many sons (*Shijing*, mao 240). This passage emphasizes a theme that is central to early Chinese views: good mothers and wives know how to rely upon, work in cooperation with, and provide support to not only their husbands and children but also the larger families of which they are a part. In other words, good mothers and wives are aware of and work to draw upon and strengthen the relationships of care and support within their families. They do not attempt to do everything themselves, nor do they avoid strained or difficult relationships, but rather they aim to find ways of working with other family members for the benefit of all; indeed, they recognize that the good of each family member is not separate from but closely tied to the good of the others. Family members have distinctive needs and distinctive contributions to make, but their needs and contributions are also interconnected. Early Confucians maintained that if the needs and contributions of family members are addressed correctly, they can be complementary in ways that promote harmony within the family, within the community, and within society as a whole.

However, although marriage was widely valued and celebrated—Mengzi refers to the titles "husband" and "wife" as "the greatest of human roles"— early Confucian texts also acknowledge that "marriage leads sometimes to misfortune, sometimes to prosperity" (*Guoyu* 1988:2.1, zhou 2).[44] *Discourse on the States* lists women such as Tai Ren, who contributed to the political success of the states they lived in and "were all able to benefit their [husbands'] families and retain close relations with their [own] families," but the text goes on to enumerate examples of women who caused discord and contributed to the failure of the state they lived in, claiming that they "all benefited strangers and were estranged from their own parents" (*Guoyu* 1988:2.1, zhou 2).[45] It is significant that the text calls attention to the fact that women who had strong relationships with their families contributed to the success of their societies, while those who were estranged from their families did just the opposite. This correspondence between familial and political contributions not only reflects the view that each society is made up of families—which means that the quality of families' lives determines the quality of a society—but it also asserts that when women were dedicated to and had good relationships with their families, their virtue provided a substantial benefit to their children, husbands, and other family members and, through them, the larger society. The influence that women had on society through their children, as we have already seen in this chapter, was strongest of all, because mothers were primarily responsible for the moral cultivation of their offspring.

An awareness of the dramatic impact that family relationships could have on a society helped to motivate early Confucian thinkers to advocate particular cultural practices aimed at developing virtues of character that would strengthen families. The *Book of Rites* offers the following description of the rituals practiced by the families of newlyweds:

> The family that has married a daughter away, does not extinguish its candles for three nights, thinking of the separation that has taken place. The family that has received the (new) wife for three days has no music, thinking her bridegroom is now in the place of his parents. After three months she presents herself in the ancestral temple, and is styled "The new wife that has come." A day is chosen for her to sacrifice at the shrine of her father-in-law; expressing the idea of her being (now) the established wife. (*Liji* 5.1)[46]

This passage highlights ritual practices that encourage husbands and wives and their families to reflect on and to process emotionally the changes in roles and contexts that a new marriage brings and the ways in which all of the members of a family are affected by these changes. The rites discussed in this passage encourage family members to think about others rather than themselves. The groom's family reflects on how a son is "now in the place of his parents," having taken on the responsibilities of carrying on the family lineage and building a home with a spouse (and perhaps soon, children), while also attending to the needs of his parents as they grow older. In sacrificing to the ancestors of her father-in-law, the bride recognizes that she is now a part of another lineage—something that expands her identity in significant ways by introducing a host of new relationships and individuals who will play pivotal roles in her life and in the lives of her children.

There are a rich variety of other stories, anecdotes, and discussions in early Confucian texts that further support the view that husbands and wives are not a distinct unit but are fundamentally interconnected with the larger families of which they are a part. One of the stories in *Collected Biographies* describes the way in which Mengzi's mother worked to bring about harmony between Mengzi and his wife after a breach in ritual propriety. Like the story above, this story depicts the role of mother and mother-in-law as particularly important in relation to promoting harmony within the family: "Once, after Mengzi had married, as he was about to enter his private apartments, he encountered his wife, who was inside the room in a state of undress. Mengzi was displeased, so he left without going in" (*Lienuzhuan* 1.11:19).[47] When Mengzi's wife told Mengzi's mother what had happened, and asked permission to leave, Mengzi's mother summoned him, saying,

> According to ritual, when you are about to enter a room, you ask if anyone is there, and that is how to convey respect. When you go into the hall, you must raise your voice to alert others to your presence. When you are about to go through a door, you must avert your gaze lest you see another's misdeed. If you fail to investigate ritual yet fault the ritual behavior of others, then you are far from being correct yourself!

Mengzi then admitted that he had been wrong and asked his wife to stay. The text notes that Mengzi's mother "understood ritual and was perceptive in the Way of the Mother-in-Law" (*Lienuzhuan* 1.11:19).

There are a number of interesting features in this story. In addition to highlighting the importance of having and knowing one's own distinctive role, inhabiting separate spaces, and knowing the rites governing those matters, this story illustrates that different family members, by virtue of their unique relationships with one another, have unique roles to play in promoting the well-being of the family as a whole. This passage also shows that early Confucians did not regard husbands and wives as a unit separate and distinct from the rest of the family. They did not expect them to resolve all difficulties independently of the rest of the family, nor did they think that the assistance and guidance of other family members was necessarily intrusive. Mengzi's wife felt comfortable telling his mother what had happened and understood that it was appropriate to do so, and Mengzi and his mother both viewed it as appropriate for his mother to intervene and provide correction. We see here a willingness to rely upon others and to draw upon the relationships of care, trust, and support within the family to resolve difficulties.

The stories of Tai Ren (King Wen's mother) and Mengzi's mother, like many of the passages discussed throughout this chapter, concern primarily the roles of mothers, not fathers. Mothers in the early Confucian tradition are often presented as smart, savvy, capable, and dedicated. They are not weak, overly emotional agents capable only of offering nurturance and love; although they provide these things, they are also firm disciplinarians who know how to communicate effectively with their children. An excellent example of this is Mengzi's mother's response when he returns home from school and answers her inquiries about his progress in his studies by saying, "I'm in about the same place as I was before." The text tells us,

Mother Meng thereupon took up a knife and cut her weaving. Mengzi was alarmed and asked her to explain. Mother Meng said, "Your abandoning your study is like my cutting this weaving. A cultivated person studies in order to establish a name and inquires to become broadly knowledgeable. By this means, when he is at rest, he can maintain tranquility and when he is active, he can keep trouble at a distance. If now you abandon your studies, you will not escape a life of menial servitude and will lack the means to keep yourself from misfortune. How is this different from weaving and spinning to eat? If one abandons these tasks midway, how can one clothe one's husband and child and avoid being perpetually short of food? If a woman abandons that with which she nourishes others and a man is careless about cultivating his virtue, if they don't become brigands or thieves, then they will end up as slaves or servants." Mengzi was afraid. Morning and evening he studied hard without ceasing . . . and became one of the most renowned classicists in the world. (*Lienuzhuan* 1.11:18)[48]

Such stories provide an excellent window into early Confucian perceptions of mothers, but what do the texts say about fathers? While the evidence is more limited, a number of passages shed light on the matter. The *Book of Rites* states that "generous affection between father and son," together with harmony between brothers and happy union between husband and wife, is one of the marks of a good family (*Liji* 5.4).[49] Similarly, Mengzi maintains that "the relationship between father and children is love" (*Mengzi* 3A4). These passages emphasize love and affection between fathers and children, as opposed to discipline or respect. Even for Xunzi, the relationship stems from care and trust, not fear and subordination: "May I inquire about how to be a person's father? I say: Be broadminded, kind, and follow the dictates of ritual. May I inquire about how to be a person's son? I say: Be respectful, loving, and have utmost good form" (*Xunzi* 12/57/24:119). These passages reflect the view that the relationship between father and child should be characterized by generosity, kindness, respect, and love.

One of the passages we examined earlier in this chapter, concerning Kongzi's response to his son Boyu in *Analects* 16.13, is also interesting to consider.[50] Although this passage is often widely read by contemporary interpreters as an instance of a cold and distant father, I have argued that there are many reasons to reject such a reading. This passage highlights some intriguing features of Kongzi's relationship with his son, including the fact that Kongzi thought it was important to encourage him to study the *Odes* and the rites; he did not leave the task of encouraging these forms of moral education entirely up to his wife or to others. Additionally, Kongzi does not simply instruct his son to study the *Odes* and the rites; he gives his son distinctive reasons for why he should study these things, specifying the benefits of doing so. This shows that Kongzi viewed it as at least partly his responsibility to see that his son was pursuing the right forms of study and activity and that he appreciated the reasons these things were important. Additionally, the description of Boyu's attitude and behavior toward his father, as well as his response to his father's instructions, tells us some important things about their relationship. First, Boyu had developed a sense of filial piety to a significant degree—seen in his hurried steps as he passed his father in the courtyard. Second, Boyu took his father's instructions seriously and did not disregard them, which indicates his respect for his father.

Analects 12.11 also sheds light on how the roles of fathers were viewed by early Confucian thinkers. In this passage, when Duke Jing of Qi questions Kongzi about government, Kongzi replies, "Let the ruler be a ruler; the subject, a subject; the father, a father; the son, a son." The duke replies, "Splendid! For if indeed the ruler is not a ruler, the subject not a subject, the father not a father, the son not a son, then although there is grain, how will I be able to eat it?" Van Norden points out that this passage can help us appreciate why some Confucians thought it was so important to use titles such as "father" in the right ways—something that came to be part of a larger teaching referred to as correcting or rectifying names: "For example, if names are used correctly, 'father' will carry the connotations of 'nurturer, protector, ethical guide.' The presence of these connotations will encourage fathers to fulfill these roles. But if people start to use the term 'father' to refer merely to a human sire, then it will seem less anomalous and objectionable that a father should be absent, indifferent, or even competitive with his children" (Van Norden 2007:84).[51] Van Norden's example can help us recognize something particularly important about the views of fathers that are expressed in early Confucian texts. While discussions of the roles of fathers in relation to their children are much more limited than those concerning mothers, especially because mothers were primarily responsible for children's early education and care, Confucian texts nevertheless maintain that the roles of fathers are important, and they do not tend to portray fathers as indifferent, wholly uninvolved in their children's lives, or completely unemotional toward their children, nor do they express approval of fathers who behave in these ways. While early Confucian texts express nothing like the view that parents should share in the work of caring for young children equally, they do maintain that fathers' roles are important and that fathers ought to relate to their children in ways that reflect their distinctive role and give rise to filial piety. Multiple texts express the view that the relationship between father and child ought to be defined by love and affection, and that the moral cultivation of children is shaped in positive ways by this relationship.

Another aspect of *Analects* 12.11, and something we have seen in this and the preceding chapter, is the seriousness with which the early Confucians regarded the relationship between the family and a good society. Indeed, in a number of places, early Confucian thinkers even suggest that rulers should emulate the concern of good parents in their rule of the people, working to embody the same virtues that are characteristic of parent–child relationships. These passages can shed additional light on how early Confucian thinkers understood the relationship between parents and children, while also highlighting their understanding of the close relationship between the family and the state. In *Analects* 2.20, Ji Kangzi asks Kongzi how he can make the people respectful, loyal, and diligent in their work. Kongzi replies, "If you are strict in overseeing them, they will be respectful. If you are filial and kind [*ci* 慈], they will be loyal. If you promote persons of goodness and teach those who are incompetent, then the people will be diligent."[52] Here we find Kongzi instructing a ruler to embody a number of virtues associated with good parents. Similarly, the *Great Learning* says that

the ruler, without going beyond his family, completes the lessons for the state. There is filial piety, with which you serve a lord. There is brotherly respect, with which you serve elders and superiors. There is kindness [*ci*] with which you treat the people. . . . It is said, "Act as if you were watching over an infant." If [a mother] is really anxious about it, though she may not hit upon [the needs of her infant] exactly, she will not be far from it. . . . From one family's humaneness, a whole state becomes humane.[53]

Although rulers at this time in China were men, the analogical reference in these passages is not exclusively to fathers watching over their children but to both parents, with particular references to mothers and the nurturing care they provide. Thus the emphasis is placed not on controlling or disciplining the people but on caring for them and attending to their needs. Attentive parents watch their infants closely out of love and concern for their well-being, in order to observe whether they are hungry or tired, and also out of protectiveness, in order to ensure their safety—both when others are caring for them and when they are playing alone. All of these things serve as helpful illustrations of the things good political leaders do for their people—watching to observe the people's needs so they can work to fulfill them before a serious problem arises, watching to be sure no one is neglected or mistreated by others, and being vigilant in order to protect their subjects from harm.

For Xunzi, too, the role of parents in caring for very young children is important and serves as a standard for other relationships, especially in governing. He writes that when we look back at good kings in history,

> Superiors all had the utmost concern for their subordinates and regulated them by means of ritual. The way superiors treated their subordinates was as though caring for a newborn [*chizi* 赤子]. . . . Therefore, as for the way that subordinates loved their superiors, they delighted in them as in their own parents, and they could be killed but could not be made disobedient. (*Xunzi* 11/54/11:110)

Here Xunzi compares the way good parents care for young children with the way superiors like rulers should care for their people. He even indicates that children who know their parents love and care for them learn to be obedient, for they come to see that their parents have their best interests at heart.

It is not surprising, then, that beginning early in the Confucian tradition, rulers are called "the father and mother of the people," a phrase that is used to emphasize the sense of responsibility that good political leaders feel for those they govern.[54] Indeed, due to the close alignment of parental relationships with the responsibilities of political leaders, some discussions of good rulers can even help us to gain a clearer picture of the virtues associated with good parental care in early Confucianism, such as *qin* 親 ("loving," "affectionate") and *ci* 慈 ("kind," "loving")—virtues we have seen in early Confucian discussions of early childhood education. The *Book of Rites* quotes from the *Book of Odes* in its discussion of this matter:

> "The happy and courteous prince is the father and mother of his people." Happy, he (yet) vigorously teaches them; courteous, he makes them pleased and restful. With all their happiness, there is no wild extravagance; with all their observance of ceremonial usages, there is the feeling of affection. Notwithstanding his awing gravity, they are restful; notwithstanding his sonlike gentleness, they are respectful. Thus he causes them to honour him as their father, and love him as their mother. There must be all this before he is the father and mother of his people. (*Liji* 29.28:340–341)

On this view, parent–child relationships serve as the paradigm for other relationships, including political relationships, and this underscores how important the role of a parent is. The paternalism inherent in this view may lead some to dismiss it, but my aim in discussing the analogy between rulers and parents is to highlight some of the qualities the early Confucians associated with good mothers and fathers and the close connection they drew between the family and political matters. Not only did the early Confucians maintain that family relationships should serve as the paradigm for political relationships, but they also argued that early childhood cultivation is the key to addressing a wide variety of social problems. This view has important implications for the kinds of policies and programs a society supports, and this is seen clearly in the contrast between some of the policies of the Qin dynasty and those of the Han dynasty, which sought to recover Confucian values and implement them. Kinney writes that the collapse of the Qin dynasty rekindled the old Confucian distrust of law as the primary means of sustaining the state and preventing antisocial behavior. Although the Han preserved much of the apparatus of the Legalist Qin state, Confucian thinkers believed that moral education would serve as a more effective deterrent to crime than the strict laws and punishments of the Qin regime. Moreover, by advocating a form of education that would promote both morals and literacy, the Confucian program would go far beyond the Qin agenda of strengthening warfare, agriculture, and social control. (Kinney 2004:16)[55]

The idea that the right kind of early childhood moral cultivation is a way of preventing crime is seen clearly in Jia Yi's *Baofu*. Jia writes,

Now, the reason the Three Dynasties lasted so long was that they used means like these [moral education techniques] in order to aid and succor the prince. When the time of the Qin came, however, they did not do it this way. Their customs certainly did not place value on yielding, but rather emphasized making accusations. Their customs certainly did not place value on ritual propriety and righteousness, but rather emphasized punishment. (*Baofu*, 14)

Jia goes on to argue that because the crown prince of Qin, Hu Hai, was educated by his tutor to use execution and remedial punishment, "if a 'Hu Hai' took the throne today . . ., he would treat killing people as if it was simply a matter of mowing down thatching grass" (*Baofu*, 14). Jia goes on to formulate his view, which we have already examined: "Now, this is the exact location of the key to the alternation between preservation and loss, and of the pivot between good government and chaos. The fate of the people depends on the crown prince and, in turn, the quality of the crown prince is determined by early instruction and the selection of the prince's attendants" (*Baofu*, 15). Later, he adds, "I therefore submit that the matters of choosing attendants and early instruction are most urgent."

* * *

An understanding of the emphasis the early Confucians placed on moral cultivation during infancy and childhood, the critical role of the family in this process, and the implications of early moral cultivation for the overall quality of a society deepens our understanding of and appreciation for Confucianism. This dimension of early Confucianism has been neglected, but we possess a better understanding of Confucian philosophy when we are aware of it. In the following chapters I will argue that there are additional reasons that this dimension of early Confucianism is important. The fact that the early Confucians gave attention to areas that we now know are critically important for moral education—and that several features of their views are supported by modern empirical evidence—also gives us good reasons to study the Confucian tradition. I will argue that there are distinctive resources in the early Confucian tradition that can augment our efforts to understand the connection between moral cultivation, the family, and early childhood. But in order to establish these claims, we must first examine what others have written about this connection.

II

HOW ARE EARLY CONFUCIAN VIEWS OF
PARENT–CHILD RELATIONSHIPS, EARLY CHILDHOOD,
AND MORAL CULTIVATION DISTINCTIVE,
COMPARED WITH VIEWS IN THE HISTORY OF
WESTERN PHILOSOPHY?

3

PARENTS, CHILDREN, AND MORAL
CULTIVATION IN TRADITIONAL
WESTERN PHILOSOPHY

O NE OF THE central arguments of this work is that the Confucian tradition can make a distinctive contribution to both our understanding of the relationship between the family and moral cultivation and our attempts to promote social and policy change relating to parent–child relationships and moral cultivation. In some areas, the Confucian tradition can lend additional support to views that some of us already hold, reinforcing convictions we already have and thereby providing added strength to our views. Additionally, the Confucian tradition has unique features that can lead us to reflect on issues, questions, and potential solutions that other resources have not put forth, and this unique potential exists in part because Confucian sources make some claims and offer some approaches that differ from those of sources in the Western philosophical tradition and in the sciences.

In highlighting these issues I am not claiming that Confucian sources are radically different from Western sources or that Western sources completely neglect the relationships between the family, moral cultivation, and the goal of creating and sustaining a good society. As this and the following chapter will demonstrate, such claims would be obviously false. As most of us know and as we shall see, there has been significant attention given to the importance of the family by both Western philosophers and social scientists. Indeed, a central part of my argument is that most of us already have a basic awareness of many of the issues that early Confucian thinkers address, and the extensive work done in the sciences on these topics gives us good reasons to think these issues are pressing for us today.

The fact that the Confucians raise issues that we already at some level know are important should lead us to examine carefully what the Confucians have to say and not dismiss them because we think we—or Western philosophers and social scientists—already know all there is to know about the topic. However, given that a range of important sources in Western philosophy and in the sciences have examined the role of the family, it is important to determine what is distinctive about Confucian views and what the Confucians can contribute to our understanding. In order to answer these questions, in the following chapters I examine Western sources on these topics, for the only way to defend the claim that specific views are distinctive and can contribute something new or different is to identify what they differ from and how. This chapter examines the views that particular Western philosophers throughout history have advanced on these topics and compares and contrasts these ideas with what we have identified in the Confucian sources; the next chapter focuses on the contributions of contemporary feminist philosophers.

Anyone who engages in careful, sustained study of the Western and the Chinese philosophical traditions will, I think, be struck by the variety of differences between them and the number of ways in which different thinkers and movements in each tradition are distinctive. In this chapter I present textual evidence that just as there is genuine diversity *within* the Chinese and the Western philosophical traditions, there are also genuine differences between some of the views of Confucian philosophers and the views of Western philosophers. This should not surprise us—particularly given all we know about the differences that exist between cultures—any more than it would surprise us that humans from different cultures, times, and places share some of the same concerns and experiences. My aim is not to offer a survey of all that Western philosophers have said about the family; rather, I confine my discussion to sources that address the subject of this study: the relationship between the family and moral cultivation. I argue that although particular themes or topics that are part of Confucian views of the family and moral cultivation are discussed in the history of Western philosophy, we do not find them addressed in the same way, nor do we find all of these features in any one thinker or school. I further argue that it is not simply the content or features of Confucian views, but the amount of weight and importance that the Confucians assign to family relationships and moral cultivation, that distinguishes Confucian views from other views.

I will focus in particular on: (1) the special role of parent–child relationships in moral cultivation (as opposed to a focus on the role of the family generally, or on the role of father–son or mother–child relationships exclusively or centrally, or on the responsibilities of parents primarily); (2) the central and foundational role of filial piety in ethics and politics; (3) the unique importance of the earliest years for moral cultivation (including the prenatal period, infancy, and early childhood); the link between early experiences within the family and virtue in general and the claim that the general ethical sensibilities we develop early in childhood are the basis for nearly every virtue; (4) the direct relationship between early childhood education within the family and the quality of a society; and (5) the poignant and powerful set of stories, anecdotes, and approaches (including specific practices) that reinforce and encourage an ethical understanding of the family and its role in moral development.

THE FAMILY AND MORAL CULTIVATION IN ANCIENT GREEK PHILOSOPHY

"Philosophers have written very little about families" (O'Neill and Ruddick 1979:3). This claim opens the introduction to Onora O'Neill and William Ruddick's *Having Children: Philosophical and Legal Reflections on Parenthood*, and as far as it concerns the history of traditional Western philosophy, it is accurate. In the preceding chapters we have seen that Confucian philosophers wrote much about families, and the sustained and extensive attention they gave to the role of the family in ethics and politics is certainly one thing that distinguishes them from most philosophers in the history of Western philosophy. O'Neill and Ruddick point out that in the work of most Western philosophers, "Family arrangements are regarded as below the level of attention of political theory, familial decisions as involving no ethical problems distinct from those which may arise between any two individuals. A territorial division of normative questions into political theory and ethics has left questions about the family in no man's land, which, perhaps significantly, is often regarded as woman's sphere" (O'Neill and Ruddick 1979:3). Here again, we find another interesting contrast with the Confucian views highlighted in the early chapters of this work: beginning early in their history the Confucians maintained that one cannot adequately address ethics or politics without addressing the critical role of the family in both of these areas. Nevertheless, O'Neill and Ruddick point out that there are some "supposed exceptions to this neglect."

Plato and Aristotle both exhibit an interest in early childhood education, and they both address—though to varying degrees and in very different ways—the role of the family.[1] In ancient Greece, cultures like Sparta advocated and practiced radically different childhood education, and thinkers in ancient Athens sought to respond to this. As we shall see, Plato and Aristotle were deeply influenced by Athenian culture, but they were also critics of it, and many of their ideas concerning how children should be educated, and especially the state's role in this process, were drawn from their observations of Spartan culture. Perhaps the most striking contrast in children's education in ancient Athens and Sparta is that Athenian parents were primarily responsible for their children's education. A father's tribe scrutinized boys at successive stages of life while girls remained at home, educated by their mothers and other women in the household. In contrast, Sparta had a state-prescribed educational program for both boys and girls. The goal of the boys' program was to train them to become the hoplite warriors the state required, while the girls' program was designed to create women who would produce the best hoplites and mothers of hoplites (Pomeroy 2002:3–4). Sparta honored its citizens according to their fulfillment of these roles and their willingness to die for them: only men who had died in battle and women who had died in childbirth were commemorated by grave markers (Pomeroy 2002:52). Although children's education was state prescribed, families, and especially mothers, still had an important role to play in children's lives.

Spartan views and practices concerning the family's role in moral cultivation clearly influenced Plato. In book 5 of the *Republic* (457c–471d), Plato presents the view that the family, as the primary object of one's loyalty, undermines one's loyalty to the city. According to Plato, when the effects of the family on the socialization of children are taken into account, it becomes clear that the family must be abolished. There should thus be no private homes, spouses, or children: "All these women are to belong to all these men in common, and no woman is to live privately with any man. And the children, in their turn, will be in common, and neither will a parent know his own offspring, nor a child his parent" (*Republic* 5, 457c–d; Bloom 1968:136). Plato leaves little doubt that these ties should be severed. At birth, children will be removed from their parents and delivered "to certain nurses who live apart in a certain section of the city." Mothers will be led to the infants when they need to be nursed, but will also be closely supervised, "so that none will recognize her own" and so that "they suckle only a moderate time and that the wakeful watching and the rest of the labor are handed over to wet nurses and governesses" (*Republic* 5, 460c–d).

As O'Neill and Ruddick note, Plato presents a restructuring of familial arrangements as a requirement for a just society in the *Republic*, wherein

> a combination of organized coupling and communal child-rearing might produce new generations whose members, besides being eugenically optimal, would feel fraternally (!) toward all their fellows and would reach positions of power by merit alone. The new men and women of the *Republic* would be liberated from the partiality, the intimacy, the divisiveness of family life. For them, indeed, the laws would be parents and all other citizens brothers. (O'Neill and Ruddick 1979:3)

Plato's interest in state-controlled education as well as eugenics is not insignificant; to some extent, his account in both the *Republic* and the *Laws* is based on an idealized picture of archaic Sparta.[2]

In the *Republic*, Plato outlines his "first-best society," but even in his discussion of a second-best society in the *Laws*, in which private property and the private family are retained, extensive legal regulation of the private family is necessary, on Plato's view. In his examination of parenting and the family in the history of Western philosophy in the seminal work *Parents and Children: The Ethics of the Family*, Jeffrey Blustein observes that Plato retains the private family "for primarily practical, not moral, reasons: he recognizes that the citizens of this city, not being gods or sons of gods, are incapable of holding their property, wives, and children in common." In the *Laws*, Plato has come to view the relation between reason and appetite differently. Whereas in the *Republic* he maintains that reason must reign in our feelings, in the *Laws* he maintains that we can develop desirable habits and traits, and that as a result, this restraint is not necessary. As Blustein points out, "On this view, though the family is still a temptation to self-seeking, reason does not require the repression of particular familial attachments. Family feeling can be enlightened by precepts of virtue, and therefore a communistic life" is no longer necessary (1982:35).

There is simply no room, in Plato's view, for the family to play a special role in moral education or moral cultivation, since he sees the family not as enabling but as a barrier to a good society. O'Neill and Ruddick correctly point out that "Plato's alleged focus on the family in his political theory turns out to be, in large part, a rejection of everything which distinguishes familial from (other) political arrangements" (1979:3). It is important to recognize, though, that Plato is deeply concerned with moral development and specifically with cultivating the traits of character that make good citizens. He also recognizes that moral cultivation occurs more easily in children, and this is what leads him to maintain that, short of banishing all of the adults from the city and starting over with the children, it will be almost impossible to bring about the ideal city of the *Republic*.

But although Plato affirms the importance of moral cultivation and maintains that childhood represents an irreplaceable opportunity for it due to the ease of cultivation, he does not believe that the family has an important role to play in this process. To the contrary, as Blustein puts it, Plato "is convinced that when familial claims are recognized and admitted into social life, they draw off energies and affections from the common purpose of the larger community and detract from the patriotism demanded of the true citizen" (Blustein 1982:32). Plato further maintains that our inborn "excessive love of self" would, "if given the opportunity, express itself through an excessive devotion to the interests of one's family and a corresponding disregard of public interests" (32). Unlike the Confucians but much like their contemporaries the Mohists, Plato maintains that attachments to our families turn us inward. While the Confucians—and, as we shall see, modern social scientists—view family relationships as providing the foundation of our capacity for positive interactions with members of the wider community and society, Plato maintains that we are prone to take an excessive interest in our families. He also views this as selfish, which marks another difference from the Confucians. From a Confucian standpoint, the family offers us our earliest lessons in compromise and making sacrifices for others, including siblings, parents, grandparents, and eventually our own children and grandchildren. Precisely because being a member of family involves learning *not* to be selfish but to think of the needs of others, the Confucians see it as the primary context for our moral development.

Plato's view, of course, did not go unchallenged in ancient Greece. Aristotle offers a critique of Plato's account of the family while also presenting a very different view of the relationship between the family and moral cultivation. In book 2 of *Politics*, Aristotle criticizes Plato's account of the abolition of the family in the *Republic*, arguing that it would not be psychologically possible for people to care for children who are not their own but are shared in the communal way Plato envisions: "For there are two things in particular that cause human beings to love and cherish something: their own and their favorite. And neither can exist among those governed in this way" (*Politics* 1262b; Aristotle 1998:31). In other words, from Aristotle's point of view we feel affection for things that belong to us and things that we like the most, and in Plato's ideal city it would be possible neither for parents to feel that their children belong to them nor for them to develop a special affection for their children. Here, even as Aristotle critiques Plato's view, he retains an important feature of Plato's account: the identification of self-love with love for one's family. In the *Nicomachean Ethics*, Aristotle writes that "a parent is fond of his children because he regards them as something of himself; and children are fond of a parent because they regard them[selves] as coming from him" (*NE* 1161b17; Aristotle 1999:132–133). Aristotle says in the *Politics* that "people give most attention to their own property, less to what is communal, or only as much as falls to them to give. For apart from anything else, the thought that someone else is attending to it makes them neglect it the more" (*Politics* 1261b; Aristotle 1998:28–29). As Blustein puts it, Aristotle's argument is that

> parents and children will not feel especially wanted, valued, and cared for by one another unless those who do the childrearing feel personally and primarily responsible for the well-being of specific children. Communal rearing, such as Plato proposes, does not extend the warmth of family feeling over the whole state, but alienates parents, so that the quality of child care and the attachment between parents and children suffer. (Blustein 1982:38)

Aristotle's tendency to see attachment to one's family as an extension of self-interest offers a contrast to the Confucian view. Both Plato and Aristotle contend that our love for our families is really an expression of self-love. As Blustein puts it, "Parents love their children because they are not completely individuated from them, because they see their children as reproducing some aspect of themselves or their lives. Parents identify with their children much the same way that painters identify with their paintings, and their love for their children closely approaches the love with which they love themselves" (Blustein 1982:41). Additionally, for Aristotle it is significant that children are biologically tied to us, making the tendency to see them as an extension of ourselves especially strong. One of the difficulties with Aristotle's view here is that adoptive parents love their children just as biological parents do, illustrating that the actual source of parental love is not in the biological ties between parents and children.

Although the Confucians noted that children are indebted to their parents for their physical bodies, compared with Aristotle the Confucians did not place as much emphasis on the biological aspects of parenthood. More importantly, the Confucian view is that the sacrifices involved in caring properly for our families teach us not to be selfish while also bringing us greater fulfillment—the kind of fulfillment that only comes from not being selfish. The Confucian view accounts for some highly significant aspects of the moral experiences of parents, most notably the fact that almost all parents would put themselves in harm's way and give their lives for their children without thinking twice. In this way, the love parents have for their children does not approach the love they have for themselves—it exceeds it. Further, parental love often compels parents to act *against* their own interests (e.g., giving up sleep, leisure time, and professional opportunities, putting themselves in harm's way in order to protect their child) or to delay meeting their own needs and desires. One can certainly argue that when parents do this, they are acting in ways that will, in most cases, eventually benefit both themselves and their children, because loving parent–child relationships provide greater fulfillment in life; this would be true, but such a view still requires admitting that devoted parents regularly act against some of their own interests—even if in pursuit of some larger ideal. We should keep in mind here that this ideal is anything but selfish, for it seeks to work for everyone's good by making personal sacrifices on a daily—and often hourly—basis. This is one of the most remarkable dimensions of the parent–child relationship and also one of the reasons that self-love does not sufficiently account for parental love.

How does Aristotle view the role of the family in moral cultivation, especially during childhood? It is telling that out of all the objections Aristotle makes to Plato's account of the family, nowhere does he claim that Plato's system would stunt or harm children's moral development, nor does he suggest that moral cultivation would not be possible without the close relationships that obtain within families.[3] This is especially notable given the various reasons Aristotle puts forth for why Plato's account would not work, including the fact that it would be impossible to prevent people from having suspicions about who their children, parents, and siblings are. Given the amount of attention Aristotle devotes to explicating why Plato's account is untenable, it is most significant that he does not claim that children would grow up without a moral foundation under such a system. Although he acknowledges that the family has a role in early upbringing and that this is important for later moral development, he does not view this period as the most important or pivotal in our moral development, nor does he specify what it entails.

Near the beginning of the *Nicomachean Ethics*, Aristotle writes that "we need to have been brought up in fine habits if we are to be adequate students of fine and just things" (*NE* 1095b5–6; Aristotle 1999:4). Unfortunately, Aristotle does not elaborate on what constitutes good upbringing, even though he does make some additional remarks about the role of the family, as we shall see later. Aristotle simply claims here that our early experiences must provide an adequate basis for ethical reflection. As Richard Kraut puts it, for Aristotle, a good upbringing is critical but "can take us only so far. We seek a deeper understanding of the objects of our childhood enthusiasms, and we must systematize our goals so that as adults we have a coherent plan of life. We need to engage in ethical theory, and to reason well in this field, if we are to move beyond the low-grade form of virtue we acquired as children" (2012: n.p.). Kraut's reading highlights the fact that although Aristotle views childhood as essential for providing the foundation for moral development, he does not view it as the most critical time in that process. It is merely a kind of waiting period that is necessary to live through if we are to progress to the later, more important, and higher forms of development.

Aristotle's view of childhood is generally negative, and he certainly does not see it as a stage that is particularly interesting or unique. In the *Eudemian Ethics* he states that "the kind of life that people live while still children is not desirable—in fact no sensible person could endure to go back to it again" (*EE* 1215b22; Aristotle 1935). Although he thinks that children (and animals) perform voluntary actions, he does not believe that children (or animals) make choices, writing that "the actions we do on the spur of the moment are said to be voluntary, but not to accord with decisions" (*NE* 1111b9; Aristotle 1999:33). This shows that he views children's actions as impulsive and not yet cultivated or learned in any substantive way. Children (and animals) do not make reasoned judgments, in Aristotle's view. Of course, Aristotle also argues that neither children nor animals can be happy, since happiness requires complete virtue and a complete life (*NE* 1100a2; Aristotle 1999:12).

This marks an important contrast with Confucian thinkers such as Jia Yi, who attributes the success of the Three Dynasties solely to the moral cultivation of the ruler's heir during early childhood. The point here is that for at least some Confucian thinkers, early childhood represents a unique and irreplaceable opportunity for moral cultivation not just because it provides a necessary foundation, as Aristotle contends, but because it is the most important stage in a person's development. If Aristotle sees childhood as analogous to building the foundation for a house—which is to say that this phase simply enables us to begin the "real work" of building the house—then thinkers like Jia Yi see childhood as linked to building not just the foundation, but also the structure of the house itself. Later years, for Jia Yi, might be analogous to installing windows and doors—important detail work, but not the most critical part of the project. Such a view allows thinkers like Jia Yi to account for why it is so difficult to remedy failures that occur during the earliest years, and why their consequences are so far-reaching.

Aristotle does make some additional claims about the family's role in moral cultivation. In the *Nicomachean Ethics*, he writes that "it is not enough if they get the correct upbringing and attention when they are young; rather, they must continue the same practices and be habituated to them when they become men" (*NE* 1180a; Aristotle 1999:169). He goes on to say, "For just as in a city the provisions of law and the types of character [found in that city] have influence, similarly a father's words and habits have influence, and all the more because of kinship and because of the benefits he does; for his children are already fond of him and naturally ready to obey" (*NE* 1180b; Aristotle 1999:169). Aristotle argues that children owe their father friendship as a result of the benefits they receive from him when young, the greatest of which is his giving them life (*NE* 1162a5; Aristotle 1999:133).[4] He writes that "we should accord honor to our parents, just as we should to the gods, but not every sort of honor; for we should not accord the same honor to a father as to a mother, nor accord to them the honor due to a wise person or a general" (*NE* 1165a25; Aristotle 1999:140).

Aristotle's view of mothers marks a deep and important contrast with the early Confucian tradition. Aristotle regards mothers as less worthy of honor, in part because he credits fathers with giving their children life.

He asserts that the father's semen provides the active principle that shapes the child in utero, while the mother provides only passive matter.[5] Aristotle does not discuss the role of mothers in maintaining pregnancies and giving birth to children, nor does he discuss mothers as educators of children. Indeed, his view of women and their proper place is the source of several of his central criticisms of Sparta. In Aristotle's view, the essential elements in the *oikos* were the father, mother, child, and slave, which formed a natural hierarchy: the father served as the authority figure in all three relationships because he alone, on Aristotle's view, possessed a fully functioning deliberative faculty. Aristotle criticized Sparta for being a state "ruled by women," for in Sparta (and unlike Athens), women not only managed the *oikos* and exercised authority in the family but could own land and manage their own property. Women's authority, according to Aristotle, hindered the realization of the good of the people.[6] Sparta is not the only culture that gave women authority in some key areas; as we have already seen, the importance of mothers and their authority in running the household and educating children is a feature of the early Confucian tradition as well, evidenced in a variety of early texts, including those documenting the lives of virtuous women and prenatal cultivation. Unfortunately, Aristotle's view of women, which reflects several features of Athenian culture, led him to neglect the importance of mothers.[7]

Aristotle correctly notes that despite what children may do for their parents, they can never repay or approximate what their parents have done for them (*NE* 1164b5; Aristotle 1999:138). However, he does not maintain that cultivating honor and deference is a distinctive virtue in its own right, or that it serves as *the* foundation—or even an important *part* of the foundation—for moral development. While the early Confucians focused on filial piety much more strongly than they did parental love—something that, as I argue later in this work, is a shortcoming in the Confucian tradition—Aristotle argues that parental love is stronger than filial love (*NE* 1161b; Aristotle 1999:133). In addition to maintaining that parents identify with their children more deeply than children identify with their parents, Aristotle argues that although parents are fond of their children from birth, "children become fond of the parent when time has passed and they have acquired some comprehension or [at least] perception" (*NE* 1161b25; Aristotle 1999:133). Blustein notes that for Aristotle, "The very young child does not really love his parents, because he is not yet capable of distinguishing them from others and understanding their special relationship to him" (1982:42).

This aspect of Aristotle's view offers a direct and powerful contrast to the account of Mengzi, who claims that even infants respond with love to their parents. Although we can debate what the necessary and sufficient conditions of "love" are, and what Aristotle and Mengzi each had in mind here, we shall see later in this work that when it comes to an infant recognizing and showing affection and preference for her parents, the evidence is in Mengzi's corner. From birth, infants show evidence of being able to distinguish their parents from others by recognizing their voices—something they begin to do in utero—and they also know their mothers by scent. Infants quickly begin to recognize and distinguish their parents' faces, something they are uniquely poised to do, because newborn infants can focus only on objects eight to ten inches away, which is the approximate distance of a parent's face when an infant is being held. By six months of age, infants clearly exhibit attachment to their parents (or other primary caregivers) or a lack thereof; this is also the age when it becomes difficult to remedy the problems associated with a lack of attachment to caregivers.[8]

As a number of recent works have noted, there are some important similarities between Aristotelian virtue ethics and Confucian virtue ethics.[9] But a deep and pervasive difference is Aristotle's emphasis on friendship and his discussion of family relationships in his section on friendship in the *Nicomachean Ethics*.[10] As Blustein argues, "Aristotle is interested in friendship as a phenomenon of family life because he believes that friendships of a close and intimate kind are a necessary constituent of the good or eudaemonistic life" (Blustein 1982:46). Yet friendship in the fullest sense, for Aristotle, is a voluntary relationship between two men who have and recognize mutual affection for each other and who can equally reciprocate that affection, which means they must be on the same social level (Hutchinson 1995:228). A man cannot have this sort of relationship with his wife, since he rules her, or with his son, since he is his son's benefactor, although a lower kind of friendship can obtain between parents and children, on Aristotle's view: "Whenever children accord to their parents what they must accord to those who gave them birth, and parents accord what they must do to their children, their friendship is enduring and decent" (*NE* 1158b22; Aristotle 1999:127). This is why Aristotle's brief discussion of family relationships is tucked into his account of friendship, which plays a more important role in the good life, on his view. Friendship is all the more important for Aristotle because he viewed women as naturally and inherently lower than men. This is one reason for his emphasis on (male) friendship, as opposed to the family, and it also explains why he did not view women as having a special role in moral education.

This, as we have seen, is in contrast to several early Confucian sources, which maintained that women have a unique and irreplaceable role in the early moral development of infants and children and which saw these early stages not just as necessary because they enabled later, more important forms of cultivation, but because they were the most important and critical stages in the development of our character. For the Confucians, then, the family played the most important role in the earliest stages of our development, while for Aristotle, the family does not play an important role in *any* stage of our development. Aristotle emphasizes the contemplative life as the best life, in contrast to the Confucian emphasis on a larger, richer picture of family relationships as an essential part of a good life. The fact that Confucians regard familial life as an intrinsic mode of human flourishing is a deep and important contrast not only with Aristotle but with other prefeminist Western thinkers as well.

THE FAMILY AND MORAL CULTIVATION IN STOIC, THOMISTIC, AND AUGUSTINIAN PHILOSOPHY

Plato and Aristotle's views both imply that beyond a certain point, it becomes extremely difficult or even impossible for adults to change themselves morally. This is a contrast to the Stoics, who do not see moral reform in adults as especially problematic. There are some important reasons for this contrast. Plato and Aristotle worried that people might suffer *akrasia*, where the strength of the nonrational parts of their soul would render them unable to follow teachings to which they rationally assented. The Stoics, however, did not share this view, and this is one reason they did not focus as strongly on childhood education as Plato and Aristotle. That is not to say that they neglected the subject of infants and children entirely, however, as we shall see.

The Stoics, like the Epicureans before them, offered what Jacques Brunschwig calls "cradle arguments," which consisted "first in describing (or in claiming to describe) the behaviour and psychology of the child in the cradle (usually in conjunction with young animals) and then in drawing (or in claiming to draw), more or less directly, certain conclusions which, in one way or another, lead to the formulation and justification of a moral doctrine" (Brunschwig 1986:113). As Martha Nussbaum points out, in offering these arguments the Epicureans suggest "that we come into the world as healthy living creatures, our faculties operating reliably and without blemish. But shortly after this we encounter external forces that corrupt and confuse us." Accordingly, "Epicurus' core idea seems to be that if in imagination we can catch the human animal before it gets corrupted, see what inclinations it has before these insidious social processes have deformed its preferences, we will have an authentic witness to the true human good, and a way of isolating, among our own desires, those that are healthy" (Nussbaum 1994:107).

Examples of "cradle arguments" from the Stoics include the claim that babies sense the need for nourishment and that is why they want to breast-feed, not because they enjoy nursing and having a full stomach; pleasure is simply a by-product. Seneca also discusses toddlers who insist on trying to stand and walk before they are able to, which results not in pleasure but pain from constant falls. However, several features of these arguments are especially important to note for our purposes. First, they are based on descriptions of physical behaviors such as seeking food and learning to walk, as opposed to descriptions of emotional responses such as Mengzi's infants' loving response to their parents. Second, these arguments do not deal in any way with the process of moral cultivation or education or with the role of parent–child relationships in moral development. As Brunschwig notes, nothing is said about "the potential roles of imitation, the help of the family environment, and its support when the child is learning to walk" (Brunschwig 1986:135). Rather, these philosophers focus exclusively on physical tendencies we have from birth, with the aim of arguing for (and against) certain views of human nature. For the Epicureans, the goal is to establish that we naturally seek pleasure; the Stoics attempt to prove that we instinctively seek to fulfill our physical needs and (against the Epicureans) that any pleasure is simply a by-product. In both cases, the implication is that "anything that cannot be seen and desired as good by the uncorrupted creature, using its untutored equipment, is not a part of the human end" (Nussbaum 1994:109).

Cicero's interest in the family is secondary to his discussion of the state. He acknowledges the critical role the family plays in the creation of the state, writing of marriage that "from such procreation and resultant offspring states have their beginnings. This blood relationship binds men together in both goodwill and affection" (*On Obligations* 1.54–55; Cicero 2000:20).[11] This is one obvious way in which his view contrasts readily with early Confucian views. Cicero considers the family to be a building block for the state, which was the most important human association in his view, while early Confucian thinkers viewed it as the most fundamental and essential part of human life. Additionally, like Aristotle, Cicero prioritizes the state over the family in certain ways. As Blustein points out, Cicero thought the state's claims on an individual's loyalty and devotion outweighed the claims of "parents, children, relatives, and friends" (1982:47).

To be sure, a variety of Stoic writings present a view that clearly rejects both the emotional reality of our attachments to our families and the idea that these connections represent genuine goods. Epictetus, for instance, cautions:

> What you love is mortal . . . you don't love something that is truly your own; it has been given to you for the time being; it is not immune to loss, won't go the distance; it is like a fig, a bunch of grapes; it's available for a fixed season of the year, and if you long for it in winter then you are a

fool. So too if you long for your son or your friend when he isn't available for you then you should realize that you are longing for figs in winter. (*Discourses* 3.24.86–87; Epictetus 2008:204)

Nevertheless, the Stoics do discuss certain aspects of family relationships constructively. Cicero thought it was important for children to show gratitude to their parents. Blustein argues that for Cicero, "the natural society of the family would be undermined if parents were not rewarded for their generosity by the gratitude and general good will of their children." Yet as Blustein next points out, beyond specifying that gratitude is only appropriate for benefits bestowed upon us "deliberately, eagerly, and generously," Cicero never elaborates on what children should be grateful to their parents for, or whether and how this debt of gratitude can ever be fully discharged (Blustein 1982:48). What this shows is that the primary focus of Cicero's moral philosophy—including his discussion of gratitude—is not the family. To the contrary, although he acknowledges that his remarks have some relevance to parent–child relationships, he almost wholly neglects their relevance. This stands in contrast to Confucian discussions of filial piety, which offer elaborate justifications for children's debts of gratitude to their parents and the impossibility of repaying the debt fully, while also outlining and presenting arguments for the specific ways in which children ought to show their gratitude. Of course, there is also more to filial piety than gratitude, on the Confucian view.

Seneca does much better on these issues, it turns out. He argues that parents who abandon their children in infancy and do not go on to nurture them have only given what "beasts and even some piddly little life forms, even some disgusting ones" give their young (*On Benefits*, book 3, chap. 30; Seneca 2011:78). This is most significant, for Seneca here acknowledges that it is not appropriate simply to be grateful that your parents granted you life.[12] He writes of the different kinds of benefits, "surely there can be none greater than the ones conferred on children by their parents. Yet they are in vain if the children are neglected in infancy, wasted unless steady devotion nurtures its own gift. . . . It is not enough to have given the gift, one must sustain it" (*On Benefits*, book 2, chap.11; Seneca 2011:39). On this view, parents fail to fulfill their obligations if they do not continue to nourish and educate children after birth. Interestingly, though, Seneca emphasizes that parents' efforts require "the support of benefits provided by many other people" and that "my origins are not my father or even my grandfather," since there are many past generations to which we owe our existence (Seneca 2011:82, 77; Bk. 3 Ch. 35, 29). While the Confucians acknowledge our debt to ancestors and take filial obligations to previous generations seriously, they nevertheless reserved special admiration for parents and did not minimize this relationship in the ways that Seneca does. Here, the Confucians seem correct: although parents are assisted by many other persons in caring for their children, the efforts of others usually are not comparable to the efforts of good parents.

Most significantly, Seneca poses the question of "whether there might be times when children can give their parents greater benefits than they have received" (Seneca 2011:76, Bk. 3 Ch. 29). Against Aristotle, he answers the question affirmatively. When a grown son saves his father's life, Seneca argues, he does more than his father did in giving him life. First, the gift of his father's life is worth more than his own life was as a newborn, since infants are irrational and lack consciousness, according to Seneca; they do not even know they are alive (78–79, Bk. 3 Ch. 31). Second, he is intentionally saving his father's life, whereas his father's act in creating him may have been unintentional, and the gift of saving his father's life clearly benefits his father, whereas simply giving an infant life does not clearly benefit the infant. Third, his father's felt need to stay alive outweighs his need as an infant to be born. All of this underscores how different Seneca's view is from Aristotle's view that children can never benefit their parents as much as their parents benefited them, because for Aristotle the gift of life is a debt that cannot be repaid. As Blustein points out, for Seneca "reverence is not a sign of inferiority, but an attitude that expresses itself through the child's continuing desire to make his parents proud of him, to bring them the happiness that can only come from witnessing his eagerness to bestow kindnesses and favors on them" (Blustein 1982:52).

Even more importantly for the present purposes, though, it underscores the contrast with the early Confucian view. If we try to imaginatively construct the response of a thinker like Jia Yi to Seneca's argument, the most important disagreement would be over Seneca's claim that the gift of his father's life is worth more than his own life was as a newborn, since infants are irrational and are not conscious of themselves or others. Based on the early Confucian view—which turns out to be correct—that the early stages of infancy represent a unique and irreplaceable stage in our development and one that is completely unrivaled in importance in adulthood, Jia Yi might argue that a parent's nurturance and attention during infancy *is* worth more than a son's actions saving his father's life when he is older. At any rate, an early Confucian would want to emphasize that a son saving his father's life by no means rivals parents' care for their children during the early stages of their development. This is not "repaying" one's parents, nor is it giving a greater benefit than one's parents gave. Indeed, Jia Yi might argue that it is impossible to give a greater benefit than parents can give their infants, precisely because of the unique and irreplaceable opportunity for cultivation that those early years represent. This response highlights some important features of the early Confucian tradition that contrast readily with Stoicism. First, the early Confucians more strongly emphasized moral cultivation than the Stoics. As a result, they would be inclined to place much more emphasis on the fact that parents help to shape and cultivate their children's character in ways that children never will be able to fully reciprocate, even if they do shape and influence their parents in significant ways. Second, they recognized that infants were much more than they seemed to be. Jia Yi's remarks about infants contrast sharply with Seneca's description of them. Third, the Confucians took filial piety much more seriously than other schools of thought. While thinkers like Aristotle, Cicero, and Seneca clearly think children should feel gratitude toward their parents and have a conception of filial piety, their accounts do not rival the depth and extent of Confucian discussions of this virtue. This is not just because the Confucians viewed filial piety as the foundation of the other virtues, although this certainly sets them apart. Confucian accounts of filial piety also stand apart because they express an understanding of the highly unique nature of the debt children owe to their parents—and not just because, as Aristotle as well as many Confucians argued, their parents gave them life. It is also because of the unique kinds of nurturance parents provide. Unlike Seneca, the early Confucians did not think that anything children could do would ever rival this investment. Clearly, early Confucian views of filial piety are lacking in certain respects, including the fact that they did not explicitly argue that the ground of filial piety lies partly in the unique nature of the early years of a child's life and the pivotal role parents play during those years. They also prioritize children's obligations over parental obligations (and tend to view these obligations as extreme and absolute), which is especially serious given early Confucian accounts of the early years of children's lives. Confucian views of filial piety are by no means perfect and need to be amended, and these are matters we will explore later in this work. But the purpose of this chapter is to highlight the ways in which Confucian views of the role of the family in moral cultivation differ from the views of these matters in the history of traditional Western philosophy. In the case of the Stoics, we can see clear and obvious contrasts, and these contrasts highlight and emphasize distinctive features of early Confucianism.

The topics of early childhood, parent–child relationships, and the need for moral cultivation are also addressed in the writings of early Christian philosophers, but within a very different framework than that of the Stoics. The writings of Augustine present a robust account of the need for moral cultivation, and his remarks on children and childhood highlight this feature of his view. However, Augustine's theological outlook leads him to argue against the view that there is a close relationship between moral cultivation and parent–child relationships, and it prevents him from viewing early childhood as a unique opportunity for moral cultivation. Augustine's account of original sin strongly shapes his views on children, parent–child relationships, and moral cultivation; due to our profound need for salvation, Augustine sees limited roles for moral cultivation and parent–child relationships in shaping our moral development. In short, for Augustine, nothing can come close to replacing the transformative power of God's saving grace.

Augustine's view of children is less than flattering. They do not exhibit any unique potential or particular malleability. In Augustine's view, as Blustein notes, "The sin of Adam is passed down to his descendants so that, like

Adam himself, children are domineering, willful, egoistic, and self-centered" (Blustein 1982:54). One might expect Augustine to grant a significant role to parents for this reason, and it is true that in his view, children who constantly have their impulses gratified by their parents and teachers will never develop the humility that is necessary to realize one's need for salvation, which means in turn that without the shaping and discipline of their parents and teachers, they will never be set on the path to finding fulfillment. For this reason, Augustine emphasizes discipline and obedience in his discussion of parent–child relationships. Yet the role of parents has important limitations in his eyes, because parents themselves are sinful and we can only be transformed through salvation and not through any program of moral cultivation or education. Partly as a result of his account of human sinfulness, Augustine does not view the relationship between parents and children as ripe with possibilities for moral cultivation. Augustine writes that parenthood is good for us because it represses our sexual desires after procreation: in marriage, "the concupiscence of the flesh, which parental affection tempers, is repressed and becomes inflamed more modestly. For a kind of dignity prevails when, as husband and wife they unite in the marriage act, they think of themselves as mother and father" (*The Good of Marriage*, chap. 3; Augustine 1955:13).[13] Passages like this help to show that Augustine sees the family in relation to his conception of original sin and sexual sin in particular.

On Augustine's view, all good things come from God, even if they come to us through other humans, but the reverse is not true; bad and evil things come from humans, not God. This is especially clear in Augustine's discussions of parents and other caregivers. In discussing his own infancy, Augustine writes in the *Confessions*,

the comfort of human milk nourished me, but neither my mother nor my nurses filled their own breasts. Rather, through them you gave me an infant's food in accordance with your law and out of the riches that you have distributed even down to the lowest level of things. You gave me to want no more than you gave, and you gave to those who nursed me the will to give what you gave to them. By an orderly affection they willingly gave me what they possessed so abundantly from you. It was good for them that my good should come from them; yet it was not from them but through them. For from you, O God, come all good things, and from you, my God, comes all my salvation. (*Confessions*, book 1, para. 7; Augustine 1960:46–47)

Later, of his mother's warnings, he writes, "Whose words but yours were those that you sang in my ears by means of my mother, your faithful servant? . . . Such words seemed to be only a woman's warnings, which I should be ashamed to bother with. But they were your warnings, and I knew it not" (*Confessions*, book 2, chap. 3, para. 7, p. 68). Augustine readily gives credit to God for the good things his mother did in these passages, but he straightforwardly assigns blame to his parents for their failings: "My parents took no care to save me by marriage from plunging into ruin. Their only care was that I should learn to make the finest orations and become a persuasive speaker" (book 2, chap. 2, para. 4, p. 67). He goes on to write that his father "took no pains as to how I was growing up before you, or as to how chaste I was, as long as I was cultivated in speech, even though I was left a desert, uncultivated for you, O God, who are the one true and good Lord of that field which is my heart" (book 2, chap. 3, para. 5, pp. 25–26). In the passage preceding the well-known pear-stealing passage, Augustine blames both of his parents for not seeing to it that he was married in order to control his sexual promiscuity, writing that his mother

> took no final care for this, because of fear that my prospects would be hindered by the impediment of a wife. These were not those hopes of the life to come which my mother herself had, but those hopes for learning, which, as I knew, both parents desired too much: he, because he almost never thought of you, and only of vain things for me; she, because she thought that the usual studies would be not only no obstacle but even of some help to me in attaining to you. Thus recalling things as far as I can, I conjecture that such were my parents' attitudes. (*Confessions*, book 2, chap. 3, para. 8, p. 69)

In all of these passages, Augustine presents his parents as providing for his formal education but not for his moral education and well-being. This he sees as their shortcoming, but he attributes the good things he received from them to God.

In the *Confessions*, Augustine openly acknowledges his love for his mother and her love for him. However, on his view, his mother's efforts to reach out and help him were not her own but God's. Additionally, none of her efforts were ultimately effective in transforming him. For this reason, Augustine's account of Monica can clarify his view. We receive no account of the ways in which Monica helped Augustine to become a better person, because in his view, she did not. This does not mean that he did not regard her devotion to her Christian faith as admirable. It does mean, though, that for Augustine, even the most outstanding parental model is insignificant in relation to our development, because God's role is so overwhelmingly important.

That is not to say that moral cultivation is wholly unimportant for Augustine. He offers a rich account of how humans must overcome their estrangement from God by remembering their original unity with God, in the process recovering their originally pure nature. Augustine's view is not that human nature must be wholly transformed by reshaping a raw nature into a perfect one; rather, Augustine thinks we must recover and return home to what was originally implanted in us—to what we were created to be.[14] Within Augustine's picture of how this transformation must occur, though, there is simply no room for the family to have a robust role in the process, nor is there room in his picture of human nature for an account of childhood as having unique potential for moral cultivation.

The account of the family offered by Thomas Aquinas differs in significant ways from Augustine's account, partly because—in contrast with Augustine, whose writings clearly show the influence of Neoplatonism— Aquinas was deeply influenced by Aristotle. His discussion of the family highlights Aristotle's influence primarily through Aquinas's focus on the debt children owe their parents. Aquinas agreed with Aristotle that children cannot discharge this debt; no benefits we can bestow on our parents will ever be as important as those they bestowed on us (*Summa Theologiae* 2a2ae, Q. 106, A. 6; Aquinas 1948:1646–1647). He also agreed with Aristotle that "parents love their children as being part of themselves . . . so that the love of a father for his children, is more like a man's love for himself" (Q. 26, A. 9;

Aquinas 1948:1295). Like Seneca in turn, Aquinas believed that parental obligations extend beyond simply bringing a child into the world; he states that parents have a duty to care for their children.[15] But Aquinas focused more heavily on the appropriate response of children to their parents, which led him to develop a set of views on filial piety.

Aquinas argues that children have two types of duties in response to their parents: duties of obedience, which are temporary, lasting only through childhood, and duties of piety, which are permanent (*ST* 2a2ae, Q. 101, 104; Aquinas 1948:1626,1639).[16] Although obedience to parents and respect for their authority are appropriate for young children, Aquinas argued that parents should receive homage or reverence—and not just honor or respect—from their children. This is an important distinction for Aquinas; he maintains that "reverence regards directly the person that excels: wherefore it admits of various species according to the various aspects of excellence. Obedience, on the other hand, regards the precept of the person that excels, and therefore admits of only one aspect" (Q. 104, A. 2; Aquinas 1948:1636). In Aquinas's eyes, our parents should be revered by us not just because they are our superiors, but because of the kind of benefits they bestow on us. Aquinas argues that one's parents and one's country are second only to God in the kinds of benefits they bestow, having "given us birth and nourishment. Consequently man is debtor chiefly to his parents and his country, after God. Wherefore just as it belongs to religion to give worship to God, so does it belong to piety, in the second place, to give worship to one's parents and one's country" (Q. 101, A. 1; Aquinas 1948:1626). Unlike Aristotle, though, Aquinas explicitly argued that parents are more important than one's country in this regard, which is why our obligations are not equal, "but chiefly to our parents, and to others according to our means and their personal claims" (Q. 101, A. 2; Aquinas 1948:1627). Blustein points out that for Aquinas it is essential that parental obligations take priority over our obligations to our country,

for it is only because parents give their children existence, food, the support needed for life, and education, that they are able to share in the benefits of homeland. Since the benefits parents bestow touch the whole of our existence, our entire personality and not just one relatively minor aspect of it, the degree of our indebtedness to them is particularly great, and it is incumbent on us to revere them in a special way, to acknowledge and pay back our debt to them by the virtue of piety. (Blustein 1982:59)

We see this view clearly in Aquinas's discussion of thankfulness, where he again argues that parents are second only to God in what they deserve from us (*ST* 2a2ae, Q. 106, A. 1; Aquinas 1948:1642–1643). In this aspect of his view, Aquinas breaks with both the earlier Greek and Roman philosophical traditions, which gave greater priority to the city or the state. Aquinas's account of the natural law underlies his emphasis on the family here. When humans act in accord with their nature, he argues, they share in God's plan, and he identifies three classes of things toward which human nature inclines human beings, one of which is to seek sexual union and to beget and educate their offspring (*ST* I–II, Q. 94, A. 2; Aquinas 1948:1009). Aquinas's emphasis on the relationship between parents and children is a natural outgrowth of this account.

Aquinas maintains that filial piety is a distinctive virtue and includes both our reverence and service to our parents. While reverence concerns one's attitude and feelings of honor for one's parents, service includes specific actions, such as visiting one's parents when they are ill and supporting them financially if they are in need (*ST* 2a2ae, Q. 101, A. 2; Aquinas 1948:1626).[17] Interestingly, Aquinas entertains a series of objections based on Christian scriptures that suggest a tension between religion and filial piety (such as Jesus's statement in Luke 14:26 that his disciples should hate their families). He responds that since religion and piety are two virtues, and since Aristotle states that good is not opposed to good, "it is impossible that religion and piety mutually hinder one another, so that the act of one be excluded by the act of the other" (Q. 101, A. 4; Aquinas 1948:1628). Here we see some of the distinctively Christian features of Aquinas's view of filial piety. He argues that

if the worship of one's parents take one away from the worship of God it would no longer be an act of piety to pay worship to one's parents to the prejudice of God. . . . If, however, by paying the services due to our parents, we are not withdrawn from the service of God, then will it be an act of piety, and there will be no need to set piety aside for the sake of religion. (Q. 101, A. 4; Aquinas 1948:1628)

There are exceptions, of course, such as cases in which "our parents incite us to sin, and withdraw us from the service of God," in which case we must "abandon and hate them." He argues that if our parents need our support and no one else can provide for them, we "must not abandon them for the sake of religion," for this would be to break the commandment to honor our parents. However, if other arrangements can be made for their care, "it is lawful to forego their service, so as to give more time to religion" or to enter religion by becoming a priest or joining a religious order. Even one who enters religion, though, must "make pious efforts for his parents' support" (*ST* 2a2ae, Q. 101, A. 4; Aquinas 1948:1628–9).

It is significant that Aquinas addresses the topic of filial piety. He does so more extensively than his predecessors in Western philosophy and explicitly acknowledges that piety is a distinctive virtue. Yet there are a number of important differences between his and early Confucian views of filial piety, including, first, that Aquinas addresses filial piety as part of his general discussion of "piety"—toward God, one's parents, and one's country.[18] The early Confucians viewed filial piety as a distinct virtue in its own right and not as an expression of a larger virtue of "piety" directed at others as well. The Confucians gave more attention to filial piety, writing considerably more about it, compared with Aquinas's discussion. Another important difference is that Aquinas, like Aristotle, fails to appreciate the unique importance of mothers, and his remarks even devalue them. Aquinas presents an argument from authority that fathers should be loved more than mothers, citing both church fathers and Aristotle for support and claiming that the father is "the active principle, while the mother is a passive and material principle. . . . In the begetting of man, the mother supplies the formless matter of the body; and the latter receives its form through the formative power that is in the semen of the father. And though this power cannot create the rational soul, yet it disposes the matter of the body to receive that form" (*ST* 2a2ae, Q. 26, A. 10; Aquinas 1948:1296). There are a few key differences in play here. First, the Confucians did not share this view of the soul; second, they appreciated the unique and pivotal nature of pregnancy; and third, they based their accounts of mothers not solely on how they viewed the origins of life but also on the critical role that mothers play in children's education, beginning in the prenatal period and extending through the early upbringing of children. As a result of all of these factors, the Confucians did not view the role of mothers as "passive."

Another crucial difference from early Confucian views of filial piety is that Aquinas maintains that one's obligations to God take precedence over one's filial obligations. The early Confucians did not have an analogous set of obligations that trumped filial obligations. This is especially clear in the story of Shun's unfailing filial piety even when his parents tried to kill him. One can only assume that Aquinas would not think that Shun's filial obligations still hold, given his view that one's filial obligations do not hold in the event that one's parents "incite us to sin, and withdraw us from the service of God." Aquinas also does not share the Confucian view that filial piety provides the foundation for our moral development or that it is a source of other virtues. If anything, Aquinas sees one's relationship with God as foundational. Nevertheless, both Aquinas and the Confucians have more to say about children's obligations to their parents, as opposed to parents' obligations to their children. Aquinas writes that it is "essentially fitting for a father to support his son: and consequently he is bound to support him not only for a time, but for all his life" (*ST* 2a2ae, Q. 101, A. 2; Aquinas 1948:1627). It seems as though it almost goes without saying for Aquinas that parents have extensive obligations to their children, and this is why he gives more attention to filial duties, which strike him as more exceptional but of course in line with Biblical commands. To some extent the same may be true of the Confucians, though the Confucians had more to say about both parental and filial obligations than Aquinas did.

THE FAMILY AND MORAL CULTIVATION IN MODERN WESTERN PHILOSOPHY

Two features of the major views of the family and moral cultivation in the history of modern Western philosophy that contrast with early Confucian views are, first, the strong emphasis on managing members of a society as opposed to cultivating them, and second, the strong separation between ethics and politics. Further, in the modern period there is a continued neglect of infancy and early childhood, pregnancy, and the role of mothers in relation to moral cultivation. As we have seen, Confucian philosophers always assumed that humans can develop or change their basic natures in significant ways, which led them to focus on moral education, self-cultivation and, of course, the role of the family. The early Confucians took a special interest in the earliest stages of development, viewing them as a unique and irreplaceable opportunity for cultivation and maintaining that mothers had a special role to play in the cultivation of their children's character. On the Confucian view, although the basic structure of a political order is important, it is significantly less important than the development of certain moral sensibilities in its members, and the family plays the most important role in that developmental process. In contrast, during the modern period of Western philosophy, the most influential political philosophers tended to focus more on how a political order can manage humans as they are, and less on the role of the family in moral cultivation. Nevertheless, thinkers such as Thomas Hobbes, Jean-Jacques Rousseau, John Locke, Immanuel Kant, and Georg Wilhelm Friedrich Hegel did hold views on the family and its role in moral education, and as we shall see, their views offer an interesting comparison with early Confucian accounts of these matters.

Much of what Thomas Hobbes has to say about the family and its role in moral development occurs within the context of his account of the state of nature. According to Hobbes, the parent–child relationship, together with voluntarily offering oneself in subservience to another and captivity, is one of three ways in which one person acquires "right and dominion over another" in the absence of civil society (*Body, Man, and Citizen*, part 2, chaps. 3–4; Hobbes 1967). In all of these cases, fear is the defining and motivating feature of the relationship, though Hobbes writes that those who choose their sovereign "do it for fear of one another," while children subject themselves to their parents because they fear them, just as those in captivity subject themselves to their captors out of fear (*Leviathan*, part 2, chap. 20; Hobbes 1968). Hobbes maintains that we are motivated by the prospect of personal gain, in all circumstances: "No man giveth, but with intention of Good to himself," and this applies to parents and children as well (*Leviathan*, part 1, chap. 15; Hobbes 1968). Hobbes maintains that children *choose* to submit to the authority of their parents. As Blustein argues, for Hobbes, "Children tacitly agree to obey parents because they instinctively want to remain alive and because they are given to understand that the parents may kill or abandon them if they do not obey" (Blustein 1982:69).[19] The obligation to obey one's parents extends into adulthood, for as Blustein puts it, on Hobbes's view "we have an obligation to keep the promise we (tacitly) made to our parents when we were dependent on them for protection" (*Leviathan*, part 1, chap. 15; Hobbes 1968).

Several things are immediately apparent here. First, Hobbes is uninterested in the role of parents as moral educators or as those who nurture and shape their children's character; the parent–child relationship mirrors the political relationship between sovereign and subject in being characterized by fear and in having absolutely binding obligations. Second, Hobbes does not view the parent–child relationship as one that evolves and develops, with parents carrying the bulk of the obligation to care for children initially and children then having an obligation to uphold filial duties to their parents. He also does not view it as a reciprocal relationship but rather a relationship characterized by fear of what might happen in the absence of children's obedience and parental care. For Hobbes, children obey their parents initially because they wish to remain alive and unharmed, and they continue to obey because they did remain alive and unharmed. Likewise, as Blustein points out, parents sustain their children so that they will not grow up to become their enemies and in exchange for their obedience in the future (Blustein 1982:72, 74). What is striking, of course, is that Hobbes focuses almost entirely on the negative omissions of parents and children here, rather than their positive actions, and he focuses on the most unlikely omissions: the failure of parents to harm their children and the failure of children to harm their parents. He acknowledges that children are grateful to have remained alive and unharmed and maintains that this motivates their obedience in the future, but even here, children are not motivated by affection or a sense of gratitude for the nurturance and education their parents provided; they are, rather, motivated by their relief and gratitude for not being harmed.

To say the least, Hobbes paints an impoverished picture of parent–child relationships. Perhaps most importantly, this account simply does not capture any of the psychological realities of parent–child relationships, such as the deep and profound love and affection parents and children have for each other. But does Hobbes offer a different account of parent–child relationships outside the state of nature? Unfortunately, Hobbes's remarks concerning the family and moral cultivation outside the state of nature do not paint a radically different picture. Hobbes did not think that infants were born with a moral sense or with concern for anyone but themselves, nor does he describe them as responding with affection toward their parents. To the contrary, he maintains that they exhibit annoyance and aggression: "Unless you give children all they ask for, they are peevish and cry, aye, and strike their parents sometimes; and all this they have from nature" (De cive, preface; Hobbes 1991:100). He also claims that compared with adults, "the dispositions of youths are not less, but much more disposed to bad habit by example than they are to good habits by precept."[20] These remarks are important, because for Hobbes, people in the state of nature are very much like infants and young children, lacking education or training. So we can see clearly that for Hobbes, infancy and childhood do not represent a unique and irreplaceable opportunity for moral cultivation; he does not view children as particularly malleable or as manifesting positive tendencies that can be developed, nor does he view parents and children as having special bonds of affection that can serve as a basis for moral development. Of course, Hobbes did not think it was impossible for people to improve their character; in the preface to De homine, he maintains that people can be made to act in a wide variety of ways and from different kinds of motives through education and training. In fact, Hobbes presents education in the Leviathan as a relatively easy process, which may account in part for the fact that he was not concerned with exploring whether childhood was a particularly opportune time to intervene. He writes, "the Common-peoples minds, unless they be tainted with dependence on the Potent, or scribbled over with the opinions of their Doctors, are like clean paper, fit to receive whatsoever by Publique Authority shall be imprinted in them" (*Leviathan*, part 2, chap. 30; Hobbes 1996:233). Eric Schwitzgebel argues that this is one of several features of Hobbes's view that distinguishes him from the early Confucian Xunzi, since "paper does not resist writing in the same way a board resists straightening" (Schwitzgebel 2007:158). Bernard Gert argues that Hobbes believed people behave in various ways "not primarily because of the way they are born, but because of the way that they have been trained. This point is made in many places, such as where he says that children 'have no other rule of good and evil manners, but the correction they receive from their parents and masters,' and then adds that 'children are constant to their rule'" (Gert 1996:167).[21] The language Hobbes uses here, however, is significant: he sees children as needing to obey the rules their parents set for them, and he views this as incredibly hard work in light of what infants and young children are naturally like. He does not view parent–child relationships as a unique context for cultivating moral sensibilities or extending natural feelings of affection and respect, for in Hobbes's view there is no such potential for virtue to begin with and affection is not the defining feature of this relationship. Instead, the power differential and the ensuing fear that motivates children's obedience is the most important feature of the parent–child relationship for Hobbes.

One of the most fascinating features of John Locke's discussion of parents and children is the fact that he recognized that mothers have an important role in the process of having and raising children, beginning with pregnancy. Indeed, Locke is the first known thinker in the Western tradition to explicitly depart from the Aristotelian view that fathers are more deserving than mothers of their children's respect because fathers give children life. In *Two Treatises of Government*, Locke argues that mothers and fathers both play a role in procreation, which gives fathers "but a joynt Domination with the Mother" over children. He further argues that mothers have "an equal share, if not the greater, as nourishing the Child a long time in her own Body out of her own Substance. There it is fashion'd, and from her it receives the Materials and Principles of its Constitution" (*First Treatise*, chap. 6, sec. 55; Locke 1988:180). Locke goes on to argue, against the views of his predecessors, including Aristotle and Aquinas, that the rational soul could not inhabit an unformed embryo and that "if it must be supposed to derive any thing from the Parents, it must certainly owe most to the Mother" (Locke 1988:180). In these passages from the *First Treatise*, Locke notes that women not only offer their bodies for the growth of a child but also must actively maintain their bodies for this purpose during pregnancy. This is especially significant given the arguments of his predecessors, who as we have seen, held that women are "passive recipients." Locke presents a more accurate picture. As Blustein points out, Locke argues that "childbirth is not the only kind of labor in which the mother engages; pregnancy itself is work. Whether or not husband and wife are equal in marriage—and Locke believes they are not—they *are* equal in the family, for power in the family, which consists in the exercise of parental authority over children, is equally shared between them" (Blustein 1982:77).

What is Locke's view of the role of the family in relation to moral education? Locke maintains that parents have a God-given obligation to "nourish, preserve, and bring up their Off-spring" (*Second Treatise*, chap. 6, sec. 66; Locke 1988:311). This responsibility "is a charge so incumbent on Parents for their Childrens good, that nothing can absolve them from taking care of it" (Locke 1988:312). Further, Locke argues that although parents must discipline their children as a part of this obligation, the affection and tenderness that parents feel for their children will in most cases tend to rein them in and prevent them from being excessively harsh.[22] Given his argument that mothers deserve equal if not more authority over their children by virtue of the fact that they carried and nourished them during pregnancy, it is not surprising that Locke maintains that parental power proceeds not primarily from paternity but from accepting responsibility for the child's growth and development: "This power so little belongs to the Father by any peculiar right of Nature, but only as he is Guardian of his Children, that when he quits his Care of them, he loses his power over them, which goes along with their Nourishment and Education, to which it is inseparably annexed" (Locke 1988:310). As I discuss later, Locke argues that parents and children have reciprocal duties, with children owing their parents honor and support in return for the benefits their parents provide, but for him the duty parents have to educate their children "seems to have the most power, because the

ignorance and infirmities of Childhood stand in need of restraint and correction; which is a visible exercise of Rule, and a kind of Dominion" (Locke
1988:313). Locke also writes that although parents have a sort of rule and
jurisdiction over their children from birth, "The Bonds of this Subjection
are like the Swadling Cloths they are wrapt up in, and supported by, in the
weakness of their Infancy. Age and Reason as they grow up, loosen them
till at length they drop quite off" (Locke 1988:304). In these passages Locke
acknowledges both that children are very much in need of moral education,
which he views in terms of the need for restraint, correction, and support,
and that parents have a unique responsibility to provide that moral education.[23] He also maintains that what parents give children during their early
and formative years has greater power than what children can give their
parents by honoring them in return. Yet children do have a God-given

> perpetual Obligation of *honouring their parents*, which containing in it an
> inward esteem and reverence to be shewn by all outward Expressions, ties
> up the Child from any thing that may ever injure or affront, disturb, or
> endanger the Happiness of Life of those, from whom he received his; and
> engages him in all actions of deference, relief, assistance and comfort of
> those, by whose means he entered into being, and has been made capable
> of any enjoyments by life. (Locke 1988:311–312)

It is clear, then, that Locke views filial obligations as important and that
his conception of filial piety includes both one's feelings of reverence for
one's parents as well as the actions one takes to provide and care for one's
parents, both emotionally and materially.

Although Locke argues, against his predecessors, that women have
an equal claim to authority in the family and are equally entitled to the
honor of their children not only because of their investment in their children during pregnancy but also because of their role in educating them,
it is unfortunately not the case that subsequent philosophers agreed. Jean-
Jacques Rousseau writes in *Émile*, "As the true nurse is the mother, the
true preceptor is the father" (Rousseau 1979:48). According to Rousseau,
although mothers desire the happiness of their children, most women are

not smart enough to raise them properly.[24] He underscores the responsibilities of fathers, maintaining that "neither poverty nor labors nor concern for public opinion exempts him from feeding his children and from raising them himself" (Rousseau 1979:49). Nevertheless, Rousseau deserves credit for emphasizing the importance of fathers' responsibilities to their children. He argues that fathers are irreplaceable and even claims that children "will be better raised by a judicious and limited father than the cleverest master in the world; for zeal will make up for talent better than talent for zeal" (48). For Rousseau, the unique commitment that parents have to their children is the primary reason why fathers serve as unrivaled educators of their children. Blustein points out that for Rousseau, "it is only a necessary, not a sufficient, condition of the ideal education for children that their teachers conscientiously attend to their duties; the teacher should also be the child's natural father" (Blustein 1982:82–83). Rousseau also views family life generally as providing a unique and unparalleled context for children's moral development, and he warns against the dangers of failing to take the time to care for and educate one's children as well as the dangers of sending children away for educational purposes:

> There is no picture more charming than that of the family, but a single missing feature disfigures all the others. If the mother has too little health to be nurse, the father will have too much business to be preceptor. The children, sent away, dispersed into boarding schools, convents, colleges, will take the love belonging to the paternal home elsewhere, or to put it better, they will bring back to the paternal home the habit of having no attachments. (Rousseau 1979:49)

Here, Rousseau recognizes several important features of family life, including not only its unique role in moral education but the extraordinary degree of influence that mothers and fathers can have on each other through their approaches to parenting, as well as the fact that parents must make real sacrifices to care for and educate their children. If one parent fails to make important sacrifices, in Rousseau's view, the other will be likely to fail in this regard, as well.

As Rousseau's remarks indicate, he was deeply concerned about harmful effects of the widespread social practice of handing over the care and education of one's children to others. He maintained that society corrupts the education of children by imposing professional demands upon fathers that make it impossible for them to educate their children themselves and also by prescribing a mode of education that encourages conformity in children. As Blustein points out, these are interrelated and mutually supportive: "The mode of education facilitates the neglect of parental duty, and the weakening of family ties make the child more amenable to social prejudices and opinions" (Blustein 1982:83). As a remedy, Rousseau argues that children must be emancipated from social pressures so their natural dispositions can develop. For Rousseau, this means that children should grow into fully autonomous, self-sufficient adults who are not dependent in any way upon others. Children are adversely affected by being made to feel dependent on others, and educators must teach them only to be motivated by desires they can satisfy themselves. Dependence on things is natural, Rousseau argues, but dependence on people is from society (and therefore is unnatural, on his view). Here, Rousseau expresses an extreme form of individualism that ignores the social dimension of our nature. Rousseau contends, "Dependence on things, since it has no morality, is in no way detrimental to freedom and engenders no vices. Dependence on men, since it is without order, engenders all the vices, and by it, master and slave are mutually corrupted." As a result, when bringing up a child, "let him not know what obedience is when he acts nor what dominion is when one acts for him. Let him sense his liberty equally in his actions and in yours" (Rousseau 1979:85).

Rousseau maintains, though, that the educational process, *including moral education*, must not begin too early. The goal of Émile's education is to preserve his naturally good nature, for on Rousseau's view, "everything degenerates in the hands of man." As a result, he argues, "Cultivate and water the young plant before it dies. . . . Form an enclosure around your child's soul at an early date" (Rousseau 1979:37–38).[25] For Rousseau, "the only habit that a child should be allowed is to contract none" (63). But Rousseau claims that infants and young children lack adequate understanding to receive instruction, because their minds are entirely dominated by the sensations of their environment; "they perceive only pleasure and pain" (62–63). As a result, Rousseau contends, the most that can be achieved at these early stages of development is what he views as the avoidance of acquiring unnatural habits that are learned through socialization.[26] Oddly enough, this leads Rousseau to a program of education that is profoundly unnatural. For example, he thinks that children raised in clean houses are afraid of spiders because no spiders are tolerated in their homes. Rousseau claims this is unnatural, and to remedy it he suggests that Émile should be "habituated to seeing new objects, ugly, disgusting, peculiar animals, but little by little, from afar, until he is accustomed to them, and by dint of seeing them handled by others, he finally handles them himself" (Rousseau 1979:63). So we can see that although Rousseau says education should not begin during infancy, he prescribes a very proactive program of habituation for infants that by no means is a matter of simply letting them follow their natural course but involves a great deal of meddling with their environment. Rousseau justifies this by arguing that the social environment in which infants are raised is artificial and destructive, and so we must construct a "natural," therapeutic environment in order to allow a child's nature to follow its natural course of development.

Although he thought that infants could be habituated in these ways, and like other reforming educators of his time Rousseau maintained that infants should not be swaddled and young children should be allowed to run and exercise, he did *not* view these early stages as a unique opportunity for moral development. He maintains, "Reason alone teaches us to know good and bad. Conscience, which makes us love the former and hate the latter, although independent of reason, cannot therefore be developed without it. Before the age of reason we do good and bad without knowing it, and there is no morality in our actions." Rousseau offers the illustration of children wanting to upset everything they see: "he smashes, breaks everything he can reach. He grabs a bird as he would grab a stone, and he strangles it without knowing what he does" (Rousseau 1979:67). Rousseau did not believe moral cultivation or education was possible during these early years, nor did he think we should meddle with children's nature by attempting to educate them. There are obvious contrasts here with early Confucian views, and Rousseau's program of education for older children deepens this contrast. Émile, for instance, is shielded from society and social attachments, and the family is no exception to this: "The child raised according to his age is alone. He knows no attachments other than those of habit. He loves his sister as he loves his watch, and his friend as his dog" (Rousseau 1979:219). While the early Confucians view siblings as playing an important role in our moral development, second only to our parents, for Rousseau these relationships are a hindrance. In the highly controlled, artificial environment that Rousseau creates for Émile in order to protect his natural goodness so that it can follow a "natural" course of development, we see clearly the contrast between Rousseau and a thinker such as Mengzi, despite the fact that they each have optimistic views concerning human nature. In addition to the absence of familial relationships and the fact that Rousseau's infants only respond to their physical environment, unlike Mengzi's infants who exhibit early signs of possessing moral sprouts through the affection they show their parents, the fragility of any naturally good impulses children have are clearly of greater concern to Rousseau than to Mengzi. As Schwitzgebel points out, "Rousseau appears to think the sprouts of human goodness are so fragile that the slightest chill could cripple them, in contrast to Mencius who sees them as always reasserting themselves" (Schwitzgebel 2007:157).

At once one of the most significant and surprising features of Rousseau's view is that tutors are required in order to achieve the first step of Rousseau's vision, because parents are too deeply entrenched in traditional views of education and corresponding social practices to educate their own children well. Eventually, future generations of fathers who have been educated differently will replace tutors and educate their own children, according to Rousseau's vision. Nevertheless, in light of all he says about the importance of parents, it is surprising that Rousseau argues for the necessity of tutors and maintains that the family will, in fact, make it impossible for a child to be properly educated. Judith Shklar points out that Rousseau not only views parents as the transmitters of false traditions and habits but also considers the family under present circumstances "inherently inefficient as a way of educating the young. If a child is to be brought up for his own sake, to become a good and happy man, he needs constant attention. To be the perfect tutor of a single child is a lifetime's work" (Shklar 2001:170–171). Indeed, Rousseau contends that the regeneration of men through education is only possible if each child has a full-time tutor. This creates an unresolved tension in Rousseau's view: given that his perfect tutor must give a child constant, undivided attention, even in Rousseau's ideal society it would be impossible for Rousseau's ideal father, who also has duties as a husband and to his other children, to accomplish the tasks of the perfect tutor, not to mention the matter of providing financial support for the family. Blustein argues that this problem suggests a deep-seated ambivalence toward the value of family life (Blustein 1982:83–84).

The strengths of Rousseau's view are his affirmation of the unique and irreplaceable importance of parents and his critique of the willingness to hand over the tasks of caring for and educating one's children to others— and the social structure that pressures parents to do so. The early Confucians, as we have seen, maintained that parents, and especially mothers, have an irreplaceable role in the care and education of children, but even the Confucians did not note, as Rousseau does, the problems that can arise with the use of other caregivers and educators. Culturally, Rousseau's critique is worthy of our consideration as we think through such institutions as boarding schools and day care and the lack of adequate parental leave (as well as flexibility and understanding) from employers, which if granted, would enable and encourage parents to be the primary caregivers and early educators of their children. It must be noted, however, that Rousseau's emphasis on the irreplaceable nature of the family makes it all the more puzzling that he does not accord a role to the family at all in his theory of education, viewing it instead as a hindrance. As Blustein notes, this raises the question of just how seriously Rousseau in fact takes the role of the family.

The weaknesses in Rousseau's view include, of course, his rigid roles for men and women, his neglect of women as educators of their children, and the fact that in his theory of education, parents cannot be involved in the education of their children because they themselves have been corrupted by tradition and society. Rousseau maintains that tutors and the children they teach can step outside tradition and society and acquire an a-traditional, a-social perspective—a view that is also deeply problematic. Although

Rousseau views fathers as ideal educators in his ideal society, fathers are not the ideal educators in the society in which we currently live. This is why Rousseau severely limits the role of the family, something that represents a deep and abiding contrast with Confucian views of childhood education. Additionally, Rousseau denies that moral education can or should take place during infancy and early childhood, which represents another crucial difference from Confucian views. Yet another glaring difference is seen in Rousseau's contention that children ought to be educated to be fully autonomous and not dependent upon others. Not only is this an unattainable goal, but it views our connections with others as not an asset but a hindrance. This is where we see some additional contrasts with early Confucian views, in which our connections with and dependence on traditions, communities, and, most importantly, our families are inevitable features of human life to be celebrated and embraced, for they contribute immeasurably to our flourishing and happiness. The early Confucians argue that nowhere is this seen more decisively than in the parent–child relationship. We become more when we embrace our roles as loving parents and children, and only when we acknowledge our dependence upon one another at various stages of our lives can we fully appreciate the importance and meaning of those roles. As Blustein points out,

> Rousseau's strong position on the pernicious character of dependency relations does not sit comfortably with his idealization of family life. An autonomous man, in Rousseau's sense, is not likely to suffer any personal attachments. Moreover, in the family, dependency is, if anything, more difficult to overcome than in the one-on-one tutor-pupil relationship. (Blustein 1982:85)

For the Confucians, of course, dependency is not something to be overcome at all, but a reality of life that is to be embraced and that gives us good reasons to cultivate ourselves. The Confucian virtues are designed to help us to depend upon others and to make us dependable in ways that are healthy and meaningful for all.

The most important thinker Rousseau influenced with his view of autonomy was Immanuel Kant.[27] However, although Kant agreed with Rousseau

that autonomy was the proper goal of education, Kant did not view relationships as problematic for a child's moral development. This is partly
because Kant did not share Rousseau's view of human nature; since Kant
did not think children are naturally good, he did not believe that social relationships destroy or contaminate our original goodness.[28] Kant maintains
that children must be educated in ways that develop their autonomy, and
he argues that from procreation follows a duty to preserve and care for one's
offspring. From this duty "there must necessarily also arise the right of parents to *manage* and develop the child," including "the right not only to feed
and care for him but to educate him, to develop him both *pragmatically*, so
that in the future he can look after himself and make his way in life, and
morally, since otherwise the fault for having neglected him would fall on the
parents" (Kant 1991:99). In the *Lectures on Ethics*, Kant makes a number of
remarks concerning the details of his views on these matters. Children very
much stand in need of moral education, and the key to this process for Kant
lies not in the development of one's emotions but the powers of reason,
which for children begins with understanding their position in relation to
their parents and their duty to obey. A child must learn to "recognize its status as a child, and that its duties should all be derived from the consciousness of its childhood, age and capacity" (Kant 1997:219 [27:468]). If children
do not learn obedience and are not disciplined appropriately, Kant argues,
they will go on to have difficulties in social life generally, because the expectation that others follow their commands will extend beyond their relationship with their parents. Unlike Rousseau, Kant views the social setting of
the family and parent–child relationships in particular as fundamental to
good upbringing, and he uses the analogy of a forest to illustrate his view:

> The trees in a forest discipline each other, in seeking airspace to grow in,
> not near others, but up above, where they do not obstruct the rest, and
> thus grow straight and tall; whereas a tree in the open, where it is not
> confined by others, grows up quite stunted, and it is already too late to
> discipline it thereafter. So it is also with man; if disciplined early, he grows
> up straight with the rest; but if this be neglected, he becomes a stunted
> tree. (Kant 1997:219)[29]

Here Kant affirms not only the importance of discipline in a child's social setting but also the importance of beginning moral education early. How early should moral education begin, in Kant's view? Kant is aware that moral education must begin during childhood, because our behavior as children is closely tied to our behavior as adults:

> It is an established fact, that nobody starts off with the grossest crimes, but has been seduced into them by steps which had their basis in subjective principles. It is a small thing when a child thoughtlessly hits another, but habit implants a lack of sensitivity here, and the offender no longer feels anything. From this come steps to acts of violence, and with other maxims concurring in the process, the child can become a murderer. It is already necessary to block the early sources. (Kant 1997:312 [27:557])

Like Rousseau, Kant distinguishes between childhood and youth. He does not discuss infancy. On Kant's view, children should be instructed in how to behave, but they should not be offered reasons for everything. Beginning around age ten, when the period of youth begins, children are "capable of reflection," and this period is thus "accessible to reason," which makes it most significant from the standpoint of moral education (Kant 1997:220 [27:469]).

What is involved in the process of moral education? Kant mentions the importance of addressing a variety of behaviors in children, including tantrums, laziness, malice, destructiveness, cruelty, and lying. Kant also stresses the importance of learning through experience and observation and not just through the memorization of abstract rules, although he argues that methods for educating children must be adapted for different ages (Kant 1997:219 [27:468]). He also discusses the importance of moral exemplars for children's education, noting that "children take their elders as a model for their action, since imitation is encouraged, in their case, as the primary ground of education," and as a result "elders, in the presence of children, must neither swear, lie nor defame, nor give approval to others doing so," and should avoid other immodest and rude behaviors (Kant 1997:398 [27:664]). Interestingly, however, Kant warns against the practice of explicitly pointing out the good behavior of others in order to inspire one's children to do better. He argues that this practice induces jealousy and hostility in children and also encourages them to have the wrong motives. Instead, "as soon as reason holds sway, we should not seek to become perfect on the ground that others surpass us, but must desire perfection for itself" (Kant 1997:195–196 [27:438]; cf. pp. 421–422 [27:694]). This is a clear example of how Kant views emotions as a problem rather than a starting place for moral development.

Kant acknowledges that parental love for children is unique, noting that "the innate inclination towards their children arises from a natural instinct, love," but he argues that children do not owe their parents love and gratitude simply because they had them. Rather, Kant writes,

> the rearing of children up to the point of self-sufficiency, i.e., an education so ordered that the children thereby obtain contentment with their lot, and pleasure in their existence, is an *opus supererogationis* on the parent's part, a thing superadded, a kindness which involves something meritori-ous, and this is what must bring the children, by reason, to the conception of filial gratitude, and awaken in them the determination to love their parents; yet it can never be claimed that they are obligated, as a perfect duty, to render love. (Kant 1997:403–404 [27:671])

Here Kant presents his view concerning the proper ground of filial piety and love and ties it critically to the parental role in raising self-sufficient, happy, and fulfilled children. His remarks on parenting suggest that Kant conceives of parents who embrace this task as, first and foremost, discipli-narians. He does not discuss nurturing behaviors or expressions of affection by parents, but he does acknowledge that parents love their children and discipline them out of love, and he notes this even in his general remarks on ethics. For example, in distinguishing hatred from anger, which "may very well consort with the utmost love towards the other," Kant uses the example of parental anger, writing that "it is from real love that parents are angry at their children for bad behavior" (Kant 1997:416–417 [27:688]).

Like the Confucians, Kant affirms the importance of parents' roles in children's moral education and even notes that this helps to provide grounds for filial piety. Unlike the Confucians, Kant views moral education exclusively in terms of coming to grasp one's moral duties through reason alone and not through traditions and rituals, or in terms of the development of affective responses to our parents and other caregivers, or the cultivation of virtues or a particular kind of ethical character in one's children. This is because, for Kant, our inclinations are often a hindrance, and they cannot be developed or shaped to guide us reliably. Additionally, the moral law lies in our reason, and acting in accordance with it requires full autonomy and the intentional rejection of heteronomy—something Kant closely associates with tradition. Additional key differences from early Confucian views include the fact that Kant does not address the unique roles of mothers in children's moral development or the way in which the early development of infants influences the subsequent course of moral development. He also has little to say about the specific practices that are a part of moral cultivation beginning in childhood.[30] These, together with the small amount that Kant wrote about the family and moral cultivation compared with other aspects of his moral theory, all mark deep and important differences from Confucian philosophers.[31]

The writings of Georg Wilhelm Friedrich Hegel contain limited remarks on the role of parents in children's moral development. For Hegel, freedom and independence are the ultimate goals of children's education, and here the influences of Rousseau and Kant are apparent. Blustein points out that for Hegel, the process of moral development begins in the home, but it cannot end there: "Children must internalize the discrimination between their particularistic role as family members and their universalistic role as members of the community, and must eventually acquire an attachment to ethical norms that does not largely spring from ties of affection for particular individuals" (Blustein 1982:95). As Hegel writes, "In respect of his relation to the family, the child's education has the positive aim of instilling ethical principles in him . . . so that thus equipped with the foundation of an ethical life, his heart may live its early years in love, trust, and obedience" (Hegel 1952:117). According to Hegel, the education of children culminates in "the ethical dissolution of the family," since once children come of age and have families of their own, "they now have their substantive destiny in the new family; the old family on the other hand falls into the background as merely their ultimate basis and origin" (Hegel 1952:118–119). It is not surprising, then, that Hegel does not address the obligations that grown children may owe their parents or the ties that parents and children have with one another over the entire course of their lives. He also does not address the affection between parents and children, opting instead to focus solely on the affection between husbands and wives, and brothers and sisters. While Hegel acknowledges the importance of the family in moral education, he views this as the sole function of parent–child relationships and does not address the unique bonds between parents and children. Additionally, while Hegel writes that a woman "has her substantial destiny in the family, and to be imbued with family piety is her ethical frame of mind," he does not elaborate on whether or in what ways mothers are specially suited for the moral education of their children (Hegel 1952:114). Unlike the Confucians, Hegel does not outline specific ways in which parents contribute to the moral cultivation of their children, nor does he discuss the importance of infancy and early childhood in that process.

Hegel had an important influence on the work of subsequent philosophers, and Karl Marx and John Dewey are two notable examples. For Marx, families play an indispensable economic role as the producers of human capital. But he has little to say about the family, parent–child relationships, and the moral education of children. Dewey, in turn, briefly acknowledges the importance of the family in the early years of children's lives, writing that during infancy and childhood, "children learn, chiefly from mothers, the ways of behavior, the language, and much of the transmitted wisdom, of their group and people. They feel the mother's affection and develop their own emotional life in response" (Dewey 1989:40). He writes that the care that parents provide early on "enlarges affection," but he does not elaborate further on this. Indeed, his primary interest in discussing children and education is not the family and moral education but the formal education that occurs within schools.[32] He maintains that "children do not long remain children" and like Hegel, does not show an interest in the continuing role of parent–child relationships in our lives. Contemporary philosophers have not wholly neglected the family's role in moral cultivation, but with the exception of contemporary feminist ethicists, whose work we will consider in the next chapter, the extent and depth of their attention comes up short compared with Confucian views.[33]

* * *

One feature of the Western views we have examined is that they tend not to give sustained attention to the family and especially to parent–child relationships. Although some thinkers note the importance of the family, their remarks tend to be passing ones, and they certainly do not offer sophisticated and detailed accounts of the role the family has in moral cultivation. Discussions of the family for the most part are only included because they serve a function within a given philosopher's larger political or ethical theory, and in each of the cases we have examined, that role is relatively small. The Western philosophers we have examined also tend not to be as interested in the process of moral cultivation generally, compared with Confucian thinkers. An additional feature that stands out when comparing the views found in traditional Western philosophy with Confucian views is that although Western thinkers exhibit some interest in either the role of the family or the process of moral cultivation, they seldom show an interest in the relationship between the two, and if they do have something to say about it, they typically do not accord it the weight that Confucian thinkers do. None of the Western philosophers we examined maintain, as Confucian philosophers do, that the right kinds of parent–child relationships and the virtues that develop as a result of them serve as the foundation for our moral development generally.

Despite the fact that these areas were neglected by most thinkers, there are important exceptions to note in the history of philosophy, such as Aquinas, Locke, and Kant, all of whom discuss filial piety; Locke even discusses the significance of mothers' efforts and investment in their children during pregnancy. It remains important to note, however, that relative to their large bodies of work, Aquinas and Locke devote very little space to these topics. What distinguishes them is that they devote any attention at all to these topics and that they offer sophisticated views in certain respects, such as Aquinas's discussion of the relationship between one's obligations to God and one's obligations to one's parents and Locke's departure from views of parentage that are not only biologically incorrect but neglect entirely the critical role of mothers. However, it remains the case that the Confucians had not only much more to say about these topics but much more that turns out to be accurate in light of what we know now about the role of parents in the moral development of their children. The work of contemporary feminist philosophers, however, engages these topics at considerable length, and a number of feminist insights both resonate in interesting ways and contrast in deep and important ways with the insights of Confucian thinkers. It is to this body of literature that we turn in the next chapter.

4

FEMINIST AND CONFUCIAN PERSPECTIVES ON PARENTS, CHILDREN, AND MORAL CULTIVATION

W HILE MANY PHILOSOPHERS tend to think of almost all feminist philosophers, and especially care ethicists, as sharing a concern with the family, such views underestimate the diversity of views, approaches, and concerns in contemporary feminist philosophy. Even within feminist philosophy, there is not a large body of literature that focuses on the role of parent–child relationships in moral cultivation. Nevertheless, in the work of Sara Ruddick, Nel Noddings, and Virginia Held, we find a sustained and sophisticated engagement with this topic. In addition to devoting particularly extensive and detailed attention to the role of parent–child relationships in moral cultivation when compared with other care ethicists who have discussed these matters, they were also among the first care ethicists to devote this sort of attention to parent–child relationships, and their work continues to influence and shape care ethical views on these matters. Indeed, this chapter will show that they offer some of the most robust and influential accounts of the role of parent–child relationships in moral development in the history of Western philosophy, and I will argue that they effectively highlight and help us understand a variety of distinctive features of both care-ethical and Confucian views on this topic.

It is important to note the discrepancy between when early Confucian thinkers and contemporary feminist philosophers each began to address these issues. In Western philosophy it took the work of women philosophers to bring these issues to the forefront and give them sustained attention. In contrast, the early Confucians addressed the central role of the family—including mothers—in moral education and cultivation, even though most of the authors were men. Indeed, all of the Confucian texts we have examined were written by men. This helps to show that Confucian philosophers did not regard these issues as unimportant or justify their neglect by bracketing them as "women's issues" in the way many Western philosophers did. In contrast, as we have already seen, parent–child relationships were regarded as centrally important in the earliest Confucian ethical and political philosophy. As a result, the Confucians engaged these issues over a longer period of time and in an exceptionally large and diverse range of different works. The sources that are the particular focus of this work are very early, and despite the sexist views and practices that have been a part of Chinese culture throughout most of its history (and which specified, for example, set roles for women that confined them primarily to the home), it is nothing short of astonishing that the unique role of mothers as moral educators was viewed as having fundamental importance for ethics, political thought, and the general success and well-being of families, communities, and the larger society. As we have seen, this is in deep and important contrast to sources throughout the history of Western philosophy, and we should be attentive to the innovativeness of contemporary feminists writing on the role of the family in moral development; they do not have a rich tradition of philosophical writings on the family to draw upon and respond to in developing and defending their views. Likewise, it is important to remember the early dates of the Confucian texts under study here. We should not expect to find in these texts the kinds of modern liberal or progressive views of, for example, gender roles or women's rights that we find in the work of contemporary care ethicists. In other words, in order to consider these views charitably and offer a nuanced comparison, it will be important to remember the differences between their respective contexts.

STUDIES OF CONFUCIAN ETHICS AND CARE ETHICS

Over the past two decades, a series of articles published in *Hypatia* as well as a number of other works have debated the nature of the similarities between care ethics and Confucian ethics. This discussion originated Chenyang Li's argument that Confucian ethics is a form of care ethics (Li 1994:81). He maintains that the Confucian conception of *Ren* ("humaneness") and the feminist conception of care each represent the highest moral ideal and share a number of features, including being good in themselves (75). Li argues that both care ethicists and Confucians reject an emphasis on general principles and a sharp distinction between the public and private spheres, that Confucianism shares with some care ethics the view that we ought to care deeply for those closest to us and more lightly for others, and that preserving social relationships ought to take priority in ethics.

Joel Kupperman argues that Li was correct to point out that Confucian and care ethics have much in common, including taking seriously the ethical importance of becoming a certain kind of person, which "implies reflection on ways of shaping oneself and also of shaping others to come" (Kupperman 2000:53). Kupperman points out the emphasis on the centrality of special relationships seen in both feminist and Confucian thought. He goes on to argue, however, that it is important to understand the differences between them, even beyond the historical baggage including gender relations and hierarchical roles seen in Confucianism. For Kupperman the most important difference is that they offer very different views concerning "what social roles we should fill and what rituals we should perform," and he argues that while the classical Confucians do not advocate adopting new roles and inventing new rituals, feminism does (Kupperman 2000:54). For the Confucians, "What is traditional is likely to have remained in place because it was not entirely unsatisfactory. Also traditions, examined closely, often represent accretions of trial and error; and they often evolve further after they are established, in such a way that undesirable features are rubbed away or diminished" (Kupperman 2000:54). Kupperman writes that for Kongzi, traditional rituals were developed "to be beautiful and highly meaningful. To replace them from scratch with something else would point toward the likelihood of a substitute that was neither beautiful nor highly meaningful" (55). In contrast, feminist philosophers from a wide variety of perspectives have argued that despite certain merits and uses, social traditions, "through the rituals and social roles they validate have distorted the selves of most women in ways that rob them of fulfilling lives. This suggests the importance of policies of change in the roles and rituals expected of women, or that men play in relation to women" (55).

Philip J. Ivanhoe discusses two different families of views in feminist ethics and argues that features of each can be found in the differing views of Mengzi and Xunzi. The *gendered virtue* view, defined by "essentialist" claims about specific virtues that are characteristic of men and women and arise out of and reflect their basic natures, shares some important features with Mengzi's account, which presents the foundations of ethics in particular kinds of innate tendencies and attitudes and ultimately "grounds ethics in species-specific, essentialist claims about human nature" (Ivanhoe 2000b:64). Likewise, the *vocational virtue* model, which views each gender's dispositions and tendencies as socially constructed and owing to socioeconomic conditions and societal norms and practices, in certain ways resembles Xunzi's account, according to which our virtue stems not from innate tendencies but from the prolonged and continuous influence of rituals and traditions. Ivanhoe goes on to argue that these comparisons are helpful "not only because they throw into relief certain aspects of each of the theories considered but also because they can draw attention to some of their shortcomings" (65). One of the most important points Ivanhoe makes regarding care ethics and Confucianism responds to Noddings's remark (concerning Kierkegaard's use of the story of Abraham and Isaac) that "no woman could have written either Genesis or *Fear and Trembling*." Ivanhoe writes, "One could imagine a traditional Confucian thinker, particularly one of the Mencian persuasion, making a similar claim that no true Confucian could have written or even conceived of either text" (61). Although Ivanhoe emphasizes crucial differences as well as similarities between these views, he points here to the shared emphasis on special relationships and especially parent–child relationships in care ethics and Confucianism.

The conversation about care ethics and Confucianism continues with Daniel Star's critique of Li's original argument.[1] Star focuses on the contrast between particular features of Confucian ethics and care ethics and on this basis offers a critique of Li's argument, as well as the work of Henry Rosemont Jr. and Sin-Yee Chan. Star argues that Confucian ethics is "better conceived of as a unique kind of role-focused virtue ethics," wherein virtue ethics is an approach to ethics that "encourages us to cultivate virtuous characters and to view other people in virtue (that is, *aretaic*) terms" (Star 2002:78).[2] He goes on to outline the differences between care ethics and virtue ethics, arguing that care ethics focuses primarily on "the particular needs of people as they exist in concrete relationships," which follow from the unique qualities of different individuals and relationships (79). Star goes on to argue that Confucian and care ethics are two distinct kinds of particularistic ethics, in contrast to principle-driven normative moral theories, but they are not two varieties of care ethics. Star argues that Confucian care is not deeply particularistic because of the Confucian tendency to focus on roles and the resemblance between different people who find themselves in the same roles, as opposed to care ethics which focuses solely on particular relationships without an emphasis on shared roles or the resemblance between the roles of, for example, different sons (with an emphasis on the fact that they are all sons) (92–93). Against Henry Rosemont's claim that in Confucianism a person's "roles" are identical with the person, Star points out, in the words of Samantha Brennan, "It has been important for feminists to say, and be able to say, that they are more than someone's daughter, or someone's wife, to assert that one's identity transcends the roles assigned to women" (Star 2002:94; Brennan 1999:869). Star writes that "to approach others primarily through preconceived role categories could well lead to an absence of genuine care being demonstrated for the individual persons being cared for" (Star 2002:94).[3]

In another essay critiquing the attempts of Li and Rosemont to argue for the similarities between Confucian and care ethics, Ranjoo Herr argues that these works neglect the importance of ritual in Confucianism while also misunderstanding the feminist conception of care. Herr notes the importance of filial piety in Confucianism and writes that care ethics takes the mother–child relation to be the most intimate family relation and the paradigm for caring relationships (Herr 2003:472–473, 475). She also argues that Confucian family relationships bring with them absolute obligations, but in care ethics, caring relationships—which do not always characterize mothering relations—are inviolable; in care ethics, "the value of care is placed above the mere fact of blood-relatedness" (475). In addition to noting other resemblances, Herr writes that Confucianism and care ethics both "take intimate caring relationships as constitutive not only of our identities but also of our moral goals," and "regard the most intimate family relation—the parent–child relation in Confucianism and the mother–child relation in Care Ethics—as the most significant relation" (480). However, Herr writes, while care ethics requires the one caring in a relationship to be extraordinarily responsive to the cared-for, Confucian *Ren* ("humaneness") is more strongly emphasized for those in the subordinate position, and she notes "the almost complete silence with respect to parents' obligations toward children" (481). Additionally, Confucian obligations are fulfilled according to the rites, and a certain deferential distance is required in parent–child relationships, unlike the intimate relationships that are a fundamental ideal in care ethics (481–482).

In contrast, Luo Shirong argues in support of Li's basic argument by developing and amending some of these claims while also highlighting some additional affinities between care ethics and Confucianism, including the role of empathy (Luo 2007). Luo works to clarify what is meant by the claim that the Confucian concept of *Ren* is similar to the notion of caring, examines affinities with agent-based virtue ethics, and discusses the difference between the two senses of caring found in the care-ethical view that caring primarily refers to a relationship and the virtue-ethical view that caring is a virtue. Luo argues that the Confucian view, which sees caring as a relational moral virtue, can help us see that we need not choose between caring as a relationship and caring as a virtue. In this way, he argues, we can more clearly see that care-based ethical approaches and Confucian ethics do indeed share some important features. Concerning the family, Luo argues that "partiality rather than impartiality characterizes both theories; that is, people in our immediate circle should be given more attention than people with whom we do not have a direct, face-to-face encounter" (95–96). Additionally, he argues, both theories affirm our obligation to care for those outside our intimate circle. Our affection for our families is deeper and serves as a foundation we must build upon in reaching out to care for others. We must care for our own families first and then extend that care to others (96).

All of these discussions highlight the emphasis on certain dimensions of Confucian ethics and care ethics in the literature, including the similarities and differences between *Ren* and care and the fact that both Confucians and care ethicists reject and offer an alternative to general moral principles. Many of these works have made important contributions by noting, among other things, the strong emphasis on relationships in both Confucian ethics and care ethics, and some have also noted the special emphasis on family relationships. Yet none of these works focuses specifically on Confucian and care-ethical views on the role of parent–child relationships in moral development and cultivation. This chapter aims to offer a detailed account of how parent–child relationships are viewed in care ethics and Confucian ethics, with a special focus on their role in moral cultivation. Although I focus on the distinctive features of each view, I nevertheless agree that there are interesting similarities between care ethics and Confucian ethics.[4] Indeed, it is because care ethicists and Confucian thinkers both take seriously the role of parent–child relationships in moral cultivation that I am writing this chapter. Unlike much of the comparative work that has been done on care ethics and Confucianism, my goal is not to resolve the question of whether Confucianism should be regarded as a form of care ethics. Instead, I aim to highlight the distinctive features of care ethics and Confucian ethics concerning the role of parent–child relationships in moral cultivation, in order to show that each of these views has distinctive contributions to make to our understanding of these matters.

MOTHERING: THE WORK OF SARA RUDDICK

Today, most care ethicists highlight caring relationships as paramount to moral life and thereby to moral theory, and although not all care ethicists are centrally concerned with parent–child relationships, the concern that care ethicists have with the distinctive practice of caring began with Sara Ruddick's discussion of mothering. Indeed, Virginia Held locates the beginnings of care ethics with Ruddick's 1980 essay, "Maternal Thinking." In this essay, Ruddick argues that the distinctive thinking, standards, and values that arise from the caring practice of mothering can yield a distinctive moral outlook and have relevance for activities beyond mothering itself. Held writes, "Ruddick's essay showed that attending to the experience of women in a caring practice could change how we think about morality and could change our view of the values appropriate for given activities" (Held 2006:27). Ruddick's argument was nothing short of groundbreaking; mothers and mothering, as we have seen, had received little attention in Western moral theorizing up until this point. Held points out that "there was no philosophical acknowledgement that mothers think or reason, or that one can find moral values in this practice. Women were only imagined to think or face moral problems when they ventured beyond the household into the world of men" (Held 2006:26). The possibility that there might be distinctive forms of moral thought to which mothers have privileged access by virtue of caring for their children was entirely new to Western philosophy.

In order to understand the heart of Ruddick's work, one must first understand why Ruddick emphasizes the significance of a maternal perspective. In her 1989 book *Maternal Thinking*, Ruddick argues that society should properly value maternal practice and maternal thinking and that mothering best expresses the dynamics of moral life. In the preface to the 1995 edition of this work, Ruddick writes that when she first began to work on this topic, she was invigorated by the view that women had "suffered, loved, worked, and reasoned distinctively" and that women can "make that distinctiveness shine; if women's shining distinctiveness had also served to oppress us, then we would transform the conditions of our distinction so that women's interests would also be served" (Ruddick 1995:ix). Since Ruddick argues for a radical departure from our ordinary understanding and use of terms such as "mothers" and "mothering," it is important to understand that her work is motivated by a desire to embrace and make meaningful the work that has made women distinctive, despite the fact that it has often been oppressive to women. She argues that the distinctive work of mothering gives rise to the most important moral insights and experiences.

What is a "mother" and what does it mean to engage in the practice or work of "mothering"? Ruddick became increasingly interested in these questions over the years, and in her 1995 preface, she writes that mothers do not have a fixed biological or legal relationship to children, nor are mothers only female; rather, mothers are identified "by the work they set out to do." In her more particularized conception, "mothers are people who see children as 'demanding' protection, nurturance, and training; they attempt to respond to children's demands with care and respect rather than indifference or assault" (Ruddick 1995:xi). The basic view here is that being a mother is defined by the kind of work one does and the way one does it, and not by giving birth to or having legal custody of a child, nor by a single emotion like love.[5] Ruddick emphasizes that mothering is "a kind of caring labor" and maintains that "mothering in households is joined in many ways with mothering in day-care centers, schools, clinics, and other public institutions." Anyone who "commits her or himself to responding to children's demands, and makes the work of response a considerable part of her or his life, is a mother" (xi–xii). Here we see what is probably the most radical part of Ruddick's proposal: individuals other than those who have their own children can be mothers, and men can be mothers, too. On Ruddick's view, biological or adoptive fathers who make the work of responding to children's demands a considerable part of their lives are mothers. As Ruddick puts it, "While most mothering has been and still is undertaken by women, there have always been men who mother. Moreover, men are increasingly engaged in mothering. Consequently, it is not difficult to imagine men taking up mothering as easily and successfully as women—or conversely, women as easily declining to mother as men" (xii).

Interestingly, Ruddick assigns a new meaning to the term "mother," so that it means something like "caregiver to children." On Ruddick's view, the work of mothering is not just the work of a child's *primary* caregivers, for it includes work done in day-care centers, schools, clinics, and other institutions. At first glance, this seems puzzling, for Ruddick appears to have strayed from her original goal of highlighting the central importance of the work of mothers, in the traditional sense of the term. Doesn't the inclusion of those other than the primary caregivers of children as "mothers" undermine our appreciation for unique importance of what mothers normally do? And if men are included as potential "mothers," doesn't this lessen the feminist character of Ruddick's project? Ruddick acknowledges these worries, writing that "even women sympathetic to the idea of mothering as genderless work worry that a genderless mother trivializes both the distinctive costs of mothering to women as well as the effects, for worse and for better, of femininity on maternal practice and thought" (Ruddick 1995:xiii). Ruddick has been pressed on why she refers to "mothers" instead of "parents."[6] In response, she writes that she wishes to recognize and honor the fact that

> even now, and certainly through most of history, women have been mothers. To speak of "parenting" obscures that historical fact, while to speak evenhandedly of mothers and fathers suggests that women's history has no importance. Moreover, I want to protest the myth and practice of Fatherhood and at the same time underline the importance of men undertaking maternal work. The linguistically startling premise that men can be mothers makes these points while the plethora of literature celebrating fathers only obscures them. (Ruddick 1995:44)

Ruddick acknowledges the aversion that many will have to men being referred to as "mothers" but contends that if a man is undertaking maternal work, "he is identifying with what has been, historically, womanly. What is so terrible—or so wonderful—about that?" (Ruddick 1995:45). Ruddick is also motivated to speak of mothering (instead of parenting) because of its political consequences, helping us to recognize that in most cases women are still held responsible for the greater share of the work of caring for children, which "offers overwhelming economic and professional advantages to men." The consequences of holding women responsible for maternal work must be acknowledged, and Ruddick argues, "Evenhanded talk of mothers and fathers or abstractions about parenting only delay this necessary, troubling acknowledgment of difference and injustice" (45). Here, her feminist agenda is in full view: our primary understanding of the work of

responding to children's demands comes from what women have traditionally done as mothers, and Ruddick aims for a world in which women are
not held responsible for the greater share of mothering work; men aspire to
do mothering work and are honored to be called mothers; and anyone who
is committed to responding to children's demands in a sensitive and effective way is, in fact, a mother. This, on Ruddick's view, valorizes the work of
mothers by elevating the term so it carries with it a normative sense, including much-needed and well-deserved respect.

Now this does not entirely resolve the difficulty mentioned earlier,
namely that the idea of genderless mothers neglects the distinctive features
of women's contributions, and this is primarily because Ruddick rejects the
view that women make distinctive contributions as mothers that cannot be
made by male mothers. Ruddick writes that "men can participate fully and
ably in all parental activities," arguing that "if men now appear to be less
effective than women in some aspects of parenting, this is a consequence
of different preparation for parenthood" (Ruddick 1997:206). These insuf-
ficiencies are further exaggerated by "sentimental, mystifying views of the
talents of female parents" (1997:206). Ruddick maintains there is nothing
women can contribute as mothers that men cannot contribute, as well. Yet
even if we agree that exceptional fathers (or to use Ruddick's terminology,
male mothers) can provide the very same things as mothers who are women,
it seems that calling the work of responding to children's demands "mothering" ultimately devalues the unique work that a child's parents or primary
caregivers normally perform. Won't we simply need to come up with a new
word for mothers and fathers? For we still must address the distinctive role
of children's primary caregivers, over and apart from the "mothering" work
of day-care workers and teachers. There is, of course, a reason why we assign
different names to these different roles; they are, in very significant ways,
different, despite the fact that when they are performed with excellence,
they share the common goal of promoting the well-being of particular children. As we shall see later, this set of concerns is one reason why Confucian
approaches contrast sharply with Ruddick's approach. Ruddick acknowledges the importance of different roles, for she explicitly argues against
referring to "caretakers" instead of "mothers," because caring for children

is highly distinctive, just as other kinds of caretaking are distinctive; as she puts it, "different kinds of caring cannot simply be combined" (Ruddick 1995:47). Yet Ruddick maintains that mothering is not a kind of caring that is uniquely distinctive of parents or primary caregivers: "Anyone who commits her or himself to responding to children's demands, and makes the work of response a considerable part of her or his life, is a mother" (Ruddick 1995:xii). We might press the issue of just *how* committed one must be, and *how* considerable a part of one's life that work must be. Nevertheless, Ruddick's rejection of biological or legal relationships as a defining feature of mothers, as well as her claim that "mothering in households is joined in many ways with mothering in day-care centers, schools, clinics, and other public institutions," helps to show that her view of "mothers" is broader than a child's parents or primary caregivers.

Another question that arises from Ruddick's argument is whether mothers and fathers typically have distinctive roles in child-rearing, and whether this is necessarily a good or bad thing. Ruddick rejects the descriptive claim that there are "any key parental tasks that belong essentially and primarily to fathers" as well as the claim that there are distinctive paternal characteristics (Ruddick 1997:205). She also rejects the normative claim that there should be distinct paternal and maternal roles and tasks, maintaining instead that fathers can and should take up the work of mothering (Ruddick 1997:205; cf. Ruddick 1995:40–45). This is particularly interesting given that as we have seen, she acknowledges the important differences between the work of different kinds of caretakers and rejects the view that we should refer to "caretakers" instead of "mothers," because it fails to acknowledge these differences. Ruddick does not have the same worries about "fathers," because the work of fathers is not distinctive, in her view. Ruddick writes that "there may be biologically based differences in styles of mothering," but she contends that "'biology' is not fixed; we have no idea of the potentialities and limitations of male and female bodies in a society free of gender stereotypes and respectful of female humans" (Ruddick 1995:41). She goes on to write that "whatever difference might exist between female and male mothers, there is no reason to believe that one sex rather than the other is more capable of doing maternal work. A woman is no more, a man no less 'naturally' a mother, no more or less obligated to maternal work, than a man or woman is 'naturally' a scientist or firefighter or is obligated to become one. All these kinds of work should be open to capable and interested women and men" (Ruddick 1995:41).

These comments help to make clear that Ruddick endorses what Ivanhoe calls a *vocational virtue* model, viewing many women's strengths as mothers as resulting primarily from social structures. Ruddick argues for the descriptive claim that men are just as capable of mothering work *and* the normative claim that men ought to be just as involved in mothering work as women. Now, one might argue that women's obligations to do mothering work are more binding as a result of infants' physical dependency on their mothers for food and also due to certain biological tendencies.[7] But as we all know, not all mothers take those obligations to be binding; most female parents in the United States today have a variety of choices about their involvement with their infants, just as male parents do. In terms of moral obligations, fathers are surely just as responsible for ensuring their children are well nourished, whether that means supporting breast-feeding mothers emotionally, morally, and physically—something that has been shown to significantly impact rates of success in breast-feeding—or helping to purchase and feed infants formula. Ruddick maintains that men are just as obligated to respond to children's demands and are equally capable of doing so, and she seems to be on solid ground here. Following pregnancy and birth, with the exception of breast-feeding, it is difficult to think of anything relating to the care of infants and children that cannot be done by fathers.

Nevertheless, one might ask whether all of the tasks of mothers can be done *equally well* by men. One might accept Ruddick's view that parents should share the work of responding to children's demands but still argue for unique and perhaps even complementary styles of parenting that tend to be more or less characteristic of male and female parents. In response to this type of objection, Ruddick argues that given "the persistence of patriarchal ideologies, sexual difference is more likely than not to be used in the service of domination," and "any attempt to spell out difference, to say fathers are like this, mothers like that, only mothers can do this, only fathers do that, resurrects mystifying dangerous fictions of provision, protection, and authority, of domination and subordination" (Ruddick 1997:217). There is, of course, a difference between the claims Ruddick describes here and the claim that men and women have certain tendencies as parents, and as we shall see, this is one place where Confucian approaches will tend to differ from Ruddick's. In the end, Ruddick views the ideal of a distinctive Father-hood (with a capital *F*) as "more of an obstacle than an aid" in the task of enabling men to share fully in the gender-inclusive work of caring for children (Ruddick 1997:214). "Fathers, historically, are meant to provide mate-rial support for child care and to defend mothers and their children from external threat. They are supposed to represent the 'world'—its language, culture, work, and rule—and to be the arbiters of the child's acceptability in the world they represent" (Ruddick 1995:42). The important point about Fathers, she argues, is that "their authority is not earned by care and indeed undermines the maternal authority that is so earned." She maintains that "mother" and "father" are not correlative roles, because "Fatherhood is more a role determined by cultural demands than a kind of work determined by children's needs. Many women do maternal work without a Father in sight" (Ruddick 1995:43). In a moment we shall see that this represents another area in which Confucian views differ significantly from Ruddick's view. As we saw earlier in this work, the Confucian tradition offers a variety of inspir-ing examples of effective, indeed, heroic, single mothers, but traditional Confucians also contend that the roles of mothers and fathers are comple-mentary and that *both* roles are shaped by culture and tradition *as well as* by children's needs. When Ruddick claims that fatherhood is "more a role determined by cultural demands than a kind of work determined by chil-dren's needs," her remarks seem to suggest that mothering is *not* determined by primarily cultural demands but by children's needs. Yet in any culture, the roles of fathers and mothers are both shaped by cultural demands and their conceptions of their children's needs—conceptions that are themselves shaped by cultural views and demands. In addition, simply because men's authority over their children is earned differently from women's authority does not mean these roles are not correlative. Ruddick does not elaborate on what it means for roles to be "correlative," but as we saw earlier in this work, traditional Confucian views suggest a range of ways in which they might be conceived of as correlative that do not involve them being equally grounded in the same kind of work.

Ruddick's overarching point seems to be that while mothers earn authority over their children by caring for them, Fathers have authority over children's lives without sharing in the work of caring for them. As a result, these roles are not correlative and should not be viewed as complementary, nor should we regard Fathers as those who respond to the demands of children, for traditionally this work has been emblematic of mothers. In Ruddick's view, attempting to fashion a distinctive form of Fatherhood that encourages men to respond to the demands of children in ways that are distinctive will only result in encouraging men to embrace traditional roles associated with domination and authority. The only way to avoid this, she contends, is to encourage men to be mothers.

An understanding of Ruddick's argument that "mothering" is work that can be taken up by more than just women with a certain biological or legal relationship to children can help us appreciate some of the distinctive aspects of Confucian views. The most obvious difference is that Ruddick, like most feminist ethicists who address parent–child relationships, focuses most centrally on the positions and experiences of mothers. This is certainly apparent in her argument that all of those who do the work of caring for children are "mothers," but it is also a part of her remarks on moral cultivation. Her main focus is the mother's task, with all of its complexities and challenges, as opposed to a narrower focus on the child's experience of moral cultivation. To be clear, it is not that Ruddick neglects the child's experience but rather that the primary focus of her discussion is maternal practice. Ruddick focuses on three different aspects of maternal practice—preserving the life of a child, fostering children's growth, and training or shaping an acceptable child—and dedicates a full chapter to each one. She describes the complexity of mothering and what it entails over the course of children's lives beautifully and in great depth, including nuanced discussions of the specific questions and challenges that mothers face in relation to the moral cultivation of their children: "Should a child be allowed to stay indoors all weekend when all the other children are out playing? Should children be forced for their own good where they fear to go—into classrooms or to birthday parties, for example? Does a boy's identity require that he play with guns, a girl's liberation that she be denied the dollhouse she wants?" (Ruddick 1995:85) As Nel Noddings points out, where the discussions of previous philosophers were vague and nonspecific when it came to the subject of children's growth and development, Ruddick is highly specific, addressing "the complexities of fostering growth—how protecting the child may conflict with encouraging growth, how attempts to shape a child may impede or foster growth" (Noddings 2010a:268–269).

Ruddick's account also illumines the ways in which mothering is a self-cultivationist activity for mothers, too, since

> mothers train themselves in the task of attention, learning to bracket their own desires, to look, imagine. . . . Maternal thinking is a discipline in attentive love. Clear-sighted attachment, loving clear-sightedness, is the aim, guiding principle, and corrective of maternal thinking. However, neither attentive love nor any other cognitive capacity or virtue sufficiently epitomizes maternal work. (Ruddick 1995:123)

Since one of her goals is to highlight the complexity of and skill necessary for maternal work, as well as its challenges, Ruddick's discussion of what is involved in raising children well is much more extensive and detailed than those of the Western philosophers we examined in the preceding chapter. She does not focus on infancy but primarily on childhood, identifying struggles within maternal practice and proposing alternatives to prevalent views that are detrimental to mothers and children. Again, she focuses more strongly on the experiences of mothers as educators or cultivators than on the activities that are a part of the cultivation process for children. For example, she points out that

> many mothers find the central challenge of mothering lies in training a child to be the kind of person whom others accept and whom the mothers themselves can actively appreciate. . . . Training can be invigorating and happy work. Yet for most mothers, the work of training is also confusing and fraught with self-doubt. . . . The rewards of training are deeply felt,

and the failures are wrenching. Yet rapidly changing and mobile societies leave a mother without guide or firm ground to walk on, surrounded by a cacophony of conflicting advice. (Ruddick 1995:104–105)

While Confucian texts about parents, children, and moral cultivation tend to focus on the experiences, activities, traditions, and virtues that are pivotal in the process of shaping children's moral character, with the ultimate aim of providing instruction and inspiration, Ruddick describes the experiences of mothers and aims to diagnose what she considers to be "seriously flawed aspects of maternal thinking" (Ruddick 1995:104). There are, then, deep and critical differences in the overall aims of these works, despite their shared concern with the relationships between mothers and children and the unique role of mothers as educators.

One can envision a wide range of approaches and views inspired by the Confucian tradition that address the questions and issues central to Ruddick's work. My aim in what follows is to describe some of the more specific ways in which Confucian approaches would differ from Ruddick's approach, in order to highlight some of the ways in which early Confucian views of parent–child relationships are distinctive even alongside the views of philosophers who, like Ruddick, regard parent–child relationships as fundamentally important. In describing Confucian approaches to these issues, I intentionally refer to "approaches" and "views" in the plural in order to avoid suggesting there is only one Confucian approach or view. However, I will focus on some general features of Confucianism that have been shared by most Confucian thinkers and which, taken together, are distinctive of the Confucian tradition. Additionally, I do not address the historical question of what traditional Confucians thought about the issues Ruddick raises, because there is no evidence to suggest that traditional Confucians conceived of questions such as how we can best encourage men to share fully in the work of responding to children's demands. Rather, I am interested in how traditional Confucian values might be used to construct Confucian-inspired responses and approaches to the problems Ruddick addresses. The aim of such a task is not to reconstruct or thoroughly revise Confucian values but rather to draw upon and develop Confucian values in ways that will help us address contemporary concerns and challenges. Of course, this task sometimes may require the amendment or rejection of particular Confucian views or values, but the overarching goal is to further develop them in ways that are faithful to many of the core features of Confucianism.[8] By bringing Confucian views into the same century as care-ethical views and working to apply them to contemporary moral problems, we can more clearly understand the distinctive contributions that care ethics and Confucianism can make to our understanding of the role of parent–child relationships in moral cultivation. As we shall see, a significant question arises over whether it is appropriate to call amended Confucian gender roles in which husbands and wives share fully in the care of children "Confucian." One's answer to this question ultimately hinges on how one understands the necessary and sufficient conditions of "Confucian" roles.

Generally, as Kupperman has argued, the Confucians value and embrace tradition, whereas feminism rejects it, though that is not to say that Confucians did not amend or reform traditions. One of the merits of the Confucian view is that we ought to be highly selective about when and how changes occur, and the Confucian tendency to prefer gradual change in many cases seems to capture more accurately the very real challenges involved in working for social and cultural change. For example, many of us will find Ruddick's suggestion that we ought not to see anything particularly terrible or wonderful about a man identifying with what have traditionally been womanly activities quite compelling. But her suggestion that we ought to push for this sort of social change by thinking of and referring to men who care for their children as "mothers" is likely to be met with considerable resistance, because traditions and customs—sometimes for better and sometimes for worse—play a pivotal role in our thinking about ourselves and our responsibilities to others. For most men—even those who are dedicated caregivers to their children and who agree that they are just as capable and obligated to do this work as women—it will simply be difficult to find the idea of being called a "mother" appealing. It may also be difficult to see how it is helpful. Cultural expectations of men and women play an important role in shaping our tendencies and approaches to parenting, and these things are not always easily abandoned, nor should they be. One cannot simply undo all of the associations we have with "mothers," including most obviously the fact that this term has always referred to women. My point here is that there is a practical challenge to overcome in implementing Ruddick's view that may be insurmountable for most people due to the significance of tradition and custom.

How would Confucian approaches differ? One type of Confucian approach might endorse the retention of rigid gender roles—a possibility that I will discuss further later—while another type of approach might encourage gradually working to change our views of how we regard the work associated with women's and men's traditional roles and the ways in which we all might identify with these different kinds of work, regardless of our gender. On the latter type of Confucian view, changes in traditions and customs typically occur gradually over time through the accumulated wisdom of many different sages and do not involve a wholesale rejection of tradition. On this view, not only do changes *actually* occur in this way, but changes *ought* to occur this way. A Confucian who holds this type of view might argue that the best way to enable men to share fully in the work of nurturing and caring for their children is not to insist that they ought to be "mothers" but to provide men and women with examples of fathers who have shared and are sharing fully in the work of caring for their children. It would be equally important to have examples of women who expect men to share fully in this work and who insist on equal partnership, as well as models of families, communities, and societies that support and encourage it. Ultimately, this can only be achieved over time, through the accumulated experiences and examples of good fathers, mothers, families, communities, and societies, and especially through an increasing number of fathers who embrace this task fully. The intergenerational dimension of this change is pivotal, especially because it involves the way in which children are raised. Sons and daughters who are raised by fathers and mothers sharing fully in the work of responding to their needs will grow up with models of how this is done and with the expectation that both male and female parents participate in the wide range of tasks that are a part of parenting. One of the merits of this approach is that when change occurs slowly and gradually and without an attempt to fully discard tradition, we are better able to avoid the pitfalls and dangers of discarding too quickly and unreflectively things that may be worth preserving. The worry is not that there is something worth retaining in the view that women ought to care for children alone and without the assistance and support of male parents but that there are valuable practices, approaches, and insights that are closely tied to the work that women have done as mothers—and that men have done as fathers—that might be lost if we attempt to discard these roles and traditions fully or try to introduce change too abruptly.

I have so far only discussed the difference between Ruddick's approach and potential Confucian approaches to the practical challenge of enabling men to share fully in what Ruddick calls mothering work. There are some larger questions before us, though, the most pressing of which concerns Ruddick's claim that there are not any key parental tasks that belong essentially and primarily to mothers, on the one hand, and fathers, on the other. While Ruddick is prepared to jettison "fatherhood" entirely, almost anyone who takes traditional Confucianism as a basis for their view will argue that the traditional roles of fathers and mothers are both important and that even though we may wish to amend them, we ought not to discard them entirely. As Kupperman points out, here is where we see one of the most remarkable contrasts between the approaches that feminists and Confucians take to the family. As we saw earlier in this work, traditional Confucians certainly viewed the roles of fathers and mothers as correlative and complementary—a view Ruddick definitively rejects. But it is also important to understand that a number of traditional Confucian sources affirm the view that fathers are not *necessary* to the task of raising a good child, as seen, for instance, in the story of Mengzi's mother. Early Confucians do, though, emphasize the distinctive roles of mothers and fathers, as well as other caregivers in the family, such as elder siblings. Indeed, an important feature of Confucian views is that different family members have distinctive and complementary roles to play in a harmonious family and we must recognize and attend to these roles in ways that express the virtues in order to achieve harmony. The ability to cultivate harmonious relationships with parents and other family members rests in part on the understanding of the differences in our relationships to them and their relationships to others.

Calling them by different names helps to remind us of this. To offer an example that is readily seen in Chinese culture today, one does not simply refer to one's sister or one's aunt by a universal term ("sister" or "aunt") but by different terms for different sisters and aunts: one's older sister or younger sister, one's father's elder sister or one's mother's younger sister. These names correspond to the reality of social life; we use different names for these individuals because we have different relationships to them, based in part on their unique histories and relationships within our families. Not only is it important not to call one's father by the same name one uses for one's mother, it is also important not to call one's other family members by that name. Most Confucians would argue that such a practice neglects the very real differences in one's relationships with these individuals, and especially the highly unique relationship that exists between mothers and fathers and their children. If fathers are not being true or good fathers, the solution is not to refer to them as mothers and encourage them to be mothers; from a Confucian standpoint we should rectify the name "father," with the expectation that fathers live up to the name. In a Confucian-inspired view that takes into account many of Ruddick's concerns, this would mean helping fathers to be fully involved in the work of caring for and nurturing their children, but in ways that make constructive use of some of the tendencies and styles of parenting that men often demonstrate.

Here we see perhaps the deepest and most important contrast between Confucian views and Ruddick's view: almost any Confucian view will acknowledge at least some distinctive features, tendencies, and unique contributions associated with mothers and fathers and with other family members. Accordingly, Confucians would tend to object to the practice of calling many different individuals, including fathers, "mothers." From a Confucian point of view, it is not only important to acknowledge the distinctive tendencies and contributions of mothers and fathers from a descriptive standpoint but also from a normative standpoint: not only do mothers and fathers *tend* to have some important differences—something surely due to a variety of factors—but this can sometimes be good for us. Confucian views will tend to see the roles of mothers and fathers as correlative and complementary, even if we amend early Confucian views and construct a contemporary Confucian view that is compatible with at least some forms of feminism.[9] An emphasis on distinctive and complementary roles within the family is a central feature of Confucianism, and this is partly because Confucians value harmony in the family, which encourages and perhaps even requires complementarity. This means that not only would most Confucians take issue with Ruddick's argument that there is nothing distinctive about "fathers" but also with her more general contention that all caregivers for children can be called "mothers."[10] Indeed, a Confucian feminist might argue that the work of grandmothers ought to be distinguished from the role of mothers in order to more fully recognize and take into account the work that women have done and continue to do for children—and the fact that all of this work is not identical. A Confucian also might argue that due to different relationships, we are uniquely positioned to contribute to children's upbringing in different ways. And although the Confucian sources discussed earlier in this work recognize the unique roles of mothers, early Confucian philosophers certainly did not maintain that other caring roles are all expressions of mothering, much less that all caring roles are equivalent or equal in value, as well as in kind.

Now, although I have been describing a Confucian-inspired view that seeks to develop aspects of Confucian values while also retaining important features of Confucianism, a more traditional type of Confucian view would simply reject the view that we should aim to have fathers share fully in the work done by mothers. On this view, each member of a family ought to have a distinctive role, including mothers and fathers, which allows each individual to make a distinctive contribution and thus to be valued for his or her contributions. At least theoretically, this approach has the practical value of ensuring that everything gets done effectively and efficiently. Indeed, proponents of a more traditional Confucian view might question how and in what ways a father could share fully in the work of caring for children without simply becoming a second mother. The central question here is how and in what ways Confucian fathers would be distinctive if they shared fully in the work of caring for children.

There are a variety of responses to this question. The distinctive contributions of fathers could include performing different tasks related to caring for children or might simply involve performing the same tasks but in different ways. For example, when mothers are breast-feeding, they will be the primary sources of nourishment of infants, and fathers might be the primary diaper changers.[11] Parents who take this approach will both get up with young infants when they awaken at night in order to meet their needs and also in order to support one another. Both tasks are equally important in meeting an infant's needs and are highly demanding. Parents might also take turns performing the same tasks, but their approaches will differ. For example, when taking turns playing outdoors with one's children, one parent may encourage more athletic activities while the other parent may encourage imaginary play or observing the activities of ants, squirrels, and birds. All of these activities involve engaging with one's child and encouraging a love of outdoor activity. Appealing to *yin-yang* theory helps to provide a theoretical basis for this type of view; indeed, in many areas of life, thinking in terms of *yin–yang* complementarity is illuminating. One who draws upon a traditional Confucian view would argue it is good for children to have parents who differ in complementary ways. One parent might be comparatively strict (*yang*), while the other is comparatively lenient (*yin*), and likewise for intellectual (*yang*) and emotional (*yin*), organized (*yang*) and spontaneous (*yin*). Of course, it would be disastrous if two parents embodied extreme forms of opposing traits or tendencies; this would be to differ in *un*complementary ways. Confucian complementarity requires parents to agree on fundamental aims and values while drawing upon each other's differing strengths. Doing this successfully takes work, and from a Confucian standpoint it is essential for both parents to reflect upon themselves continuously and work to improve in areas in which they tend to be, for instance, excessively strict or not strict enough. But they should not aim to be exactly the same.

In each of the examples I have offered, the different activities and approaches of the two parents are complementary. The child benefits from engaging with both parents and from exposure to a wider range of approaches and activities, and the parents also benefit, not only in lessening one another's burden but also in being able to share fully in the joys of parenting. Yet none of the examples I offer here involve drawing upon "essential" female or male characteristics. None of the complementary traits I mentioned need to be associated with either gender, even if traditionally they have been. Fathers and mothers may perform these tasks equally well, depending upon their individual backgrounds, abilities, tendencies, and interests. The roles of same-sex couples could be just as complementary as those of heterosexual couples. Since essential female or male characteristics do not define the two parental roles, each mother's role and each father's role will tend to be distinctive in different ways. Of course, as discussed, there would be certain trends: when mothers are breast-feeding, they will be the primary sources of nourishment, and during the early months of a child's life one of the only other roles that is similarly demanding is diapering, which makes it a natural role for the other parent to take up. But neither a father's role nor a mother's role would be fixed in the sense of requiring all fathers and all mothers to perform many of the same activities—a characteristic feature of traditional Confucian roles based on the rites. This is an important amendment and one that, for some, might mean that such a view of parenting is not "Confucian." But it also must be remembered that *any* contemporary Confucian view is going to look significantly different from traditional Confucian views.[12] Families today must reckon with such things as technology, different forms of employment, different laws and forms of government, and differently structured societies than those of earlier periods in history. Although aspects of some Confucian rites have been retained in some East Asian cultures, the rites are not fully in practice anywhere, and even if they were revived, they would not be exactly the same. The view I am describing significantly amends traditional Confucian views concerning the roles of fathers and mothers, but it also retains important Confucian features.

In addition to preserving the view that Confucian parents should have roles that are complementary and distinctive, a Confucian "distinctive fatherhood" would also likely have an important self-cultivationist dimension that would acknowledge that men have not historically been involved in the work of caring for children and that as a result, at least in many cases, men will have some different approaches to the work of caring for children. Acknowledging and reflecting on this can help us find ways of helping men to share in the work of caring for their children more effectively. From a self-cultivationist standpoint, it would be important not to deny that there have been and continue to be different cultural expectations of men and that there are differences between men and women—regardless of whether their origin is primarily biologically determined or culturally constructed. A Confucian self-cultivationist approach would not simply dismiss or reject those differences out of hand as being wholly or necessarily patriarchal or oppressive; instead, such an approach would encourage us to reflect on those differences and their role in our approaches to and feelings about caring for our children. In this way, the distinctive challenges and experiences of both men and women could be used as a basis for self-cultivation. For Confucian approaches, this involves reflection on our relationships to others and our responsibilities to them, and the hard work of changing our attitudes and behaviors in ways that cultivate and express Confucian virtues such as humaneness, benevolence, reciprocity, and sympathetic understanding. Because Confucians tend to view specific roles and relationships as opportunities for self-cultivation, Confucian-inspired approaches are likely to view a distinctive fatherhood not as an obstacle but as a necessary aid to helping men share in the work of caring for their children. Of course, whether or not a distinctive fatherhood helps men to do this depends upon what that distinctive fatherhood is. But Confucians would not view the acknowledgement of distinctive roles for mothers and fathers as an obstacle per se, as Ruddick does. One difference this helps to remind us of is that Ruddick's interest in moral cultivation is focused more on mothers' experiences than on those of children or fathers. Ruddick views a distinctive fatherhood as problematic partly because she views it as the acceptance of a set role, while Confucians would tend to view the acknowledgement of one's role as a father as the beginning of the process of self-cultivation and thus the beginning of reflection and improvement.

This discussion also points to Ruddick's emphasis on mothering work, as opposed to the special relationship that defines our ordinary understanding of what constitutes a mother. Ruddick associates a distinctive fatherhood with the view that men ought to do different work, but

Confucian views of fathers and mothers do not focus primarily on work in the way that Ruddick's view does. Confucian understandings of mothers take seriously a wide variety of defining features of mothers beyond the work they do, including the biological relationship that is fundamental to early Confucian discussions of prenatal cultivation and some accounts of filial piety (which regard one's body as a gift from one's parents), as well as the love and affection that mothers have for their children. Indeed, there is a fundamental difference between Ruddick and the Confucians concerning the necessary and sufficient conditions for being a mother. This can help us further appreciate why it would be difficult for a Confucian view to accommodate the claim that all of those who make the work of caring for children a regular part of their lives ought to be called "mothers." Most Confucians would object to taking certain kinds of work as the defining feature of mothers because that approach does not focus centrally on the profound love and affection parents have for their children, which in the vast majority of cases is unrivaled by anyone else who cares for them. In addition, though, Confucians would tend to argue that a focus on *the work* of responding to the demands of children generally neglects *the relationship* that obtains between parents and *specific children*—their *own* children. In the case of grandparents, aunts, uncles, older siblings, and others, there are additional distinctive relationships to be taken into account. There are really two differences here, between focusing on the work and the relationship (and especially the love and affection parents have for their children) and between focusing on all children and one's own children.[13] Most Confucians would worry that Ruddick's approach neglects the special relationship parents have with their children, a relationship that stems not only from the profound love and affection they have for their children but also from sharing a home together and being their children's primary caregivers. Some caregivers come and go in a child's life, but not her parents. Ruddick's definition of mothers does not incorporate these things. She rejects the view that a biological relationship or a legal relationship makes one a mother, and most Confucians would, I think, agree that these are not sufficient conditions for being a true or good mother, but most Confucians would focus primarily on the nature of a child's relationship with her parents instead of biological or legal issues. Few among us are confused as to who our parents are, and this is because we know our mothers and fathers as a result of the highly unique, special relationship we have with them—a relationship that is primarily determined by profound love and affection. Mothers and fathers are those who are primarily responsible for raising particular children, and Ruddick is right to point out that this involves certain kinds of work. Confucians would worry about her failure to fully recognize the unique work that parents do by virtue of sharing a home with their children and being their primary caregivers—as opposed to others who do what she calls "mothering work." Indeed, these are additional reasons why almost any Confucian approach would reject using the term "mother" or "mothering work" to refer to those who are not our mothers or to the work that good day-care workers, teachers, or clinicians do with children. The parent–child relationship almost always involves an unparalleled love and affection for particular children, living with or having lived with those children, and an accompanying legal relationship. With the important exception of adoption, the parent–child relationship usually involves a biological relationship. These factors should not be excluded, because they help to distinguish the uniqueness of the parent–child relationship compared with the relationships children have with others who care for and nurture them, often in critically important ways but not in ways that rival the parent–child relationship.

In her more recent work, Ruddick more strongly emphasizes the importance of the relationship between mothers and children in addition to the work of mothering, as well as the special nature of certain relationships among the relationships of all those who do mothering work. She writes, "As much as care is labor, it is also relationship . . . caring labor is intrinsically relational. The work is constituted in and through the relation of those who give and receive care. . . . More critically, some caring relationships seem to have a significance in 'excess' of the labor they enable" (Ruddick 1998:13–14). She gives the example of a father who brings his child to day care and the day-care worker who receives the child. While they both reassure the child, the character and meaning of the father's actions in doing this, from Ruddick's standpoint, may be "in excess of the labor they enable."

The father's work is a response to the relationship, while the day-care worker's relationship with the child is most likely a response to the work. However, it is important to add that the latter is paid to do this work and would not care for the child outside of this financial arrangement; thus, the day-care worker's care is conditional, whereas the parent's is not. Ruddick still frames things primarily in terms of the work, but these remarks include the importance of the relationship and the distinctive nature of the parent–child relationship—though she does not prioritize these things in the way that most Confucian views would. In the preface to the second edition of her work, Ruddick also writes that emphasizing mothering work "does not give adequate weight to the myriad cultural, domestic, and personal relationships that structure anyone's experience of mothering and that precede and usually long outlast the years of intensive child care." It also neglects the importance of pregnancy and giving birth, namely that "all mothering, whether done by men or women, depends on some particular woman's labor; to be 'pregnant' with new life is still and only to be a woman whose body and embodied willfulness is the ground and condition of each new and original being who lives" (Ruddick 1995:xiii). These are important amendments and ones that would bring Ruddick's view a bit closer to aspects of the Confucian views we examined earlier in this work. But although Ruddick maintains that all mothering depends on some woman giving birth, she also points out that childbearing comes to nothing without someone to mother the infant, and in the end, she argues that childbearing and mothering are distinct activities (Ruddick 1995:xiii). This type of view, as we shall see in a moment, will not come quite so easily for Confucians who take seriously early Confucian views concerning early moral cultivation, and this is the final contrast between Ruddick's view and Confucian views that I wish to discuss.

Unlike Ruddick, early Confucian sources did not argue for the need to distinguish childbearing from mothering. This is at least partly because giving birth and mothering usually are different aspects of the same role or relationship—and it is important to note here that Confucians, as I noted earlier, have not tended to view childbearing and mothering as "activities" or "work," as Ruddick does, but in terms of relationships. But the difference between Ruddick and Confucian thinkers concerning giving birth and mothering highlights a further set of differences between these views as well. We have seen how strongly early Confucian sources advocate prenatal cultivation; in contrast, Ruddick argues that

> pregnancy, birth, and lactation are different in kind from other maternal work and, measured by the life of one child, are brief episodes in years of mothering. A scrambling, temperamental toddler in reach of poisons under the sink, a schoolchild left out of a birthday party, a college student unable to write her papers—these children are more emblematic of the demands on a mother than is a feeding infant, let alone a silent fetus. (Ruddick 1995:48)

These remarks are especially important for our purposes, not only because they highlight the contrast with the Confucian emphasis on the earliest stages of infancy and the view that one's parental responsibilities begin before birth, but also because they highlight another critical difference from Ruddick's outlook, namely, that she does not view the earliest years of a child's life as critically important in the ways that the early Confucians do. While for Ruddick pregnancy and breast-feeding are "brief episodes in mothering" compared with the long lives of children, early Confucian thinkers maintained that these early years are unique and irreplaceable in their importance for a child's development compared with the years to follow. This is a view that, as we shall see in the next chapter, is now broadly supported by a large body of empirical evidence from multiple disciplines. Additionally, as we shall see, these early stages and experiences are critically important for first-time mothers. The demanding and rewarding experience of breast-feeding an infant over time is one activity that helps to cultivate a number of the virtues and capacities that good mothers need—especially the ability to prioritize a child's needs and to make both personal and professional sacrifices in order to serve the child's best interests. It is an experience that prepares one for later experiences and challenges as a mother and that helps to cultivate virtues that serve one well more generally in life. However, one can only appreciate this if one does not simply view it as a physical act but appreciates the important emotional and moral dimensions of this experience for both mothers and children.

The early Confucians did not view the work of pregnant mothers and mothers of young infants as "different in kind from other maternal work" as Ruddick does, and it is pivotal to appreciate just how deep the contrast is here. Ruddick writes that "neither pregnancy nor birth is much like mothering. Mothering is an ongoing, organized set of activities that require discipline and active attention." Pregnant women "usually engage projectively in maternal tasks—making clothes or buying a crib, for example. But these tasks relate directly not to the fetus but to the baby it will become. A mother takes care of her fetus by taking care of herself" (Ruddick 1995:50). In addition to the political and metaphysical views that Ruddick expresses in distinguishing between a "fetus" and "baby," another motivation for minimizing the connection between pregnancy, birth, breast-feeding, and other mothering work is perhaps Ruddick's desire to defend her larger view that men are equally capable of mothering work. There are good reasons to question her view from a scientific standpoint, including the connection that has been well-established between breast-feeding and a variety of issues relating to the later health and well-being of children and mothers. The evidence suggests that these early stages of development and the relationships that are formed between infants and their parents both in utero and during the first years of a child's life—including attachment theory and research concerning prenatal care and breast-feeding, which will be discussed in the following chapters—should not be viewed as disconnected from, or different in kind from, what occurs subsequently in children's lives and in the lives of their parents. But my present concern is to show how Ruddick's view contrasts with Confucian views, and perhaps the deepest and most important contrast is that early Confucian texts argue explicitly for the view that pregnant mothers can and should engage in "an ongoing, organized set of activities that require discipline and active attention"—to use Ruddick's words—and that contribute irreplaceably to the moral, emotional, and physical development of their children.

CARING AND PARENTING: THE WORK OF NEL NODDINGS AND VIRGINIA HELD

Ruddick's work is especially important in relation to discussions of parent–child relationships and moral cultivation for a variety of reasons, including its sustained attention to these topics, the fact that it marks the beginnings of care ethics, and Ruddick's remarkable influence over subsequent care ethicists, including Nel Noddings and Virginia Held. Noddings is the care ethicist who has been discussed most in relation to Confucian ethics. Indeed, Noddings is the most widely known proponent of care ethics. Her work is also important for the present study because Noddings writes extensively about moral education.

In between the publication of Ruddick's "Maternal Thinking" in 1980 and Noddings's first book, *Caring: A Feminine Approach to Ethics and Moral Education* in 1984, the developmental psychologist Carol Gilligan's book *In a Different Voice* (1982) appeared. Gilligan's empirical work helped to provide impetus for the development of the ethics of care. Challenging a number of Lawrence Kohlberg's conclusions, Gilligan's work focused on the way that many girls and women interpret, reflect on, and describe moral problems, including a greater concern with context and human relationships and less reliance on abstract rules and individual conscience. Although only some of the women in Gilligan's studies manifested these tendencies, almost none of the men did, leading Gilligan to write that "if women were eliminated from the research sample, care focus in moral reasoning would virtually disappear" (Gilligan 1987:25). This, she argues, merits our attention. Held points out that the importance of Gilligan's work for moral theory has been

its suggestion of alternative perspectives through which moral problems can be interpreted: a "justice perspective" that emphasizes universal moral principles and how they can be applied to particular cases and values rational argument about these; and a "care perspective" that pays more attention to people's needs, to how actual relations between people can be maintained or repaired, and that values narrative and sensitivity to context in arriving at moral judgments. (Held 2006:27–28)

While Gilligan argued that both perspectives are needed in order for a person to have an adequate morality—a view that most care ethicists have not shared—she did not indicate how they are to be integrated or woven together into a coherent moral theory. For the purposes of this study, it is important to note just how diverse the responses to Gilligan's work have been, especially as they relate to the question of how strongly a "care perspective" is tied to biology, on the one hand, and culture, on the other. Scholars of Confucianism are not the only ones who have noted that other cultures exhibit certain resonances with a "care perspective": Sandra Harding points out that African men showed some of the same tendencies in interpreting moral problems as the women Gilligan studied (Harding 1987).

When feminist philosophers found that Gilligan's work resonated with their own dissatisfaction with the dominant moral theories, the work of developing a viable alternative became a central focus. Like Gilligan and Ruddick, Noddings was motivated by an awareness of male bias in moral theory and in studies of moral development. In *Caring* (1984) and subsequent works, she offers an account that goes a long way toward establishing care ethics as an alternative to other moral theories. Noddings discusses the activities of care, including attending to the feelings and needs of others and identifying with another's experience of reality. One of several distinctive features of Noddings's view is her argument that caring involves *engrossment*, which means being receptively attentive—either continually or momentarily—to the needs expressed in an encounter (Noddings 2010b:47–48). She maintains that this does not involve imagining oneself in another's place "by analyzing his reality as objective data and then asking, 'How would I feel in such a situation?' On the contrary, I set aside my temptation to analyze and to plan. I do not project; I receive the other into myself, and I see and feel with the other. I become duality" (Noddings 1984:30).[14] Noddings rejects the approach she associates with the golden rule, "do unto others as you would have them do unto you," because in her view this involves attributing to others "the same pains, feelings, and passions that we undergo." She argues that in caring encounters "I receive the other person and feel what he or she is feeling even if I am quite sure intellectually that I would not myself feel that way in the given situation" (Noddings 2002b:14). Luo Shirong points out that Noddings is not wholly correct in claiming that the golden rule is a peculiarly Western, rational, and masculine way of looking at "feeling with," since the golden rule or principle of reversibility is a part of early Confucian teachings (Luo 2007:98; cf. Ivanhoe 2008b; Tiwald 2010). As a result, this is one of several ways in which her view—at least as she understands it—offers a contrast to Confucian views.

Noddings distinguishes "caring for" or "natural caring," which takes place when one person (the carer) cares directly and in person for another (the cared-for), from "caring about" or "ethical caring," which concerns strangers or people with whom we do not have direct contact (Noddings 2002b:21–22). We *care for* those who are in our circle of family, friends, and acquaintances; in calling this "natural caring," Noddings means "a form of caring that arises more or less spontaneously out of affection or inclination" (Noddings 2002b:29). However, Noddings stresses, "I do *not* mean to suggest that the capacity for natural caring does not need cultivation. On the contrary, I will argue that it needs continuous and sensitive cultivation" (Noddings 2002b:29). In contrast to natural caring, when we *care about* a needy stranger, we draw upon our capacity to care for family and friends, asking ourselves how we would respond if this was someone we knew: "In doing this, we draw upon an ethical ideal—a set of memories of caring and being cared for that we regard as manifestations of our best selves and relations. We summon what we need to maintain the original 'I must'" (Noddings 2002b:13).[15] *Caring for* takes precedence over *caring about* in a couple of ways, on Noddings's view: "Chronologically, we learn first what it means to be cared for. Then, gradually, we learn both to care for and, by extension, to care about others" (Noddings 2002b:22). This is one area in which Noddings's view is in agreement with Confucian views. Noddings emphasizes the importance of what occurs in children's emotional worlds when they are cared for, writing that caring "arises as a product of actual caring and being cared-for and my reflection on the goodness of these concrete caring situations" (Noddings 1984:84). In addition to learning to care for before we learn to care about, Noddings argues that caring about strangers is secondary, because its main importance is that it enables us to care for our loved ones: "The preferred state is natural caring; ethical caring is invoked to restore it" (Noddings 2002b:14).

Noddings's discussion of parent–child relationships and children's moral education is strongly influenced by Ruddick's work. In *Starting at Home: Caring and Social Policy*, Noddings writes that although Ruddick writes from the perspective of mothers, whereas her own main focus is on the child, "the accounts are largely complementary. Ruddick acknowledges that maternal interests are anchored in 'demands'; my preference is to speak of needs and wants" (Noddings 2002b:176). As we have seen, Ruddick's discussion focuses intentionally on "mothers" and "mothering," and although Noddings does not use this specialized terminology and opts for more general terms like "parenting," she nevertheless accords a special place to the relationship between mothers and children. In *The Maternal Factor*, Noddings argues that the caring relation develops from the original caring relation established by maternal instinct. She writes that the mother–child relation is "the primary example of natural caring, but unlike other relations of natural caring, it still has firm roots in instinct" (Noddings 2010b:59). Noddings's view, much like Ruddick's, valorizes the virtues and values traditionally linked to women, and her examples of carers are more often women than men, though like Ruddick, she clearly and explicitly emphasizes that men can and should be carers.

Noddings writes in detail about the specific practices and attitudes that help to define good, caring parent–child relationships and the way in which these things give rise to caring children beginning from the time they are newborns. These things mark important similarities with Confucian discussions. Noddings attends to the process of moral cultivation, although she describes it in different terms, preferring to talk more in terms of growth and development than cultivation. This is not simply a matter of terminology; there is a key difference between Noddings's care-ethical approach, which centers on empathy due to its connection to her conception of caring, and Confucian approaches, which focus more on the cultivation of virtues. Noddings writes,

Moral education at home and in schools often concentrates on the acquisition of virtues and/or moral reasoning. Both have something valuable
to contribute to moral growth, but there is a fundamental difference in
emphasis between these programs and programs aimed at increasing
empathy. When we try to inculcate honesty, courage, obedience, or courtesy as personal virtues, attention is directed to the moral agent, the one
who "possesses" the virtue. In contrast, when we try to promote empathy,
attention is directed to others—to those who are affected by our actions.
(Noddings 2010b:63–64)

Many if not most Confucian approaches—and especially those of a
more Mengzian character—combine aspects of the two types of approaches
Noddings describes here, but Noddings's approach is unquestionably
different in its strong focus on feeling with others and the way in which this
sort of caring, and not the development of a set of virtues, ought to be our
primary aim. She maintains that care theory

suggests a more explicit, a firmer, foundation on which to build the formation of such habits. It insists upon receptivity, vulnerability to the
suffering of others, acceptance of the obligation to respond as carer to
the expressed needs of the cared-for (which may involve meeting those
needs, diverting them, or sensitively rejecting them), and at least one
absolute injunction: never inflict unnecessary pain. (Noddings 2010a:284)

This sort of language and the things that Noddings emphasizes are a
marked contrast to early Confucian views. Even in the case of those virtues that resonate with the moral sensibilities Noddings describes, such
as reciprocity or sympathetic understanding (*shu*) and humaneness (*Ren*),
the process of cultivation involves not just exercising certain kinds of feelings and sensitivities to others but practicing the rites and role-specific
duties, such as those tied to filial piety. Indeed, Noddings's discussion of
the things that are a part of learning to care contrast deeply with Confucian accounts of moral cultivation. It is not that there are no shared concerns here; Noddings emphasizes the importance of things such as bodies,

selves, and places—especially homes—that are a part of moral cultivation in almost any culture or tradition. Confucian moral self-cultivation includes coming to view and understand one's body in certain ways and developing a certain understanding of oneself, and this work occurs in places of significance—especially the home. But Noddings's care-ethical account and Confucian self-cultivationist accounts of these things differ, especially because they aim to produce different kinds of people. Another important contrast is that Confucians focus strongly on filial piety as the defining characteristic of the parent–child relationship and the root of the other virtues that good parent–child relationships promote. The cultivated person embodies the virtues of ritual propriety and filial piety as well as a wide range of other virtues, while in her descriptions of carers, Noddings focuses on the maintenance of caring relations and growth in the capacity to care. Noddings rejects the type of approach that is characteristic of filial piety, which involves an acknowledgement of parental authority and control and views this as an asset in moral cultivation. Noddings writes that "control, in the hands of maternal thinkers, is aimed at transfer. Such caregivers want to reduce their own overt control and pass it to the child, and their control of the child is accompanied by attentive love" (Noddings 2002b:135). Although both Noddings and the Confucians aim to help children cultivate self-control, and although they seem to share the view that parental control should be accompanied by attentive love, there is nevertheless a larger difference here concerning the overall character of parent–child relationships. For Noddings, as we shall see in a moment, the reverence that is a part of filial piety is antithetical to the kind of reciprocity and interdependence that is the aim of the ethics of care.

One of the strengths of Noddings's work and one of its distinctive features—especially when compared with Confucian views—is her appreciation not just of the importance of what loving, attentive parents do for their children and the fact that this merits gratitude on the part of children, but of the response of children to their parents and the fact that parents should feel and express gratitude for that response. She emphasizes the contribution of the cared-for, explicitly including the contributions of infants and children: "By recognizing the carer's efforts, by responding in some supportive way, the cared-for makes a distinctive contribution to the relation and establishes it as caring. In this way, infants contribute to the parent–child relation, patients to the physician-patient relation, and students to the teacher-student relation" (Noddings 1984:xiii-viv). In *Starting at Home*, Noddings writes, "Parents and teachers recognize the contribution of the cared-for, at least implicitly, when they express their own delight with responsive infants, children, and students. Indeed, caregivers at every level find their work more satisfying when the recipients of care respond positively in some way" (Noddings 2002b:207). She argues that the cared-for make an irreplaceable *contribution* when they respond positively to the carer, one that elicits gratitude from the carer and that in turn has an important role in moral education: children whose parents and teachers feel and express gratitude to them develop an appreciation for the importance of expressing gratitude not only to carers but also to those who are in the position of the cared-for. There is, Noddings argues, a need for appreciative response in both directions; "Appreciation of interdependence should be extended into the wider world. Children need to see that salespeople, service workers, and all other legitimate workers should be treated with courtesy and, when appropriate, with gratitude for their contributions" (Noddings 2002b:208). Interdependence is a key part of Noddings's account of moral education and, specifically, of how children learn to care. She writes that "we must ask how best to develop attitudes and habits that will enable our children to recognize and live by what is understood about moral interdependence, material interdependence, and social interdependence" (Noddings 2002b:212).

Noddings explicitly offers an alternative to "a long legacy from Aristotle and others who believed that love and appreciation are required *from* the less powerful *for* the more powerful. This attitude is revealed when we, as parents and teachers, think that our children should be responsive and appreciative because we are doing something for them" (Noddings 2002b:208). It is particularly important to acknowledge this aspect of Noddings's work, because I have argued that although several Western philosophers discuss filial piety, none of them devote as much attention to it as Confucian philosophers, nor does it play as fundamental a role in other traditions of thought. A closely related aspect of Confucianism is the emphasis it places on respect for the elderly and for older persons more generally. Indeed, because Confucians emphasize these things more strongly and give them more attention than Western philosophers, the contrast between the Confucians and Noddings here may be even deeper than the contrast with thinkers like Aristotle. Although Confucians emphasize the importance of reciprocity, they place tremendous emphasis on the importance of children feeling and expressing gratitude and reverence toward their parents, and this emphasis is not matched by discussions of parents' love and gratitude for their children. Confucian writings do not suggest that children ought to learn about gratitude from parents expressing gratitude to them, nor do they emphasize that parents ought to be grateful to their children; this is simply not a characteristic of the relationship. While the Confucians viewed filial piety as the root of the other virtues, Noddings suggests that children's moral development rests in part on a deeply appreciative response in *both* directions.

Another pivotal difference is that caring is clearly *the* central concept in Noddings's work, while Confucian views present multiple virtues and themes as central. I have argued in this work that one such theme in Confucian ethics is the central importance of the family, which is also a feature of Noddings's work. But even in works such as *Starting at Home*, which argues that caring is a way of life that is learned in the home, Noddings's central focus is caring; her discussions of parent–child relationships revolve around, contribute to, and depend upon her larger discussion of caring. For example, in her chapter on "Learning to Care," she discusses how children become caring individuals through their encounters with others, especially parents and teachers: "A smile or cuddle from an infant, a look or nod of gratitude from an older child, a sigh of relief from an elderly patient—all contribute to the maintenance of caring relations. In classrooms, eager hands raised, suggested projects pursued, and expressed needs to read or question are the kinds of responses by which teachers judge their own effectiveness" (Noddings 2002b:208). For Noddings, it is significant that caregivers in families share much with caregivers in other areas. Indeed, though Noddings acknowledges the important role of the family, one of her aims is to emphasize, as Ruddick does, that caring in households is joined with caring in other places and contexts.

This picture is very different from the one Confucian thinkers present. While the Confucian emphasis on the family is not unrelated to virtues like humaneness (*Ren*), which includes a conception of caring that has been fruitfully compared with those of care ethicists, this virtue has other dimensions as well, including its deep connection to filial piety and ritual propriety. And while Noddings's discussions of parent–child relationships typically revolve around her larger discussion of caring, it is not clear that Confucian discussions of parent–child relationships take a single idea as central in the same way. If anything, Confucian texts present parent–child relationships as critically tied to filial piety, but it seems inaccurate to highlight filial piety alone when Confucian views of parent–child relationships ultimately rest upon a broader conception of moral cultivation. While there is a single organizing idea in care ethics that takes precedence, Confucian views rest upon a conception of moral cultivation in which a number of different virtues and practices combine to play this sort of role.

One might still point to Noddings's extensive discussions of parent–child relationships as representing shared ground with Confucian views. This is an important resemblance, but we must also take care to note the important differences and those that Noddings—like other feminists—intentionally emphasizes herself. In *The Maternal Factor*, Noddings briefly discusses her views on the differences between care ethics and Confucian ethics and offers a critique of Chenyang Li's argument. The difference that Noddings most strongly emphasizes is that Confucianism is "male oriented," with roles and duties that are male defined and a strong emphasis on tradition. She contends that these things are likely to prevent the reforms that are necessary in order for Confucianism to widen its domain of application and embrace female equality. Noddings argues that "Confucianism would have to admit that it was wrong to claim the inferiority of women and, then, patiently locate and repudiate all the doctrines based on this claim" (Noddings 2010b:140). Whether or not one agrees, it remains the case that one of the deepest differences between the work of care ethicists and Confucian views is the centrality of women and women's relationships in care ethics and the related goal of female equality. Noddings writes that "caring for others may be clearly identified as a female tradition," and like Ruddick, she focuses heavily on the experiences of mothers, arguing that caring mother–child relationships are—at least in some critically important ways—a paradigm for moral life in general (Noddings 2010b:138). Although I have emphasized in this work the role of mothers in early Confucian accounts of moral cultivation, the Confucians did not take mother–child relationships to be paradigmatic in a special way over and above father–child relationships. Despite the fact that many Confucian texts emphasize the unique and irreplaceable role of mothers in moral cultivation and view this cultivation as fundamentally important in every major area of ethics and politics, Confucian roles are, at least in most traditional Confucian texts, predominantly cast in male terms. I would argue that if we take all of these views and consider them together, there is a good basis for saying that the early Confucians maintain that *parent–child* relationships—including the relationships that both mothers and fathers have with their children—help to form the foundation for developing other virtues. In contrast, care ethicists like Ruddick and Noddings insist that the mother–child relation and feminine approaches to caring have a particularly unique importance in our understanding of caring and therefore in our understanding of the moral life generally.

This difference is significant, because Noddings and Ruddick emphasize both the unique sort of care that good mothers provide and feminine approaches to caring, while the Confucians emphasize the role of both fathers and mothers. For Noddings and Ruddick, the caring relationship between mothers and children has a special role in accounting for our moral development. For traditional Confucians, parent–child relationships that are characterized by filial piety have a special role to play in moral cultivation, because filial piety is understood as the root of the other virtues. As we have seen, Noddings rejects this type of view due to its emphasis on filial piety as opposed to a more reciprocal sense of gratitude, but additionally, Noddings focuses more on *the caring relationship*, whereas the Confucians focus on the origins of our capacity to become good. This concern in Confucianism is a function both of virtue-ethical and self-cultivationist orientations. Confucians do, of course, emphasize the way in which parent–child relationships are a model for other kinds of relationships—especially political ones, seen in the idea of a ruler as "the mother and father of the people." Yet there remains an important contrast here between the Confucian tendency to view parent–child relationships as accounting for the origin of our capacity to become good (by developing the virtue of filial piety), and the emphasis of Noddings and Ruddick on the kind of relationship on which we should model other relationships (seen in their discussions of engrossment, natural caring, and mothering). So while some care ethicists and early Confucian thinkers share an emphasis on parent–child relationships and argue that those relationships have a foundational role in moral development, they diverge in their accounts of which relationships are basic, which is seen in the Confucian emphasis on parents and the feminist emphasis on mothers and also the ways in which these relationships are foundational, which is seen in the Confucian emphasis on filial piety and the feminist emphasis on paradigmatic relationships. This provides us with two very rich and detailed accounts of how parent–child relationships ought to inform our understanding of morality, accounts that nevertheless differ in fundamentally important ways.

One of the important contributions of the work of Noddings and Ruddick is that they have helped to inspire a rich variety of works focused on caregiving, some of which build upon mothering while also extending beyond it.[16] Virginia Held develops in new ways the view that mother–child relationships are fundamental to moral and political life, arguing that "relations between mothers and children should be thought of as primary, and the sort of human relation all other human relations should resemble or reflect" (Held 1987:114–115). She contends that those who are "thoughtfully involved in the work of bringing up children or caring for the dependent may design better public institutions for child care, education, health care, welfare, and the like—not just better in terms of efficiency but in embodying the relevant values" (Held 2006:78). Additionally, political institutions that govern activities where care is obviously relevant may be improved "by considering their design from the perspective of mother/child relations rather than only from the perspective of the liberal rational contractor" (78). Though the Confucians affirm the connection between the political and parent–child relationships, there is an important contrast here: for Held, it is not simply a matter of cultivating a particular virtue like filial piety, which will, in turn, help to enable the rest of our moral development. Rather, the parent–child relationship is something we must continually draw upon and reference in order to reason well from a moral standpoint. This is certainly a view that contemporary Confucian-inspired views could easily incorporate, but it was not an explicit part of traditional Confucian views.

Another distinctive feature of Held's view is her strong emphasis on the way in which persons are relational and interdependent, which accounts for one of the reasons why she argues that mother–child relationships are paradigmatic in a special way. She writes,

> Every person starts out as a child dependent on those providing us care, and we remain interdependent with others in thoroughly fundamental ways throughout our lives. That we can think and act as if we were independent depends on a network of social relations making it possible for us to do so. And our relations are part of what constitute our identity. This is not to say that we cannot become autonomous; feminists have done much interesting work developing an alternative conception of autonomy in place of the liberal individualistic one. Feminists have much experience rejecting or reconstituting relational ties that are oppressive. (Held 2006:13–14)

Held's remarks here highlight both similarities and differences between her perspective and Confucian views. On the one hand, interdependence and social relationships are an important part of Confucian views as is the insight that this begins (and continues) within the context of parent–child relationships, but on the other hand, as we have already seen and as Kupperman points out, Confucians are not as ready as feminists are to reject traditional views and practices. Held notes an additional difference from Confucian views, based on the recent comparative discussions of care ethics and Confucianism: "A traditional Confucian ethic, if seen as an ethic of care, would be a form of care ethics unacceptable to feminists" (Held 2006:22). As we have seen, this is a view that Noddings shares. Yet Held also points out an area of shared concern:

One way in which the ethics of care does resemble Confucian ethics is in its rejection of the sharp split between public and private. The ethics of care rejects . . . a public sphere of mutually disinterested equals coexisting with a private sphere of female caring and male rule. The ethics of care advocates care as a value for society as well as household. In this there are some resemblances to the Confucian view of public morality as an extension of private morality. (Held 2006:21)

As we saw earlier in this work and as Pauline Lee argues, "The Confucian inner/outer delineation, which is graduated and permeable, can be envisioned as a series of nested concentric circles with the family as the fountain of moral energy at the center of the well-ordered political and economic world" (Lee 2000:17).

* * *

The work of care ethicists is marked by a deep and profound regard for the contributions of women and the way in which they have been denigrated and devalued. Care ethicists argue that the experience of mothering and the relationships between mothers and children serve as a unique resource for understanding our capacities and our development as human beings, especially concerning our capacity to care for others. Additionally, caring clearly takes precedence in the work of care ethicists, and their views on parent–child relationships are critically tied to their conceptions of caring. In contrast, Confucian views of parent–child relationships and moral cultivation do not center on women's experiences or give a single idea or role precedence.

Perhaps the deepest and most important contrast between Confucian views and Ruddick's view is that almost any Confucian view will acknowledge at least some distinctive features, tendencies, and unique contributions associated with mothers and fathers, as well as other family members. Confucian views will also tend to see the roles of mothers and fathers as correlative and complementary, even if we amend early Confucian views and construct a contemporary Confucian view that is compatible with at least some forms of feminism. In this view, not only will two parents tend to have distinctive tendencies and styles, but this often can be good for both children and parents. A final area of contrast with Ruddick's view is that Ruddick does not view the earliest years of a child's life as critically important in the ways the early Confucians do. This is particularly important, because one of the main arguments of this book is that these views enable the Confucians to make some distinctive contributions to our understanding of parent–child relationships and moral cultivation.

As we have seen, Noddings's work also helps to highlight a variety of ways in which Confucian views are unique, even alongside other views that emphasize the importance of parent–child relationships in relation to moral cultivation. Noddings critiques the type of view that is characteristic of Confucian filial piety—including the emphasis on the positive role of parental authority in moral cultivation, as well as the unique sort of reverence that children ought to feel for their parents. In Noddings's view, just as children should feel gratitude for their parents, parents ought to express gratitude to their children. In contrast, Confucian views tend to focus on the *different* kinds of feelings and expressions that are appropriate for children and parents in the course of moral cultivation. All of these features help to highlight the fact that Noddings's care-ethical account and Confucian self-cultivationist accounts aim to produce very different kinds of people. For Confucians, mastery of ritual propriety and filial piety is absolutely essential. For Noddings, feminist values and a rejection of traditional hierarchical practices is essential. By "essential," I mean that on each view, these are defining features of cultivated persons. These differences help to show just how diverse views that emphasize the role of parent–child relationships in moral cultivation can be.

Without question, there are ways in which feminist views can push Confucian views to engage topics they have neglected or engaged poorly. First and foremost among these are the range of possibilities that are open to women and the roles and responsibilities of fathers. Ruddick's contention that men can and should share fully in the work of caring for children ought to be taken seriously by anyone working to construct contemporary Confucian views, and as we work to promote change in this area in the United

States and other Western countries, one would hope that amended Confucian views might help to promote change in contemporary East Asian cultures, where father involvement is sadly lacking. Confucian views can also be amended and augmented in compelling ways by Noddings's emphasis on parents' gratitude for their children, which can help us recognize that Confucianism places far too much emphasis on the contributions of parents and the reasons why they deserve respect and reverence. Held's view, too, highlights ways of augmenting Confucian views through her argument that parent–child relationships do not just nurture our moral development through a foundational virtue like filial piety; rather, we must continually draw upon and reference parent–child relationships in order to reason well from a moral standpoint. Whether or not an amended view that incorporates these perspectives ought to be called "Confucian" depends, of course, upon how one understands the necessary and sufficient conditions for being a "Confucian" view. For the purposes of this work, it is not important whether or not we call this view "Confucian" or whether we describe it as a view that incorporates features of Confucianism; my aim is simply to demonstrate that Confucian values and ideas can help us address contemporary moral problems.

There are also ways in which the Confucian tradition can serve as a constructive resource for feminist philosophy. Confucian views should encourage care ethicists to attend more carefully to the role of pregnancy and early childhood in moral cultivation. Confucian views should also lead feminist philosophers to examine whether their analyses focus on the welfare and rights of individuals in ways that are prone to neglect rather than draw upon the role of relationships of care and support within families. The next chapter examines the empirical evidence that lends support to these and other aspects of Confucian views, which I argue gives us good reasons to take them seriously.

III

WHY DO CONFUCIAN VIEWS OF THE
RELATIONSHIP BETWEEN PARENT–CHILD
RELATIONSHIPS, EARLY CHILDHOOD, AND MORAL
CULTIVATION WARRANT SERIOUS CONSIDERATION,
AND WHAT CAN THEY CONTRIBUTE TO OUR
UNDERSTANDING OF THESE AREAS?

5

EARLY CHILDHOOD DEVELOPMENT AND EVIDENCE-BASED APPROACHES TO PARENTS, CHILDREN, AND MORAL CULTIVATION

W E HAVE THUS far seen that Confucian philosophers make a range of distinctive claims about the specific role of parent–child relationships in moral cultivation during the earliest years of a child's life and its implications for the development of a good society, including the claim that the general ethical sensibilities we begin to develop during infancy and early childhood, and even during the prenatal period, are the basis for nearly every virtue and that early childhood education within the family has a *direct bearing* on the quality of a society. Further, as we have seen, the Confucian tradition brings a unique, particularly poignant, and powerful set of stories, anecdotes, practices, and approaches to reinforce and encourage an ethical understanding of the family and its role in moral cultivation. However, distinctiveness alone is not a reason to accept a particular set of views, even though it might be a good reason to include them in our study of a given topic, since studying diverse perspectives can help us more fully explore the problems and challenges that are a part of particular issues—and assist with the process of formulating potential solutions and new approaches to those problems. But in order for us to accept a set of views, we normally want to know whether or not they are true. This chapter argues that several aspects of Confucian views on infancy, childhood, parent–child relationships, and moral cultivation cohere with the evidence we have concerning children's development, how and when various aspects of it occur, and the role that parents play in that process. As a result of this coherence, I argue, we have good reasons to take Confucian views of parent–child relationships seriously.[1]

While there is much excellent research relating to parent–child relationships and the family, this poses a particular challenge for this work—a work in the humanities that aims to engage and apply work from the sciences constructively. This sort of interdisciplinary task is especially daunting when there are large numbers of studies and theoretical materials that are potentially relevant to one's work. As a result, I have narrowed my focus in this chapter. In anticipation of my argument in the next chapter that Confucian views can serve as a resource for promoting social and policy change, I focus on an unusually successful early childhood intervention program that has been implemented at the level of policy and its theoretical foundations in attachment theory and human ecology theory. I argue that the evidence supporting these theories and the policy research relating to the program help to show that several key features of early Confucian views concerning parent–child relationships and moral cultivation are accurate.[2]

EVIDENCE-BASED APPROACHES TO EARLY CHILDHOOD INTERVENTION AND PARENTAL CAREGIVING: AN OVERVIEW OF THE NURSE–FAMILY PARTNERSHIP

In recent years, there has been increasing recognition that brain development is most rapid during a child's first three years of life and that opportunities to influence the course of a child's life are greatest during those years. As a result, policy makers have been increasingly pressured to fund early childhood intervention programs that focus on the first three years of life (Shore 1997; Olds et al. 2000; Olds 2002). Early childhood intervention programs share the assumption that "children's earliest experiences play a fundamental role in shaping their life opportunities and that parental caregiving is the most important of these earliest experiences" (Olds et al. 2000:110).[3] Although these programs have a wide range of goals and service elements, many are home-visiting programs that aim to reach high-risk families with young children by bringing services to them. Early findings in studies of one particular program of home visitation by nurses, a maternal and early childhood health program known as the Nurse–Family Partnership (NFP), intensified interest in this type of service and prompted a proliferation of home-visiting programs. However, few programs have rivaled the success of this one (Olds et al. 2000:109, 115).[4] Indeed, a variety of new studies cast doubt on the effectiveness of home-visiting programs that do not adhere to the elements of the model studied in NFP trials, including the use of nurse visitors and evidence-based program protocols designed to promote adaptive behavior (Olds 2010:59).[5] As NFP program founder David Olds points out,

Many early childhood intervention programs fail because they are not based on a thorough understanding of the following factors: (a) the risk and protective characteristics in the targeted population as they relate to the outcomes of interest; (b) the likely developmental pathways leading to the negative outcomes the interventions intend to prevent and the positive outcomes they intend to promote; and (c) the mechanisms, based on sound theory and evidence, through which their designers expect the programs to produce behavioral change. (Olds 2010:50; cf. Olds and Kitzman 1993)

In contrast, the success of the NFP's efforts to intervene in the lives of at-risk families continues to be measured in the remarkable outcomes of three randomized, controlled trials, evidenced not only in the lives of the mothers but in the lives of the children whose mothers enrolled in the program before they were born and who are now adults.

The NFP is a thirty-seven-year old program of research that aims to achieve long-term improvements in the lives of at-risk families through intensive efforts aimed at children's early years and the pivotal role that parents play in shaping children's lives.[6] The program provides first-time,

low-income mothers with home visits from public health nurses beginning early in pregnancy and continuing through the first two years of the
child's life. Nurse–Family Partnership nurses are trained to engage clients
in activities associated with: (1) improving pregnancy outcomes by helping
women to improve prenatal health; (2) improving child health and development by helping parents to provide sensitive and competent caregiving; and
(3) improving parental life course and economic self-sufficiency by helping parents to develop plans for the future, including completing their education, finding work, and engaging in family planning (Olds 2006:11–13).
The program has been tested in three separate, large-scale, randomized
controlled trials in Elmira, New York (begun in 1977), Memphis, Tennes-
see (begun in 1987), and Denver, Colorado (begun in 1994). Not only the
impressive longitudinal dimension of these studies but also other characteristics are important to note: randomized, controlled trials represent the
most rigorous research method for measuring the effectiveness of an intervention, but due to their cost and complexity, they are not often used to
evaluate complex health and human services. Follow-up studies of the long-
term outcomes for mothers and children in the three trials continue today.
Since 1997 the NFP has helped other communities develop the program
outside of a research context, and the program currently serves first-time
mothers and their babies in 37 states, operating in 280 counties nation-
ally.[7] The success of the program has also increased interest among policy
makers in other countries, and since 2004 the Nurse–Family Partnership
International Program has been tested and implemented in several countries abroad, with Australia, Canada, England, the Netherlands, Northern
Ireland, and Scotland currently taking part.[8]

The NFP shows remarkable promise for reducing some of the most damaging and widespread problems faced by low-income children and families
in the United States today, many of which have far-reaching consequences
for other members of society and for the overall quality and character of
our society as a whole. Consistent program effects include improvements
in a range of areas for nurse-visited mothers and children compared with
mothers and children in the control group, who were randomly assigned not
to receive the program. These effects include improved prenatal health, fewer

childhood injuries, fewer unintended subsequent pregnancies, increased intervals between births, increased father involvement, increased maternal employment, reductions in families' use of welfare and food stamps, better infant emotional and language development, and improved school readiness for children born to mothers with low psychological resources.[9] A twelve-year follow-up study found less role impairment (at work, with friends, or with family members) owing to alcohol and other drug use, longer partner relationships, a decrease in closely spaced subsequent pregnancies, and greater sense of mastery in overcoming challenges among the nurse-visited mothers compared with the control group. Among the twelve-year-olds in the study, the program reduced the use of cigarettes, alcohol, and marijuana; lowered their likelihood of internalizing disorders (e.g., anxiety and depression); and improved the academic achievement of children born to mothers with low psychological resources (Kitzman et al. 2010, Olds et al. 2010). Fifteen-year follow-up studies found fewer arrests, convictions, and days in jail for mothers; reduced child abuse and neglect; and reduced arrests and convictions among the fifteen-year-olds (Olds 2006:5).[10] A nineteen-year follow-up showed fewer lifetime arrests and convictions and indications of greater sexual restraint and responsibility among the nineteen-year-olds, with particularly significant results among the female children of nurse-visited mothers. The intervention delayed the age at which girls had been (if at all) first arrested and reduced the incidence of arrests for serious and violent crime by the girls (Eckenrode et al. 2010).

The frequency of home visits changes with the stages of pregnancy and is adapted to meet parents' needs; when parents are experiencing crises, the nurses are permitted to visit more frequently than program protocol specifies (Olds 2010:57). Women were enrolled in the NFP trials no later than the end of the second trimester, after which nurses completed an average of 9, 7, and 6.5 visits during pregnancy and 23, 26, and 21 visits from birth to the child's second birthday (in Elmira, Memphis, and Denver, respectively). Each visit lasted approximately 75–90 minutes. Nurse–Family Partnership nurses follow detailed visit-by-visit guidelines. During pregnancy, they work to educate women about and help them to improve behaviors and practices that contribute to pregnancy complications and poor birth outcomes, including the quality of their diet, adequate weight gain, ciga-rette smoking, and use of alcohol and illegal drugs. Nurses' activities include teaching women to identify the signs of pregnancy complications, encour-aging them to seek medical attention for these complications and also to use preventive care, and helping to facilitate womens' compliance with doc-tors' recommendations and treatment (Olds 2010:57–58). The nurses also work to prepare the expectant mothers for parenthood through discussions of infant behavior and care and conversations about the women's hopes and expectations and their own childhood experiences with their parents. Dur-ing home visits following the birth of the child, in addition to assessing and providing education on infant/toddler nutrition, health, and environmental safety, nurses assess parent–child interaction, model activities that promote sensitive parent–child interactions and that in turn facilitate developmental progress, and guide parents in fostering social support networks.

Short-term outcomes of the studies (changes that occur by completion of the program, when the child turns two) report substantial improvements in sensitive and competent parental caregiving for infants and toddlers, including decreases in child-rearing beliefs associated with child maltreat-ment, increases in stimulating home environments, and increased father involvement in childcare and support. Intermediate outcomes (changes that are measured within 2–6 years of program completion) include con-tinued improvements in stimulating home environments, higher rates of fathers living with the mother and child, and higher rates of marriage. Long-term outcomes (changes that require a greater time to measure, often 10 or more years following program completion) include a decrease in arrests and adjudication for incorrigible behavior involving the children (e.g., truancy, destroying property), and fewer arrests, convictions, and days in jail for the parents. In addition to reducing involvement with the crimi-nal justice system for both mothers and children, low-income, unmarried nurse-visited women are more likely to participate in the workforce than their counterparts in the control groups (Olds, Henderson, and Kitzman 1994; Olds et al. 1998; Kitzman et al. 2000). It is important to understand that in the case of many of these findings, the difference between nurse-visited families and the control group is substantial. For example, in the

Elmira study, during the first two years of life, nurse-visited children born to low-income, unmarried teens had 80 percent fewer verified cases of child abuse and neglect than their counterparts in the control group; that is a difference of one case (or 4 percent) in nurse-visited families versus eight cases (or 19 percent) in the control group (Olds 2010:60). Another striking difference was seen in the intervals between the birth of the mothers' first and second children: these intervals were *more than 30 months longer* in nurse-visited mothers than mothers in the control group (Olds 2010:61). The risk of rapid, successive pregnancy is high in the population the NFP serves, and it has an enormous impact on these families, both in relation to maternal educational achievement and workforce participation and to the health and well-being of the children—something we shall examine later in this chapter.

An economic evaluation of the NFP by the Rand Corporation, which extrapolated the results of the 15-year follow-up study in the Elmira trial, found that the savings to government and society for serving families in which the mother was low-income and unmarried at registration exceeded the cost of the program by a factor of four over the life of the child (Olds 2002:164). The return on the investment was realized before the child's fourth birthday, with primary savings found in reduced welfare and criminal justice expenditures and increases in tax revenues. More recently, a cost–benefit analysis of preventive interventions conducted by the Washington State Institute for Public Policy (WSIPP) relied on data from all three trials of the NFP and estimated that on a per-family basis, government and society realize a $17,000 return on investment over the life of the child (Aos et al. 2004; Olds 2010:69). In contrast, many of the other early childhood interventions examined in the WSIPP analysis failed to realize a return on investment, despite large per-child investments in preventive services beginning early in life. This helps to show that although early interventions have the potential to produce savings to government, not all of them do, and policy makers would be wise to invest in those programs that have demonstrated their effectiveness. The way in which the NFP helps to lower government spending is significant not only because a number of different sources of spending are affected but also because the savings are

seen consistently over many years. For example, one NFP twelve-year follow-up study showed that during the twelve-year period following the birth
of the children, government spent less per year on food stamps, Medicaid,
and Aid to Families with Dependent Children and Temporary Assistance
for Needy Families for nurse-visited families, compared with families in the
control group. The government savings outweighed the program cost (Olds
et al. 2010). Nurse–Family Partnership findings also show that both the
functional and economic benefits of the program are greatest for families at
greater risk. As Olds points out,

> Cost analyses suggested by the program's cost savings for government
> are primarily attributable to benefits accruing to this higher risk group.
> Among families at lower risk, the financial investment in the program
> was a loss. This pattern of results challenges the position that these kinds
> of intensive programs for targeted at-risk groups ought to be made avail-
> able on a universal basis. (Olds 2010:68–69)

Such a practice would not only be wasteful from an economic standpoint;
it would carry the risk of diluting NFP services for families who most need
them due to insufficient resources to serve everyone effectively.

One of the distinctive features of the NFP is its grounding in epidemiology and developmental theory. In the following sections of this chapter,
I will focus on some of the theoretical foundations of the NFP and how
Confucian views stack up with this evidence. But it is important to begin
by noting that there are a number of more general areas in which the
approaches of the NFP resonate strongly with early Confucian views of
parent–child relationships, moral cultivation, and the role of the family in
creating and maintaining a good society. The NFP focuses on promoting
the distinctive kind of parental caring that, on the view of the early Confucian thinkers we have examined, provides the foundation for a child's
moral development. The long-term findings of NFP studies show that
the impact of the program is seen far beyond the home, which illustrates
the Confucian belief that good nurtured within families naturally extends
out to society. The NFP and the early Confucian views we have examined

share the view that many if not most societal problems have their deepest origins in the family and more particularly in parent–child relationships. They also share at least two of the reasons for having this view; first, that the prenatal period, infancy, and early childhood together represent a unique and irreplaceable time to intervene in a person's life; and second, that parents have a highly unique role in shaping their children through the care they provide. The NFP and the early Confucian thinkers we examined earlier in this work share an interest in the process of self-cultivation for both parents and children, and they both endorse the view that working to strengthen relationships of care and support within families and communities is the most successful approach to solving some of the most intractable social problems. These approaches contrast readily with—and can, in the right contexts, be more effective than—approaches that focus primarily on offering financial assistance or providing support for individuals without also enlisting the support of an individual's family and community.

The early Confucians obviously did not have access to the sort of scientific evidence that provides the foundation for the NFP, but their observations led them to some of the same conclusions that motivate the NFP. For many early Confucian thinkers, it is critical that we give attention to the early months and years of children's lives, because this is when the beginnings of our moral inclinations and responses, like fragile sprouts, require the greatest protection, care, and nurturance. Jia Yi's account of prenatal cultivation and its implications for moral development further extend this view, and as we shall see in this chapter, some of his reasons for advocating prenatal cultivation resonate with the reasons why the NFP enrolls women during pregnancy. The NFP and most other early childhood intervention programs share the same basic underlying assumption seen in the views of these early Confucian thinkers: "Early childhood—the prenatal period through the beginning of school—is a unique developmental period that serves as a foundation for behavior, well-being, and success later in life" (Karoly, Kilburn, and Cannon 1998:106). Like the NFP, a range of early Confucian thinkers contend that this period has greater potential for success as a time to intervene in the life of a child.

In addition to emphasizing the unique and critical nature of early infancy and childhood, the NFP and early Confucian thinkers further emphasize the role of parent–child relationships during these early years. When Mengzi writes that "among babes in arms, there is none that does not know to love its parents" he is describing an observable response in infants that he believes indicates significant moral potential, and in distinguishing "treating our elders as elders" from "treating our young ones as young ones," he exhibits an awareness that the way we interact with and care for our children is unique, as is the response of children to their parents. The NFP seeks to intervene in the lives of parents out of an awareness that parents are uniquely positioned to impact their children's lives, and vice versa. This is why the NFP seeks to intervene in parents' lives even before the birth of a child and includes program goals that concern the mother's well-being, including continuing education, employment, and future pregnancies. This aspect of the program is grounded in the realization that it is exceedingly difficult to intervene effectively in the lives of children without intervening in the lives of their parents. For example, mothers who participate in the workforce are more likely to expect their children to work as adults. But even more significant than the economic benefits of this is that it shows that nurse-visited families are more inclined to see themselves as members of and participants in a society, and thereby have a greater appreciation for shared societal standards and norms. Parents have an unequaled ability to instill this sort of appreciation in their children, and the NFP encourages this in part by helping parents to learn appropriate techniques for and approaches to disciplining their children. There is a marked difference between nurse-visited families and those in the control group on this count. Olds and his colleagues write,

> The higher rates of involvement and punishment and improved safety of their households, we believe, are reflections of their greater belief that their children must be disciplined and protected for them to succeed in school, work, and mainstream society. The relative lack of involvement and reduced use of punishment on the part of mothers in the comparison group, we hypothesize, reflects lower expectations for their children's participation in

mainstream society, and reduced efforts to promote discipline, conformity, and safety. (Olds, Henderson, and Kitzman 1994:95–96)[11]

The findings of the NFP have received a great deal of attention, in part because, as the *Journal of the American Medical Association* has noted, they stand in contrast with a range of other early childhood interventions. Although a number of other programs were designed to improve economic conditions as well as parental caregiving in low-income families, most have failed or produced only minimal effects; indeed, nearly every home-visitation program that has attempted to promote economic self-sufficiency has failed (Kitzman et al. 2000:1983).[12] Program founder David Olds notes that home-visiting programs differ in a variety of fundamental ways and the contrast between the NFP and other programs is striking in a number of areas, including the degree to which program goals and objectives are grounded in developmental research and epidemiology; the degree to which carefully specified theories of behavioral change underlie the clinical operation of the program; the specific populations offered the service; and the background, training, and qualifications of home visitors (Olds et al. 2000:110, 137–139). Distinctive features of the NFP include hiring registered nurses as home visitors, targeting women who have had no previous live births (in addition to focusing recruitment on women who are low-income, unmarried, and adolescents), and beginning the program during pregnancy.[13]

One of the most distinctive features of the NFP, compared with other early childhood intervention programs, is the degree to which solid theoretical foundations inform the design of the program. Since the original trial conducted in Elmira, the program has increasingly focused on its theoretical foundations, because they show how the program works. Accordingly, the NFP is an excellent example of how theory can influence practice. By integrating theoretical perspectives in psychology, including two that we will examine in this chapter—human ecology theory and attachment theory—the NFP is "substantially more effective than programs that are built on more limited theoretical foundations or without any theoretical foundations at all" (Olds et al. 1997:24).[14] It is to these theoretical foundations that we now turn.

HUMAN ECOLOGY THEORY, CONFUCIAN
SELF-CULTIVATION, AND THE FAMILY

Much of the NFP's success rests on having a carefully designed and reliable program of behavioral change, since it aims to help women to improve their prenatal health behaviors (e.g., reducing use of tobacco, alcohol, and illegal drugs; developing healthy eating habits; identifying obstetric complications and seeking treatment promptly) and to learn how to provide sensitive, competent care for their infants (e.g., reading and responding to babies' communicative signals, playing with them in ways that promote emotional and cognitive development, creating a household that is safe for children). In addition, nurse visitors "help women envision a future consistent with their deepest values and aspirations; they help women evaluate different contraceptive methods, child care options, and career choices; and they help women develop concrete plans for achieving their goals" (Olds 2010:54–55). All of these things involve helping women to change their way of seeing themselves and their children and to alter their behavior in positive ways as a result of and in connection with those changes. Yet as NFP founder David Olds points out, "Changing behavior is enormously challenging and usually requires more than simply educating parents about the consequences of their behavior. . . . It is here that having a theory of behavioral change . . . is crucial in devising promising preventive interventions" (Olds et al. 2000:137). By attending to the theoretical underpinnings of the program, the NFP aims to develop a theory of preventive intervention that is designed to promote adaptive behavioral change.[15] The theoretical foundations of the program help to explain how and why the program works, but they also continue to shape the program:

> In describing how these theories have shaped the design of the program and its refinement over time, we emphasize the continuity and change in the program and the role that theory has played in influencing practice. We view the program model as a work in progress that will continue to be

informed by clinical experience, scientific evidence, and theoretical developments related to its implementation and effects. (Olds et al. 1997:10)

Confucian philosophers would likely refer to the aspects of the program that address behavioral change as a program of self-cultivation, but one of the important differences between Confucian approaches to self-cultivation and the theoretical foundations of the NFP rests on the distinction between a "program" or "approach" and a "theory," in the technical scientific sense. It is critically important to understand that the theoretical underpinnings of the NFP are not "theories" in the ordinary language sense, which would make them somewhat akin to Confucian "programs" or "approaches" to self-cultivation, which—although they were refined informally over time—were not systematically studied and tested to determine their overall effectiveness. In contrast, the theories that form the foundations of the NFP are *scientific* theories. As Jerry Coyne points out, "in science, a theory is much more than just a speculation about how things are: it is a well-thought out group of propositions meant to explain facts about the real world," and in order for a theory to be considered scientific, "it must be *testable* and *make verifiable predictions.* That is, we must be able to make observations about the real world that either support it or disprove it" (Coyne 2009:15). All of the theories that underpin the NFP have been tested, and their predictions have been verified repeatedly through studies that meet certain standards (such as being randomized, controlled, and replicated in different settings); they are supported by large bodies of empirical evidence. It is important to understand this, because much of what these theories posit may sound like common sense to the average observer, but the insights and observations they provide are not just the perspectives or views of their founders and the scientists who conducted the studies, nor are they hypotheses that have been confirmed through only a few studies.

I will refer to the NFP's theory of behavioral change as a theory of self-cultivation, because it addresses the process of changing one's views, attitudes, and feelings as well as one's behavior. In this way, the NFP takes an interest in many of the same things that early Confucians referred to as self-cultivation. Much of the NFP's theory of self-cultivation is grounded in human ecology theory, which attends to the role that a parent's social context plays in the quality of her parenting, and self-efficacy theory, which attends to the way that a person's beliefs about potential outcomes and her own abilities influence the likelihood that she will change certain behaviors. However, I will focus on the former because of its particular continuities with the Confucian views that are the focus of this book.

Bronfenbrenner's (1979) theory of human ecology emphasizes the importance of the evolving relationships between different aspects of a person's social context and the way in which these relationships influence human development. The ecological environment "is conceived as a set of nested structures, each inside the next, like a set of Russian dolls. At the innermost level is the immediate setting containing the developing person," and other settings extend outward (Bronfenbrenner 1979:3). Bronfenbrenner's aim, though, is to look beyond single settings to the relations between them. According to human ecology theory, "such interconnections can be as decisive for development as events taking place within a given setting. A child's ability to learn to read in the primary grades may depend no less on how he is taught than on the existence and nature of ties between the school and the home" (3). Further, ecologic theory is grounded in research showing that "the person's development is profoundly affected by events occurring in settings in which the person is not even present," such as the impact of the conditions of parental employment on young children (3–4). Not only whether parents are employed outside or inside the home, but the kinds of employment they find, the environments in which they work, and the attitudes of parents' employers and coworkers toward employees with children all have a potential impact on the developing child. Additionally, Bronfenbrenner emphasizes that certain kinds of changes in the ecological environment— including those levels of the environment that are not the most proximate or innermost ones—can have a lasting effect on behavior and development:

> For example, research results suggest that a change in maternity ward practices affecting the relation between mother and newborn can produce effects still detectable five years later. In another case, a severe economic crisis occurring in a society is seen to have a positive or negative impact on the subsequent development of children throughout the life span,

depending on the age of the child at the time that the family suffered financial duress. (Bronfenbrenner 1979:4)

Human ecology theory highlights just how complex our environment is, and especially the fact that different contexts are not completely separate—even though they may appear to be—but often are related and influence one another in surprising ways. Additionally, human ecology theory highlights the multiplicity of ways in which these contexts impact us deeply, showing that the factors influencing children's development are not always simple and direct.

Even Bronfenbrenner's research models worked to take account of these features of human development. By applying human ecology theory to the laboratory and testing room, Bronfenbrenner had an important impact on research methods. Although the literature in developmental psychology often made reference to one of the basic units of analysis at the innermost level of the ecological schema, known as the *dyad*, or the two-person system, in practice, the principle was often disregarded due to the traditional focus on a single experimental subject. As Bronfenbrenner explains, this way of proceeding can be problematic when dealing with dyads, because data is typically collected about one person at a time, for example, about either the mother or the child but rarely for both simultaneously. When data is collected for both the mother and the child simultaneously, though,

the emerging picture reveals new and more dynamic possibilities for both parties. For instance, from the dyadic data it appears that if one member of the pair undergoes a process of development, the other does also. Recognition of this relationship provides a key to understanding developmental changes not only in children but also in adults who serve as primary caregivers—mothers, fathers, grandparents, teachers, and so on. (Bronfenbrenner 1979:5)

This approach highlights what Confucians would call the self-cultivationist aspects of Bronfenbrenner's work, and one aspect of his research that resonates with Confucian approaches to self-cultivation is his emphasis on the social nature of the process of cultivating the self. Instead of focusing solely on the individual and her volitional, emotional, and intellectual resources for change, Bronfenbrenner highlights the role that relationships play in our capacity to change and develop ourselves. As we saw earlier in this work, this is something the Confucians discussed at length, but ecology theory grounds such a view in a robust body of research concerning how we bring about change in ourselves and others. Not only does Bronfenbrenner emphasize the capacity for development and cultivation in adults as well as children, but also the impact that self-cultivation in parents has on developing children. In these ways, human ecology theory not only emphasizes self-cultivation but also the key role that parent–child relationships play in it, as well as the role of the larger family, community, and social context of which one is a part.

From this perspective, parents' care of their infants is influenced by a variety of factors, including the larger social context in which parents live: their relationships with family and friends, as well as the structural characteristics of and interrelations between their social networks, neighborhoods, communities, and cultures. Bronfenbrenner points out that "whether parents can perform effectively in their child-rearing roles within the family depends on role demands, stresses, and supports emanating from other settings" (Bronfenbrenner 1979:7). Parents' evaluations of their capacity to function and the way they view their children

> are related to such external factors as flexibility of job schedules, adequacy of child care arrangements, the presence of friends and neighbors who can help out in large and small emergencies, the quality of health and social services, and neighborhood safety. The availability of supportive settings is, in turn, a function of their existence and frequency in a given culture or subculture. This frequency can be enhanced by the adoption of public policies and practices that create additional settings and societal roles conducive to family life. (7)

These influences play a role in the quality of parenting and a person's willingness and ability to change and develop parenting skills, and they have a dramatic impact on developing infants and children. This impact can be negative, as Bronfenbrenner's example of an economic crisis suggests, or it can be positive. As NFP findings show, "To the extent that parents have networks of family members and friends who share a commitment to the child, for example, parents' efforts to care for the child are enhanced" (Olds et al. 1997:11).

More recently, Bronfenbrenner (1992) has expanded upon human ecology theory to further refine the role of persons and processes in human development with the *person–process–context* model of human development. Whereas the original formulation of human ecology theory focused primarily on how various contexts shape children and families, Bronfenbrenner's person–process–context model gives greater attention to the role that parents sometimes play in selecting and shaping these contexts. This is done by focusing on the characteristics of persons and processes, in relation to contextual influences, and this model is an important part of the NFP's use of human ecology theory, because NFP nurses aim to help women identify the aspects of their environment that they can influence and to teach them how to take a proactive role in selecting and shaping those contexts. Here we can see another way in which human ecology theory presents evidence for a view that the early Confucians describe and argue for in their discussions of moral cultivation and parent–child relationships. While Confucian thinkers note we can select and shape certain contextual influences, seen for example in Kongzi's view that our efforts to bring about change in ourselves will be influenced by the degree to which we seek out friends who share our commitment to self-cultivation, the most powerful examples of this influence are seen in stories and anecdotes about parents who worked to shape the environments in which their children were being raised. Mengzi's mother moved three times, each time seeking to improve her son's context, because she recognized that her choices about where to live were having an impact on her son's development. This is a tangible illustration of Bronfenbrenner's view that parents sometimes play an important role in selecting and shaping their children's contexts.

The person–process–context model is seen in the NFP's emphasis on program processes, which are seen in the ways the nurse visitors work with parents; processes within parents, which are seen as the influence of parents' psychological resources (such as developmental histories, mental health, coping styles) on behavioral adaptation; and processes that occur within the context of parents' interactions with their children and with others (Olds et al. 1997:12). The program views parents as developing persons, which makes them the primary focus of the intervention:

> Particular attention is focused on women's progressive mastery of their roles as parents and as adults responsible for their own health and economic self-sufficiency. The home-visitation program emphasizes the development of the parent because parents' behavior constitutes the most powerful and potentially alterable influence on the developing child, particularly given parents' control over their children's prenatal environment, their face-to-face interaction with their children postnatally, and their influence on the family's home environment. (11–12)[16]

Human ecology theory, then, not only leads the NFP to acknowledge and respond to the ways in which parents' contexts shape and affect the kinds of parents they become but also the ways in which parents are themselves growing individuals who are capable of change and capable of impacting—to varying degrees and in varying ways—the contexts in which they live.

One of the main hypotheses of human ecology theory is that "the capacity of the parent–child relationship to function effectively as a context for development depends on the nature of other relationships that the parent may have" (Olds et al. 1997:12). Parent–child relationships are enhanced when these other relationships involve mutual positive feelings and are supportive of the parent–child relationship, and they are impaired when the parent's other relationships involve antagonism or interference with the parent–child relationship (Bronfenbrenner 1979:77). As a result, human ecology theory is particularly evident in the degree of emphasis the NFP places on encouraging the involvement of other family members and friends in mothers' attempts to improve health-related behaviors and to prepare for parenthood. The NFP aims not only to acknowledge the impact of their relationships with family members, friends, neighbors, and other members of their communities, but also to help parents to negotiate these relationships. Nurses spend considerable time working with mothers on the roles and responsibilities of fathers and encouraging the father's involvement in all aspects of the program, so long as the mother wants him to be involved and there is a constructive basis for the relationship (Olds et al. 1997:11; Olds 2002:156). Rates of marriage are higher among nurse-visited women in the program, as are rates of fathers' involvement, which is significant, because marriage has been shown to increase the likelihood of economic self-sufficiency and lowers children's risk for a range of different problems (McLanahan and Carlson 2002; Olds 2002). Yet as Olds points out,

> It would be a mistake to conclude that simply promoting marriage for unmarried pregnant women is the right approach, without considering the quality of the possible relationship and the risk for domestic violence. The decision to marry is complex and requires careful consideration of whether the father (or other prospective partner) can be a good spouse and positive caregiver. (Olds 2010:54)

Accordingly, nurses help women to reflect carefully on their options and the many different aspects of their decisions concerning marriage and fathers' involvement. Interestingly, Olds writes that although the fathers are sometimes ambivalent, unprepared, abusive, or involved in criminal activities, in the majority of cases, fathers are eager to be supportive partners and providers for their children (Olds 2010:54). This is significant, because it helps to show that although high-risk families may not know how to provide support or may not believe they are capable of doing so, they may nevertheless wish to be supportive. This is why the NFP gives attention to improving partner communication and commitment.

The NFP also works to involve other family members, including grandparents. In the Elmira study, by the end of the fourth year after the delivery of the child, other family members played a greater role in the care of the children than did family members in the comparison group (Olds et al. 1997:13). There are some very tangible ways in which the presence of supportive family members and friends enhance a child's environment, some of which go directly to the safety and basic care of the child. Isolation from supportive family members and friends is associated with higher rates of abuse and neglect, something that is particularly important, because it shows that simply encouraging women to be more independent or providing material forms of support is not an adequate solution (Gabarino 1981). Although the NFP aims to address material factors such as unemployment, poor housing, and household conditions—all of which are also associated with higher rates of abuse and neglect—and although the program also encourages women to recognize the control they do have over their life circumstances, this is done in concert with the process of helping women to cultivate their relationships with and reliance on others. This aspect of the program is especially interesting from a Confucian point of view, because the program aims to help not by focusing on individuals in isolation but by addressing them in relationship to others and primarily to family members. As we have seen, beginning very early, the Confucian tradition emphasized the idea that members of families and communities ought to rely upon one another and cultivate complementary roles in order to function harmoniously. Early Confucian thinkers denied that addressing material conditions primarily or alone was adequate for helping to improve the overall quality of people's lives, and they argued that reliance on and cooperation with others—and especially family members—is good for all of us. Central among those family relationships, from a Confucian standpoint, is the parent–child relationship, and this relationship continues to serve as a special and unique source of support for both parents and children, not just during childhood but throughout the entire course of our lives. We have seen in this work that the Confucian emphasis on the fact that parent–child relationships continue to have an important role throughout our lives is unique alongside most views in the history of Western philosophy.

The early Confucians also maintained that the family plays a special role in self-cultivation and that the right sorts of relationships can help us bring about change in ourselves. Research in ecology theory also provides support for this view. There are some highly specific ways in which the informal support (or lack of support) of family and friends is seen in human ecology theory. For example, women's attempts to quit or reduce cigarette smoking during pregnancy "are affected by whether individuals close to them believe that smoking is bad for pregnant women and the fetus, and whether they actively support women's efforts to quit" (Olds et al. 1997:13). Similarly, the involvement of family members, friends, and boyfriends or husbands is "especially important in helping women practice contraception, finish their educations, and find work" (13). This type of evidence helps to show how important it is for nurse visitors to encourage the involvement of other family members and friends and enlist their support. Nurses make every effort to conduct some of the discussions of family planning and contraception when mothers' boyfriends or husbands are present, and in recognition of the fact that finishing school or finding a job depends on finding appropriate childcare, nurses help mothers to identify safe and nurturant care within their social network or, if none is available, to find appropriate subsidized care elsewhere. This task is enormously difficult, and although NFP families do much better than the control group, the level of participation by others during the nurses' visits is lower than first expected. In the Memphis program, only 14 percent of nurses' visits were completed with grandmothers participating, even though two-thirds of the sample were under the age of nineteen at registration and living at home and in spite of nurses' offers to schedule visits in evenings and on weekends (13–14). It is partly because these mothers are not situated in supportive families and social contexts that they are at risk in the first place, but it is also because they are, in many cases, adolescents asserting their independence. When the NFP examined the reasons why grandmothers were not more involved, many of the adolescent mothers indicated that they preferred to have the nurses to themselves and did not want their mothers present (14). Yet regardless of whether or not the mothers wish for their own parents to be involved in a supportive capacity, the evidence shows that mothers improve their chances of success when their social support networks are engaged. It is important to understand that this evidence does not undermine the view that we ought to empower women, but it does undermine the view that empowering women means always encouraging them to do things on their own. Rather, this evidence suggests that mothers are more able to succeed in reaching their goals—and, in turn, become more confident in themselves—when they are actively supported by a network of family and friends. Mothers are capable of change and improvement, but the right conditions—especially being surrounded by supportive family and friends and having those individuals recognize that their contribution is important—play an enormous role in their success or failure.

In addition to this emphasis on working to build, enhance, and deepen mothers' informal social support networks and their skills for navigating and drawing upon family and friends, human ecology theory also focuses NFP nurse-visitors' attention on assessing families' needs and helping them to make use of community services. This includes not only various forms of financial assistance but subsidized housing and assistance with finding clothing and furniture. An especially important part of the program is the way in which nurse visitors work to link mothers with their primary-care physicians and nursing staff. With the mothers' permission, the visitors maintain contact with the mothers' and children's primary-care providers, sending them written reports communicating their health and social needs and following up by phone as needed to devise a plan of care. This plays an important larger role in the way mothers view their doctors, since "the visitors can clarify and reinforce recommendations made by the office staff and thus help ensure greater compliance with physician and nurse recommendations" (Olds et al. 1997:15). Nurses work to teach parents to attend to their own health during pregnancy and to observe their children's indicators of health and illness, instructing parents on such things as how to use a thermometer and when to call the doctor's office. In providing instruction in these areas, nurses aim not only to improve overall health outcomes for mothers and babies but to increase preventive care and decrease inappropriate use of emergency and primary care. Nurse–Family Partnership nurses have also improved the health and human service system in the communities where they worked in significant ways. For example, in Elmira, the nurses advocated against and helped to abolish required fees for childbirth education classes, which made them more accessible to low-income families. In Memphis, NFP nurses challenged a group of school principals who were not allowing pregnant girls to attend school, despite the fact that this practice conflicted with state law.

Another important way in which human ecology theory has influenced the NFP is its decision to enroll women who have had no previous live births and to enroll them no later than the second trimester of pregnancy and to continue services through the child's second birthday. These factors are important, because according to human ecology theory, people are more likely to change their behavior when they are undergoing a major role change known as an *ecological transition*. Bronfenbrenner highlights the developmental significance of ecological transitions—"shifts in role or setting, which occur throughout the life span" (Bronfenbrenner 1979:6). Examples include the arrival of a younger sibling, entry into school, graduating, finding a job, marrying, having a child, changing jobs, moving, and retiring. Bronfenbrenner writes, "The developmental importance of ecological transitions derives from the fact that they almost invariably involve a change in *role*, that is, in the expectations for behavior associated with particular positions in society. Roles have a magiclike power to alter how a person is treated, how she acts, what she does, and thereby even what she thinks and feels" (Bronfenbrenner 1979:6). The evidence shows that first-time mothers are indeed more likely to change their behavior than women having a second or third child, and the prenatal period, together with the first two years of life, marks the most significant period of transition for new parents. This illustrates one of several ways in which the NFP is evidence-based; the evidence supporting human ecology theory is why the NFP enrolls first-time mothers during pregnancy and the program continues through the child's second year of life, and NFP findings lend further support to this body of research, especially because the NFP has been more successful than other intervention programs that begin after pregnancy, do not extend through the second year, or target the preschool years.

The research concerning ecological transitions is extraordinarily significant for our understanding of parent–child relationships and moral cultivation. Ecologic theory helps to explain why parents' behavior constitutes the *most potentially alterable* influence on the developing child, as it is based on evidence of the potential humans have to change their attitudes and behaviors, and the conditions and processes that help to facilitate successful change (Olds et al. 1997:12). This provides a solid foundation on which to build an account of moral cultivation, and it gives us good reasons to attend to many of the things the early Confucians highlighted in relation to moral cultivation, including parent–child relationships and the prenatal period. Although we have seen that the specific beliefs associated with early Confucian prenatal cultivation do not align with what we know about the influences on the developing fetus, the early Confucians were correct to highlight the unique importance of the prenatal period as the beginning of a child's development and the beginning of parents' responsibilities to their children. In addition to the evidence that pregnancy is part of an ecological transition, which means that women are especially able to bring about change in themselves during this unique period, there is abundant evidence concerning the observable effects of mothers' behavior and environment during pregnancy on the unborn child. Prenatal exposure to tobacco, alcohol, and illegal drugs are established risks for poor fetal growth, preterm birth, and neurodevelopmental impairment (e.g., attention deficit disorder or poor cognitive and language development).[17] These risks in turn give rise to cascading effects:

> Children born with subtle neurological perturbations resulting from prenatal exposure to substances such as tobacco and alcohol and to maternal stress and anxiety during pregnancy are more likely to be irritable and inconsolable and to have difficulty habituating to auditory stimuli in the first few weeks of life, making it more difficult for parents to find enjoyment in their care. (Olds 2010:53)[18]

This is one example of how the quality of the uterine environment can directly influence the quality of parent–child relationships and parental caregiving during the critical weeks and months following a child's birth. These factors, too, are influenced by a person's social context:

> Parents who are mature, married to supportive spouses, and have adequate incomes and few external stressors are more likely to manage the care of difficult newborns better than those parents without these resources. Unfortunately, children with subtle neurological vulnerabilities are more

likely to be born into households where these salutary conditions are not present, multiplying the likelihood that caregiving will be compromised. (Olds 2010:54)

The effects of the prenatal environment have long-term consequences, as well. Children who develop early-onset antisocial behavior, a kind of disruptive behavior that often characterizes children who grow up to become violent adolescents and, sometimes, chronic offenders, are more likely to have subtle neurodevelopmental deficits, sometimes due to poor prenatal health combined with abusive and rejecting care early in life (Olds 2010:55).[19] Further evidence indicates that prenatal tobacco exposure is a unique risk for conduct disorder and youth crime (55).[20] Adverse prenatal influences on fetal development are sometimes exacerbated by adverse experiences during infancy and early childhood, but it remains the case that a mother's behavior (and the support of the mother by the father and other family members) during the prenatal period plays a critical role in the development of her child. This includes the impact of a mother's behavior during pregnancy on the child's future moral development, seen, for example, in the established connection between adverse prenatal influences and youth crime. The early Confucians were correct to claim that a mother's behavior and environment during pregnancy have a direct and observable impact on her developing child, including, sometimes, long-term effects on the child's moral character. They were incorrect, of course, about the specific things that are harmful and the kind of impact they can have, and this is one area in which the Confucian view should be amended and developed further in light of what the evidence shows. For example, while it is not the case that there is a simple and direct relationship between the things that a pregnant mother looks at and her child's physical and moral character, it is the case that when pregnant mothers successfully bring about changes in themselves, it can have an enormous impact on a child's physical and moral character. While eating rabbit will not result in particular physical deformities, as some early Chinese thinkers believed, the things that a mother consumes do impact the developing child in critically important ways, many of which can have long-term consequences. Indeed, one of the evidence-based practices of the

NFP is that nurses help pregnant women to complete 24-hour diet histories on a regular basis and plot weight gains at every prenatal visit. Nurse–Family Partnership mothers improved the quality of their diets during pregnancy to a greater extent than mothers in the control groups, which, combined with reduced use of cigarettes, contributed to the superiority of their pregnancy and birth outcomes, including fewer preterm deliveries and low-birth-weight babies and fewer cases of neurodevelopmental impairment compared with the control groups (Olds 2010:58–68). These types of outcomes can help ground Confucian arguments for prenatal cultivation in a defensible and evidence-based view that would be acceptable to a contemporary audience.[21]

Together, human ecology theory, NFP findings, and Confucian views of prenatal cultivation should lead us to consider the experience of pregnancy more carefully, especially the way in which this unique experience might contribute to a person's capacity for self-cultivation. The research concerning ecological transitions and first-time mothers helps to show that parent–child relationships have a unique role in moral self-cultivation, because they impact both the parent *and* the child in deep and profound ways, and the evidence shows that this process begins before birth. While this evidence may concern some liberals and progressives because of its potential to be used in debates about abortion rights, ecologic theory and NFP findings deal with the impact of attributive personhood—regarding the developing fetus as a developing person and behaving accordingly—as opposed to the metaphysical question of when one becomes a person. The NFP enrolls women who have already decided not to end a pregnancy, just as Bronfenbrenner's research focuses on the ecological transitions of pregnant women who wish to carry their babies to term. The research shows that in these cases, the sooner there is attributive personhood, the better the outcomes will be for both mothers and babies. Nevertheless, we ought not to ignore scientific evidence simply because we worry that it might undermine our political or religious views. Anyone who takes scientific evidence seriously ought to be willing to reconsider her views in light of our best science; this applies equally to those who hold liberal or conservative views. The fact that a mother's behavior during pregnancy has an impact on her unborn child and that what happens in utero impacts a child's characteristics is well-established and uncontroversial. Whether this evidence ought to lead one to support restrictions on abortion is an open question.

In addition to its strong emphasis on the role and influence of families and communities in our lives, particularly in relation to self-cultivation, one of the clearest ways in which the NFP's application of human ecology theory resonates with Confucian ethics is in the view that parent–child relationships in particular have a special role in self-cultivation. Human ecology theory and NFP findings support the view that not only do parents shape their children's lives and character in unparalleled ways, but becoming a parent for the first time has unique potential to help shape a person's character. An interest in self-cultivation is a defining feature of Confucian ethics, and it is also a central feature of the theoretical foundations of the NFP. The fact that the program design is based on the theory that first-time pregnant mothers are more likely to cultivate themselves, something that appears to be an important factor in the success of the program, suggests a number of important things.[22] First, we have good reasons to be hopeful about the capacity for self-cultivation even in adults in some of the most challenging circumstances, as the target population of the NFP has always been low-income and often unmarried and adolescent. The most powerful evidence for the claim that self-cultivation is possible even in high-risk individuals may be that the impact of the program was consistently greater on those mothers and children who were at greater risk for the problems being measured (Olds 2010:6).[23] The economic benefits of the program are also greatest for families at greater risk (Olds 2002:153). This evidence shows that it is possible for people to make significant, lasting changes in their attitudes and behaviors, but there are particular circumstances under which this sort of change is more likely to occur, and these circumstances are dramatically shaped by changes in social roles. All of this is important, because it helps to show that the Confucians were right to focus so much of their attention on the nature of self-cultivation and how it works. As the Confucians maintained, we are capable of changing ourselves in deep and profound ways, even as adults, but this process is long and difficult, and we require a great deal of support along the way.

Human ecology theory and NFP findings also show that the experience of having and raising children is distinctive in terms of the way it impacts a person's willingness to work to change and improve herself. This should prompt us to consider some of the reasons why the early Confucians viewed having and raising children as such an important part of a good life. This feature of Confucianism is quite distinctive and marks an important contrast with many other ethical views. It is seen in the centrality of filial piety but also in the inclusion of parental roles in discussions of important social roles. Texts devoted to women's lives and virtues, such as *Collected Biographies of Women*, clearly express the idea that being a parent is a constitutive feature of the good life and document the critical role of mothers in a good society. Of course, there are multiple reasons why the Confucians emphasized the importance of having and raising children, including religious reasons and practical concerns about ensuring the care of oneself and one's family as one ages. However, another reason for having and raising children—and one that is deeply grounded in and inspired by the Confucian tradition of moral self-cultivation—is that it makes us better people. Although early Confucians did not explicitly argue for this view, a wide range of teachings and stories from the Confucian tradition express and illustrate the view that becoming a parent represents a unique opportunity for self-cultivation, including the descriptions of mothers who practiced prenatal cultivation and stories about the sacrifices that parents make for the good of their children. For example, earlier in this work, we saw that according to multiple early Confucian texts, the exemplary King Wen's virtue resulted in part from the fact that his mother, Tai Ren, practiced prenatal cultivation while she was pregnant with him and continued to exemplify a variety of virtues throughout his early childhood. The descriptions of Tai Ren's activities during pregnancy and her son's early childhood include following the rites and surrounding herself with people and things that are inspiring and virtuous—activities that were consistently a part of early Confucian accounts of moral self-cultivation and that surely not only furthered the moral cultivation of young King Wen but also that of Tai Ren. Even though she was already dedicated to following the Way, nothing in these stories suggests that her dedication to prenatal cultivation and her virtuous behavior during her son's early years did not also result in her own moral cultivation; from a Confucian standpoint, activities such as following the rites, when done in the right way, continually have a positive impact on the development of one's character. Indeed, the stories about Tai Ren suggest that she was more intentional about several aspects of moral self-cultivation when she became pregnant, and this surely resulted not only in her son's moral cultivation but hers as well. Although the Confucian view involves nothing as specific as Bronfenbrenner's claim that the ecological transition of having children enables self-cultivation in a unique way, such a view is certainly compatible with the early Confucian views we have examined and could be used to support and augment them. Indeed, this is one way in which the Confucian view could be developed to lend support to the claim that having and raising children is good for us from a self-cultivationist standpoint.

Human ecology theory has a clear link to important features of Confucianism in its emphasis on what we might call holistic approaches to problem solving, seen in the degree of attention given to the role of families and communities in helping the mothers to become good parents. Without question, one of the distinctive features of Confucian ethics is the amount of emphasis it places on the cultivation of a range of virtues that enable one to flourish within a family and community, as well as an emphasis on the good of the family, community, and society over against a narrower concern with the good of individuals. Human ecology theory and the findings of the NFP also underscore the importance of these things. Indeed, the results of the program reinforce the view that caring for a person produces tangible, quantifiable benefits, and this is true for both the mothers and their children. As we have seen, in addition to working to strengthen supportive relationships within families, nurses exemplify care and concern, and their impact on the families illustrates the difference that relationships of care and concern make in the lives of families. The NFP is explicitly designed to reduce social isolation and promote supportive and engaged families and communities who ideally participate together with women in caregiving and decision-making (Olds 2006:12). Although women often become more confident and effective agents through the NFP program—something that is seen in areas such as economic self-sufficiency—this is not primarily achieved by helping them to recognize their individual rights or autonomy but through relationships of care and trust and through a carefully designed program of self-cultivation. One of the strengths of the program is that it enlists family and friends in a common cause; rather than highlighting the individual alone with her rights, it embeds her in a supportive community. In doing so, the program promotes the development of individuals in ways that "go-it-alone" or strongly self-reliant views do not.

EARLY CHILDHOOD AND PARENT–CHILD RELATIONSHIPS IN ATTACHMENT THEORY AND EARLY CONFUCIANISM

Human ecology theory emphasizes the role of families and communities in the process of moral cultivation, which is something that Confucian thinkers emphasize more strongly than Western philosophers, historically. Yet Confucian views include more specific claims about the role of the family, including those concerning the unique and irreplaceable role of parent–child relationships in moral cultivation and the especially pivotal role that those relationships play before birth and during infancy and early childhood. Another main part of the NFP's theoretical foundations, attachment theory, explains these features of parent–child relationships by focusing on how the bonds between parents and children impact a child during the earliest stages of development.

In his groundbreaking 1969 work, *Attachment*, John Bowlby maintains that an infant's emerging social, psychological, and biological capacities cannot be understood apart from its relationship with its mother.[24] Bowlby's theory of attachment posits that "human beings (and other primates) have evolved a repertoire of behaviors that promote interaction between caregivers and their infants (such as crying, clinging, smiling, signaling), and that these behaviors tend to keep specific caregivers in proximity to defenseless youngsters, thus promoting their survival, especially in emergencies"

(Olds et al. 1997:19). This organization of behavior toward an infant's primary caregivers is *attachment*, and it has its origins in our biology; in order to promote survival, humans are biologically predisposed to seek proximity to caregivers in times of stress, illness, or fatigue—something we share with many other species. Attachment, then, is instinctive behavior associated with self-preservation, and it is a product of the interaction between one's genetic endowment and one's early environment. Not surprisingly, then, it is particularly apparent and "readily activated especially by the mother's departure or by anything frightening, and the stimuli that most efficiently terminate the systems are sound, sight, or touch of the mother" (Bowlby 1969:179). Attachment begins during the earliest hours and weeks of a child's life; as we shall see, by six months, there are dramatic differences between the behavior of infants who are securely attached to their primary caregivers and those who are not. Bowlby hypothesizes that the attachment system is readily activated until the end of the third year of life, when "some maturational threshold is passed," something that is supported not only by studies in attachment theory but also by our understanding of brain development (Bowlby 1969:205).[25]

Attachment theory further hypothesizes that children's trust in the world and their later capacity for empathy and responsiveness to others, including their own children, is traceable to their child-rearing histories and attachment-related experiences and specifically to the degree to which they formed an attachment with caring, responsive, and sensitive adults (Main, Kaplan, and Cassidy 1985; Olds 2002:156, 2006:14). Following Darwin's early observation that the first means of communication between a mother and an infant are facial expressions and other movements of expression in the body, research in attachment theory confirms the importance of "facial expression, posture, tone of voice, physiological changes, tempo of movement, and incipient action," all of which is experienced "in terms of value, as pleasant or unpleasant" and "may be actively at work even when we are not aware" of it (Bowlby 1969:120, 110–112). Bowlby stresses that the mother–infant attachment relation is "accompanied by the strongest of feelings and emotions, happy or the reverse," and that infants' capacity to cope with stress is correlated with particular maternal behaviors (Bowlby 1969:242, 344).

In addressing the fundamental dynamics of the attachment relationship, Bowlby writes that infants are active in seeking interaction and mothers' maternal behaviors are reciprocal to infants' attachment behaviors. The development of attachment is related to the sensitivity of the parent in responding to the baby's cues as well as to the amount and nature of their interaction (Bowlby 1969:346).[26] Accordingly, the set goal of the attachment system is not just proximity to the attachment figure but access to one who is emotionally available and responsive.[27] Neurobiological studies now identify the control system Bowlby described with the orbitofrontal cortex, an area that has been shown to mediate "the highest levels of control of behavior, especially in relation to emotion" (Price, Carmichael, and Drevets 1996:523; see also Schore 1994, 2003a, 2012). There are remarkable differences in the behavior of securely and insecurely attached individuals, and psychoneurobiological studies of the effects of positive and negative parental environments reveal important differences in brain organization as well.

This research is critically important, because it demonstrates that things such as our ability to control our behavior and our emotional health are heavily shaped by our earliest experiences with our parents and specifically the degree to which they cared for us in sensitive, responsive ways.[28] Attachment theory, then, helps us to appreciate why parent–child relationships during the earliest weeks, months, and years are so unique in their potential for changing the entire course of children's lives. Attachment behaviors highlight the unique ways in which children respond to their parents and the impact that good parental caregiving has on infants right from the start.

Attachment behaviors are established during the first months of a child's life, and their long-term consequences are well documented. Bowlby notes that a child's attachment is seen in a number of different forms of behavior as they occur in a variety of circumstances (Bowlby 1969:334). For example, Bowlby discusses an early study of the development of a child's attachment behavior by Mary Ainsworth and her colleagues, in which a sample of twelve-month-old infants from white middle-class families was observed in an unfamiliar ("strange") playroom they had not seen before that was equipped with a generous supply of toys. The infants were observed as they entered the room with their mothers and explored it first with their mothers present, and then as an unfamiliar adult entered the room and their mothers remained, as their mothers left the room while the other adult remained, and as their mothers returned to the room. Bowlby explains, "The procedure presents a cumulative stress situation in which there is opportunity to study individual differences in an infant's use of his caregiver as a base for exploration, his ability to derive comfort from her and the attachment-exploration balance as it changes during the series of changing situations" (Bowlby 1969:336; see also Ainsworth et al. 1978). During the initial period, when the infants were with their mothers only, most of the infants spent their time exploring the playroom while at the same time keeping an eye on mother. There was virtually no crying. Although the arrival of a stranger reduced the exploration of almost all infants, there was still virtually no crying. However, when mothers left the children with the stranger and then returned after a brief absence, the behavior of over half of the children changed abruptly; the differences in their behavior became much more evident and the existence of different patterns of attachment became apparent as well (Bowlby 1969:336–337). In one group were the infants who explored the unfamiliar room freely, using their mothers as a secure base, who were not distressed by the arrival of a stranger, who showed awareness of their mothers' whereabouts during her absence, and who greeted her on her return. Some infants showed some distress during the brief absence of their mothers while others weathered it without upset. In the other group were infants who were much alarmed by the stranger, who dissolved "into helpless and unoriented distress" in their mothers' absence, and who, when their mothers returned, did not greet them. Some of these infants also did not explore the room, even initially, when their mothers were present (Bowlby 1969:337).

Bowlby points out that an especially valuable index of the security of a child's attachment is the way the child responds to her mother when she returns after a brief absence. Securely attached children exhibit an organized sequence of behavior: after welcoming and approaching mother, they seek to be picked up and to cling or else remain close to her. Responses shown by other children are of two sorts: one appears to be disinterested in mother's return or avoids her, while the other is an ambivalent response, half wanting and half resisting mother. Three main patterns of attachment emerge when these criteria are applied to the way infants perform in this type of study: *securely attached* infants (a majority in most samples of this kind) are active in play, seek contact when distressed after a brief separation, are readily comforted, and soon return to absorbed play; *anxiously attached and avoidant* infants (about 20 percent in most samples) avoid their mothers during reunion, especially after a second brief absence, and many of them treat a stranger in a more friendly manner than their own mothers; *anxiously attached and resistant* infants (about 10 percent) oscillate between seeking proximity and contact with their mothers and resisting contact and interaction with them. Some are noticeably more angry or more passive than others (Bowlby 1969:337–338).

Research in this area has evolved and expanded to include diverse populations, including high-risk families such as those the NFP serves. Studies that examine the long-term consequences of attachment have been especially important for highlighting the critical importance of attachment, something that Bowlby notes even in his early work. In multiple studies, infants were revisited nine months later, at twenty-one months old, and given an opportunity to engage in free play and in play with an adult stranger. Those who had been classified as securely attached "engaged for a longer time in each episode of play, showed more intense interest in toys and gave more attention to detail, and they laughed or smiled more frequently than did those earlier classified as avoidant or ambivalent. In addition, the secure infants were more co-operative, both with mother and with other persons" (Bowlby 1969:362). A further study of this kind observed three-and-a-half-year-old children who had been classified as securely or anxiously attached as infants. In a nursery-school environment, with mothers absent, children who had been classified as securely attached infants "showed themselves to be more competent socially, more effective in play and more curious, and also more sympathetic to other children's distress, than those earlier classified as insecurely attached" (362). These findings have been replicated in a wide range of studies. Noteworthy features of securely attached children include the fact that they fare better not only emotionally, but also socially and intellectually. For example, as we shall see, even such things as language development are affected by attachment. This helps to show that one's emotional, social, and intellectual capacities are not completely separate domains; emotional health and well-being are closely related to social life and intellectual development.

This research also provides evidence in support of the claim that parent–child relationships provide the foundation for our moral development generally, serving as something like the root of a wide range of other virtues as well as moral capacities or sensibilities such as empathy. This is most significant in relation to early Confucian views, since one of the truly distinctive features of Confucian views is that they see the right kinds of parent–child relationships as providing the foundation for almost every virtue and moral capacity. Since attachment has such a dramatic impact on wide-ranging areas, including emotional vitality, empathy and sympathetic concern for others, social engagement, and intellectual development, this body of research lends support to a view that sees parent–child relationships not just as one of several roots of our development but as *the* root of our development in just about every area of human life. Here, then, we see the empirical evidence for the Confucian claim that a deep-seated love, appreciation, and respect for one's parents serves as the root of virtues such as reciprocity and sympathetic understanding, as well as one's enjoyment of and dedication to such activities as learning and reflection, and one's trust in others as well as one's own trustworthiness. The Confucian emphasis on a love of learning is not inconsequential here. Although we might expect attachment theory simply to confirm the role of parent–child relationships in preparing children to have healthy emotional and social lives, there is a close relationship between secure attachment in infancy and intellectual curiosity during infancy and childhood, including curiosity about our environment and our willingness to explore it.

Two aspects of early Confucian views on these matters stand in particular need of further refinement, based on what attachment theory tells us. The first is the specific nature of filial piety and the tendency of Confucians to focus more on respect and reverence than love and affection for and trust in one's parents—which seems clearly to characterize the attachment relation early on, even though this surely tends to give rise to respect for one's parents. The second is the importance of parents' loving, sensitive, and responsive feelings and actions toward the child, which elicit the child's response and therefore are the ultimate foundation for a child's development. Since the child's feelings and attitudes toward the parent are a response to the parent's caregiving, it is ultimately the parent's virtues (and not the child's filial piety) that serve as the foundation for the child's development. Although a number of early Confucian sources discuss the role of good parents in early childhood, including prenatal cultivation, and also offer anecdotes and stories about good parents (especially mothers), the virtues associated with good parental care, such as *qin* 親 ("loving," "affectionate") and *ci* 慈 ("kind," "loving"), still receive considerably less attention in Confucianism than does filial piety.[29] There is simply an imbalance in the amount of attention given to and the number of traditional stories and anecdotes about filial piety compared with good parental care, and this is an area in which Confucian views of parent–child relationships need to be amended and augmented by a fuller discussion of the ways in which filial piety depends upon good parental care.

One way of amending the Confucian view while retaining a strong emphasis on filial piety would be to account for the origins of filial piety by taking seriously the claim that filial piety is best understood as "the sense of gratitude, reverence, and love that children naturally feel when they are nurtured, supported, and cared for by people who do so out of a loving concern for the child's well being" (Ivanhoe 2007:299). If we link this view with the Confucian claim that filial piety is the source or root of the other virtues, then a particular view of parent–child relationships and moral cultivation emerges: good parental caregiving enables the development of filial piety, which in turn enables the development of the virtues. This type of view requires us to reject one of the central justifications for filial piety found in the Confucian tradition, namely the view that children ought to be filial to their parents simply because they owe their existence to them. But some early Confucian thinkers also recognized that the love and nurturance of good parents is one of the most powerful bases for filial piety, which reminds us that in embracing this view, while we are rejecting one of the main Confucian justifications for filial piety, we are accepting and affirming another Confucian justification.[30]

This line of argument could be extended by providing a fuller description of good parental caregiving and offering empirical support for this view. Attachment theory is an excellent resource for this type of support, and some of the evidence resonates with and complements early Confucian views in particularly compelling ways. For example, in *Analects* 17.21, Kongzi offers the intensive care that parents provide for their children during their first three years as a reason why it is appropriate for children to observe a three-year mourning period following the death of their parents. As we have seen, the first three years are the most pivotal time when it comes to attachment, and brain development is most rapid during the first three years, helping to explain why this serves as a particularly critical time developmentally. In offering the sustained care that parents provide during those early years as a reason why it is appropriate to follow the three-year mourning period, Kongzi suggests that good parental caregiving during the early years should give rise to filial piety on the part of children. Kongzi makes a normative claim here, but it seems reasonable to conclude that this normative claim is based on observations about children and their dependence on their parents during these early stages of development—even though it is not, of course, based on modern scientific research. We can see here how some early Confucian sources offer or at least suggest a more defensible basis for filial piety than the claim that children owe their existence to their parents. This example also shows how some Confucian observations about early childhood and parent–child relationships were accurate in surprising and even startling ways, such as the focus on the first three years of life.

There are dimensions of Confucian views of filial piety that are readily accounted for with reference to attachment theory, including evidence that loving, supportive parent–child relationships contribute immeasurably to the development of children's moral character.[31] The fact that parent–child relationships provide the foundation for children's moral development is seen in the emotions, attitudes, sensibilities, and inclinations of children who have been cared for in a sensitive, responsive manner, compared with those who have not. Attachment behaviors are often assessed through growth in infants' "emotional vitality" during the first year of life, including the dual features of emotional expression (reactivity) and an infant's increasing capacity to share emotional experiences with caregivers (reliance on mother). One thing that attachment theory highlights is the critical role of primary caregivers in supporting expression and regulation of emotions during the earliest months of a child's life: "The emotional vitality of the infant is a striking feature of its development during the first year of life. By 6 months of age, emotional expressions are well developed and contextually meaningful. Emotion responses have become shaped through interpersonal exchanges to reflect increasingly clear motivations and affective experiences" (Robinson and Acevedo 2001:402). Emotional vitality can be observed in infants' facial, vocal, and bodily cues, as well as in the duration of expressed emotion (Thompson 1994; Robinson and Acevedo 2001). These things can be observed over the course of an infant's earliest months, and the development of specific attachments during this period greatly impact emotional vitality, which is shaped by transactions with caregivers that encourage expressions of emotion and also help to regulate them, partly by sharing in them. Studies are increasingly finding that the causes of low emotional vitality are traceable to the earliest stages of development, including some that begin even before birth. Poor maternal prenatal diet and substance abuse during pregnancy may contribute to low birth weight and low emotional vitality, even in the absence of preterm birth.[32]

A wide range of studies have now examined attachment theory in low-income, ethnically diverse families with other high-risk factors and in earlier and later stages of infancy and childhood. A number of studies have examined the association between patterns of emotional reactivity and reliance on mother in infancy and cognitive and language developments in the same children as toddlers. For example, infants who displayed a pattern of combined high reactivity and high reliance on mother in response to positive, anger, and fear emotional challenges had higher cognitive and language skills at two years of age compared with infants who displayed patterns of low emotional reactivity and low reliance on mother. Children who showed high fearful distress and low reliance on mother and whose mothers had low psychological resources had especially poor outcomes developmentally (Robinson and Acevedo 2001:402–415). In the Robinson and Acevedo study, emotional vitality and vulnerability was measured at six months of age through infants' emotional reactions and the tendency to look at their mothers in response to fear, joy, and anger stimuli. An infant's social referencing or visual engagement of her parents in the face of uncertainty is a significant indicator of attachment. This behavior stems from infants' experience of responsive, attentive, sensitive care; infants do it because they are seeking comfort, reassurance, and assistance, and infants who do not turn to their parents are less effective in recruiting these kinds of support and may develop other strategies for diminishing their distress, such as dissociation and gaze aversion (Klinnert et al. 1983; Tamis-LeMonda and Bornstein 1989; Robinson and Acevedo 2001). Indeed,

> securely attached infants have the expectation that emotions will be responded to sensitively, hence, they communicate negative as well as positive emotions freely and share them with the caregiver. A pattern of minimizing and averting attention from emotion is thought to be typical of insecure/avoidant infants, whereas heightening fearful expressions are typical of insecure/ambivalent infants. (Robinson and Acevedo 2001:413–414)

This research helps to show that behaviors such as looking and reaching for parents, even when an infant is just six months old, are important indicators of attachment, which has enduring consequences for a child's emotional vitality. Infants are classified as emotionally vulnerable in response to fear stimuli if they have high distress reactions to fear stimuli, which coincide with limited efforts by the infants to look at or seek assistance or comfort from their mothers. Infants are classified as having low emotional vitality if they lack lively expressions of joyful and angry affect and do not share these expressions with others. Infants who are securely attached typically reference (or look at) their mothers and examine their mothers' expressions when they are presented with fear, joy, and anger stimuli. They also tend to have low distress reactions to fear stimuli and lively responses to joy and anger stimuli, while sharing these reactions with their mothers by referencing them and exchanging expressions. In contrast, infants who have had negative attachment experiences tend not to reference their mothers, have high-distress reactions to fear stimuli, and do not express joyful or angry affect in a lively way.

What this shows, of course, is that attachment behaviors relate not only to one's bond with one's parent or primary caregiver—seen in the tendency of infants to look at their mothers and to seek assistance or comfort from them—but also one's more general emotional health—seen in whether or not infants express joy and anger in a lively way and whether they are easily frightened. A key factor is how their emotional reactions to fear, joy, and anger stimuli *are joined with* their reactions to their mothers. Infants who have been cared for by their parents in a sensitive, responsive way will reference their parents when they encounter something new, are uncertain, or are frightened, because they have learned that their parents will provide support, comfort, and guidance. They reliably expect these things from their parents, because their parents have reliably provided them. Likewise, they reference their parents when encountering something enjoyable, because they have learned that lively expressions of joy are shared and encouraged. Infants enjoy seeing their parents' smiles, as parents enjoy seeing their infants' smiles. These are all important aspects of attachment behaviors.

There are important relationships between infants' attachment-related behaviors at six months and their subsequent development in a wide range of areas. The NFP has found that "six-month-old infants classified as 'vulnerable' in response to fear stimuli (high reactivity and low looking at mother) and 'low vitality' in response to joy and anger stimuli (low reactivity and low looking at mother) exhibited poorer language and cognitive development at twenty-one and twenty-four months than infants exhibiting high emotional vitality (high reactivity and frequent looking at mother)" (Olds et al. 2002:489). At six months, infants of nurse-visited mothers were less likely to exhibit emotional vulnerability in response to fear stimuli than those in the control group, and those born to women with low psychological resources were less likely to display low emotional vitality in response to joy and anger stimuli. At twenty-one months, nurse-visited children were less likely to exhibit language delays than children in the control group (491). This is a clear illustration of the far-reaching consequences of helping parents to provide more sensitive and responsive care for their children during the earliest months of life.

Attachment theory further demonstrates how direct and observable the consequences of good parental caregiving are over the entire course of a person's life, a main focus of the NFP, which seeks not only to nurture positive attachment experiences in infants but also to address the negative attachment experiences of mothers and their impact. Attachment theory posits that the capacity for empathy and responsiveness to others has its origins in our child-rearing histories and specifically in our attachment-related experiences. Forming an attachment with a caring, responsive, sensitive adult is a critical part of what normally enables one to become a sensitive and responsive parent (Main, Kaplan, and Cassidy 1985; van IJzendoorn 1995). A growing body of research suggests that our attachment-related experiences are encoded in "internal working models" of self and others that give rise to styles of emotional communication and relationships that buffer the individual in times of stress or lead to maladaptive patterns of affect regulation and feelings of worthlessness. Differences in internal working models, according to attachment theorists, have enormous implications for mothers' capacities for developing sensitive and responsive relationships, especially with their own children (Olds et al. 1997:19). This means that one of the keys to affecting the attachment experiences of young children is finding ways to address and try to repair the damage inflicted by the negative attachment experiences of their parents. Accordingly, attachment theory has affected the design of the NFP home-visitation program in three main ways, the first two of which explicitly deal with the attachment histories and tendencies of the mothers. It is important not to overlook this, for it shows once again that the NFP aims not simply to affect children but also their parents, and the program acknowledges that changing the lives of the children through preventive intervention requires changing the lives of their parents. This change, in turn, presupposes the ability of adult human beings to change their attitudes and behaviors in significant ways (i.e., to evidence the capacity for moral self-cultivation).

Nurse–Family Partnership nurses help mothers and other primary caregivers review their own child-rearing histories through discussions of how they were disciplined as children and through identification of parents (either their own or others) they felt had done a good job of bringing up their children (Olds et al. 1997:20). Nurse visitors in the three trials introduced these topics at increasingly earlier stages. In the Elmira program, discussions began when the babies were around eight months old, in anticipation of the child becoming mobile, when discipline issues are likely to emerge. In the Memphis study, nurses introduced these topics around the sixth month; and in Denver, they began discussions with some families during pregnancy. Although flexibility is needed due to different families' readiness to address certain kinds of issues, nurse visitors often found that discussing these issues during pregnancy helped women and other caregivers to develop more accurate views concerning infant motivations and methods of communicating (20–21). This is particularly important, because nurse visitors found that parents with histories of unmet needs and hurtful treatment "often have distorted beliefs (working models or attributions) about themselves, others, and relationships that can interfere with their accurately reading children's cues and their own capacity for responsive nurturance" (21). It is most significant that simply getting mothers to reflect on their own experiences (and the experiences of others) can help them recognize that they should work to do things differently. Nurses then work to help women learn alternative strategies and methods of interaction. The fact that this is an integral part of the program shows the practical value of normative reflection on both one's own experiences and the experiences of others.

Another way in which attachment theory informs the program is through the "explicit promotion of sensitive, responsive, and engaged caregiving in the early years of the child's life" (Olds et al. 1997:19). Program protocols have been designed to offer a systematic presentation of how infants communicate through nonverbal cues and crying behavior, and how mothers and other caregivers can effectively read and respond to these cues. A great deal of emphasis is placed on effective ways to respond to the emotional needs of infants and toddlers, since it is within the context of these responses that infants attach to their parents (21). In recognition of how important this aspect of the program is, increasingly comprehensive parent–infant curricula were incorporated into the program in each of the three trials.[33] It is important not to underestimate the long-term effects of this process; as the evidence supporting attachment theory helps to show, the early relationship between parents and infants provides the foundation for just about every aspect of children's lives as they grow:

> Parents who empathize with their infants and sensitively read and respond to their babies' communicative signals are less likely to abuse or neglect them, and they are more likely to read their children's developmental competencies accurately, leading to fewer unintentional injuries. Competent early parenting is associated with better child behavioral regulation, language, and cognition. As children enter early elementary school, responsive and positive parenting can provide some protection from the damaging effects of stressful environments and negative peers on externalizing symptoms and substance use. In general, poor parenting is correlated with low child serotonin levels, which, in turn, are implicated in stress-induced delays in neurodevelopment. (Olds 2010:52–53)[34]

Nevertheless, despite the remarkable impact of helping women to review and reflect on their child-rearing histories and helping them to learn strategies and approaches that promote sensitive, responsive caregiving, it is likely that the most important way in which attachment theory has affected the design of the NFP program is something that is a much less explicit part of the curriculum: the kind of close, caring relationship that the nurses cultivate with the mothers. Specifically, nurse visitors aim to develop an empathic relationship with the mothers and, whenever possible, with other family members as well. The development of this sort of close, therapeutic alliance demonstrates to the mothers that "positive, caring relationships are possible. The parent begins to see herself as someone who deserves support and attention and by extension, sees her child as deserving the same" (Olds et al. 1997:19–20).[35] The reason why this aspect of attachment theory's influence on the NFP program is so important is that a mother's determination to avoid repeating neglectful and harmful behaviors to which she was subjected as a child, as well as her commitment to caring for her own child in a sensitive, responsive way, depends in some important ways on her own experience of having been cared for. Indeed, because many NFP mothers have little experience with consistently caring, supportive relationships, this may be the most important aspect of the NFP program as a whole. Through their own relationships with the women, the nurses model the kind of care and support that good mothers provide, which gives the mothers firsthand experience with how it feels to be cared for in these ways. The goal is to provide a "corrective" experience for those who experienced neglectful and abusive relationships in their own childhood and, unfortunately, in many cases, over the entire course of their lives so far. In each of the studies conducted, a sizable number of the mothers reported that they had never before experienced the sort of consistent care and support they received from the nurse visitor. Many noted that the care shown to them by the nurse visitor differed from the way their own parents related to them (Olds et al. 1997:20).

There is an important parallel between parental acts of love and care and the way the nurses enter into the lives of those they seek to help through empathy and care. The NFP reports that

> A critical feature of the program process was the development of a close therapeutic alliance between the nurse and the mother. That relationship, we hypothesize, enabled them to participate in and understand one another's worlds. . . . The connection of their separate social systems through their relationship strengthened the power of the program to produce significant shifts in the life course development and caregiving of the nurse-visited women. (Olds, Henderson, and Kitzman 1994:96)

The nurses serve not only as teachers but offer models or paradigms for how to care; they offer the mothers a sense of being cared for and this elicits a sense of gratitude. Like good parents, the nurses' actions express the priority of care over power and prerogative. Accordingly, they constitute the kind of relationship they seek to elicit from the mothers and others. The mothers, as a result of having been cared for in these ways, are more inclined to "give back" this care to their children, and this results not just from having seen the nurses model caring behavior toward their infants; it comes from having been the recipient of the nurse's consistent care and support.

This aspect of the NFP program resonates strongly with early Confucian views of Virtue or moral power (*de*). As we saw earlier in this work, a number of early Chinese thinkers maintained that humans have a natural tendency to gravitate toward and be influenced by those who are virtuous. The fact that nurses, in caring for the women, elicit a greater desire and capacity in the mothers to care for their own children is an example of this type of effect. Of course, in the NFP program, the caring relationship between the nurses and mothers is not a magic bullet; other forms of intervention are required, too, and even when nurturing, caring relationships between the nurses and mothers emerge, women still must work hard to bring about changes in themselves. But there is something to the Confucian view that moral behavior elicits the same from others, and since a major part of the NFP program is the way in which the nurses develop a caring, empathic relationship with the mothers, NFP findings provide tangible evidence of this view.

Since the hiring of nurses as home visitors was one of the major distinguishing factors between the NFP and other less successful home-visitation programs, a study was conducted to evaluate whether nurses are more effective than paraprofessionals (those with no formal training in the helping professions) as home visitors (Olds et al. 2002). Both nurses and paraprofessionals in the study received the same home-visiting guidelines, training, and supportive supervision in the NFP program model. For most outcomes on which either paraprofessional visitors or nurse visitors produced significant effects, including mother–infant responsive interaction, paraprofessionals typically produced effects that were approximately half the size of those produced by the nurses. Indeed, nurses produced more significant effects on a wide range of maternal and child outcomes, had lower drop-out rates among families visited, and had a lower number of attempted visits in which women were not at home (Olds et al. 2000:136, 2002:486, 494). Discussing the reasons for the nurses' effectiveness, the NFP cites their clinical experience, the fact that they are viewed as authorities due to their formal training in women's and children's health, as well as the public's rating of nurses as having the highest standards of honesty and ethics of all professionals (Olds et al. 2002:494; Olds 2006:15).[36] This explanation, however, could be augmented by a discussion of the virtues that are distinctively associated with nursing. An account of the character traits that help nurses to succeed in their profession and of traits that nursing provides unique opportunities to cultivate might help us to more fully understand the factors that enable nurses to help bring about change in the lives of high-risk mothers and potentially in other groups as well. Such a discussion might also shed light on how to more effectively cultivate these virtues in others.[37]

Several aspects of NFP studies indicate that the early Confucians were right to think that a child's response to the unique nurturance and care that good parents provide during the earliest stages of development serves as the foundation for a range of other moral (and even intellectual) virtues and capacities. As we have seen, attachment theory demonstrates that parents' behavior as caregivers directly impacts a child's emotional and moral development. As Olds and colleagues note, "Attachment security is considered a reflection of the quality of parental caregiving and is associated with subsequent behavioral adaptation with peers" (Olds et al. 2000:135; see also Carlson and Sroufe 1995). Attachment theory provides evidence for some important aspects of Confucian views, including the beliefs that parent–child relationships provide the foundation for a person's moral development and that much of this foundation is built during the earliest stages of infancy. Without question, attachment theory establishes the claim that quality of parental caregiving during the earliest years has a unique and irreplaceable importance for a child's development.

Of course, there is nothing in attachment theory or NFP findings that necessarily indicates that *filial piety* develops in response to good parental caregiving, even though it is clear that children do seek proximity to their caregivers and that good parental care fosters their emotional, intellectual, and moral development.[38] Although one could use this evidence to ground a compelling account of filial piety, one could also describe the response of children to good parental care in other ways. Another important difference between Confucian views and attachment theory is that while the NFP focuses on parent–child relationships, the *Analects* and the *Mengzi* repeatedly discuss both filial piety *and* brotherly respect, which indicates that older siblings have a critical role to play along with parents in younger children's moral development. Indeed, *Analects* 1.2 includes both parental and sibling relationships in its discussion of the "root" of humaneness. Although the NFP actively encourages the involvement of other family members, something that is a part of its application of ecologic theory, the intervention targets mothers who are having their first child, and attachment theory does not provide evidence that parents and siblings play similarly critical roles, as some early Confucian texts suggest. A wide range of cross-cultural studies support attachment theory and affirm the unique importance of a child's attachment experiences with the mother in particular, but the role of elder siblings in a child's moral development is an area worthy of further consideration, even if it is not ultimately related to attachment theory. Indeed, support for the importance of siblings as well as grandparents, aunts, uncles, and other family members might instead be found in ecologic theory.[39]

* * *

The evidence examined in this chapter lends support to a number of early Confucian claims about the critical role that families play in our lives, and especially the role that parents play in the lives and moral development of their children. Such evidence highlights the unique and irreplaceable importance of parent–child relationships during the earliest stages of infancy and childhood and shows us the unparalleled consequences of sensitive, responsive parental care during these early weeks, months, and years of children's lives. As the Confucians argued, even during the prenatal period, a mother's behavior can have a tremendous impact on the future development of her child. This research supports the Confucian view that children's responses to parental caregiving serve as the foundation for the development of their character.

The Confucians further argued that these are not tangential issues in relation to political questions, nor do discussions of the family, parent–child relationships, and early childhood moral education belong to some separate, private realm. Rather, as a number of Confucian thinkers argued, the question of how to support and nurture the right kinds of parent–child relationships during the early years of children's lives is the single most important question to address in working to create and sustain a good society. The evidence examined in this chapter lends support to this view as well, but as we shall see in the next chapter, our policies and social practices in the United States do not even begin to conform to the evidence. The bulk of public spending on children in the United States currently occurs not during early childhood but during the school-age years. The United States is one of the only countries that does not require employers to offer paid leave to new parents, and the duration of unpaid leave for new parents is extremely short compared with the duration of paid leave offered in other Western countries. These and many other aspects of our public policies as they relate to parents and young children do not cohere with what the evidence tells us we should be doing, not only from the standpoint of raising good citizens and sustaining a good society but also from the standpoint of fiscal responsibility.

Now that we have seen how Confucian views of the relationship between parent–child relationships, early childhood, and moral cultivation are distinctive, and also the ways in which some of the central tenets of these views are supported by our best science, an important question remains. What is the constructive value of Confucian views in relation to the kinds of challenges mentioned above? How can Confucian views serve as a resource to inform and enhance our understanding of these problems and their potential solutions, as well as our efforts to promote not only changes in public policy but also positive social change within our own families, communities, and the larger culture in which we live? In the final chapter of this work, I consider these important questions.

6

THE HUMANITIES AT WORK

Confucian Resources for Social and Policy Change

HOW MIGHT EARLY Confucian views of parent–child relationships and early childhood moral cultivation serve as a constructive resource for us today? I contend that Confucianism can help us reconsider the role of parent–child relationships in a good society and that if we take Confucian views seriously, we will be led to endorse certain kinds of social and policy change. I begin by addressing how early Confucian views on these matters can contribute to discussions in contemporary political philosophy, but in the remainder of this chapter, I argue that Confucian views can make contributions that go beyond theoretical discussions. I highlight the critical role that cultural attitudes and norms play alongside public policy in promoting change, and I offer an account of how Confucian views can serve as a unique resource in our efforts to take seriously, in both our policies and practices, the central role of parent–child relationships during the earliest years of children's lives. I focus on a number of specific areas, arguing, for instance, that while a significant period of paid leave for new parents ought to be mandated in the United States, new parents also must understand why it is important and worthwhile to take a significant period of time off from work after having a child, and they must be confident that they will not be penalized for doing so. The feelings, attitudes, and beliefs that new parents have on these matters are shaped by the attitudes and beliefs of their families, friends, employers, and coworkers, and I argue that Confucian sources can serve as a helpful resource for promoting needed change in this area. I further propose that this serves as a helpful illustration of how the humanities can serve as an important resource for promoting social and policy change. Indeed, in arguing for the contemporary relevance of early Confucian views, I am offering an example of how the sciences and the humanities can come together in mutually supportive ways to promote real change.

PARENTS, CHILDREN, AND JUSTICE: HOW CONFUCIANISM CAN INFORM WORK IN POLITICAL PHILOSOPHY

One of the most influential political philosophers of the last century, John Rawls, emphasizes the role that political institutions—and in particular, principles of justice—ought to play in working to address the forms of injustice that stem from three different kinds of moral contingencies. Each of the following contingencies, in Rawls's view, shapes citizens' lives in pivotal ways:

> (a) their social class of origin: the class into which they are born and develop before the age of reason; (b) their native endowments (as opposed to their realized endowments); and their opportunities to develop these endowments as affected by their social class of origin; (c) their good or ill fortune, or good or bad luck, over the course of life (how they are affected by illness and accident; and, say, by periods of involuntary unemployment and regional economic decline). (Rawls 2001:55)

Rawls argues that societies are structured in such a way as to contain various social positions and that people begin their lives in social positions not of their own choosing and that do not result from their own actions. These social positions shape our hopes and expectations, and the opportunities we have to fulfill those hopes and expectations are determined in part by the political system as well as economic and social circumstances. Rawls writes that

> the institutions of society favor certain starting places over others. These are especially deep inequalities. Not only are they pervasive, but they affect men's initial chances in life; yet they cannot possibly be justified by an appeal to the notions of merit or desert. It is these inequalities, presumably inevitable in the basic structure of any society, to which the principles of social justice must in the first instance apply. (Rawls 1999:7)

For Rawls, the concept of social justice entails the idea that citizens should not automatically be penalized for the disadvantages they face through no choice of their own. When Rawls says that citizens work for the ideal of justice for all, he is positing a good they all value—the good of having choices and control over their own lives and the good of not suffering for the inequalities in their prospects in life that arise from contingencies.

Throughout Rawls's discussion, when it comes to the development of one's capacities, including moral capacities, he continually returns to social class of origin, as opposed to the sort of family in which one is raised. Indeed, the family is not among the moral contingencies Rawls discusses, and yet it would be the very first and most important moral contingency on which Confucians would likely focus.[1] Of course, we can assume that in mentioning class position, Rawls means that our life prospects are deeply affected by the class position of the family we are born into, and it is true that class position has a substantial effect on the lives of families. Nevertheless, there is much about the kind of family one is born into that class position does not capture and that marks a deeper source of inequality between individuals born into a society than any other single factor.[2] Additionally, the other contingencies Rawls discusses, including native endowments and good or ill fortune over the life course, are both dramatically shaped by our families. We have seen that there is substantial empirical evidence to show that our "native endowments" or our capacities at birth can be shaped in highly significant ways by mothers' behavior and experiences during pregnancy, including nutrition, substance abuse, and the diagnosis and treatment of complications. Good or ill fortune in life in many cases stems from the family one has, and it is certainly mitigated substantially if one has a supportive, nurturing family to serve as a safety net when one suffers ill fortune. Of course, a family's class position matters as well, for this determines the extent to which we have financial resources to draw upon in cases of ill fortune. But it is important not to think about a family's resources in solely financial terms. Nurse–Family Partnership findings show that even when families continue to have limited financial resources, there can be marked improvements in other areas. For example, the program has been shown to help high-risk families to rely less on public assistance and to achieve economic self-sufficiency, but this does not mean there is a radical transformation in their class position. Nevertheless, in those same families there often are remarkable improvements in sensitive and competent parental caregiving for infants and toddlers and decreases in cases of child abuse and neglect. These latter qualities are not measured by class position, but they impact children's development in unparalleled ways.

Further, as we have seen, the family is a much more effective context for intervention if one wishes to address injustice. The most important point here is that NFP findings actually show that those who benefit most from the program are families at the highest risk. This is important, because it shows that intervening at the level of the family through evidence-based programs, and specifically those that address parent–child relationships during the prenatal period through the first two years of life, is more effective than many other forms of support at addressing the moral contingencies Rawls discusses and the profound injustices that stem from them. Now, this has some interesting implications for Rawls's "difference principle," because it shows that when we examine at least some forms of evidence-based policy, there is empirical evidence to support Rawls's view that those who are worst off ought to receive the greatest assistance. Nurse–Family Partnership findings consistently show that the families at highest risk benefit the most from the program. The economic benefits of the program are also greatest in those cases. Such data support the view that those who ought to receive such services are those who are most at risk, because they demonstrate that these families actually benefit most from intervention. In turn, society benefits most from early childhood interventions that target such families, most importantly in terms of the overall quality of society, seen in such areas as lower crime rates, but also because of the financial savings, which ideally would allow government to invest more of those dollars in other ways of supporting families.

The larger point I want to make, though, is that on a Confucian-informed view, the family ought to be our primary concern when addressing moral contingencies. It is more foundational and more influential than any of the other moral contingencies that Rawls discusses, seen in the fact that intervening into the lives of families can have a substantial impact on the other contingencies Rawls mentions. As we have seen in this work, remarkably, it is also the most potentially alterable aspect of a child's earliest experiences. One has absolutely no control over the family one is born into or adopted into as an infant or young child, and one cannot choose to exit one's family; even in those rare cases in which one chooses estrangement or is subjected to it, one still experiences the consequences of having spent the early years of one's life within a particular family. As we have seen, these consequences are nothing short of dramatic for us, emotionally, physically, and morally. Together, these things make the family an excellent candidate for the most important moral contingency we ought to focus on when examining the sources of injustice. It is not that we should not attend to other moral contingencies as well; clearly, families who endure hardship by virtue of their class position or in the form of injuries or disabilities, for example, ought to receive forms of support that work to address these disadvantages, which often give rise to pervasive forms of injustice. Class position and socioeconomic brackets are also important to attend to, because they can help us determine which families are most likely to benefit from a program such as the NFP. But since the inequalities owing to one's class position, native endowments, and good or ill life fortune are deeply shaped, mitigated, or deepened by the family, and also since the family (and especially the quality of parent–child relationships during the early years) has a greater influence on one's overall capacity to flourish in life than any other single factor, we have good reasons to prioritize the family in relation to the task of addressing the sources of social injustice. Although I have argued elsewhere that Rawls gives more attention to the family than he receives credit for, in this particular area of his political philosophy—and in the work of most Western political philosophers today—the role of the family is neglected. This represents a flaw in Rawls's account of the things that principles of justice ought to address, and this is one area where Confucians can help us not only develop a more plausible theoretical account of the role of the family in relation to the basic structure but also an account that is supported by and can be put into practice with evidence-based policy. I am not arguing that Confucian views provide us with all of the answers; they can, however, serve as a constructive resource in highlighting and working to improve upon areas within political philosophy that are lacking.

Now, others have insisted that the family deserves a more primary place in political theory and have engaged at length some of these same issues. For example, Susan Moller Okin argues that a just family is first among social institutions and an essential foundation of a just society, because it plays a fundamental role in sustaining justice (Okin 1991:17).[3] The most important thing for families to do, she argues, is to teach justice, including gender equality. However, as Philip J. Ivanhoe has argued, one of the difficulties with Okin's view is that it imposes a narrow liberal social agenda upon the family and obscures many of the goods one finds within family life (Ivanhoe 2010a). While families play an important role in cultivating many different moral attitudes, they do not exist solely or primarily for promoting justice, gender equality, or other specific political ends. As we have seen in this work, Confucian views offer a contrast to the type of view that Okin presents. Confucians defend the view that the kinds of love and care that are characteristic of nurturing families provide the foundation for our moral development. It is within the context of supportive parent–child relationships that children first experience what it means to be loved and cared for, for one's own sake. This experience, according to a number of the early Chinese sources we have examined, sparks a sense of gratitude and indebtedness and the beginnings of a desire to respond in these ways toward others—a view supported by a substantial body of research in the social sciences.[4]

These aspects of Confucian views give us good reasons to regard families as special kinds of social institutions—distinctive for being founded on intimate, interlocking personal relationships that provide the basis for most of our moral capacities (Ivanhoe 2010a). In this work, we have seen there is significant evidence to support the view that this is true not only for children but for parents as well; becoming a parent represents a unique opportunity for moral cultivation by strengthening individuals' capacity for change. In contrast with the views of both Rawls and Okin, Confucian accounts point away from the unique importance or centrality of justice. While early Confucian sources acknowledge that families help cultivate in us an initial sense of justice, this capacity is but one of many moral capacities nurtured in this context. Although there are good reasons to think that a sense of justice guides our future thinking about and concern for other members of society, justice does not have a unique or foundational place in our early moral development generally. As we have seen, the unique forms of support, responsiveness, nurturance, and love that parents offer, and children's subsequent responses to the care they receive, play the most important role in the early moral development of infants and children. Confucian accounts emphasize these aspects of our early experiences within the family, and as a result they offer a model of an account that does not take justice to be central to our early development.

The fact that early Confucian views align closely with our best science concerning early development and its long-term consequences suggests we have good reasons to question views that place justice at the center of discussions of the family in relation to political philosophy and ethics. It also suggests the family ought to be viewed as a special kind of social institution, one with an absolutely pivotal role in the basic structure of society. This means that not all matters relating to the family, especially those relating to the care of children, ought to be considered part of a private realm not to be intruded upon by the kinds of laws and policies governing the public realm. Given the fact that a number of central Confucian claims concerning these matters are supported by evidence-based approaches, political philosophers ought to accord the family more support and attention as a part of the basic structure of society. Specifically, our social and public policies ought to extend further than they currently do by providing certain forms of support for families. Evidence-based policy—with the NFP being an excellent example—shows that the early Confucians were right in claiming that parent–child relationships during the earliest stages of a child's development represent a unique and irreplaceable opportunity to nurture members of a society and to impact the quality of a society more generally. More than any other social institution, the family represents an opportunity to intervene in the lives of future and current members of society in ways that make a real difference. In the next section, I will specify the particular kinds of policies this type of approach would support, but for now I want to point out that in viewing the private and public spheres as permeable and in endorsing the view that the family constitutes a special kind of social institution deserving of support, I am not arguing that families should be monitored, regulated, and policed, or that our public policies should force individuals to make certain types of choices with respect to their families. As I will argue in the following section, one of the distinctive features of early Confucian political views is that they explicitly argue against approaches that place a strong emphasis on laws and policies. I am, however, calling for a more moderate view, wherein families are offered greater support because of their unique role as a social institution. This type of support, as we shall see, ought to provide more options and greater flexibility to families who wish to make choices that nurture and strengthen familial relationships and children's development (e.g., paid leave for new parents); it in no way imposes an agenda upon or forces families to make certain kinds of choices. We should, though, give families certain options and help them understand why taking advantage of those options is worthwhile. As I will argue in the next section, this process will involve not only certain forms of policy change but also changes in some of our cultural attitudes, beliefs, and practices.

The larger point to be made here is that we have good reasons to think that the tasks of nurturing parent–child relationships and creating and sustaining a good society are more closely related than most political philosophers treat them, and early Confucian views can provide a resource for working to expand our understanding of how we ought to view the basic structure of society in light of this relationship. This should be of interest not only to political philosophers, though; one reason why we should deal with the boundary between the private and public spheres in a more fluid, permeable way is that the same virtues nurtured within the context of the family, including attitudes and behavior toward others, are important in our lives as members of a larger society. Confucians maintain that our attitudes toward our own family members, for whom we have great love and affection, serve as a basis for our interactions with others. They ought to expand our capacity to see others more sympathetically and to act in ways that reflect such attitudes. Parent–child relationships in particular tend to shape in dramatic ways how we think about and relate to others. Loving, attentive parents have heightened feelings of concern for other children in harm's way, feelings that stem from their love and concern for their own children. Likewise, children who love and appreciate what their own parents have done for them have heightened feelings of concern for other parents that stem from their feelings for their own parents. These are irreplaceable capacities in citizens, for they enable us to understand our fellow citizens more sympathetically, even when we have no existing relationship. Upon seeing a child who is lost, a loving parent will be more likely to help reunite the child with her parents, knowing that her own child could be in the same situation; upon seeing an elderly couple who need directions, a filial daughter will be more likely to offer assistance, knowing that her own parents could be in the same situation. Here we can see the kind of "extension" that Mengzi describes; one feels greater concern for others as a result of one's concern for one's own parents and children. This example also illustrates how the possession of certain virtues is a necessary complement to our roles and relationships. Not all parents and children experience this type of extension; those who possess some measure of the virtues associated with good parents and children, such as filial piety, do. Additionally, this type of extension helps to show why ethics and political philosophy should not be pried apart but must, as the Confucians contend, inform and support one another.

Having reviewed some of the differences between Confucian views and Okin's view, it will be helpful to extend this comparative analysis to care ethics. How do Confucian views on these matters differ from the views of contemporary care ethicists? Although Okin's work points in a different direction, might we not gain some of the same things the Confucians offer by reading and learning from contemporary feminist philosophy? For Confucians and for many feminists, the critical role of the family in creating and sustaining a good society is not a tangential matter; it ought to be among the primary concerns of ethicists and political philosophers. This means that we can gain *some* of the same things from reading their work, for they challenge ethicists and political philosophers to take these questions seriously. But as I argued in chapter 4, Confucian views on parent–child relationships, early childhood, and moral cultivation differ in a wide range of deep and important ways from contemporary feminist views, and while ethicists and political philosophers who have not seriously engaged the role of the family may initially hear all of this talk about the family as being the same, one of the aims of this work is to encourage philosophers to recognize the distinctive value of these accounts. Just as different accounts of justice have important differences, different accounts of the family do as well, and they are equally deserving of the kind of close study that political philosophers give to topics such as justice.

Especially in light of the important differences between contemporary feminism and early Confucianism concerning these matters, I do not think their shared emphasis on the family ought to be seen as a threat to the value of studying either one of these views. On the contrary, the fact that contemporary feminists challenge some of the same features of contemporary ethics and political philosophy helps to show that neither the early Confucians nor contemporary care ethicists are discussing issues relevant only to their own time and place, nor are they describing values that are culturally specific or entirely foreign to us. This can provide added support to their efforts to elicit the attention of other philosophers. Unlike a number of issues in contemporary philosophy, this set of concerns is not a reflection of a particular culture, society, or era. Additionally, one might argue that the fact that perspectives as different as contemporary feminism and early Confucianism each affirm the central importance of parent–child relationships demonstrates there is potential for agreement on some of these issues in a modern liberal democracy as diverse as the United States. This is not an insignificant point, for it highlights the potential for bringing about the kinds of social and policy change I will describe in the following section of this chapter.

POLICY CHANGE, SOCIAL CHANGE:
HOW CONFUCIANISM CAN HELP CHANGE
HOW WE TREAT FAMILIES

Even if one accepts the view that Confucian views of parent–child relationships, early childhood, and moral cultivation can contribute to and guide work in ethics and political philosophy in some distinctive ways, one might still wonder how Confucian views might contribute to the larger task of working to bring about change in our society at the practical level. In this work, I have argued for and presented empirical support in favor of evidence-based public policy. One might ask, then, why can we not simply rely upon the scientific evidence we have to promote change in these areas? Why should we look to the resources found in any area of the humanities, let alone Chinese philosophy? What might Confucian views on these matters help us to achieve at the level of promoting real change? In addition to the specific question of what contributions Confucian philosophy can make toward promoting social and policy change, there is also the larger, more general question of what work in the humanities can contribute to our efforts to promote change. I have argued that those in the humanities ought to attend to work in the sciences and that the scientific evidence in particular areas can sometimes give us good reasons to take particular views more seriously, but one might wonder whether this leads to a privileging of the sciences, and indeed, those working to promote social and policy change tend not to view the humanities as a resource for their work, at least not to the same extent that the sciences serve as a resource for them. In this part of the chapter, I will argue that Confucian views of early childhood moral cultivation serve as an excellent illustration of how the humanities can augment work in the sciences to help promote change in a society. Not only can Confucianism support efforts to promote change at the level of public policy; even more importantly, it can serve as a helpful resource for promoting social change, which is, as the early Confucians suggest, a necessary complement to legal and policy change.

Another question we must consider, however, is why we ought to look to the resources of other cultures—including very ancient, unfamiliar cultures—in our efforts to address contemporary moral and political problems. I have argued throughout this work that we ought to attend to early Confucian views of the family not simply because we find a larger, richer fund of resources on this topic in Confucianism than in Western philosophical and religious texts, but also because Confucian views align better with what we now know is true of parent–child relationships, early childhood, and moral cultivation. As we have seen, early Confucian thinkers make a range of distinctive and nuanced claims about the specific role of parent–child relationships in moral development during the earliest years of a child's life and in the development of a good society. This means that Confucian philosophers offer us a direct and powerful theoretical justification for programs like the NFP. Further, as I have noted, the Confucian tradition brings a unique, particularly poignant and powerful set of stories, anecdotes, and approaches to reinforce and encourage an ethical understanding of the family and its role in moral development. These illustrations show how families perform this role in our ethical and political lives, and these themes are found not only in well-known stories such as those about Mengzi's mother, but in philosophy, religion, art, and literature throughout the Chinese tradition. Such resources offer a practical source of inspiration and guidance. Not only are these resources more extensive and robust compared with the resources found in American culture on this subject, but they also present us with the opportunity to reflect on the resources within our own culture and the reasons why we hold the views we do.

For instance, as we have seen earlier in this work, a range of early Confucian thinkers maintain that social change begins (and continues) with parent–child relationships, but they also note that people often tend to look toward what is distant or farther away as the key to change.[5] This tendency is not confined to ancient societies. One contemporary expression of this view in the United States is the tendency to reserve special admiration for those who prioritize the needs of the many (or work to achieve "the greatest good for the greatest number") over the needs of their special relations, particularly their families. This sometimes leads individuals to prioritize their work life over their family life, because they feel their impact will be greater if they influence a larger number of people through their work—compared with the relatively small number of children they will have.[6] But this measures influence only in numbers, when in fact we must also measure the depth and extent of one's influence. In the vast majority of cases, the extent and depth of influence that parents will have over their children's lives will far outweigh the extent and depth of their influence on the lives of others—even though we are certainly likely to influence and be influenced by others in meaningful and profound ways. While there are rare exceptions—seen, for instance, in the lives of such individuals as Martin Luther King Jr. and Nelson Mandela—most of us will not have this kind of widespread influence. Most of us will, however, have the opportunity to shape the course of our children's lives—who they will become, what they will value, and how they will respond to others and the world around them. As we have seen, there is abundant evidence to show that the influence of parents over their children is highly unique and nothing short of remarkable in its depth and extent. In the vast majority of cases, no one else will play such a foundational role in shaping our character, including our emotional health and well-being; our capacity for empathy; our intellectual life and abilities; and our overall attitude toward life and others we encounter. This is profoundly meaningful work for parents. Almost none of us will ever do anything as grand as leading the civil rights movement, but we can help build a great family.

Yet the widespread attitudes, beliefs, and practices found in our culture and society do not reflect an appreciation for the unique and foundational importance of parent–child relationships. Although many if not most people in the United States would agree that good mothers and fathers and caring sons and daughters deserve more praise than they get, there is not a widespread tendency to reserve special admiration for—and seek moral inspiration from—the stories of good mothers and fathers.[7] Indeed, we often admire those who prioritized their efforts to promote social and political change over spending time with their families. This kind of prioritization tends to be viewed as regrettable but laudable, and when individuals make such a choice, it is often taken as a mark of their extraordinary concern for others and willingness to sacrifice their own personal concerns for the greater good. What is particularly interesting about these views is that caring for one's children is viewed as a "personal" concern or preference and not as something that involves a significant sacrifice and investment in others or something that serves the greater good of society—as Confucians insisted it did. The assumption seems to be that it is easier for people to care for their own children and that doing so aligns with personal preferences and desires, whereas working for the good of others is harder and involves a kind of "selflessness," because it does not align with personal desires and preferences. Yet this view is clearly flawed. Good parents are anything but focused on their own personal desires and preferences; indeed, this is what typically distinguishes sensitive, responsive parents from their counterparts. Good mothers and fathers regularly set aside and sacrifice their own personal and professional needs and desires for the well-being of their children, and doing so seldom involves the kind of attention and accolades that often come with helping large numbers of people. Additionally, the assumption that those who choose humanitarian work over time with their families are not doing what they personally desire to do is problematic; these individuals have made personal choices to dedicate their time and energies to certain causes. While they may have conflicting desires and feel regret over missed time with their families, to suggest they are not acting on personal desires and preferences simply does not present an accurate picture of the complex motives and desires that shape our choices in life.

Now, it is not impossible to find these types of exemplars in ancient China. As we saw earlier in this work, the sage-king Yu, who was highly regarded by both the early Confucians and Mohists, is said to have left his family for several years in order to work to tame the floodwaters that were wreaking havoc in much of the land. But although his actions certainly promoted the best outcome for the greatest number and were seen as warranted, Confucian texts still emphasize the toll it took on his family, something seen clearly in the biography of Tu Shan, Yu's wife. Indeed, although Confucians certainly admired individuals who made sacrifices for the greater good—which they tended to understand as expressions of humaneness—they also reserved deep admiration for good parents and children, and this is why there are many more stories of good mothers, fathers, sons, and daughters that act as a source of inspiration throughout East Asia, even today. As we have seen, the story of Mengzi's mother—memorialized in the popular saying, "Mengzi's mother moved three times," is a well-known example. There are relatively few well-known stories and sayings of this sort in American culture, by comparison. This difference is another reason why Confucian views can serve as a new and helpful resource for us in reconsidering our approaches to the family and in creating a more constructive view of the family, both in relation to policy and in our own daily lives.

There are additional reasons why Confucianism is a particularly good resource for us in this area. The Confucian tradition, as we have seen, contains rich and varied sources that can help us explore and work to understand the importance of the family. Many of the philosophical discussions of the family found in early Confucianism are highly accessible and can be read and appreciated not just by philosophers but by a wider audience. This is partly because they are often accompanied by illustrative stories and anecdotes that engage readers in a highly personal way. It is also because many early Chinese philosophers were more interested in eliciting a therapeutic result than proving a theoretical point, and this led them to teach and write in ways that reach out to their audience and help them to reflect on their attitudes, feelings, beliefs, and practices. Ivanhoe argues, for example, that Mengzi uses "thought experiments" as a way of getting readers to reflect on their own feelings and experiences: Mengzi "invokes hypothetical scenarios and then asks us to imagine what would occur were such conditions to obtain" (Ivanhoe 2000a:19). For example, in order to argue for the existence of natural moral sensibilities, Mengzi tells us to imagine someone who suddenly and unexpectedly saw a child about to fall into a well, and asks us whether that person would not feel alarm and concern motivated by genuine sympathy for an innocent child.

A fascinating aspect of such moral thought experiments is that if Mengzi is right, all of us, in contemplating this hypothetical scenario and reflecting upon it, will imaginatively experience our own moral sprouts. That is to say, we will feel a "stirring in our hearts" that testifies to our own standing disposition to feel sympathetic concern for a fellow human being.

Mengzi will have encouraged us to take the first step in our own moral self-cultivation (Ivanhoe 2000a:19).

Similarly, as we saw earlier in this work, other early Confucian texts are filled with engaging stories, anecdotes, and descriptions of approaches and experiences that are a part of everyday life. Of course, for contemporary readers, these stories can sometimes be difficult to understand due to differences in time and place, but what is truly extraordinary about early Confucian texts is the extent to which readers can, even in a contemporary Western setting, read them and not only understand much of what they are working to communicate but also find it compelling. Many Confucian stories and anecdotes have a unique quality that makes them broadly accessible and appealing, and this quality distinguishes them from much (though certainly not all) of the work encountered in the history Western philosophy. This quality is traceable not only to the way in which early Confucian texts are written and the aims of their authors and editors, but also to the fact that, as it turns out, the early Confucians were right about a number of things they argued for, including much of what they have to say about the role of parent–child relationships in a good life and a good society. This—combined with the reasons I have already offered—constitutes a further reason why we ought to seek them out as a potential resource for helping us rethink and work to reshape the attitudes, beliefs, practices, and policies related to the family that are found in our own society.

My argument that Confucianism can serve as a constructive resource in helping to promote social and policy change in this area is, of course, premised on the claim that there is a need to change our views, practices, and policies as they relate to parent–child relationships, early childhood, and the role of the family in a good society. I have presented quite extensive empirical evidence for the view that parent–child relationships, especially during early childhood, serve as a unique and irreplaceable context for our moral development and that this has direct consequences for the quality and success of society in many ways, but it is important to appreciate the extent to which American culture and society do not currently recognize this reality. What I mean is that if we look to our public policies in areas that relate to parents, children, and the early years of children's lives, and if we examine the widespread attitudes, beliefs, and practices among members of our society concerning the role of parent–child relationships during the earliest years of children's lives, we do not find views, practices, and policies that align with what our best science tells us. There are many examples showing that the critical role of parent–child relationships is not something that is fully recognized or taken seriously in laws and public policy in the United States. The bulk of public spending on children in the United States presently occurs during the school-age years, in the form of expenditures on primary and secondary schools, criminal justice, youth employment, and other youth programs (Karoly, Kilburn, and Cannon 1998:108; Isaacs 2009). Federal law only requires employers to offer twelve weeks of unpaid leave to new parents, and due to the eligibility require- ments specified by the law, only about 60 percent of American employees are eligible.[8] These examples do not reflect anything like the view that parent– child relationships during the early years of children's lives are the foundation of a good society, even though we have an abundance of scientific evidence showing just how critical those relationships are and despite recent increases in funding for early childhood programs.

Although many if not most people in the United States would say that they know parent–child relationships are foundational for us in an impor- tant way and that early childhood is especially important developmentally, these views are not reflected in our policies or in the widespread attitudes and practices found within our culture. These two areas are, as I will argue, closely related: in many cases, people are unable to dedicate more of their time to their children because their employers do not provide them with paid leave when their children are very young and do not give them the subse- quent kinds of accommodations that reflect an understanding of the impor- tance of parent–child relationships. Additionally, cultural attitudes and beliefs concerning work-related achievement and the satisfaction and rewards that it can bring sometimes leads people to decide to dedicate substantially more of their time to their work than to their families. And the fact that putting infants and young children into full-time day care is a widespread practice perpetuates it: one is more likely to embrace the options that one's extended family and friends have embraced. Again, none of these factors operate in iso- lation; for many families, it is not an option to do anything but put their chil- dren into full-time day care because taking time off is not financially feasible.

It might also be detrimental to one's professional life in the long term. Additionally, of course, many infants and children do quite well in full-time day care, and so many families may not view this as a pressing issue. However, the question I am interested in is how we can optimize the resources for nurturing parent–child relationships during the early years of children's lives, since we know that it is well worth the investment. So the question is not whether children can still flourish if their parents are not offered (or do not accept) a significant period of paid parental leave, but whether in most cases, all things considered, it would be better for everyone involved if this option did exist and was embraced by all—including not just parents but their larger support networks and social contexts. If indeed most of us already know "deep down" that parent–child relationships during the early years of life have a unique and irreplaceable importance, then one of the ways in which early Confucian views have contemporary relevance is that they can help us recognize and give voice to what our own moral sensibilities implicitly tell us and prompt us to work toward ensuring that our public policies as well as our attitudes and day-to-day lives reflect those sensibilities more accurately and effectively.

As we saw earlier in this work, early Confucian philosophers maintain that it is not enough for a society to simply address its problems through laws and policies. Drawing on this aspect of the Confucian tradition, my argument is not that we ought to focus primarily or exclusively on public policy reform with respect to early childhood and the family but that these efforts should be balanced and complemented by efforts to promote social change—seen in the attitudes, beliefs, and practices that are a part of our daily lives. To be sure, social change is incredibly difficult to bring about, for it involves changing citizens' ways of thinking and acting. Indeed, it is precisely because of the challenges involved in getting people to reflect on and reconsider their own perspectives that sources in the humanities have an important role to play in relation to social change. The sciences, too, bring much that is needed in our efforts to understand the importance of parent–child relationships during the early years of our lives. The empirical evidence is a necessary guide in our efforts to reform policy and to promote social change. However, since our views and practices are heavily shaped by culture, it will be helpful to make use of resources in both the sciences and the humanities in order to bring about change that encompasses not only our public policies but the views and practices within individual families as well. Confucian thought can serve as a new, important, and highly unique resource in this process. In Confucianism, and in a rich variety of works throughout the humanities more generally, we find texts that engage our hearts and imaginations in lively ways and push us to reflect on ourselves and our way of being in the world. We need citizens to reconsider their views on the importance of the earliest years of a child's life and the dramatic and tangible ways in which the right kinds of parental caregiving during these early stages can shape the entire course of a person's life. The kinds of stories, anecdotes, and specific approaches we find in the texts of early Confucianism can make an important contribution to this process.

My argument is not that working for policy change and working for social change are entirely separate, disconnected endeavors. Rather, they are mutually supportive endeavors. Just as laws and policies often help promote social change, shifts in citizens' attitudes, beliefs, and practices can promote policy change, especially in a liberal democracy. In what follows, I offer some specific examples of social and policy change that I think early Confucian views of parent–child relationships and early childhood (as well as our best science) support. I also describe how Confucianism can serve as a helpful resource in working for change in each of these areas. My aim is not to offer a thoroughgoing overview of areas in need of social and policy change relating to the family but to offer a few examples of the kinds of change that Confucian views and the empirical evidence commend and the ways in which Confucianism can augment our efforts to promote change in these areas.

SUPPORTING AND STRENGTHENING THE NURSE–FAMILY PARTNERSHIP

One who takes the view presented by early Confucian philosophers seriously and works to apply it in a contemporary setting will maintain that we ought to devote a significantly greater share of our resources and attention not only to expenditures on children but to preventive interventions focused specifically on parent–child relationships in the earliest years of a child's life and even during the prenatal period. As we have seen, the NFP represents an example of a highly effective program of this sort. The evidence associated with NFP findings—including short- and long-term benefits and financial and qualitative benefits that impact citizens' quality of life and their desire and capacity to be contributing members of society—indicates that our society as a whole stands to benefit in a number of ways from investing in this program,. The NFP is a model of the type of program worthy of robust support so that it can serve more of the kinds of families who have been shown to benefit significantly from the program and also so that the program can augment its efforts as necessary.

Jurists and legislators, as well as our fellow citizens, need to see that programs like the NFP are worth investing in, and discussions of the kinds of qualitative issues that early Confucian philosophers focus on can further strengthen efforts to convey the value of the program. While data from the sciences and economic evaluations of the program can help us appreciate the quantifiable difference the program makes and the reasons why investing in the program makes financial sense, works in the humanities, such as those in the Confucian tradition, can help us more fully appreciate the qualitative changes the NFP brings about in the lives of families. The program does much more than help families to rely less on public assistance and to reduce their encounters with the juvenile and criminal justice systems—even though these are important results; it also does much more than generate financial savings to government—even though this is one measure of the program's effectiveness. The most important achievement of the NFP, however, is that it helps families to lead happier, more satisfying, and ethically better lives. Certainly, this difference is partly enabled by the quantitative differences the program makes in areas such as economic self-sufficiency, but the program's achievements cannot be reduced to these quantifiable aspects of its success. In order to fully appreciate the value of the program, we need to appreciate the difference it makes not just in families' material living conditions but in the overall quality of the lives that parents and children enrolled in the program are leading.

We can see here one example of how the humanities and the sciences can work together in mutually reinforcing ways to address some of the problems facing societies in places like the United States today. The NFP already brings multiple, inspiring stories of success and well-documented statistics to support our investment in the program. These things alone ought to be sufficient to convince jurists, policy makers, legislators, and other citizens that the program is worthy of our support. However, the task of gaining support and working for policy change is challenging. My aim is simply to show that there are productive, helpful resources in Confucianism for helping us think through the role of parent–child relationships in a good society and that the stories, anecdotes, and approaches the Confucian tradition brings have the potential to engage people's hearts and minds in a way that is conducive to promoting change by generating further support for programs such as the NFP. Resources from the Confucian tradition could augment existing efforts to convey to jurists, policy makers, legislators, and other citizens the importance of investing in parent–child relationships during the earliest years of children's lives. Confucian resources might reinforce or prompt us to reflect more deeply on reasons we already have for supporting a program like the NFP and thereby provide added strength to our views. A range of other resources in the humanities can also be drawn upon to help us with this process, including the work of ethicists who have written about the role of the family in relation to social policy. Of course, the findings of the NFP and its theoretical foundations must be the primary focus of such efforts, but resources from the Confucian tradition might potentially serve in a supportive role in helping citizens to become aware of the fact that we have good reasons to support the NFP.

There are also some ways in which Confucian views might have the potential to serve as a constructive resource in relation to the NFP. Program founder David Olds points out that there are some areas in which the program would like to improve and expand its efforts (Olds et al. 1997:23). In examining common challenges faced by home visitors in the Memphis trial, the NFP found that many challenges grew out of nurses' efforts to address the unique needs of families while simultaneously addressing the broad goals and objectives of the program (Kitzman et al. 1997). One of many factors that shape the unique needs of families is their cultural background, and the NFP has an excellent record of working to take into account cultural influences and differences. For instance, in order to refine the program model for African-American families in Memphis, the NFP relied on scholarship on African-American family life, a national program advisory committee, a local community advisory committee, participant focus groups, and individual participant feedback. At the same time, training sessions stressed that not everything can be learned up front, because much diversity exists among families of particular races and classes, and nurses must work to learn about the values, goals, and needs of individual families in the course of their work (Kitzman et al. 1997:97). One way in which Confucian thought might serve as a helpful resource for the NFP is in working with Asian-American families. Those who have ethnic roots in East and Southeast Asia come from cultures strongly influenced by Confucian values, and early Confucian views of parent–child relationships and the family would be a rich resource for nurse visitors working with families from these cultural backgrounds. Indeed, as we have seen in this work, many of the stories and anecdotes found in the Confucian tradition are widely known and serve as a source of inspiration for many parents and families of East Asian descent. So in addition to helping nurse visitors gain a better sense of the cultural background of families with East Asian roots, some of the specific stories and anecdotes found within the Confucian tradition might serve as a potential resource for nurse visitors to draw upon explicitly. Additionally, the NFP continues to explore the potential for the program in other countries, and should the NFP expand its offerings to parts of East Asia, Confucianism will serve as a rich resource for those working to understand and address the unique needs and challenges of families in East Asia.

NEW PARENT LEAVE, BREAST-FEEDING SUPPORT, AND PRENATAL CARE

If we take seriously what NFP findings and the theoretical foundations of the program tell us, then we will be led to see that there are some key areas in which our policies ought to be reformed. Indeed, NFP findings can serve as a helpful guide to further policy change, because some of the difficulties that NFP families encounter are more widespread problems that are encountered by families throughout our society. The challenges involved in new parents returning to work or school are a prime example. The NFP reports,

> As expected, there were times that mothers could not simultaneously address their caregiving responsibilities and their personal goals for school, work, and family life. Which goal(s) to focus on was a major concern of the nurses. For example, with young adolescents, should the nurse focus her energies on facilitating the youngsters' return to school, knowing that early separation from infants may interfere with their becoming fully engaged in the care of the baby and fully assuming the maternal role? Similar tensions existed with the goal of job training or employment for the older woman. These tensions were exacerbated when family obligations further complicated decisions about priorities. Heeding the simultaneous demands of caring for a young child and attending school or work is a challenge even for women with considerable personal, social, and material resources. This challenge was even greater for many young women in the program, given their limited resources. (Kitzman et al. 1997:104)

This is one area in which our laws can make a big difference in the lives of families by mandating paid parental leave for all new parents who wish to take it. Obviously, many NFP mothers face separate challenges such as being unemployed, enrolled in job-training programs, or still being in high school, and such cases would require the availability of more specific forms of support. But paid parental leave would be a good place to begin. Most other Western societies do much better than the United States, and not just because they require employers to offer paid leave to new parents; they also offer a longer period of leave—which aligns much better with what the empirical evidence tells us about the relationship that is established between parents and children during the early weeks, months, and years of children's lives. The United States is unusual worldwide, because it does not mandate paid parental leave, and it is unusual among Western countries (especially European countries), because of the short duration of parental leave (twelve weeks). The United Kingdom provides thirty-nine weeks of paid leave for mothers; Sweden provides sixteen months of paid leave, which is available to both mothers and fathers. These examples are important, because they show that liberal democracies can have better policies.[9]

If we take seriously what the evidence tells us about the early weeks and months of children's lives and the ways in which investing in the quality of parent–child relationships during these early stages translate to a wide variety of goods not just for individuals and families but for a larger society, we will support mandated paid parental leave for a longer period of time. Two-thirds of all mothers with children under the age of six in the United States work outside the home (Bok 2010:150). Yet despite these numbers and despite an abundance of evidence demonstrating the importance of parental leave, the laws concerning parental leave have yet to change in the United States. As Derek Bok points out,

America has been especially backward in encouraging the kinds of interaction between parents and newborns that research has shown to be critically important to a child's later development. Most working parents would like to take time off when a child is born, but the United States is the only advanced, industrialized country that does not require employers to offer paid parental leave. Moreover, it allows only a three-month absence from work. . . . In sharp contrast to America, other highly advanced industrialized democracies require an average of ten months of paid parental leave, and Scandinavian countries actually provide for periods ranging from eighteen months to three years. There is no convincing reason why the United States should not follow these examples and insist on paid parental leave for at least six months for all families. Such a requirement would put the well-being of parents and infants ahead of questionable claims of burdening business and hampering economic growth that have not been persuasive in other advanced nations. (Bok 2010:146)[10]

One of the important points Bok makes here is that there is a strong tendency in the United States to base our support for laws and policies on their potential to foster economic gains. Indeed, in offering justifications for programs that aim to improve the quality of life for parents and children in the United States—both in terms of their physical living conditions and their overall happiness and well-being—there is a strong tendency to focus on whether such programs are "good investments" financially. So the primary questions considered in deliberations about various forms of legal and policy change frequently include whether there will be an economic "return on the investment" and if so, how long it will take to see that return. The amount of money saved by investing in programs designed to improve the lives of families tends to be the primary justification offered to and by legislators and policy makers for funding such programs. Obviously, such matters need to be a part of deliberations concerning whether or not to invest in any program; a government should be a good steward of citizens' tax dollars and responsible about budgetary matters. But the financial value of a program should not be the only or primary matter on which legislators and policy makers focus. We must also consider the way in which citizens' lives—including their happiness and overall flourishing—might be improved by particular laws and policies and the consequences of individual citizens' quality of life for society as a whole. The issue of parental leave highlights how damaging it can be for a society when the financial value of a program becomes the primary deciding factor in its value to society. Indeed, it is primarily a concern with promoting economic growth *over a concern for the well-being of children and their parents* that has motivated America's backward policies concerning parental leave.

One of the distinctive roles the humanities can play in the task of creating and sustaining a good society is to remind us not to neglect matters relating to human flourishing in favor of economic gains—something that can be an especially strong temptation in a culture and society so strongly shaped by capitalism. The absence of humanistic or qualitative reasons for investing in programs is one of the reasons why resources in the humanities—such as those found in the Confucian tradition concerning parent–child relationships—can augment our efforts to promote changes in our laws and policies, as well as social change. It is not that such reasons are disconnected from a society's overall well-being, including its financial well-being; as we have seen in this work, there is a direct relationship between, for example, supportive parent–child relationships during the earliest years of children's lives and such things as economic self-sufficiency and lower incarceration rates. But we should not be arguing for investing in early childhood intervention programs exclusively or even primarily on the basis that they will help us to lower expenditures on the criminal justice and prison systems. We ought to reflect on, be primarily motivated by, and offer reasons that reflect the desire to improve the overall quality of life and happiness of our citizens. Bok points out that the way in which parental leave can do this is clear: "If parents could take paid parental leave for adequate lengths of time, they might feel less torn between the necessity to work and their desire to care properly for their infant children" (Bok 2010:146). This would increase the overall happiness and satisfaction parents feel, and families would also be leading ethically better lives. They would be able to fully experience and appreciate the rich variety of goods that come from being able to care for one's children on a day-to-day basis during the earliest stages of their development, and parents would also benefit from the opportunities for growth and moral development that come from responding to demands and challenges of parenting. Perhaps most importantly, as we have seen throughout this work, the benefits to children of nurturing, supportive parent–child relationships are unparalleled and have an impact on virtually every aspect of a child's development. These benefits will be enhanced if parents are provided with greater opportunities to cultivate their relationships with their children during the early weeks, months, and years of their children's lives. And these benefits, in turn, are passed on to society, not just in financial savings in areas such as juvenile and criminal justice but in the form of citizens who are healthier and happier and who have a greater capacity for empathy and for reflection on themselves and the world around them. The latter benefits—to both individuals and society—are tied to areas such as improved school readiness—things that can help children benefit from an education in ways that enable them to become better citizens.

In addition to the tendency to focus strongly—and sometimes exclusively—on the financial value of laws, policies, or programs, legislators and citizens have also exhibited a tendency to resist evidence-based policy. This is seen, for example, in the proliferation of laws banning the use of handheld cell phones while driving and the use of "hands-free" cell phones as an alternative. The evidence shows that hands-free phones do not significantly reduce the risks associated with cell phone use while driving, because the source of the risk is distraction (e.g., Strayer, Drews, and Johnston 2003). In the case of this example, legislators seem to be embracing legislation that permits the use of hands-free devices because their constituents (including the cell phone industry as well as individual citizens) will be happier with this option—and therefore happier with their legislators—than with a strict ban on cell phone use while driving. Though not uncommon, such an approach to lawmaking is hazardous. But here we can see where the humanities can make a contribution to the political process in relation to law- and policy making. Citizens must be made to reflect on their attitudes and beliefs and how they relate to the evidence concerning cell phone use. Critical reflection on stories and anecdotes have an important role to play here: citizens need to reflect on the accounts of those who have lost loved ones as a result of cell phone–related accidents, as well as the stories of those who have accidentally killed or maimed others in order to answer a phone, and they need to understand how much they can increase or decrease the likelihood of such accidents through their actions. Perhaps even more importantly, citizens ought to reflect on their reasons for feeling they need to use their cell phones at all times: Does this reflect unreasonable (and sometimes dangerous) expectations from one's superiors, coworkers, and clients? Does it reflect an unhealthy attachment to one's work or an attempt to be "present" in the lives of loved ones without actually being physically with them? Or does it simply reflect a habit that one has acquired because it is a convenient, time-saving measure? Reflecting on these kinds of questions is only a first step, but it is an important first step in the process of helping citizens to change their behavior, and such reflection can not only help create a safer society, it can also help people to see ways in which they might be able to improve the quality of their lives, the time they spend with others, and the way in which they balance the demands of work and family. The humanities are a rich resource for developing citizens' skills for this type of reflection and their willingness and capacity to change, and can augment the evidence the sciences provide, all in an effort to encourage citizens to lead safer and richer lives.

In some ways, convincing lawmakers and citizens of the need for paid parental leave ought to be easier than convincing them of the need for a ban on cell phone use while driving, even though an abundance of empirical evidence supports both types of legislation. This is because the general view that parent–child relationships are fundamentally important is not something that most people would contest. Upon reflection, almost all of us recognize that we have been shaped by our parents in important ways. So instead, the challenges of gathering support for this type of legislation would likely be primarily financial, based on the worry that government subsidies of employers could lead to higher tax rates. Yet there is good evidence to show that denying workers paid new parent leave does not, in fact, lead to long-term economic gains. Instead, providing good working conditions—including various forms of paid leave—leads countries to be more competitive economically (Heymann and Earle 2009).[11] Here again, attending to the evidence can help us make better legal and policy decisions. In addition, there are a variety of alternatives to consider in relation to paid leave, and we can look to actual policies and outcomes in a number of countries for guidance. For instance, different countries provide different percentages of a worker's salary in connection with parental leave, as well as differing lengths of leave.[12]

Resistance to mandated paid parental leave might also be tied to the fact that not everyone can immediately see how he or she would personally benefit, but while none of us benefit from *all* of the laws and policies governing the workplace, most of us benefit in a variety of ways of which we are not fully aware. For example, guarantees of safe working conditions and policies that prevent discrimination based on one's ethnic background, race, or gender provide benefits to most of us that did not exist for our grandparents (and perhaps not even for our parents).[13] But some might also doubt that parental care during the early weeks and months of children's lives is really necessary or superior enough to day care to make such an investment worthwhile. In addition to the empirical evidence that offers support for parental leave, Confucian views can serve as a resource in helping legislators and citizens reflect on these issues. As we have seen, the theoretical foundations of the NFP and early Confucian philosophy alike emphasize the unique and irreplaceable importance of supportive parent–child relationships during the early years of children's lives. In addition to helping legislators and citizens to understand that the empirical evidence indeed supports the view that this investment in parental care for children during the early months of children's lives is worthwhile—and worthwhile not just for individual families but in terms of short- and long-term consequences for society in a variety of areas—it will be necessary to help citizens to appreciate what this evidence tells us about the nature of a society. Confucian views can provide assistance here, because they clearly articulate the view that individual families are related to a larger society in the way that concentric circles are related. Families are not separate from society; they constitute it; and what we do for families and developing children has direct and observable consequences for society. Confucian views ought to push us to look more closely at such policies and their benefits and to reflect on our attitudes and beliefs about work, family, and the care of young children. Confucian thinkers encourage us to imagine ourselves in others' positions, and to think about ourselves and those we love not just in our current position but over the entire course of a life: What challenges and experiences did my parents encounter in caring for me when I was young? What was my experience like as a parent when my children were young? What do I hope things will be like for my children, nieces or nephews, grandchildren, and friends? Here again, the kinds of stories, anecdotes, and approaches that are a part of the Confucian tradition can serve as a rich resource in helping us to reflect more deeply on what we believe and why and the ways in which these beliefs can be translated into action. We have good reasons to think that the early Confucians were right about the formative nature of the early interactions between parents and children and that these relationships provide the foundation for and directly impact a society in tangible ways. One clear and direct way of supporting and nurturing parent–child relationships during the earliest stages of a child's development is to ensure that all parents are able to care for their young children, if they so desire.

This last qualification is a significant one, for it reminds us that even if an extended period of paid parental leave was widely available, some parents might be hesitant to take full advantage of it. Our actions, of course, are not shaped wholly or even primarily by laws and public policies. This is one of the reasons why Confucian thinkers would emphasize that it is not enough simply to change our laws and policies; we must work to promote social change at a deeper level as well, including working to change people's attitudes toward work and family and toward those who take time off from work to care for their young children. This is a clear example of how, in addition to policy change, we will also need to work to change citizens' ways of thinking about the family and their corresponding behavior. Even if the law requires employers to offer new parents leave with pay for an extended period, there is nothing to guarantee that employers will encourage their employees to do so or will help them to feel supported in making this choice. The attitudes of one's coworkers and clients, and how they view one's dedication to the job and the proper order of one's priorities, play an influential role as well. Bound up in a parent's decision to take an extended period of leave from work to care for her young child are cultural attitudes and beliefs concerning work–family balance, the praiseworthiness of those who show an unqualified dedication to their careers, and the demands and rewards of caring for one's child as an infant and toddler. The attitudes of employees who do not have children or who did not or could not take time off to be with their children will be especially important to address, for these individuals are sometimes prone to view parental leave as a special dispensation that gives some individuals "time off" or as something that is frivolous.

There are additional challenges to consider in relation to cultural attitudes and beliefs concerning child care, especially among those who could not or did not take time off—or much time off—when their children were small. Those who placed their children in full-time day care, nursery school, or preschool are likely to encourage others to do the same if they feel that it worked well. But particular attitudes, feelings, and beliefs are complex here; we often choose to highlight and focus on the benefits of the things we do out of necessity, especially when there is no alternative and when it concerns something very close to our hearts, such as the care of our children. In some cases, then, parents will highlight for other parents the positive features of day care, nursery school, or preschool, because this enables them to put a more positive spin on an inevitable situation. Since a majority of infants, toddlers, and preschoolers in the United States are placed in some form of out-of-home care while their parents work, there is a growing expectation that all families will place their children in out-of-home care, especially as they become toddlers, and parents who do not do this may be subjected to pressure from other parents to do so, on the basis that it would be better for their children.[14] These social attitudes and beliefs mirror the culture for parents in the workplace that has been established in the United States. In addition to working for legal and policy change in areas such as parental leave, citizens need to reflect on their own attitudes and practices in relation to child care. Parents should have a choice to care for their children, at least for a significant period of time, without sacrificing their careers. Additionally, those who choose to stay home with their young children should feel supported in doing so and should not be pressured to make another choice.[15]

Not only is encouragement and support important, but supervisors and coworkers within the workplace also ought to be well educated about the policies and should make sure new employees, as well as clients, are well informed. These are things that should be followed up on in person, not just in the large volume of written guidelines issued to employees. The larger point here is that any policy impacting the family should not be treated as just another policy; the impact is simply too great and merits a greater investment by all. None of these things concern the content of our policies; what they concern are the attitudes, feelings, and beliefs about parents and children that are commonly found within our society and within individual places of employment. While some of these things can be mitigated and shaped by revising our laws, policies, and guidelines concerning these matters, there is no replacement for the difficult task of helping citizens to reflect critically on their own assumptions, attitudes, and beliefs concerning families and their role in a good society. Since the early Confucians not only argued that laws and policies are not enough to transform a society but stressed the nature and possibility of working to bring about change in ourselves, including our attitudes, feelings, and beliefs, this represents a clear illustration of how their view has continuing relevance for us today.

In addition to the wide range of benefits relating to parent–child relationships we have already reviewed in this work, there are additional benefits to providing mothers with an extended period of paid parental leave to care for their infants. One example is the established relationship between breast-feeding rates and parental leave. Studies have shown that the length of maternity leave is a significant factor in a mother's decision to try to breast-feed initially, as well as in the early cessation of breast-feeding. The numbers are significant: new mothers who were at home for thirteen weeks or more had greater odds of initiating breast-feeding and continuing any breast-feeding beyond six months, and they were about twice as likely to predominantly breast-feed beyond three months (Ogbuanu et al. 2011). This is not a minor matter when it comes to children's (and women's) health. As the American Academy of Pediatrics (AAP) states, "Breastfeeding and human milk are the normative standards for infant feeding and nutrition. Given the documented short- and long-term medical and neurodevelopmental advantages of breastfeeding, infant nutrition should be considered a public health issue and not only a lifestyle choice" (AAP 2012). The AAP recommends exclusive breast-feeding for about six months, followed by continuation of breast-feeding for one year or longer as mutually desired by mothers and infants. The AAP stresses that contraindications for breast-feeding are rare, but because breast-feeding support is not what it should be in our society and culture, the rates of breast-feeding in the United States are low. According to Centers for Disease Control and Prevention (CDC) statistics for 2011, among infants born in the United States, only 35 percent were exclusively breastfed through three months of age, and 23.8 percent were still breast-feeding at all at one year of age (CDC 2011). While many Americans tend to see breast-feeding as a personal matter, the AAP stresses that it is a public health issue. Indeed, breast-feeding serves as another example of why a sharp separation between public and private is inadequate. The implications of low breast-feeding rates in the United States for the larger society are important to understand. According to a recent study that conducted a cost analysis for all pediatric diseases for which risk ratios favor breast-feeding, "If 90 percent of families in the United States could comply with medical recommendations to breast-feed exclusively for six months, the United States would save $13 billion per year and prevent an excess of 911 deaths, nearly all of which would be in infants" (Bartick and Reinhold 2010). More important than the cost savings, of course, are the saved lives, which have an immeasurable impact on families' capacity for happiness and fulfillment.

The early Confucian sources we have examined in this work stress the moral importance of cultivating the unique relationship between mothers and infants. It is important to recognize, then, that the benefits of working to promote paid parental leave and breast-feeding are both tangible—since they are financial and health-related—as well as moral. Additionally, these benefits extend not just to individual infants, mothers, and families, but also to society as a whole. While some might worry about attempts to pressure women into breast-feeding, we shall see in a moment that most women desire to breast-feed but are either unsuccessful initially or quit earlier than they wish to. Our aim, then, should be to provide resources that will enable women to succeed in this important endeavor by offering greater support and encouragement. The reasons why women in the United States stop breast-feeding or do not attempt to breast-feed can help us see how policy change needs to go hand in hand with social change, including changes in cultural attitudes and beliefs and better education about infant nutrition and growth. Studies have found that women often believe that breast milk does not satisfy their infants' nutritional needs, even during the earliest months of a child's life—a belief even more common among Hispanic and low-income families (Li et al. 2008). Younger women and those with limited socioeconomic resources are more likely to stop breast-feeding within the first month, and the leading reasons for cessation include physical pain and discomfort, concerns about adequate milk supply, infants having difficulties, and concerns that the infant is not satiated (Ahluwalia, Morrow, and Hsia 2005). These findings are important, because they confirm that women frequently desire to continue breast-feeding but stop as a result of problems.

Many of these problems are preventable with proper care, education, and good support. Reviews of randomized controlled studies have shown that providing extra support for breast-feeding mothers, from either professionals or laypeople with training, results in an increase in the length of time that women continue breast-feeding (both exclusively and after the introduction of complementary foods). Face-to-face support that is offered without women needing to request it has been most successful; support that is only offered if women seek help is significantly less likely to be effective, which suggests that women should be offered predictable, scheduled, ongoing visits (Renfrew et al. 2012). In addition, families and close friends play an important role in women's success in breast-feeding. In particular, mothers who have family members or friends who have successfully breast-fed a child are more likely to succeed, partly because women are more likely to share concerns within their network of family and friends (Dix 1991:222–225; Kuan et al. 1999:4–5.[16] One study found that husbands and grandmothers provided the greatest degree of emotional and instrumental support, while doctors and nurses provided more information, which also played an important role in establishing lactation: "Long-term breastfeeding mothers were those who had adjusted most optimally to pregnancy and motherhood, were most likely to characterize their marriages as satisfying and loving during the prenatal period and throughout the first postpartum year, and were most satisfied with the nature and extent of support received from husbands" (Isabella 1994). This highlights once more the important role that the attitudes and beliefs of family members play in the lives of mothers and infants. It also shows how the family serves as an irreplaceable complement to good educational support and care from medical providers. This is a helpful illustration of how changes at the policy level and social change, in terms of the attitudes, beliefs, and experiences of family and friends, can be mutually supportive and need to go hand in hand to bring about successful change.

All of this supports the idea that promoting something like breast-feeding through policy is only one part of the picture. Employers must understand that providing dedicated space and time for breast-feeding and workplace lactation support results in a number of key benefits for employers, including greater retention of employees, reduction in sick time taken by parents, and lower health-care and insurance costs.[17] Additionally, providing longer periods of leave for women can enable breast-feeding, as we have seen, and there is also a need for greater public funding for evidence-based lactation support services. But this issue also must be addressed by working to change citizens' attitudes and beliefs about breast-feeding. In addition to understanding the benefits of breast-feeding for both mothers and children, people ought to understand the remarkable demands on women who breast-feed, including feedings that come every two hours in the early months of infants' lives. Employers and coworkers need to understand the unique demands and time constraints on breast-feeding mothers, even when they are pumping milk in the workplace during the day. Perhaps most importantly, fathers and other family members must be encouraged and helped to understand the pivotal role they can play in breast-feeding success. The need for cultural and social change to accompany policy change in the case of both new parent leave and breast-feeding represents a clear illustration of how the Confucian view that laws and policies are not enough to transform a society has continuing relevance for us today. Not only should early Confucian views of parent–child relationships during early childhood lead us to support these kinds of social and policy changes, but Confucian views can also serve as a resource in helping to promote these forms of change.

An added benefit of applying Confucian views in these ways is that it shows how Confucian views can be amended and expanded in a contemporary setting to take proper account of women's experiences. There is a basis for this in early Confucian texts, which deal extensively with topics such as prenatal cultivation and the irreplaceable role of mothers in children's moral education. But the Confucian tradition has also been strongly patriarchal throughout its history. Earlier in this work, I noted Nel Noddings's claim that Confucianism needs to locate and repudiate all of its doctrines associated with the inferiority of women. Identifying and critiquing the ways in which Confucianism has perpetuated the view that women are inferior is an important task, as is developing the existing resources within Confucianism that empower women and emphasize the need to respect and value women's experiences. I have argued that many of the views and practices found in early Confucianism can be used to inform policies, as well as attitudes, beliefs, and practices that support mothers in a contemporary setting. Providing paid parental leave and supporting the desire and choice to breast-feed are two ways in which our laws and policies ought to be amended to support women and their families in our society. We also ought to work to cultivate greater support within our culture and society for women who choose to take time off from work to care for their infants and toddlers, who work to balance nurturing young children with their jobs or careers, and who choose to breast-feed. This includes working to change the attitudes, feelings, and beliefs of those who surround women in their families, communities, and places of work.

These aims and goals ought to be supported by those with different perspectives and from diverse backgrounds in our culture and society. Although many of the issues I discuss might at first glance seem most appealing to conservatives and communitarians who stress the goods associated with having and raising children and with family life more broadly, as I have shown in this chapter, these issues also relate directly to the status of women in our society, especially in the workplace. Indeed, a number of the aims I describe here converge with aims of feminist philosophers. Sara Ruddick writes,

> The best-intentioned individuals can do little to transcend gender until communities support the work of mothering and the well-being of children with free and effective medical services, day-care centers, flexible working hours, and pervasive respect for maternal work. Restructuring the work life requires acknowledging that women are still held responsible for mothering and that this genderization offers overwhelming economic and professional advantages to men. (Ruddick 1995:45)

Ruddick shares with the Confucian-informed view I am describing an emphasis on the need for social change as well as policy change, and specifically the need for communities to support parents and children in new and tangible ways. A number of feminist philosophers who have argued for the political implications of care ethics have been led to similar conclusions.

Joan Tronto argues that we should view care as both a moral and political ideal and as "the highest social goal" (Tronto 1993:175). She writes that "Caring activities are devalued, underpaid, and disproportionately occupied by the relatively powerless in society" (Tronto 1993:113). Diemut Bubeck and Eva Kittay have both argued that care ought to be seen as a public concern and not as the private responsibility of women or private charities (Bubeck 1995; Kittay 1999). Virginia Held writes, "Given how care is a value with the widest possible social implications, it is unfortunate that many who look at the ethics of care continue to suppose it is a 'family ethics,' confined to the 'private' sphere." She goes on to say,

> Instead of seeing the corporate sector, and military strength, and government and law as the most important segments of society deserving the highest levels of wealth and power, a caring society might see the tasks of bringing up children, educating its members, meeting the needs of all, achieving peace and treasuring the environment, and doing these in the best ways possible to be that to which the greatest social efforts of all should be devoted. (Held 2006:18–19)

In addition to their central emphasis on care, feminist philosophers working from a care-ethical perspective emphasize the importance of recognizing the sexist characteristics of our current arrangement and also tend to be more eager to address legal and policy issues, while Confucian sources place more emphasis on the role of the family and relationships within families both in relation to individuals and the larger society, but these are, in many ways, complementary strategies, with each bringing needed strengths. They support many of the same solutions, while offering different reasons as well as some different alternatives and potential solutions. In areas such as paid parental leave and support for breast-feeding, feminist and Confucian approaches can come together to help promote change in some innovative ways, highlighting how the humanities can help us reflect critically on ourselves and the world around us and also lead us to work for change both in our own families and communities and also at the level of law and policy.

One further area in which early Confucian views can augment and encourage efforts to promote social and policy change is in the area of pre-natal care. One of the truly distinctive features of early Confucian views on early childhood is the emphasis they place on the prenatal period, and the idea that parent–child relationships, including a mother's responsibilities to her child, begin before birth. Early Confucian views, then, ought to encourage us to provide greater support for women during the prenatal period. The percentage of pregnant women who receive timely and continuous prenatal care in the United States still lags behind several other advanced democracies, which accounts in large part for the fact that the United States trails most other leading democracies in the incidence of infant mortality and premature births. The United States currently has the forty-third lowest infant mortality rate in the world, with an average of 7 deaths per 1,000 live births.[18] Similarly, the number of low-weight, premature births in the United States exceeds that of most other prosperous countries (Reichman 2005:91–92; Bok 2010:149). In addition to supporting the NFP and other programs that have demonstrated their effectiveness in bringing about change this area, additional legislation ought to augment our efforts to ensure that all prospective mothers receive adequate prenatal care. As a first step, greater funding must be made available to fund prenatal care for low-income women. As Bok points out, "while the federal government has long made an effort to supply proper nutrition to low-income mothers and infants, the program has never been funded sufficiently to accommodate more than 60 percent of the eligible mothers, even though it is widely thought to yield savings in Medicaid and other costs that could more than repay the added cost" (Bok 2010:149).

As Confucian thinkers would be quick to point out, passing legislation that adequately funds prenatal care for those who cannot afford it, while necessary, is only a first step. Here again, we can see how the humanities can make an important contribution to our understanding of what makes a real difference in the lives of families in areas such as prenatal care. While many who work on policy are inclined to address problems such as the availability and affordability of prenatal care primarily by providing financial assistance, one of the things that our best science in areas such as this shows—and this is seen clearly in NFP findings—is that once prenatal care is paid for, a number of challenges still remain. Pregnant mothers must be educated about why prenatal care is important, encouraged to make and attend their appointments, and if needed, offered assistance in finding transportation to and from their appointments. Additionally, women must be educated about pregnancy complications and when they should call the doctor. They also must be educated about and supported in their efforts to improve their nutrition and other important elements of prenatal care that occur in the home. Clearly, ensuring that women have healthy pregnancies is not simply a matter of paying for their medical care and food—even though this ought to be a part of our efforts to address prenatal care. The point is that financial assistance in these areas is a necessary but insufficient solution for addressing such areas as infant morality rates, low birth weight, and premature births. These problems typically originate well before a child is even born, and no amount of financial support can replace the kind of one-on-one support and care for pregnant mothers that is provided, for example, by the nurse visitors and the support system they work to encourage and cultivate within families. Making a difference in these areas involves "investing" in the lives of families not just financially but in the form of caring, supportive relationships.

There is some potential shared ground between Confucian views and care-ethical views in the area of prenatal cultivation, even though one might expect this to be the least likely potential area of resonance, due to feminist concerns about abortion rights. Noddings writes, "When we move to social policy, it is obvious that the very first consideration should be the health of wanted fetuses and the mothers who will bear and care for them. Clearly, in every culture, it is in everyone's best interest to produce healthy children and to maintain the health of their caregivers" (Noddings 2002b:121). Noddings's remarks here underscore the fact that an emphasis on the importance of the prenatal period should not be viewed as a threat to abortion rights. Nevertheless, an augmented Confucian view would likely refer to wanted children or babies, because Confucian views will generally aim to emphasize the unique relationship between parents and children, and attributive personhood during pregnancy plays an important role in helping parents to understand the ways in which their child's life already depends upon their choices and actions. Feminists, in contrast, tend to be concerned about the political implications of using such language, because the abortion debate in the United States has focused on the metaphysical status of persons.[19] However, as Noddings's remarks show, feminists have good reasons to support a stronger emphasis on prenatal care, and this ought to be separated from feminist concerns about abortion rights.

MARRIAGE

Despite these important areas of agreement between feminist philosophers and Confucian thinkers, there are nevertheless some more distinctive areas in which Confucian views do, I think, point to the need for social change in relation to the family. Indeed, some feminists would undoubtedly resist certain types of change that Confucian views would support, and one example is marriage. In a 2012 article in the *Washington Post*, Isabel Sawhill, a senior fellow and codirector of the Center on Children and Families at the Brookings Institution whose research has focused on domestic poverty and single mothers, argued that we have good reasons to be concerned about a significant demographic shift in America.[20] The number of children born outside of marriage in the United States has increased dramatically over the past two decades, from roughly 30 percent in 1992 to 41 percent in 2009. More than half of the babies born to women under the age of 30 are born out of wedlock, and the only group of parents for whom marriage continues to be the norm is the college-educated (Sawhill 2012:n.p.). As a result of the increase in the number of children born out of wedlock, the percentage of children living with a single parent has risen (Bok 2010:141).[21] At first glance, these statistics might strike one as benign, yet as Sawhill points out, there is significant empirical evidence to suggest that the marital status of parents affects children's well-being in a variety of areas. Sawhill highlights three reasons why we ought to be concerned. First, she writes, marriage involves a commitment that cohabitation does not, including taking vows before friends and family to support one another, which "signals a mutual sense of shared responsibility that cannot be lightly dismissed." This view is supported by the evidence: "cohabiting parents split up before their fifth anniversary at about twice the rate of married parents. Often, this is because the father moves on, leaving the mother not just with less support but with fewer marriage prospects. For her, marriage requires finding a partner willing to take responsibility for someone else's kids." Second, Sawhill points out,

> a wealth of research strongly suggests that marriage is good for children. Those who live with their biological parents do better in school and are less likely to get pregnant or arrested. They have lower rates of suicide, achieve higher levels of education and earn more as adults. Meanwhile, children who spend time in single-parent families are more likely to misbehave, get sick, drop out of high school and be unemployed. (Sawhill 2012:n.p.)[22]

Sawhill writes that it is not clear why children who live with their unmarried biological parents do not do as well. Adults who marry may have different tendencies and character traits than those who have children outside of marriage: "People in stable marriages may have better relationship skills, for instance, or a greater philosophical or religious commitment to union that improves parenting." There are practical considerations as well: "Raising children is a daunting responsibility. Two committed parents typically have more time and resources to do it well." Third, Sawhill writes, marriage brings economic benefits: "It usually means two breadwinners, or one breadwinner and a full-time, stay-at-home parent with no significant child-care expenses." Although this difference does not account for the differences between children of married parents and children of cohabiting parents, these things do translate into tangible differences in the lives of most children living in single-parent homes. Indeed, child poverty rates are higher in single-parent homes. There are also interesting studies pointing to how we might bring about positive change in this area; for example, as Sawhill points out, "if individuals do just three things—finish high school, work full time and marry before they have children—their chances of being poor drop from 15 percent to 2 percent." These statistics are especially significant, because they show that a set of interlocking issues affect one's socioeconomic position; marriage is not a magic bullet, but it is among the significant factors that shape the lives of families in dramatic and tangible ways.

It is important to understand that the points Sawhill makes, and the empirical evidence on which she bases her claims, do not suggest that there are not outstanding single parents and children who thrive even though they do not live with their married biological parents. It is not *necessary* for a child to have married parents in order to flourish, but the evidence shows that there is a statistically significant difference in the lives of families in which children live with their married biological parents, compared with those who do not. This is not something that should be viewed as undermining the efforts and the success of single parents; to the contrary, it shows that when single parents raise children who flourish, they are beating the odds in significant ways, which makes them even more admirable. The same is true of families in which there has been a divorce and remarriage; when children flourish in these cases, parents have done a particularly good job of offsetting the factors that normally create difficulties for children, and this is a significant and admirable achievement. This evidence also should not be viewed as undermining women. For example, there is no empirical evidence that suggests that women or children benefit when women remain in abusive marriages. But it is also important to remember that abusers are not always husbands; they include live-in boyfriends.

Indeed, many of Sawhill's points ought to be viewed as feminist in character—as working to empower women and not to undermine them. She stresses that stronger public support is needed for single-parent families, including subsidies or tax credits for child care and the earned-income tax credit. Sawhill's view should not be mistaken for the "family values" view propagated by many conservative Republicans. Yet she also points out that certain things are a reality, from an empirical standpoint. If we are honest about what the evidence tells us, we must recognize that "no government program is likely to reduce child poverty as much as bringing back marriage as the preferable way of raising children." There are a variety of accompanying points to be made here, especially pertaining to the fact that this view should not be viewed as undermining or opposed to feminism. Most women do not choose, as an expression of autonomy or as a simple lifestyle choice, to be single parents. Rather, this is a situation that one normally enters into wishing that things were different. Efforts to encourage marriage should not be viewed as undermining single mothers, but encouraging men to be accountable to and responsible for both the mothers of their children and their children—and not just financially. This is something that, all other things being equal, helps women, not only in the difficult task of caring for their children but also in their careers and in other areas of their lives. One can maintain that women are fully capable of raising children on their own and yet still defend the view that it is better for all of us—women, men, and children—when there are two parents to share in this experience and when those two parents remain committed to sharing in the joys and challenges of this task together over the course of their lives. Perhaps most importantly, being loved and cared for within the context of a marriage—and here I say marriage rather than "committed relationship," because the statistics show that the most successful committed relationships are usually marriages—is good for us as human beings and not just financially or in terms of domestic labor. Being loved and cared for in these ways helps us to lead happier, more satisfying lives.

Derek Bok argues that the deep and sustained relationship between parents that occurs within the context of marriage is one of the greatest factors influencing happiness for both parents and children. Repeated surveys have found that "married couples are more satisfied with their lives than individuals who are single, divorced, separated, or cohabiting but unwed. People who are married tend to live longer and are less likely to become depressed, commit suicide, or experience health problems than persons who are divorced or separated" (Bok 2010:17). Indeed, as Bok points out, the research shows that marriage has a much greater effect on longevity than income (Bok 2010:216n30). Now, Bok is aware that many will contend that marriage does not necessarily *cause* happiness; perhaps those who marry are simply happier to begin with and their disposition contributes to marital success. This is something that researchers have studied, and the evidence suggests that the causation runs both ways: "People who marry, at least if they are below the age of 30, are happier on average than those who stay single. But studies of people before and after they get married also show that marriage and the courtship leading up to marriage often produce a significant increase in well-being" (Bok 2010:7).

The impact of successful marriages appears to have more lasting effects on children: "In one study that divided adults into seven groups according to the quality of their parents' marriage, investigators found that the happiest group was made up of individuals who grew up in a home where parents were content and seldom in conflict with one another" (Bok 2010:140; see Gohm et al. 1998:319). At first glance, this may appear to be mundane and unrevealing; one would, of course, expect children to be happier if their parents are content and get along well. But what is especially noteworthy about this evidence is that it indicates that good marriages have an *enduring effect* on children's happiness, even into adulthood. Given the evidence we have examined in this work concerning the unique and irreplaceable importance of children's early experiences for their overall development, this should not be surprising, but it suggests that parents' marriages are an important component of children's lives and development. The evidence we have indicates that marriage should not be viewed as tangentially related to children's well-being over the course of their lives but as a direct and powerful factor in their current and future well-being.

This evidence clearly supports the view that if a government wishes to help facilitate happiness and well-being in a variety of areas for its citizens, it should support the formation and maintenance of families with married parents. What might be done to encourage and nurture healthy marriages as a way of supporting children and families in the United States? Bok contends that "warm human ties are so important to happiness that it is worth considering whether policies exist that can do something to strengthen marriages and families in ways that will foster caring relationships and promote the healthy development of children" (Bok 2010:139). He maintains that educational efforts can make a difference, especially in relation to reducing teenage pregnancy, which would reduce the number of children born out of wedlock, but also in "teaching better skills of communication and conflict avoidance to young couples before and during marriage, or imparting parenting skills to couples expecting their first child" (Bok 2010:143). Effective programs aimed at helping teenagers to understand how and why to avoid becoming pregnant can reduce teenage pregnancy by as much as 50 percent among those enrolled, and the cost of such programs is low (Amato and Maynard 2007). As Bok points out, reducing teenage pregnancy does much to increase opportunities for young women and improve their well-being, and it also has benefits for children, since the risks of premature birth and low birth weight are higher among infants born to teenage mothers. As we have seen, these early risk factors are correlated with other problems down the road. In targeting teenage pregnancy, of course, the aim is to reduce the number of children born out of wedlock, but evidence-based programs that offer marital and premarital education also have potential to lower the incidence of divorce; a study of one government program of this sort found that only 4 percent of couples who had received instruction had split up after five years, compared with 25 percent of couples who had not received instruction. Since only about 40 percent of recently married couples in the United States receive any counseling or education to help them build a successful marriage, Bok points out that expanding and improving our efforts to support evidence-based programs that strengthen marriage is a promising approach (Bok 2010:144).

Bok also points out that some of our existing policies in the United States actually discourage low-income couples from marrying. He writes,

Large majorities of poor women would like to have a husband and agree that a lasting marriage would be best for them and for their children. Their reasons for not marrying are much more likely to be financial rather than resulting from a frivolous attitude toward family and parenthood. Either they cannot afford to lose the child care subsidies, earned income tax credits, or welfare benefits they would forfeit by marrying a wage-earning man, or they cannot find a mate who has steady work and an income large enough to support a family. (Bok 2010:145; see also Edin and Reed 2005)

In one study, over 80 percent of couples sampled cited economic factors as a reason for not getting married, and 78 percent of the men who met the couples' economic threshold were married to the mother of their child within the next four years (Bok 2010:238n27). This evidence suggests that policy change could have a significant impact on rates of marriage in low-income families. Bok suggests a variety of measures that might help alleviate the economic obstacles to marriage in these circumstances, including a higher minimum wage, better job-training programs, and a reduction of the financial disincentives to marriage that poor women face (145).

Yet as Sawhill points out, "The government has a limited role to play. It can support local programs and nonprofit organizations working to reduce early, unwed childbearing through teen-pregnancy prevention efforts, family planning, greater opportunities for disadvantaged youth or programs to encourage responsible relationships." But the task of encouraging and nurturing healthy marriages is not a matter to be addressed primarily through laws or public policies; rather, we must work to change citizens' attitudes, beliefs, and practices. This is why Sawhill suggests that it will be important to have "the media, parents and other influential leaders celebrate marriage as the best environment for raising children."

In addition to serving as an illustration of the Confucian view that laws and policies are not sufficient for bringing about all or even most of the change that our society needs, early Confucian views support the view that we should not "go it alone" and that the family involves complementary roles for parents—as well as other family members—that are mutually supporting. In addition, Confucian thinkers encourage us to think about human flourishing not in individual terms by focusing on what is best for one member of a family or by seeing the interests of one member of a family as taking priority over the others for reasons relating to individual freedom or autonomy, but to consider the overall flourishing of the family, with special attention given to the ways in which the well-being of each of its members is closely tied to and influences the well-being of the others. As we have seen in this work, Confucians maintain that family members' fates are closely tied, and in making decisions about the family one ought to consider the impact of one's decisions on all family members. Parents have a particularly pressing obligation to prioritize their children's needs, because parent–child relationships play a unique and irreplaceable role in children's development. This in turn means that parents ought to do all they can to ensure that they are present in the lives of their children in every possible way; no other factor will be more important in their children's development. The most effective way to do this is to have two parents working together as a team in mutually supportive, complementary roles, so neither parent is completely or consistently overwhelmed. Indeed, for this reason and other reasons as well, a complementary model of parenting helps to make each parent a better parent.

Confucian thinkers tend to embrace traditions such as marriage and contend that although traditions evolve, change, and can be improved and refined over time, we nevertheless ought to view them as assets rather than adversaries. They should not be abandoned easily, and changes should not be taken lightly, for despite changes in cultures over time, we remain human, and many of our traditions are designed to serve uniquely human needs. Grieving rituals are an important illustration; the therapeutic value of having contexts in which grief is expressed and acknowledged openly and communally is not something that has changed in human cultures over time. We still have the same basic needs emotionally, but because some cultures too quickly abandoned traditions and rituals relating to grief, many are left without a way of grieving in healthy ways. Marriage serves as another good example of a tradition that empirical evidence shows is—so long as it involves a supportive relationship—good for us, for a wide variety of reasons.

How, specifically, might Confucian views serve as a resource for promoting social change with respect to marriage? As I have argued in this chapter, social change is shaped and driven in important ways by helping members of a society reflect critically upon their attitudes, beliefs, and practices. Confucian discussions of the family challenge us to think more about our own commitments and the absence or presence of certain kinds of attitudes, beliefs, and practices in our own culture and society. As I have already pointed out, many of these works are broadly accessible; they are readable and engaging. Most importantly, early Confucian sources consistently accord the family the most central place in a good life. They highlight the unique and irreplaceable importance of parent–child relationships for our moral development, beginning even before we are born and continuing in highly significant ways throughout infancy and childhood. They also highlight the unique partnership parents have within the context of a marriage, and the ways in which spouses can serve in roles that complement one another and augment one another's individual strengths and abilities. While few of us today would want to adopt the roles of husbands and wives seen in early Confucian texts, there remains much that can be gleaned from these texts and much that they can prompt us to consider. In this chapter I have argued that works in the humanities can help us reflect more deeply on ourselves and the world and also help motivate us to work for change in ourselves and our society in areas such as the family. Works that effectively achieve these goals need not always describe views or practices that we wish to accept or adopt wholesale. Indeed, it is often the case that works that present and examine perspectives that are in certain ways flawed and in need of amendment offer some of the greatest opportunities for us to think hard about and respond critically and constructively to institutions such as marriage and their role in a good life.

Now, particularly with respect to a topic such as marriage, many will have a desire to avoid the force of the evidence, which may not square easily with certain liberal values, beliefs, and attitudes. But philosophical fallibilists and naturalists ought to be willing to revise their values and beliefs in order to bring them in line with our best science. At the beginning of this section, I acknowledged that some feminists will not be as eager to embrace this type of social change as some of the other changes I have discussed in this chapter. The hesitance of some feminists to support efforts to strengthen and encourage healthy marriages stems in part from a deep and important difference between feminism and Confucianism: their respective attitudes toward traditions. Many feminists worry about traditions, because so many of them have a long and disturbing history of oppressing women, and much of this oppression continues within traditions today. Another expression of this difference is seen in the Confucian emphasis on filial piety and the Confucian view that hierarchical relationships have a constructive and necessary role to play in moral development and self-cultivation. For Confucians, the power differential between parents and children and the fact that children feel and show respect and reverence for their parents, as well as love and affection, are primary features of this relationship that enable it to have a special role in moral cultivation. As we have seen, many feminist thinkers disagree, partly because hierarchy and tradition have historically been sources of women's oppression.

The work that feminist thinkers have done on these issues merits our attention, especially because it can heighten our awareness of the problems that traditions sometimes present. Yet from the standpoint of moral cultivation, Confucian views of the constructive value of hierarchical relationships are not without merit. The NFP serves as a helpful resource in looking at these issues. As we saw earlier in this work, when the NFP conducted a study measuring the effectiveness of paraprofessionals as home visitors who received the same guidelines, training, and supportive supervision as the nurse-visitors, the latter were substantially more successful in promoting positive outcomes. One of the interesting features of this study is that although the paraprofessionals chosen for the program were much closer to being peers or equals of the women, since they lacked formal training in a helping profession and came from similar backgrounds, they were less effective in helping the women to bring about positive change in themselves and their families. One crucial difference is that women view the nurses as authorities, and the data suggest that this has a positive effect on them. Even more interesting is the fact that at least in many cases, the women come to see the nurses as, in some important ways, resembling the mother they never had, with women noting they had never had someone care for them in the sensitive, supportive, and consistent ways that the nurse-visitor did, and that this care and support contrasts with what their parents offered them. Although the nurses do not "lord it over" the women or explicitly emphasize that they are authorities, the women view them as such, and they are correct to do so. This is one of the reasons why the nurses are more effective in their efforts to intervene in the lives of these women, especially with respect to helping them recognize their capacity for successful change.

From a Confucian point of view, this illustrates the importance of hierarchical relationships in regard to moral cultivation. Although relationships characterized by reciprocity and equality certainly have an important place in many areas of our lives, so, too, do relationships characterized by certain forms of authority and hierarchy. One example of such a relationship that most of us have experienced and benefited from is that of teachers and students. The example of good teachers, like the example of NFP nurses (who also serve as teachers in the program), shows that authorities do not need to be heavy-handed or power-mongers to be viewed and respected as authorities. To the contrary, when authorities such as teachers or nurses do not wield or use their authority in heavy-handed ways, they typically elicit greater respect and are therefore able to do their work more effectively. This is also a characteristic of good parents, and a wide variety of early Chinese thinkers argued that this is what good rulers are like, too. *Analects* 10.2 states that Kongzi talked with lower-ranking officers "in a relaxed and affable way," wearing his authority lightly.

There is an important analogue to be found in marriage. Like certain aspects of traditions associated with grieving and particular aspects of traditions associated with hierarchical relationships, there is evidence to suggest that the tradition of marriage has redeeming value for us today. Now, we would be wise to attend to feminist concerns about marriage, for they can serve as a helpful resource as we work to address and amend traditional aspects of marriage that have harmed women. But early Confucian sources, too, can serve as a helpful resource, by encouraging us not to entirely reject traditions that have value. Confucians would highlight the variety of qualitative goods that come from supportive marriages and would argue that marriage serves as yet another example of how we can work to enrich our lives and deepen our own fulfillment by deepening our commitment to and appreciation for the unique and irreplaceable opportunities that family life brings.

CONCLUSION

N THIS WORK I have argued that early Confucian accounts of the role of parent–child relationships in moral cultivation have much to teach us. When compared with philosophers throughout the history of Western philosophy, Confucian philosophers stand alone in recognizing and giving sustained attention to the unique and irreplaceable importance of parent–child relationships in moral cultivation, especially during the earliest years of our lives. Even when compared with the work of contemporary feminist philosophers, some of whom do emphasize the unique value of parent–child relationships, the work of Confucian philosophers stands out for its insistence on the importance of the earliest stages of our development, during the prenatal period and early infancy, and its contention that filial piety—which stems from the right kinds of parent–child relationships—serves as the foundation for nearly every other virtue and moral capacity. The work of early Confucian philosophers is also distinctive when compared with other views, because the Confucians argued that there is a direct relationship between the quality of parent–child relationships and the quality of a society and emphasized the nature and possibility of moral cultivation and how it occurs. They further propose that alongside the highly specific roles mothers play in children's moral cultivation, other members of a family—including fathers, elder siblings, and grandparents—have identifiable roles as well.

I have argued that in addition to being unique in the history of philosophy both for what they wrote about these topics and for the amount of space they dedicated to them, early Confucian accounts of parent–child relationships, early childhood, and moral cultivation merit our attention because they align with much of what our best contemporary science tells us about the relationship between these areas. At the same time, while several important features of Confucian views of parents, children, and moral cultivation are supported by the most reliable empirical evidence we have on these matters, others can be augmented, amended, or further developed as a result of sustained engagement with this evidence. In arguing for this view and in showing how the sciences can help us improve upon some of the accounts offered by early Confucian thinkers, I have attempted to show how the sciences can inform work in the humanities in some important ways. I have also argued that this task is worthwhile because early Confucian views can serve as a distinctive and helpful resource for promoting policy change as well as social change relating to the family, and because allowing work from the sciences to inform these views helps to make them more readily applicable in a contemporary setting.

Just as I work to show how the sciences can augment work in the humanities, I also aim to show how the humanities can contribute to ongoing efforts to understand and apply what we know about parent–child relationships, early childhood, and moral cultivation. One of the aims of this work is to offer an example of how the humanities can contribute in important ways to our understanding of issues that are often regarded as primarily the domain of fields such as developmental psychology, while also contributing to our efforts to address these issues practically—something often regarded as the domain of public policy. While policy makers often readily draw upon research in the sciences when advocating for certain forms of policy change, they do not often regard the humanities as a helpful resource. The constructive value of work in the humanities for promoting societal change tends to be overlooked, partly as a result of the strong emphasis on policy change (as opposed to other approaches to promoting societal change) and the accompanying emphasis typically placed on the financial benefits of "investing" in programs that support families, especially during the early years of children's lives. Since the sciences measure outcomes that are often quantifiable, the sciences typically are a more appealing resource when gathering this type of support for policy change.

Following the Confucian view that changes in laws and policies alone are insufficient for bringing about widespread social change (even though, as I argue, they are certainly necessary), in discussing early Confucian views of parent–child relationships, early childhood, and moral cultivation, I offer an example of how work in the humanities can be a resource not only in working for certain forms of policy change but also in relation to the difficult task of promoting social change within individual families, communities, and places of work. There are some good reasons to think that the changes in attitude, belief, and practices that I describe in this work are more difficult to bring about than changes in policy, even when we consider the sometimes almost insurmountable bureaucracy one faces in bringing about policy change. For one thing, working to change the attitudes, beliefs, and practices of individual families and communities in a society requires adapting one's message for different contexts and audiences, giving them reasons they can relate to and find compelling, and getting individual citizens to reflect critically on themselves and the world around them. In contrast, working for policy change typically involves crafting arguments for smaller, more specific, and more consistently well-educated audiences (e.g., legislators). Perhaps most importantly, though, I have argued in this work that policy change often relies upon social change in important ways. In order for policy changes that take seriously the importance of parent–child relationships to be successful, we need citizens to reconsider their views on how important the early years of children's lives are and the dramatic and tangible ways in which the right kinds of parental caregiving can shape the entire course of a person's life. Scientific evidence from successful, evidence-based programs such as the Nurse–Family Partnership and theoretical perspectives such as attachment theory ought to have an important role in convincing citizens and policy makers alike that social change is necessary, but the kinds of stories, anecdotes, approaches, and practices we find in the texts of early Confucianism can also make an important contribution to this process. This is an excellent example of how the humanities can contribute alongside the sciences to our efforts to promote both social change and policy change.

One of the most unique features of Confucian views of parent–child relationships and early childhood development is that they focus on the qualitative difference that loving, supportive parent–child relationships can make in our lives. I have cited the evidence that frequently serves as the most readily given justification for programs, policies, and laws that support parent–child relationships during the earliest years of children's lives: they lead to a return on the financial investment that is seen in savings to government in areas such as welfare and crime. However, what the early Confucians would focus on is that these children and their parents are leading happier, more fulfilling, and ethically better lives; they exhibit a greater capacity for empathy and are more readily able to imagine themselves in another person's place, to reflect critically on their decisions, and to stand up to peer pressure. These are things that the humanities seeks to nurture in us, in contrast with disciplines that tend to focus more on profit.

In *Not for Profit: Why Democracy Needs the Humanities*, Martha Nussbaum highlights the strong tendency to focus on profit and economic value not only in policy making, but in education—a tendency that is reflected in a steep decline in the percentage of students majoring in the liberal arts and the sciences and a corresponding increase in preprofessional undergraduate degrees. Nussbaum quotes the following observation of former Harvard president Drew Faust: "Higher learning can offer individuals and societies a depth and breadth of vision absent from the inevitably myopic present. Human beings need meaning, understanding, and perspective as well as jobs. The question should not be whether we can afford to believe in such purposes in these times, but whether we can afford not to" (Nussbaum 2010:124). Nussbaum points out that the pressure for economic growth has led many universities—especially in Europe and Britain, but in the United States as well—to pressure disciplines within the humanities whose contribution to profit is not obvious to "emphasize those parts of its own scope that lie closer to profit, or can be made to seem to." For instance, philosophy departments are in many cases encouraged to focus on highly applied and "useful" areas, such as business ethics, rather than the study of Plato, or skills of logic and critical thinking, or reflections about the meaning of life—which might ultimately be more valuable in young people's attempts to understand themselves and their world. "Impact" is the buzzword of the day, and by "impact" the government clearly means above all economic impact. (Nussbaum 2010:128)

This tendency to understand "impact" primarily as *economic* impact is an expression of the same tendency I have highlighted, whereby the value of "investing" in children and families is measured primarily in economic terms.[1]

This tendency and the assumptions that motivate it should not go unchallenged. Why should programs that support parents and children demonstrate that they will bring a return on our "investment" in parents and children that is financial in character? One potential response to this question is that a financial return is what demonstrates the effectiveness of a particular program or policy, and it is true that programs that are effective at bringing about improvements in parent–child relationships during the early years of children's lives *often* bring a financial return on their investment. At least in some respects, this helps to show that the Confucians were right about the close relationship between the quality of parent–child relationships and many of the larger challenges a society faces. For instance, when breast-feeding mothers are supported and encouraged, more women breast-feed successfully, which helps more infants to avoid illness, and in turn there is less of a burden (financial and otherwise) on a society's health-care system and on employers, due to fewer employee absences to care for a sick child. Similarly, children and parents who are enrolled in the NFP have fewer encounters with the juvenile and criminal justice system, which, once again, has both financial benefits and benefits concerning the overall safety and desirability of our society. However, it is important to remember that these quantifiable measures of success are not the only measures of success, nor are they the most important ones. Indeed, the financial benefits of successful early childhood intervention programs or policies that support and encourage breast-feeding or provide parents with paid parental leave, though significant, do not represent the biggest changes that are typically seen in the lives of families; even families who are transformed in remarkable ways by the NFP typically are not catapulted from a low-income bracket to the middle class. But this program, as we have seen, brings about changes in the lives of families that are nothing short of extraordinary and that represent the things most of us value more highly than anything else—including, most notably, the experience of being cared for, nurtured, and supported by our families for our own good, and the experience of knowing, by virtue of those expressions of care and support, that we are loved. This is true not only for high-risk families but for other families, too, who experience the benefits of policies as well as social and cultural attitudes and practices that support, encourage, and nurture the relationships between parents and children. We should want to pursue such programs for moral reasons, even if money were no object.

A number of the changes that programs such as the NFP and policies such as mandated paid parental leave bring about in the lives of families *can* be measured quantifiably, but the most important changes are seen in the quality of the relationship between parent and child and the ways in which this relationship enriches the lives of families and shapes the moral character of both children and their parents. Through the NFP, for instance, as we have seen, many mothers come to feel for the first time in their lives that someone genuinely cares about them. They learn how to show their children that they love and care about them, and those feelings of parental love and affection are nurtured and developed in new ways, in turn giving rise to deeper, more meaningful expressions of love and nurturance for their children; the children, in turn, feel loved and cared for. These things translate into a wide variety of observable, sometimes even quantifiable changes in their lives, but in too strongly emphasizing the quantifiable changes, we often lose sight of the more important changes, such as the experience of being loved and cared for unconditionally and the way in which relationships of love and trust within families contribute to our overall happiness and well-being. We ought to support programs such as the NFP and policies that effectively nurture parent–child relationships not solely or primarily because they are "good investments" financially; we ought to support them because they improve our lives and the lives of our fellow citizens by contributing the most important goods life has to offer—none of which, as most of us know, are financial.

Nussbaum writes that political leaders in the United States often rightly emphasize the importance of making all Americans capable of pursuing the "American dream." But as she points out, "The pursuit of a dream requires dreamers: educated minds that can think critically about alternatives and imagine an ambitious goal—preferably not involving only personal or even national wealth, but involving human dignity and democratic debate as well" (Nussbaum 2010:137). Nussbaum argues for the crucial importance of the humanities but notes that they do not make money: "They only do what is more precious than that, make a world that is worth living in, people who are able to see other human beings as full people, with thoughts and feelings of their own that deserve respect and empathy, and nations that are able to overcome fear and suspicion in favor of sympathetic and reasoned debate" (143). In light of my argument in this work, I would add that the pursuit of the American dream requires that the hearts and minds of all of our children be prepared for the kind of formal education Nussbaum argues for, which includes the development of their capacities to think critically about and feel empathically for others in their own society and throughout the world. This is something that can only occur if they are nurtured in the right ways during the earliest years of their lives—and throughout their childhood—by loving, supportive relationships with their parents and families. This kind of nurturance depends upon parents recognizing and taking an active interest in the unique and irreplaceable role they have in their children's moral development.

Here, we can begin to see more clearly how the humanities can make a distinctive contribution to our efforts to promote social change. My argument is that in addition to highlighting and supporting the evidence-based policies that our best science recommends, we need to reflect on and communicate the most important goods that come from nurturing parent–child relationships during the early years of children's lives—the goods that many works in the humanities highlight for us. In this work, I have argued that more than any other tradition or philosopher, early Confucian thinkers communicate these goods to us in moving, vivid ways that speak to the heart, prompt reflection, and inspire change. As the opening lines of the *Great Learning* say,

> Those of antiquity who wished that all people throughout the empire would let their inborn luminous virtue shine forth put governing their states well first; wishing to govern their states well, they first established harmony in their households; wishing to establish harmony in their households, they first cultivated themselves.[2]

NOTES

INTRODUCTION

1. Because the kinds of social problems and public policy issues I discuss in this work differ in some important ways across different societies and cultures, my primary focus is the way in which Confucian views might inform efforts to promote certain kinds of social change and public policy change in the United States. I occasionally note how Confucian views might be applied in other settings, but I also discuss the differences in practices and policies relating to the family in the United States as compared with a number of other societies, which should help to clarify for readers some of the reasons I am focusing on the United States and not Western countries in general; the United States faces some unique and particularly pressing challenges in this area.

2. Anne Behnke Kinney offers excellent historical studies of Chinese views of childhood (Kinney 1995, 2004). Lisa Raphals (1998) presents an insightful study of early Confucian views of women, including mothers and daughters. Although Kinney and Raphals both discuss some of the sources I deal with in this book and I will draw upon their work in presenting my argument, each of their works has a focus and disciplinary orientation different from mine.

3. For a detailed discussion of this aspect of the discipline of philosophy, see Cline 2013a: chap. 1.

4. A number of works have examined and argued for the contemporary value of Aristotle's work. Some influential examples are Anscombe 1958; Cooper 1986, 1999; Nussbaum 1986; Annas 1993; Hursthouse 1999; MacIntyre 1999.

5. This is a claim I have made previously, and in this work I present the details of this view and offer an argument in support of it, with respect both to specific Confucian stories, anecdotes, and approaches (discussed in chaps. 1 and 2), and to the views of Western

philosophers throughout the history of Western philosophy (discussed in chaps. 3 and 4). For my previous discussions of this kind of view, see Cline 2012, 2013a:214–230.

1. MORAL CULTIVATION, FILIAL PIETY, AND THE GOOD SOCIETY IN CLASSICAL CONFUCIAN PHILOSOPHY

1. For a study of self-cultivation in the history of Confucian thought, see Ivanhoe 2000a.
2. Throughout this book, all translations from the *Mengzi* follow Van Norden 2008 unless otherwise indicated.
3. I use the *Analects*, *Mengzi*, and *Xunzi* to introduce readers to early Confucian views on the family, moral cultivation, and politics for multiple reasons. First, the *Analects* (the most influential record of Kongzi's thought) and the *Mengzi* are the most influential Confucian texts in which these views are advanced, while also being two of the earliest works to develop some of the distinctive claims I focus on in this work, including the assertion that filial piety is the root of or foundation for our subsequent moral development. Second, Mengzi and Xunzi offer the earliest Confucian discussions of (and debates about) human nature and moral cultivation, and they are detailed, sophisticated, and even systematic, thus making them good sources for philosophical study; i.e., they offer clear and well-formulated views on matters that are the central focus of my study.
4. On the early Confucian notion of a flourishing life, see Van Norden 2007:99–117.
5. The *Analects* (*Lunyu*) is the most influential record of Kongzi's thought. When I use the name "Kongzi" in this chapter, I am referring to the family of thinkers and the philosophical vision that are associated with him in the *Analects*, and in this study I am primarily concerned with explicating the account we find in the received text of the *Analects*. For all the topics I consider in the *Analects*, including moral cultivation and filial piety, I present textual evidence supporting the view that there is reasonably consistent, unified treatment of these themes in the text. For a detailed account of textual matters relating to the *Analects*, see Cline 2013a:20–23.

   Throughout this book, all quotations from the *Analects* follow the numbering found in the Chinese University of Hong Kong Institute of Chinese Studies Ancient Chinese Texts Concordance Series (Lau and Chen 2006). Translations follow Watson (2007), except where I have indicated that the translation is my own. In all quotations from Watson, I have changed the translation of *junzi* to "cultivated person" (from "gentleman").
6. For an insightful study that examines the lively debates about questions of innovation in ancient China, see Puett 2001.
7. For a detailed discussion of this aspect of the rites in Kongzi's ethics, see Ivanhoe 2000a:4–8.
8. See also Kongzi's remarks on correcting or rectifying names (*zhengming* 正名) in *Analects* 13.3. For a discussion of Kongzi's view of rectifying names, including both its role in his philosophy as a whole and contemporary scholarship on this matter, see Van Norden 2007:82–96.

9. On the idea of being bound to others in important ways, see Christine Swanton's account of love as a form of bonding between people (2005:104–109). For a helpful discussion of the role of the rites in Kongzi's thought, see Wilson 2002.

10. My translation.

11. For later thinkers like Mengzi, and in some places in the *Analects*, the same term refers to the virtue of benevolence.

12. For recent discussions of filial piety, see Ivanhoe 2007. See also three thematic issues of the journal *Dao*: 6, no. 2 (2007), 7, no. 1 (2008), and 7, no. 2 (2008).

13. My translation.

14. See chaps. 1 and 9 of the *Classic of Filial Piety* (Lau and Chen 1992). The translation is my own.

15. For a comprehensive study of early Chinese religious life, see Puett 2002.

16. For a helpful discussion of this aspect of early Chinese religious life, see Sommer 2003:207–208.

17. For a discussion of the religious view that is presented in the *Analects*, including passages concerning spirits, see Cline 2013b. The view that Kongzi doubted the existence of spirits is difficult to defend for several reasons. For instance, the text clearly specifies that Kongzi performed ancestral sacrifices and that he did so with a reverential air (e.g., 10.8). Kongzi also maintained that one should not simply "go through the motions" but must be sincere and have the right attitudes and feelings when performing rituals. Indeed, as my earlier discussion indicates, the early Chinese generally believed that in order to be effective, sacrificial rituals must be performed with a genuine attitude of reverence.

18. Zilu goes on to ask about death, and Kongzi answers, "When you don't yet understand life, how can you understand death?" For an excellent analysis of this passage and other passages concerning death in the *Analects*, see Ivanhoe 2011.

19. Zhu Xi maintains that Kongzi responds in this way because he thinks Zilu is not ready to learn about these things, while some other commentators maintain that Kongzi responds in this way because his teachings deal solely with our concrete daily lives. The disagreement here concerns whether Kongzi knew teachings about death and spirits but simply chose not to share them with Zilu.

20. For a discussion of this understanding of filial piety, see Ivanhoe 2007:305.

21. Quoted in Ivanhoe 2007:299.

22. For further discussion of these reasons, see Ivanhoe 2007:300.

23. Quoted in Ivanhoe 2007:303.

24. Meng Jiao, "The Wandering Son," quoted in Ivanhoe 2007:303–304.

25. Most traditional Confucian commentaries on the *Analects* maintain that emotional attitude and not just one's physical behavior is important when it comes to being filial. For some traditional Chinese commentators' remarks on this issue, see Slingerland 2003:11. For an alternative interpretation of this aspect of early Chinese thought, see Fingarette 1972, and for an analysis and critique of Fingarette's view, see Schwartz 1985; Ivanhoe 2008a.

26. My translation. The *Analects* also asserts that those who are humane help others to cultivate themselves (6.30; 12.16).

27. For detailed studies of this idea, see Ivanhoe 1999, 2000a:ix–xvii; Nivison 1996:17–57. I follow Nivison and Ivanhoe in capitalizing "Virtue" to distinguish *de* from the ordinary term "virtue."

28. Kongzi also maintains that when the ruler is correct, he does not even need to issue official orders—his will is put into effect immediately (13.6). When a ruler is not correct, the people will not do what he says, even if he issues official orders.

29. My translation.

30. For studies of Mengzi's theory of human nature, see Graham 1990:7–66; Lau 2000. For more general studies of Mengzi's moral philosophy, see Nivison 1996; Shun 1997; Ivanhoe 2002a. See also Liu and Ivanhoe 2002; Chan 2002. Virtually all scholars of early Chinese thought who have published on the *Mengzi* agree that Mengzi offers an account of human nature. The notable exceptions are Ames (1991) and Behuniak (2005); for critiques of these views, see Bloom 2002; Eno 2005.

31. Kongzi's explicit remarks on human nature in the *Analects* are limited (5.13; 17.2), but commentators agree that Kongzi had views on human nature. For a study of *Analects* 5.13, see Ivanhoe 2002b. Kongzi's remark in 17.2 ("In nature (*xing* 性) [humans are] close to one another, in practice far apart") suggests that human nature does not determine people fully; their nature is in some sense malleable. This, of course, ties Kongzi's view of human nature to his view of self-cultivation. As we have already seen, passages like 1.2 also express a view of human nature (without using the term *xing* 性).

32. Translation from Legge (1970a). The *daren* 大人, lit. "the large/great person," is often discussed in contrast to the *xiaoren* 小人, "the small/petty person." In addition to highlighting the difference between worrying about "great" matters like moral character and "petty" matters like wealth, these terms illustrate that early Confucian thinkers such as Kongzi and Mengzi viewed cultivated persons as possessing a variety of virtues that expand and enrich their lives as human beings, making them more than they were before, whereas the lives of those with poor character are diminished.

33. This is one of several aspects of Mengzi's thought that suggests his view is best understood as a virtue ethical one. For a carefully argued, textually grounded account of these matters see Van Norden 2007.

34. For a detailed discussion of the four sprouts, see Van Norden 2007:247–277.

35. See Ivanhoe 2000a:25n17; emphasis in original. Ivanhoe notes that Mengzi uses a number of different terms for "sprout" throughout the text, including *meng* 萌, *nie* 蘗 (buds), and *miao* 苗 (sprouts of grain). He does not, however, use the word for "seed," which would have illustrated a tendency that is hidden, unlike the active, visible moral senses Mengzi envisions (Ivanhoe 2000a:18, 25n16).

36. See, e.g., *Mengzi* 4B12; 6A8; 6A10.

37. Translation slightly modified from Ivanhoe (2000a:20).

38. Mengzi is making a generic and not a universal claim here, i.e., a claim about how most human beings (those who have a normal range of capacities) are. See Ivanhoe 2002c:222–223.

39. Translation from Legge (1970a:322–323).

40. My translation.

41. Translation adapted from Legge (1970a).
42. Translation slightly modified.
43. Translation slightly modified.
44. Van Norden 2008:176.
45. See also *Mengzi* 4B16.
46. Compare with the use of water as a metaphor for Virtue, or moral power (*de*), in the *Daodejing* (see esp. chaps. 8, 61, 66, and 78).
47. Translation adapted from Legge (1970a:184).
48. Cf. 7A12. It is worth considering the Cultural Revolution in China (1966–1976) as an example of a political movement in which children were called on to attack their elders (including family members). Memoirs written by Red Guards who participated in this movement indicate that although in many cases children did terrible things to their parents and elders during this time, they experienced significant psychological distress and were deeply conflicted about their actions. It is important to note that people did not simply fall into this kind of behavior; they were driven to act in these ways by living under a cruel totalitarian regime, and as Daniel Bell points out, these events were short-lived (2006:150n118).
49. One might object to Mengzi's claim on the grounds that having a bad family is worse than having no family at all. However, even in our modern society, we take seriously the potential deformity or damage done to children who do not have families. Governmental agencies tend to be hesitant about removing children from their homes, even when there are serious problems, and this course of action is regarded as justifiable only in extreme cases. Even then, the goal known as "family preservation" is almost always pursued by working to rehabilitate, guide, and strengthen families so there can be reunification. (The U.S. Department of Health and Human Services reports that each year around 300,000 children are temporarily removed from their homes, but only 65,000–70,000 of those children are eventually permanently removed due to a termination of parental rights.) (Bergner 2006). When children are removed from their homes, temporarily or permanently, the first preference is to place them with relatives so they remain within their own extended families, and the second preference is to place them with new families (such as a foster family or an adoptive family). Placing a child in an orphanage or group home is typically regarded as the least desirable option, precisely because that is not a family environment.
50. For a detailed discussion of *Analects* 13.18, see Cline 2013a:157–163.
51. Thanks to Philip J. Ivanhoe for this point.
52. Translation slightly modified. The other two unfilial things are "by a flattering assent to encourage parents in unrighteousness" and "not to succour their poverty and old age by engaging in official service" (Legge 1970a:313). In 4B30, Mengzi lists five unfilial things: laziness without attending to the nourishment of one's parents; gambling, chess-playing, and fondness for wine without attending to the nourishment of one's parents; being fond of material things and selfishly attached to one's wife and children without attending to the nourishment of one's parents; following one's desires and bringing disgrace to one's parents as a result; and being fond of bravery, fighting, and quarreling so as to endanger one's parents.

53. Translation from Ivanhoe (2002a:64–65). For a helpful discussion of these issues, see Ivanhoe 2002a:64–67.
54. Translation slightly modified.
55. Translation from Legge (1970a:343–344).
56. For the detailed argument for these models see Ivanhoe 2000a:29–32. See esp. the beginning of chap. 1 of the *Xunzi*.
57. Throughout this book, all references to the *Xunzi* follow the numbering (chapter/page/line) in the Hong Kong Concordance Series (Lau and Chen 1996), accompanied by the page number in Hutton 2014. All translations follow Hutton unless otherwise noted.
58. Translation slightly modified.
59. Translation slightly modified.
60. See, e.g., Xunzi 19/98/1:215-16.
61. There is an interesting analogue in the way military trainers look for young men and women with "spirit" to forge into soldiers. Such individuals usually are problematic in normal society because their spiritedness leads them into trouble, but with discipline, their energy can be channeled, making them highly effective soldiers.
62. Translation slightly modified.
63. Translation slightly modified.
64. The third case in which the filial son does not follow orders is when "following orders requires a beastly act, but not following orders requires cultivation and decorum" (*Xunzi* 29/141/20–29/142/1:325).
65. There are clear examples of how Xunzi's remarks here are relevant in our modern society, including cases involving members of the military who had to choose whether to follow unlawful orders. (Articles 91–92 of the U.S. Uniform Code of Military Justice address such cases.)
66. See *Xunzi* 9/35/7–8; 11/54/12; 11/55/26. Xunzi does not specify a particular policy for addressing the needs of the latter groups.
67. Translation slightly modified.
68. Translation slightly modified.

2. INFANTS, CHILDREN, AND EARLY CONFUCIAN MORAL CULTIVATION

1. For a discussion of childhood moral education in neo-Confucianism (in Zhu Xi's work), see T. H. C. Lee 2000, esp. 456–459.
2. As we shall see in this chapter, the *Book of Rites* helps to confirm that early Confucians believed children and youth ought to behave in certain ways toward their parents and elders and that they had to fulfill a variety of filial obligations. These behaviors and attitudes, then, were not expected only of adult children.
3. Van Norden cites Wong 1989. Wong refers to the *Analects, Mengzi, Zhongyong* (*Doctrine of the Mean*), and *Daxue* (*Great Learning*).
4. My translation.

5. Another passage that emphasizes these themes is *Analects* 14.43, in which Kongzi observes a man waiting for him who is sitting with his legs sprawled out, rather than in the posture and attitude proper for receiving an honored guest. His posture implies a lack of both ritual propriety and filial piety, which are exhibited in many aspects of human behavior, including actions and speech but also, as we see here, in demeanor. Kongzi says, "Young but not properly submissive, grown and no one speaks well of you, old and you still don't die—a real pest!" Kongzi then raps the man on the shin with his staff. By emphasizing the failure of the young to exhibit filial piety and respect, and by noting the long-term implications of this failure in early moral cultivation, this passage resonates with *Analects* 1.2. Both express the view that children and youth who do not develop the virtue of filial piety will fail to develop a sense of responsibility to others and will become a burden on society or, worse, will directly undermine it.

6. My translation.

7. On the age for capping (a traditional Chinese coming-of-age ritual), see Kinney 1995:34. See also *Liji* 10 ("Neize"), sec. 2, v. 34. For a translation see Legge 1885:478. This passage also says that at the age of capping, one "attended sedulously to filial and fraternal duties." I will discuss the significance of this claim later in this chapter.

8. "Sprinkling" (*sa* 洒) refers to sprinkling earthen floors with water, in order to maintain them properly.

9. For a translation, see Slingerland 2003:198.

10. For example, James Legge maintains that Confucius's response to Fan Chi "was likely to make him doubt the existence of spiritual beings, or at least to make him slight their worship. . . . And indeed the worship of ancestors and of the departed great was a practice of doubtful propriety, and so liable to abuse, that I am pleased to think that Confucius wished to guard his disciples and others against the superstition and other evils to which it might lead" (Legge 1880:140–141). Roger Ames quotes this passage as evidence for the claim that in classical Confucianism, "the focus of religiousness is reverence for the continuity of one's lineage and its community expressed through family feeling (*xiao*), rather than any 'worship' of dead people" (Ames 2009:265). Ames suggests here that "keeping the spirits at a distance" implies a rejection of the traditional practice of ancestor veneration.

11. My translation.

12. Translation from Legge 1970a:265.

13. Translation slightly modified from Hutton 2014.

14. My translation.

15. My translation.

16. My thanks to Eric L. Hutton for pointing this out.

17. All translations from the *Liji* come from Legge 1885 (unless otherwise specified), with book (and sometimes verse) followed by page numbers.

18. All translations from *Baofu* follow Csikzentmihalyi 2006, with page numbers.

19. There is more to be said about the analogy between language acquisition and moral development, and how this analogy can be instructive. For a discussion of how the empiricist

view of language acquisition can illustrate Xunzi's account of moral education, see Ivanhoe 2000a:34.

20. This term is literally translated as "prenatal education" or "fetal instruction," but in this work I will render it "prenatal cultivation," because this more accurately captures the meaning of the term. The passages I discuss later, which describe the activities that were a part of *tai jiao* show that *tai jiao* did not consist of "instructing" fetuses. The connotations of *jiao* included not only the more literal sense of "teaching" and "instructing," but also "cultivating."

21. See *Guoyu, Jinyu* 晉語 4, sec. 24. Also see Kinney 2004:10–11.

22. All translations from the *Lienuzhuan* follow Kinney 2014, with chapter, story, and page number.

23. For Dong Zhongshu's view, see *Hanshu* 56. Jia Yi mentions prenatal cultivation in the *Xinshu* ("Taijiao zashi"), while his writings in the *Hanshu* (which we have been examining) stress early childhood education. Liu Xiang's view is found in the *Lienuzhuan*, which I discuss in the next section.

24. One silk manuscript from Mawangdui on fetal development and childbirth is referred to as *Taichanshu* 胎產書 ("Book of the Generation of the Fetus"). For a translation of this work, see Harper 1998:372–384.

25. The evidence concerning the unique importance of the prenatal period for children's development is discussed in later chapters.

26. According to ecology theory, people are more likely to change their behavior when they are undergoing a major role change, referred to as an *ecological transition*. First-time mothers have been shown to be more likely to change their behavior than women having a second or third child, and the prenatal period, together with the first two years of life, constitutes the most significant period of transition for new parents. Ecology theory helps to explain why parents' behavior constitutes the *most potentially alterable* influence on the developing child, as it is based on evidence of the potential humans have to change their attitudes and behaviors and the conditions and processes that help to facilitate successful change. See chap. 5 for further discussion.

27. For a translation of the *Lienuzhuan*, see Kinney 2014. On the textual history, authorship, and interpretation of the *Lienuzhuan*, see also Raphals 1998:87–138. As Raphals notes, a significant number of the *Lienuzhuan*'s intellectual virtue stories are corroborated by pre-Han texts.

28. The legend of sage-king Yu taming the floodwaters appears in a number of early Confucian texts, including the *Mengzi* (3A4; 3B9).

29. Translation slightly modified.

30. The *Lienuzhuan* includes a story in which Mengzi's mother provides correction to her son as a young man (after he is married), discussed in the final section of this chapter.

31. Pauline Lee (2000) argues that women were believed to be capable of cultivating the same virtues as men, even though their roles differed.

32. Many of Zhu Xi's remarks on this topic are found in *Conversations of Master Chu, Arranged Topically*, chap. 1, "Lesser Learning" (Gardner 1990:88).

33. The view that women should obey their husbands emerges quite early in the Confucian tradition; see, e.g., *Mengzi* 3B2.

34. There are a number of outstanding studies of women's lives during the Song, Ming, and Qing dynasties; see, e.g., Ebrey 1993; Ko 1994, 2001, 2005; Mann 1997. For a vivid illustration of how views of women changed between the early periods in Chinese history and later periods, see Lisa Raphals' revealing discussion of the Ming recensions of the *Lienu-zhuan* (Raphals 1998:113–138).

35. For an excellent essay on this topic, see Raphals 2002; she discusses two women who were praised by Kongzi, one of whom is Ji of Lu (Jing Jiang), mother of Gongfu Wenbo, who is celebrated in both the *Guoyu* and the *Lienuzhuan*.

36. Translation from Legge 2003:59–60.

37. Translation from Legge 2003:57.

38. Translation from Legge 2003:56.

39. Raphals (1998:224–227).

40. See Raphals's (1998:139–193) discussion of the history of views concerning *yin* and *yang*, especially in relation to gender roles in early China.

41. For an outstanding study pertaining to correlative cosmology in early China, see Puett 2002.

42. Translation from Csikszentmihalyi 2003:168.

43. I discuss these issues in greater detail in chap. 4.

44. For Mengzi's view, see also *Mengzi* 3B3: "When a man is born his parents hope he will find a wife; when a woman is born her parents hope she will find a husband. All parents feel like this."

45. For a discussion of this passage, see Raphals 1998:15–16.

46. The text attributes this quotation to Kongzi. Translation from Legge 2003:52.

47. Translation slightly modified. Commentators suggest that on this occasion, Mengzi walked in on his wife when she was on the chamber pot.

48. Translation slightly modified.

49. Translation from Legge 2003:52.

50. I want to reiterate that my concern here is not with the historical accuracy of the events described in the passages I examine but rather with the views presented concerning parent–child relationships and moral cultivation.

51. See, for instance, *Analects* 13.3. See Van Norden (2007:82–96) for an excellent discussion of Confucian teachings concerning correcting names.

52. Translation slightly modified.

53. Translation adapted from Legge 1971:370.

54. This idea is not altogether foreign to our own culture. Americans commonly refer to "the founding *fathers*" of the United States. Such references are typically accompanied by a sense of reverence and respect, and appeals to the actions and intentions of the founding fathers usually rest on the assumption that these early leaders had the best interests of the people in mind. In such cases we want to recapture their sensibilities at least partly because we think they resemble the sensibilities of a wise and caring parent. Thanks to Michael R. Slater for pointing this out.

55. For studies that take account of other aspects of the political climates of the Qin and the Han, see Loewe 1974; Bodde 1986; Powers 1991; Lewis 1999.

3. PARENTS, CHILDREN, AND MORAL CULTIVATION IN TRADITIONAL WESTERN PHILOSOPHY

1. The Greek *oikos* refers to people related by blood, marriage, and adoption, and to property held by the family, including slaves. It may be translated as "family," "household," or "estate," but the fact that the *oikos* includes human and nonhuman possessions obviously distinguishes it from the modern Western family. See Pomeroy 1999:20–23.

2. See Pomeroy 1999:44. Allan Bloom also points out that Plato's city in many ways resembles Sparta, and he argues that Socrates adopts the opinions of his interlocutors, who have special attachments to Spartan culture—Adeimantus "because it is austere, secure, and aristocratic; Glaucon because it is warlike" (Bloom 1968:380).

3. See *Politics* 1261a-1263a; Aristotle 1998:26–31 (book 2, chaps. 1–4).

4. Nancy Jecker (1989) identifies the view that parents are owed gratitude from children simply because they had them as the "Law of Athens" and argues against this claim.

5. See, e.g., Aristotle, *Generation of Animals* 738b20–26; 729a10. Athenian law affirmed the precedence of the father's parentage over the mother's; children belonged to the father's *oikos* (Pomeroy 1999:96–97).

6. See for example Aristotle, *Politics* 1252b10–12; 1269b12–1270a6. For a helpful discussion of this issue, see Pomeroy 1999:42–43, 2002:69.

7. Aristotle's remarks about mothers are always offered as asides and are never developed at any length. For instance, as an example of the fact that friendship "seems to consist more in loving than in being loved," he mentions "the enjoyment a mother finds in loving" (*Nicomachean Ethics* 1159a28–35). But he goes on to describe how "sometimes she gives her child away to be brought up, and loves him as long as she knows about him; but she does not seek the child's love. . . . She would seem to be satisfied if she see the child doing well." What is especially noteworthy about this example is that, first, Aristotle does not focus on the obvious and ordinary cases of mothers who raise their children and exhibit love for their children in a variety of self-sacrificing ways each day. This shows a lack of understanding of parenting generally, in that he fails to recognize that in no case is a parent's love fully reciprocated by a child; he does not need to offer a scenario in which a mother cannot interact with her child to show this. Second, Aristotle shows no appreciation for the pain that a mother would feel in the scenario he describes; rather, he claims that she seems to be satisfied as long as the child is doing well.

8. I discuss this evidence in detail in chap. 5.

9. In addition to Van Norden 2007, which contrasts Confucian views of filial piety with those of Plato, Aristotle, and Aquinas (122), two recent works comparing the thought of Kongzi and Aristotle briefly address the role of the family in moral cultivation as mentioned by these two thinkers. Jiyuan Yu writes: "both Aristotle and Confucius value the role of the family in cultivation" and "taking the family seriously in moral philosophy is one point that sets both Confucius and Aristotle apart from modern ethics" (Yu 2007:121). However, Yu also points out, contra Confucius, filial piety is not the root of the virtues for Aristotle, and the state plays a much more important role than the family in moral education, on

Aristotle's view (129). May Sim writes that "Aristotle's talk of familial responsibility sounds very similar to the Confucian filiality . . . and his talk of amity (*philia*, standardly translated as 'friendship') sounds similar to the Confucian ren" (Sim 2007:116), though she does not elaborate on these similarities or discuss obvious differences between these accounts. Sim also writes, "Beginning from the home or one's family is the way to proper self-cultivation for both Confucius and Aristotle" (118). As readers will see, my view is that the resemblance between early Confucian views and Aristotle's views on this matter turns out to be quite thin when closely examined.

10. See *Nicomachean Ethics*, book 7, chap. 12, "Friendship in Families" (Aristotle 1999:132–134).

11. Although there were numerous Stoic treatises entitled "On Appropriate Action," Cicero's transmutation, expansion, and romanization of Panaetius's version, "On Obligations," is the only survivor. For a translation, see Cicero 2000. For a helpful overview of Stoic ethical works, see Schofield 2003:254.

12. Blustein points out that Seneca does not discuss the conceptual difficulty of this issue, namely that "unlike saving a life, creating a life is not conferring a benefit upon someone, for it is only through the creation of life that there *is* anyone at all upon whom to confer benefits" (Blustein 1982:49–50). Indeed, existence seems to be a condition for the possibility of the conferral of benefits, not a benefit proper. In his critique of the traditional Confucian grounds of filial piety, Philip J. Ivanhoe argues that "it is not at all evident that bare existence per se can be considered a good," and that even if this could be shown, this good would not be a legitimate basis for gratitude (2007:300).

13. For a helpful discussion of these features of Augustine's view, see Blustein 1982:55–56.

14. Given these features of his account, Augustine's view appears to be close to a "recovery model" of self-cultivation, discussed by Philip J. Ivanhoe in relation to the neo-Confucian thinker Zhu Xi (Ivanhoe 2000a). Aaron Stalnaker compares Augustine and the early Confucian thinker Xunzi, though Stalnaker maintains that Augustine and Xunzi are both examples of a re-formation model of self-cultivation and that, studying them in relation to various models of self-cultivation does not adequately flesh out the details of their views (Stalnaker 2006:39–40). I think a good case can be made for the view that Augustine's account of moral cultivation more closely resembles a recovery model of self-cultivation, but since it is tied to a particular conception of God, original sin, and a range of other distinctive ideas, I would argue that Augustine's view is distinctive enough to require its own model.

15. See *Summa Theologiae*, 2a2ae, Q. 26, A. 9 (Aquinas 1948:1295). Blustein (1982:57) writes that Aquinas thought parents should provide their children with physical, mental, moral, and religious education.

16. For further discussion, see Blustein 1982:57.

17. On piety as a distinctive virtue, see *ST*, 2a2ae, Q. 101, A. 3 (Aquinas 1948:1627).

18. For a comparative study of the general accounts of virtue, especially the virtue of courage found in Aquinas and the early Confucian thinker Mencius (Mengzi), see Yearley 1990.

19. Following Gordon Schochet, Blustein (1982:71) points out that Hobbes may have "future-oriented consent" in mind, since he maintains both that there is tacit consent given by children and that children lack the rational capacities for meaningful consent. In the case

of future-oriented consent, Blustein writes, "Though children, as children, do not actually consent, eventually they will come to see that obedience was a small price to pay for protection and that in obeying they only did what they would have wanted to do if they were fully rational." See Schochet 1975:232. Another alternative, as Blustein points out, is that Hobbes may be referring to immature children, who cannot consent, and mature children, who can consent (1982:71–72).

20. Hobbes's discussion is found in Hobbes 1967 (*De homine*, chap. 13, sec. 7). For a helpful discussion of Hobbes's view of human nature and education and an insightful comparison of this view with Xunzi, see Schwitzgebel 2007. On Hobbes's view of human nature, see esp. p. 159.

21. Gert cites *Leviathan* (Hobbes 1968) chap. 11.

22. We can see evidence here of Locke's view that people are naturally sociable and that parents especially want to promote their children's welfare. In this respect, Locke's view contrasts readily with Hobbes's view.

23. Locke's emphasis on the nature and importance of education stems in part from his denial that morality has any innate aspect, something that is reflected in his choice of metaphor (which is more Xunzian than Mengzian). For a helpful discussion of this aspect of Locke's view, see Schneewind 1994, esp. 200–206. For an insightful comparison of Confucian moral self-cultivation and Locke's views concerning self-transformation, see Kim 2009.

24. Rousseau discusses this in book 1 of *Émile*. See Shklar 2001:170.

25. The metaphor merits a comparison with Mengzi's moral "sprouts," but as we shall see, it is significant that Rousseau discusses "young plants" and not "sprouts," for he does not think infants exhibit moral tendencies that can be cultivated. Rousseau also uses this metaphor to defend a very different view, arguing in favor of isolating the young plant in a hothouse environment to protect it from the harmful influences of socialization.

26. For a helpful discussion of these aspects of Rousseau's view, see Parry 2001:253–255.

27. For a study of Kant's views concerning autonomy and their relationship to other views in the history of Western philosophy (including Rousseau), see Schneewind 1997.

28. Rousseau's view of human nature and the destructive role of socialization is closer in certain respects to early Daoist views than to Mengzian views, but the early Daoists would strenuously object to Rousseau's account of education, which would strike them as profoundly unnatural. For a helpful discussion of naturalness in relation to these issues, see Schwitzgebel 2007.

29. Compare with Kant's remark that "One cannot hope to make anything perfectly straight out of such crooked timber as man is made" (Kant 1959). These remarks underscore Kant's belief that our inclinations can never become a reliable guide to morality, while his remarks about trees in a forest in the *Lectures* concerns the role of discipline in helping us to develop our understanding of moral duty. Both remarks provide an interesting comparison with Xunzi's metaphors in his account of human nature and moral cultivation. Ivanhoe notes the contrast between Xunzi's optimism concerning the possibility of cultivation (including the transformation of our inclinations) and Xunzi's trust in the methods of past sages, compared with Kant's trust of an a-historical, a-social conception of reason as the standard and guide. See Ivanhoe 2000a:36.

30. Kant does, however, offer a robust view of the duty to cultivate one's natural powers. For a discussion and defense of Kant's views on the duty to cultivate one's natural capacities, talents, abilities, and the like, see Johnson 2007.

31. There are also questions about whether Kant's remarks on these matters are fully compatible with his moral theory.

32. For a detailed discussion of Dewey's views on education, see Noddings 2010a.

33. Another example is the work of John Rawls. I have argued that Rawls's discussion of the family's role in moral development has been neglected, but even when we consider what Rawls has to say, it simply does not compare with the extent and depth of Confucian writings on this subject. For discussion of Rawls's account of the family's role in moral education and for my argument that Confucianism can serve as a constructive resource in further developing these and other aspects of Rawls's view, see Cline 2013a.

4. FEMINIST AND CONFUCIAN PERSPECTIVES ON PARENTS, CHILDREN, AND MORAL CULTIVATION

1. In the same issue of *Hypatia*, Lijun Yuan also offers a critique of Li's argument, but since Yuan's essay seems to be primarily concerned with what constitutes feminist ethics and my main concern in this section is the literature that has explored the features of care ethics and Confucian ethics in a comparative light, I will not focus on Yuan's essay further here.

2. Star cites Rosemont (1997) and (Chan) 1993.

3. In his reply to Star, Li writes that "in comparison with Kantian ethics, utilitarian ethics, and contractarian ethics, Confucian [*Ren*] ethics and feminist care ethics often speak in similar voices on such issues as moral ideals, the nature of self, impartiality, universality, and flexibility with rules" and contends that "these similarities are philosophically significant" (Li 2002:132). He argues that virtue ethics and care ethics, and roles and care ethics, can go hand in hand and are not mutually exclusive.

4. On the need for studies of the differences as well as the similarities between them, see Li 2002:131.

5. Ruddick rejects the view that mothers—understood in the more traditional biological and legal sense—are "naturally" loving. Ruddick writes that many different emotions are a part of mothers' experiences and that "maternal love itself is a mix of many feelings, among them: infatuation, delight, fascination, pride, shame, guilt, anger, and loss. Although maternal work is often entrenched in passion and . . . is provoked and tested by emotion, the idea of work puts the emphasis on what mothers attempt to do, not on what they feel" (Ruddick 1995:xi).

6. bell hooks, for example, has argued that the word "maternal" will simply reinforce the view that caring for children is primarily women's work and that women are inherently better at parenting (hooks 1984:138–139).

7. For example, new and nursing mothers' brains are especially sensitive to the sounds their infants make, which normally leads them to awaken more quickly when their infants cry out at night.

8. The thorny issue of whether one is simply developing a view or fundamentally changing it—or both—is one that presents challenges for any tradition, and there are many examples of this throughout history. Sometimes developing a view involves little change to the existing view, other than extending and applying it in new ways; at other times it involves amending or changing parts of the view in question. Developing a view can also involve completely rejecting aspects of the view in question, though when substantial or very important parts of a view are rejected, it seems less appropriate to refer to it as "developing a view" and more appropriate to refer to it as amending or reconstructing a view. Of course, in these cases, much rests on which parts of the existing view one regards as most important or substantial and whether various parts of a view can be rejected without losing others as well. Here, different members of traditions often diverge, with some arguing that others' views and practices represent such fundamental changes that they are no longer representative of that tradition. For one take on these issues, see Van Norden 2007:323.

9. For an argument that Confucian philosophy is not inherently sexist and an account of what Confucian feminism might look like, see Rosenlee 2006. See also Van Norden 2007:330–332.

10. There is a kind of homogeneity in the views of some feminist ethicists, including Ruddick, on the issue of how best to conceive of the roles of caregivers, in the sense that they present a single, often "maternal" or "feminine" model to which all caregivers are expected to conform. This is a kind of value-monist view, and it is coupled with a kind of "revaluation of values" in which patriarchal (i.e., traditional) social norms are devalued.

11. Those who would view the mother's role here as significantly more appealing than the father's are likely neglecting two important features of these experiences. First, such a view romanticizes breast-feeding and neglects the very real challenges it entails. Second, such a view neglects the fact that frequently one of the only times that young infants awaken and observe and engage with their world is, quite naturally, during diaper changes. This affords fathers who dedicate themselves to this task a unique period of interaction with their children. Neither breast-feeding nor diaper changes are all "sweetness and light" and both are demanding and challenging, but both activities also provide unique opportunities for bonding and interaction with one's children. This is one of the things that makes them complementary activities.

12. No Confucian today could be a third-century B.C.E. Confucian, just as no contemporary Christian could be a first-century C.E. Christian. Neither is a "live option," as William James would point out.

13. As we shall see, Virginia Held focuses more strongly on relationship.

14. Noddings's account of what it means to apply the principle of reversibility (or the "golden rule") sometimes borders on a caricature. Imagining oneself in another's place does not necessarily (or usually) entail analyzing another person's experience "as objective data" or attributing to others the same feelings we have. For a helpful account of Confucian perspectives on what this kind of "sympathetic understanding" entails, see Ivanhoe 2008b; Tiwald 2010.

15. Confucians highlight the value of traditions in these kinds of deliberations. Specifically, in addition to memories of caring and being cared for, members of traditions—whether moral or religious—also draw upon stories or narratives, anecdotes, and ethical teachings.

16. Especially notable examples include Eva Feder Kittay (1999) and Virginia Held (2006); the latter's work is discussed in the text.

5. EARLY CHILDHOOD DEVELOPMENT AND EVIDENCE-BASED APPROACHES TO PARENTS, CHILDREN, AND MORAL CULTIVATION

1. The final chapter of this work addresses what it might mean to take Confucian views seriously, including the specific ways in which these ideas and approaches can inform our efforts to promote social and policy change.

2. I have previously argued that there are important resonances between aspects of the Nurse–Family Partnership (NFP) and Confucian ethics (Cline 2012; Cline 2013a:220–230). This chapter examines these issues in greater detail and gives specific attention to the theoretical foundations of the NFP and how these theories support early Confucian claims.

3. For studies of early childhood interventions, see Karoly et al. 1998; Karoly, Kilburn, and Cannon 2005.

4. The program was previously known as the Nurse Home Visitor Program.

5. On the effectiveness of other home-visitation programs, see Gomby, Culcross, and Behrman 1999; Olds et al. 2000.

6. Sociodemographic risk factors include young maternal age, being unmarried, low caregiver education (less than twelve years), and being unemployed. All of the trials have examined program impact with women who have had no previous live births, and each has focused recruitment on low-income, unmarried, and adolescent women, because the problems the program is designed to address—including poor birth outcomes, child abuse and neglect, and diminished economic self-sufficiency of parents—are concentrated in these populations. See Elster and McAnarney 1980; Furstenberg, Brooks-Gunn, and Morgan 1987; Overpeck et al. 1998.

7. On these aspects of the program, see www.nursefamilypartnership.org/about /program-history.

8. On this part of the program, see www.nursefamilypartnership.org/communities /NFP-Abroad.

9. Mothers with low psychological resources are those who scored lower on tests measuring intelligence, mental health, and sense of mastery (discussed in more detail later) at baseline.

10. For a sampling of the published results of the NFP, see Olds, Henderson, and Kitzman 1994; Olds et al. 1997, 1998; Kitzman et al. 2000.

11. There is evidence to suggest that higher levels of discipline and restriction by parents in low-income communities are associated with greater competence on the part of children when they reach adolescence. See Baldwin, Baldwin, and Cole 1990.

12. On programs that have failed or been minimally effective, see Maynard et al. 1993; Olds and Kitzman 1993; St. Pierre et al. 1995; Quint, Bos, and Polit 1997. The most careful and thorough review of the evidence regarding the extent to which these programs have been effective, and their comparative success or failure, is Olds et al. 2000:109–141. For a strong critique of home-visiting programs based on failed programs, see Gomby, Culcross, and Behrman 1999.

13. The fact that nurses are the home visitors in this program is one reason why the NFP is more successful than other early intervention programs. I discuss the evidence for this later in this chapter.

14. Self-efficacy theory is the third major part of the NFP's theoretical foundations.

15. Adaptive behavioral change is behavioral change that occurs in response to one's environment.

16. Ecologic theory provides strong empirical evidence against views of human nature as strongly "fixed," such as Hobbes's view, discussed in chap. 3. As we shall see later in this chapter, it also challenges strongly individualist views of the self, moral agency, and moral cultivation, seen in the views of thinkers such as Rousseau (also discussed in chap. 3), Ralph Waldo Emerson, and Jean-Paul Sartre.

17. On the impaired development of children whose mothers used substances such as tobacco, alcohol, marijuana, and cocaine while pregnant, see the following studies: Fried et al. 1987; Kramer 1987; Mayes 1994; Olds, Henderson, and Tatelbaum 1994; Streissguth et al. 1994; Millberger et al. 1996; Olds 1997.

18. For studies of these difficulties, see Saxon 1978; Streissguth et al. 1994.

19. On the long-term effects of poor prenatal health (including maternal smoking during pregnancy) seen in older children, adolescents, and teenagers, see Moffit 1993; Raine, Brennan, and Mednick 1994; Streissguth et al. 1994; Millberger et al. 1996; Olds 1997; Wakschlag et al. 1997.

20. On maternal smoking during pregnancy and adult male criminal outcomes, see Brennan, Grekin, and Mednick 1999. See also Moffit 1993; Wakschlag et al. 1997.

21. In the next chapter I will discuss the constructive value of Confucian accounts of prenatal cultivation; that is, I will discuss why we ought to amend and further develop this view rather than simply abandoning it and instead discussing the scientific data we have in this area.

22. Olds notes that serving first-time mothers beginning during pregnancy is thought to be part of the reason why the NFP has had such successful results. See Olds et al. 2000:136.

23. This finding is consistent with results of other preventive interventions. See Brooks-Gunn et al. 1992.

24. Bowlby 1969 is the first of three volumes. For a broad overview of the field at the end of the century, see Goldberg, Muir, and Kerr 1995; Cassidy and Shaver 1999.

25. Interestingly, the early Confucians observed that children are particularly dependent upon their parents during the first three years of life and developed views concerning the appropriateness of children mourning the loss of their parents for three years, something that suggests at least some level of appreciation for the idea that filial piety is a response to

parental caregiving, even if this was not consistently how they presented the ground of filial piety. I discuss this later in this chapter.

26. For a helpful overview of these aspects of attachment theory, see the foreword to Bowlby's work by Allan Schore (1973:xi–xxii).

27. For further discussion, see Schore's foreword in Bowlby's *Separation* (1973:xvii).

28. Sensitivity is typically defined as a combination of warmth and responsivity, seen in the extent to which a parent takes the child's perspective, accurately perceives her signals, and promptly and appropriately responds to those signals.

29. Other traditional societies also do not give equal weight to the virtues and qualities associated with good parents and those associated with good children. For example, while the biblical Ten Commandments specify that children should honor their parents, they do not include any specific commandments for parents with respect to the way they should treat their children. Thanks to Michael R. Slater for pointing this out.

30. As we saw earlier in this work, there is evidence for the claim that early Confucians recognized that good parental care was a powerful basis for filial piety in texts such as the *Shijing* and in literature such as Meng Jiao's "The Wandering Son."

31. Strengthening parent–child relationships has even been shown to lower children's likelihood of being susceptible to negative peer influences. See Emde and Buchsbaum 1990.

32. On the impact of prenatal diet and substance use on emotional vitality, see Zuckerman and Brown 1993. On the role of attachment in emotional vitality more generally, see Schore 1997; Robinson, Emde, and Korfmacher 1997.

33. Another way in which the NFP program promotes healthy attachment-related experiences between mothers and infants is through its educational efforts relating to family planning and contraception. Since rapid, successive pregnancy affects a mother's ability to succeed as nurturing caregiver for the children she already has, this can have a significant impact on children's attachment behaviors, while also affecting women's educational achievements and workforce participation (Olds 2006:12). For studies examining these issues, see Furstenberg, Brooks-Gunn, and Morgan 1987; Musick 1993.

34. For studies of these issues, see Baumrind 1987; Hart and Risley 1995; Peterson and Gable 1998; Bremner 1999; Grant et al. 2000; Pine 2001, 2003; Bremner and Vermetten 2004.

35. I further discuss the unique role of nurses in the NFP later in this chapter.

36. The NFP cites the Gallup organization, "Nurses Remain at Top of Honesty and Ethics Poll," November 27, 2000; http://www.gallup.com/poll/2287/nurses-remain-top-honesty-ethics-poll.aspx.

37. For works focused on the qualities associated with good nurses, see Kuhse 1997; Sellman 2011. See also Noddings 2003:139.

38. This is an area well worth further study. It would be interesting to learn more about the attitudes and actions of children who have benefited from the NFP toward their parents, compared with those in the control group.

39. The idea that siblings play an important role in one's conception of oneself and the world is widely recognized, as is the fact that parents of "only children" sometimes face unique challenges in helping their children to take a wider view and realize that

everything does not revolve around them. These challenges are a concern in American culture as well as in Chinese culture. Indeed, due to an increase in the number of only children in China as a result of the "one-child" policy, this is a growing area of concern in Chinese society.

6. THE HUMANITIES AT WORK

1. For a detailed study of these aspects of Rawls's theory of justice in comparison with the view found in the Confucian *Analects*, see Cline 2013a.
2. There is much research that supports this, including the NFP findings. Although the families the NFP serves usually come from the same or similar socioeconomic classes, there are nevertheless deep and important differences between them, from their basic living conditions, to their views of child care and parental responsibilities, to family dynamics and levels of support. Indeed, in the trials, nurse visitors found that the tremendous variability in the needs and strengths of the families constituted one of the most significant challenges in helping families. For further discussion, see Kitzman et al. 1997:102–103.
3. For a helpful introduction to the extensive body of secondary literature on Okin's work, see Satz and Reich 2009.
4. As we have seen, Confucian conceptions of filial piety as well as *de* ("Virtue," "moral power") play important roles in their views here.
5. "The Way lies in what is near, but people seek it in what is distant; one's task lies in what is easy, but people seek it in what is difficult. If everyone would treat their parents as parents and their elders as elders, the world would be at peace" (*Mengzi* 4A11).
6. Of course, many individuals are motivated to spend more time working than with their families simply by a desire to make more money and/or the desire to advance to a more prestigious, influential position. These motivations, like the view that it is better to promote the greatest good for the greatest number, reflect certain kinds of attitudes and beliefs that lead individuals to minimize the importance of prioritizing the family. Later in this chapter I argue that we have good reasons to work for change in these areas, but these kinds of attitudes, beliefs, and practices cannot simply be addressed through legal or policy change.
7. Consider, for example, the reasons why Gandhi, Mother Teresa, Martin Luther King Jr., Albert Schweitzer, and Nelson Mandela are widely considered sources of moral inspiration.
8. Five states offer maternity leave that goes beyond the federal law: California, Hawaii, New Jersey, New York, and Rhode Island offer partial wage compensation to women following the birth of a child. Only about one-fourth of U.S. employers offer fully paid maternity leave of any kind. See Ray, Gornick, and Schmitt 2009.
9. I would like to stress that I am *not* arguing that we should model our laws and policies in this area after East Asian countries. With respect to parental leave policies (including both the length of leave and the availability of paternal leave in addition to maternal leave), European countries tend to do better than East Asian countries. Cultural factors in some East Asian countries partly account for this difference. For

example, in China there is a widespread expectation that grandparents will provide in-home care for infants and children. Views and standards concerning women's equality and the treatment of women also help to account for the difference between countries that mandate paid leave for a significant period of time and those that do not, which represents another reason why it is nothing short of scandalous that that the United States lags so far behind in this area.

10. For further discussion, see Waldfogel 2001:99. For an argument concerning the financial feasibility of paid parental leave in the United States, see Heymann and Earle 2009. I discuss the financial aspects of this issue later in the chapter.

11. I am not arguing we should mandate paid parental leave because it will lead to economic gains. Rather, I am pointing out that the evidence does not support the view that paid parental leave is economically disadvantageous for a country; as a result, it is not a good reason to reject mandated paid leave.

12. Sweden offers 16 months at 80 percent of the worker's salary, while Canada offers 17 weeks at 55 percent; Japan offers 14 weeks at two-thirds pay. Any of these would make an enormous difference in the lives of American families.

13. It is important to remember the rampant discrimination against immigrants to the United States from different parts of Europe, the United Kingdom, and Ireland over the past 150 years, because this can remind us that not too long ago most of us would have been the victims of work-related discrimination. Here we see another example of how the humanities can contribute significantly to our efforts to promote social and policy change through the careful study of history.

14. The question of whether out-of-home care can be more beneficial for children than being cared for by their own parents is complex and depends upon a variety of factors, including the situation and needs of the child, the background of the child's parents (including their educational background and emotional resources), the quality of the out-of-home care (including the educational level and background of the teachers and the caregiver/teacher–child ratio, as well as the curriculum), and the amount of time the child spends there. Most investigators agree that the cognitive effects of high-quality care are consistently positive, but many parents are capable of providing high-quality care for their children if given the opportunity (and if they desire to do so and are committed to it). Perhaps most importantly, though, most centers that are of high quality charge rates that are out of reach for most families. There is, however, substantial evidence to show that small children from low-income families can benefit from particular types of programs. For instance, the Perry Preschool Project offered two-and-a-half-hour classes with low student–teacher ratios and weekly visits with parents and children in their homes to low-income African-American children aged three and four with very low IQs. The program was successful in part because of its efforts to strengthen parent–child relationships and parental engagement with the child, instead of simply delegating that task to someone else. For an overview, see Schweinhart 2010.

15. Whenever possible, parents of young children should also be accorded greater flexibility by their employers in terms of the hours they work and the choices they make concerning the responsibilities they take on at work. Due to technological progress, it is increasingly

possible for employees to do at least some of their work and even participate in meetings from remote locations. Various kinds of flexibility ought to be offered to full-time employees but can be augmented by expanding the kinds of positions available to parents of young children. Bok suggests, for example, "Greater efforts might also be made to increase part-time jobs in the public sector for mothers of small children so that they can work but still have ample time for parenting. Sweden has had such success with this approach that Swedish mothers spend more time with their small children than American mothers even though a higher percentage are employed" (Bok 2010:147).

16. This study also confirms the important role that nurse home visitors can play in breast-feeding success.

17. See *The Business Case for Breastfeeding*, a comprehensive employer-education program sponsored by the U.S. Department of Health and Human Services Office on Women's Health: https://www.womenshealth.gov/breastfeeding/government-in-action/business-case-for -breastfeeding.pdf.

18. Data are from the United Nations World Population Prospects, the 2010 revision (for the years 2005–2010). Compare the U.S. ranking with the top-ranked country, Singapore (2 deaths per 1,000 live births); Japan (ranked sixth with 3 deaths per 1,000 live births); France (ranked twelfth with 4 deaths per 1,000 live births); and the United Kingdom (ranked thirty-first with 5 deaths per 1,000 live births).

19. This marks a further difference from Confucian approaches. See Ivanhoe 2010b.

20. Sawhill is president of the National Campaign to Prevent Teen Pregnancy and senior editor of the *Future of Children*.

21. Bok writes that the percentage of children living with a single parent increased from 8 percent in 1960 to 28 percent in 2005.

22. Bok writes that these factors persist even after controlling for income, education, and other observed factors. For empirical evidence concerning the impact of the involvement of both mothers and fathers on early childhood development, see Ryan, Martin, and Brooks-Gunn 2006; Martin, Ryan, and Brooks-Gunn 2007, 2010.

CONCLUSION

1. Indeed, Nussbaum points out that President Obama has defended early childhood interventions by saying, "For every dollar we invest in these programs, we get nearly ten dollars back in reduced welfare rolls, fewer health care costs, and less crime" (Nussbaum 2010:137). Nussbaum and I would like to see more emphasis on the fact that effective programs of this sort lead human beings to lead happier, more satisfying, and ethically better lives, and help children to become reflective, empathic citizens, in part by cultivating the capacities that will later enable them to benefit from an education.

2. Translation from Gardner 2007:4–5.

BIBLIOGRAPHY

Ahluwalia, Indu B., Brian Morrow, and Jason Hsia. 2005. "Why Do Women Stop Breastfeeding? Findings from the Pregnancy Risk Assessment and Monitoring System." *Pediatrics* 116:1408–1412.

Ainsworth, Mary D. Salter, Mary C. Blehar, Everett Waters, and Sally Wall. 1978. *Patterns of Attachment: A Psychological Study of the Strange Situation.* Hillsdale, N.J.: Lawrence Erlbaum.

Amato, Paul R., and Rebecca A. Maynard. 2007. "Decreasing Nonmarital Births and Strengthening Marriage to Reduce Poverty." *Future of Children* 17:117–141.

American Academy of Pediatrics. 2012. "Breastfeeding and the Use of Human Milk." *Pediatrics* 129:e827–e841.

Ames, Roger T. 1991. "The Mencian Conception of *Ren Xing*: Does It Mean 'Human Nature'?" In *Chinese Texts and Philosophical Contexts. Essays Dedicated to Angus C. Graham*, ed. Henry Rosemont Jr., 143–175. Chicago: Open Court.

——. 2009. "Becoming Practically Religious: A Deweyan and Confucian Context for Rortian Religiousness." In *Rorty, Pragmatism, and Confucianism*, ed. Yong Huang, 255–276. Albany: State University of New York Press.

Annas, Julia. 1993. *The Morality of Happiness.* New York: Oxford University Press.

Anscombe, Elizabeth. 1958. "Modern Moral Philosophy." *Philosophy* 33:1–19.

Aos, Steve R., Roxanne Lieb, Jim Mayfield, Marna Miller, and Annie Pennucci. 2004. *Benefits and Costs of Prevention and Early Intervention Programs for Youth.* Olympia: Washington State Institute for Public Policy.

Aquinas, Saint Thomas. 1948. *Summa Theologiae.* 5 vols. Trans. Fathers of the English Dominican Province. New York: Benzinger.

Aristotle. 1935. *Athenian Constitution. Eudemian Ethics. Virtues and Vices.* Trans. H. Rackham. Cambridge: Harvard University Press.

——. 1998. *Politics.* Trans. C.D.C. Reeve. Indianapolis: Hackett.

——. 1999. *Nicomachean Ethics.* Trans. Terrence Irwin. Indianapolis: Hackett.

Augustine. 1955. *The Good of Marriage.* Trans. C. T. Wilcox. New York: Fathers of the Church.

——. 1960. *The Confessions of Saint Augustine.* Trans. John K. Ryan. New York: Image.

Baldwin, Alfred L., Clara Baldwin, and Robert E. Cole. 1990. "Stress-Resistant Families and Stress-Resistant Children." In *Risk and Protective Factors in the Development of Psychopathology*, ed. Jon Rolf, Ann S. Masten, Dante Cicchetti, Keith H. Neuchterlein, and Sheldon Weintraub, 257–280. New York: Cambridge University Press.

Bartick, Melissa, and Arnold Reinhold. 2010. "The Burden of Suboptimal Breastfeeding in the United States: A Pediatric Cost Analysis." *Pediatrics* 125:e1048–e1056.

Baumrind, D. 1987. *Familial Antecedents of Adolescent Drug Use: A Developmental Perspective.* Washington, D.C.: U.S. Government Printing Office.

Behuniak, James, Jr. 2005. *Mencius on Becoming Human.* Albany: State University of New York Press.

Bell, Daniel A. 2006. *Beyond Liberal Democracy: Political Thinking for an East Asian Context.* Princeton: Princeton University Press.

Bergner, Daniel. 2006. "The Case of Marie and Her Sons." *The New York Times Magazine.* www .nytimes.com/2006/07/23/magazine/23welfare.html?pagewanted=all&_r=0

Bloom, Allan, trans. 1968. *The Republic of Plato.* 2nd ed. New York: Basic.

Bloom, Irene. 2002. "Mengzian Arguments on Human Nature (*Ren Xing*)." In *Essays on the Moral Philosophy of Mengzi*, ed. Xiusheng Liu and Philip J. Ivanhoe, 64–100. Indianapolis: Hackett.

Blustein, Jeffrey. 1982. *Parents and Children: The Ethics of the Family.* New York: Oxford University Press.

Bodde, Derk. 1986. "The State and Empire of Ch'in." In *The Cambridge History of China*, vol. 1, ed. Denis Twitchett and Michael Loewe, 21–102. Cambridge: Cambridge University Press.

Bok, Derek. 2010. *The Politics of Happiness.* Princeton: Princeton University Press.

Bowlby, John. 1969. *Attachment and Loss.* Vol. 1, *Attachment.* New York: Basic.

——. 1973. *Attachment and Loss.* Vol. 2, *Separation.* New York: Basic.

Bremner, J. D. 1999. "Does Stress Damage the Brain?" *Biological Psychiatry* 45:797–805.

Bremner, J. D., and E. Vermetten. 2004. "Neuroanatomical Changes Associated with Pharmacotherapy in Posttraumatic Stress Disorder." *Annals of the New York Academy of Sciences* 1032:154–157.

Brennan, P. A., E. R. Grekin, and S. A. Mednick. 1999. "Maternal Smoking During Pregnancy and Adult Male Criminal Outcomes." *Archives of General Psychiatry* 56:215–219.

Brennan, Samantha. 1999. "Recent Work in Feminist Ethics." *Ethics* 109:858–893.

Bronfenbrenner, Urie. 1979. *The Ecology of Human Development: Experiments by Nature and Design.* Cambridge Harvard University Press.

——. 1992. "The Person-Process-Context Model in Developmental Research Principles, Applications, and Implications." Unpublished manuscript, Cornell University, Ithaca, NY.

Brooks-Gunn, Jeanne, R. T. Gross, H. C. Kraemer, D. Spiker, and S. Shapiro. 1992. "Enhancing the Cognitive Outcomes of Low Birth Weight, Premature Infants: For Whom Is the Intervention Most Effective?" *Pediatrics* 89:1209–1215.

Brunschwig, Jacques. 1986. "The Cradle Argument in Epicureanism and Stoicism." In *The Norms of Nature: Studies in Hellenistic Ethics*, ed. Malcolm Schofield and Gisela Striker, 113–144. Cambridge: Cambridge University Press.

Bubeck, Diemut. 1995. *Care, Gender, and Justice*. Oxford: Oxford University Press.

Carlson, Elizabeth A., and L. Alan Sroufe. 1995. "Contribution of Attachment Theory to Developmental Psychopathology." In *Developmental Psychopathology*, ed. Danti Cicchetti and Donald J. Cohen, vol. 1, *Theory and Methods*, 581–617. New York: Wiley.

Cassidy, J., and P. R. Shaver, eds. 1999. *Handbook of Attachment: Theory, Research, and Clinical Applications*. New York: Guilford.

Centers for Disease Control and Prevention. 2011. Breastfeeding Report Card and CDC National Immunization Survey: "How Many Infants Born in the United States Are Breastfed?" www.cdc.gov/breastfeeding/faq/index.htm.

Chan, Alan K. L., ed. 2002. *Mencius: Contexts and Interpretations*. Honolulu: University of Hawaii Press.

Chan, Sin Yee. 1993. "An Ethic of Loving: Ethical Particularism and the Engaged Perspective in Confucian Role-Ethics." PhD diss., University of Michigan.

Cicero. 2000. *On Obligations*. Trans. P. G. Walsh. New York: Oxford University Press.

Cline, Erin M. 2012. "Confucian Ethics, Public Policy, and the Nurse–Family Partnership." *Dao: A Journal of Comparative Philosophy* 11 (3):337–356.

——. 2013a. *Confucius, Rawls, and the Sense of Justice*. New York: Fordham University Press.

——. 2013b. "Religious Thought and Practice in the *Analects*." In *The Dao Companion to the Analects*, ed. Amy Olberding, 259–291. New York: Springer.

Cooper, John. 1986. *Reason and Human Good in Aristotle*. Indianapolis: Hackett.

——. 1999. *Reason and Emotion*. Princeton: Princeton University Press.

Coyne, Jerry A. 2009. *Why Evolution Is True*. New York: Penguin.

Csikzentmihalyi, Mark, trans. 2003. "Luxuriant Gems of the Spring and Autumn (Chunqiu Fanlu)." In *Images of Women in Chinese Thought and Culture*, ed. Robin R. Wang, 162–169. Indianapolis: Hackett.

Csikzentmihalyi, Mark, ed. 2006. *Readings in Han Chinese Thought*. Indianapolis: Hackett.

Dewey, John. 1989. *The Later Works, 1925–1953*. Vol. 7, *1932/Ethics*. Carbondale: Southern Illinois University Press.

Dix, Dustine N. 1991. "Why Women Decide Not to Breastfeed." *Birth* 18:222–225.

Ebrey, Patricia Buckley. 1993. *The Inner Quarters: Marriage and the Lives of Chinese Women in the Song Period*. Berkeley: University of California Press.

Eckenrode, John, Mary Campa, Dennis W. Luckey, Charles R. Henderson Jr., Robert Cole, Harriet Kitzman, Elizabeth Anson, Kimberly Sidora-Arcoleo, Jane Powers, and David Olds. 2010. "Long-Term Effects of Prenatal and Infancy Nurse Home Visitation on the Life Course of Youths: Nineteen-Year Follow-up of a Randomized Trial." *Archives of Pediatric and Adolescent Medicine* 164:9–15.

Edin, Kathryn, and Joanna M. Reed. 2005. "Why Don't They Just Get Married? Barriers to Marriage Among the Disadvantaged." *Future of Children* 15:117–137.

Elster, A. B., and E. R. McAnarney. 1980. "Medical and Psychosocial Risks of Pregnancy and Childbearing During Adolescence." *Pediatric Annals* 9:89–94.

Eno, Robert. 2005. "Review of James Behuniak Jr., *Mencius on Becoming Human.*" *China Review International* 12:359–363.

Epictetus. 2008. "Discourses." In *The Stoics Reader: Selected Writings and Testimonia*, trans. Brad Inwood and Lloyd P. Gerson, 195–205. Indianapolis: Hackett.

Fingarette, Herbert. 1972. *The Secular as Sacred.* New York: Harper and Row.

Fried, P. A., B. Watkinson, R. F. Dillon, and C. S. Dulberg. 1987. "Neonatal Neurological Status in a Low-Risk Population After Prenatal Exposure to Cigarettes, Marijuana, and Alcohol." *Journal of Developmental and Behavioral Pediatrics* 8:318–326.

Furstenberg, F. F., J. Brooks-Gunn, and S. P. Morgan. 1987. *Adolescent Mothers in Later Life.* Cambridge: Cambridge University Press.

Gabarino, J. 1981. "An Ecological Perspective on Child Maltreatment." In *The Social Context of Child Abuse and Neglect*, ed. L. Pelton, 228–267. New York: Human Sciences.

Gardner, Daniel K., trans. 1990. *Learning to Be a Sage: Selections from the Conversations of Master Chu, Arranged Topically.* Berkeley: University of California Press.

——. 2007. *The Four Books: The Basic Teachings of the Later Confucian Tradition.* Indianapolis: Hackett.

Gert, Bernard. 1996. "Hobbes's Psychology." In *The Cambridge Companion to Hobbes*, ed. Tom Sorell, 157–174. New York: Cambridge University Press.

Gilligan, Carol. 1982. *In a Different Voice: Psychological Theory and Women's Development.* Cambridge: Harvard University Press.

——. 1987. "Moral Orientation and Moral Development." In *Women and Moral Theory*, ed. Eva Kittay and Diana Meyers, 19–32. Lanham, Md.: Rowman and Littlefield.

Gohm, Carol, Shigehiro Oishi, Janet Darlington, and Ed Diener. 1998. "Culture, Parental Conflict, Parental Marital Status, and the Subjective Well-Being of Young Adults." *Journal of Marriage and the Family* 60:319–334.

Goldberg, Susan, R. Muir, and J. Kerr. 1995. *Attachment Theory: Social, Developmental, and Clinical Perspectives.* Hillsdale, N.J.: Analytic.

Gomby, Deanna S., Patti L. Culcross, and Richard E. Behrman. 1999. "Home Visiting: Recent Program Evaluations—Analysis and Recommendations." *Future of Children* 9:4–26.

Graham, A. C. 1990. *Studies in Chinese Philosophy and Philosophical Literature.* Albany: State University of New York Press.

Grant, Kathryn E., Jeffrey H. O'koon, Trina H. Davis, Nicola A. Roache, LaShaunda M. Poindexter, Mashana L. Armstrong, Joel A. Minden, and Jeanne M. McIntosh. 2000. "Protective Factors Affecting Low-Income Urban African American Youth Exposed to Stress." *Journal of Early Adolescence* 20:388–417.

Guoyu 國語. 1988. Vol. 2. Shanghai: Shanghai guji 上海古籍出版社.

Harding, Sandra. 1987. "The Curious Coincidence of Feminine and African Moralities." In *Women and Moral Theory*, ed. Eva Kittay and Diana Meyers, 296–315. Lanham, Md.: Rowman and Littlefield.

Harper, Donald J., trans. 1998. *Early Chinese Medical Literature: The Mawangdui Medical Manuscripts.* London: Kegan Paul International.

Hart, B., and T. R. Risley. 1995. *Meaningful Differences in the Everyday Experience of Young American Children*. Baltimore: Brookes.

Hegel, G.W.F. 1952. *The Philosophy of Right*. Trans. T. M. Knox. New York: Oxford University Press.

Held, Virginia. 1987. "Non-contractual Society: A Feminist View." *Canadian Journal of Philosophy* 13:111–135.

——. 2006. *The Ethics of Care: Personal, Political, and Global*. New York: Oxford University Press.

Herr, Ranjoo. 2003. "Is Confucianism Compatible with Care Ethics? A Critique." *Philosophy East and West* 53:471–489.

Heymann, Jody, and Alison Earle. 2009. *Raising the Global Floor: Dismantling the Myth That We Can't Afford Good Working Conditions for Everyone*. Stanford: Stanford University Press.

Hobbes, Thomas. 1967. *Body, Man, and Citizen*. Ed. R. S. Peters. New York: Collier.

——. 1968. *Leviathan*. Ed. C. B. Macpherson. Baltimore: Penguin.

——. 1991. *De cive*. In *Man and Citizen*, ed. Bernard Gert. Indianapolis: Hackett.

——. 1996. *Leviathan*. Ed. R. Tuck. Cambridge: Cambridge University Press.

hooks, bell. 1984. *Feminist Theory: From the Margin to the Center*. Boston: South End.

Hursthouse, Rosalind. 1999. *On Virtue Ethics*. New York: Oxford University Press.

Hutchinson, D. S. 1995. "Ethics." In *The Cambridge Companion to Aristotle*, ed. Jonathan Barnes, 195–232. New York: Cambridge University Press.

Hutton, Eric L. trans. 2014. *Xunzi: The Complete Text*. Princeton: Princeton University Press.

Isaacs, Julia B. 2009. "How Much Do We Spend on Children and the Elderly?" and "A Comparative Perspective on Public Spending on Children." Working Paper. The Brookings Institution Center on Children and Families.

Isabella, Patrice H. 1994. "Correlates of Successful Breastfeeding: A Study of Social and Personal Factors." *Journal of Human Lactation* 10:257–264.

Ivanhoe, Philip J. 1991. "A Happy Symmetry: Xunzi's Ethical Thought." *Journal of the American Academy of Religion* 59:309–322.

——. 1999. "The Concept of *de* ('Virtue') in the *Laozi*." In *Religious and Philosophical Aspects of the Laozi*, ed. Mark Csikszentmihalyi and Philip J. Ivanhoe, 239–257. Albany: State University of New York Press.

——. 2000a. *Confucian Moral Self Cultivation*. 2nd ed. Indianapolis: Hackett.

——. 2000b. "Mengzi, Xunzi, and Modern Feminist Ethics." In *The Sage and the Second Sex: Confucianism, Ethics, and Gender*, ed. Chenyang Li, 57–74. Chicago: Open Court.

——. 2002a. *Ethics in the Confucian Tradition: The Thought of Mengzi and Wang Yangming*. 2nd ed. Indianapolis: Hackett.

——. 2002b. "Whose Confucius? Which Analects?" In *Confucius and the Analects: New Essays*, ed. Bryan W. Van Norden, 119–133. New York: Oxford University Press.

——. 2002c. "Confucian Self Cultivation and Mengzi's Notion of Extension." In *Essays on the Moral Philosophy of Mengzi*, ed. Xiusheng Liu and Philip J. Ivanhoe, 221–241. Indianapolis: Hackett.

——. 2007. "Filial Piety as a Virtue." In *Working Virtue: Virtue Ethics and Contemporary Moral Problems*, ed. Rebecca L. Walker and Philip J. Ivanhoe, 297–312. New York: Oxford University Press.

———. 2008a. "The Shade of Confucius: Social Roles, Ethical Theory, and the Self." In *Polishing the Chinese Mirror: Essays in Honor of Henry Rosemont Jr.*, ed. Ronnie Littlejohn and Marthe Chandler, 41–56. New York: Global Scholarly.

———. 2008b. "The 'Golden Rule' in the *Analects*." In *Confucius Now: Contemporary Encounters with the Analects*, ed. David Jones, 81–108. Chicago: Open Court.

———. 2010a. "A Confucian Contribution to Justice, Gender, and the Family." Presented at Confucian and Liberal Perspectives on Family, State, and Civil Society, December 7, 2010, City University of Hong Kong.

———. 2010b. "A Confucian Perspective on Abortion." *Dao* 9:37–51.

———. 2011. "Death and Dying in the *Analects*." In *Mortality in Traditional Chinese Thought*, ed. Amy Olberding and Philip J. Ivanhoe, 137–152. Albany: State University of New York Press.

Jecker, Nancy. 1989. "Are Filial Duties Unfounded?" *American Philosophical Quarterly* 26:73–80.

Johnson, Robert N. 2007. "Self-Development as an Imperfect Duty." In *Moral Cultivation: Essays on the Development of Character and Virtue*, ed. Brad K. Wilburn, 125–146. Lanham, Md.: Lexington.

Kant, Immanuel. 1959. "Idea for a General History with a Cosmopolitan Purpose." In *Theories of History*, trans. Patrick Gardiner, 22–34. Glencoe, Ill.: Free Press.

———. 1991. *The Metaphysics of Morals*. Trans. Mary Gregor. New York: Cambridge University Press.

———. 1997. *Lectures on Ethics*. Trans. Peter Heath. Cambridge: Cambridge University Press.

Karoly, Lynn A., Peter W. Greenwood, Susan S. Everingham, Jill Hoube, M. Rebecca Kilburn, C. Peter Rydell, Matthew Sanders, and James Chiesa. 1998. *Investing in Our Children: What We Know and Don't Know About the Costs and Benefits of Early Childhood Interventions.* Santa Monica, Calif.: RAND Corporation.

Karoly, Lynn A., M. Rebecca Kilburn, and Jill S. Cannon. 2005. *Early Childhood Interventions: Proven Results, Future Promise.* Santa Monica, Calif.: RAND Corporation.

Kim, Sungmoon. 2009. "Self-Transformation and Civil Society: Lockean vs. Confucian." *Dao* 8:383–401.

Kinney, Anne Behnke, ed. 1995. *Chinese Views of Childhood.* Honolulu: University of Hawaii Press.

Kinney, Anne Behnke. 2004. *Representations of Childhood and Youth in Early China.* Stanford: Stanford University Press.

Kinney, Anne Behnke, trans. 2014. *Exemplary Women of Early China: The Lienü Zhuan of Liu Xiang.* New York: Columbia University Press.

Kittay, Eva Feder. 1999. *Love's Labor: Essays on Women, Equality, and Dependency.* New York: Routledge.

Kitzman, Harriet J., Robert Cole, H. Lorrie Yoos, and David Olds. 1997. "Challenges Experienced by Home Visitors: A Qualitative Study of Program Implementation." *Journal of Community Psychology* 25:95–109.

Kitzman, Harriet J., David L. Olds, Kimberly Sidora, Charles R. Henderson, Carole Hanks, Robert Cole, Dennis W. Luckey, Jessica Bondy, Kimberly Cole, and Judith Glazner. 2000. "Enduring Effects of Nurse Home Visitation on Maternal Life Course: A Three-Year Follow-Up of a Randomized Trial." *Journal of the American Medical Association* 283:1983–1989.

Kitzman, Harriet J., David L. Olds, Robert E. Cole, Carole A. Hanks, Elizabeth A. Anson, Kimberly J. Arcoleo, Dennis W. Luckey, Michael D. Knudtson, Charles R. Henderson, and John R. Holmberg. 2010. "Enduring Effects of Prenatal and Infancy Home Visiting by Nurses on Children: Follow-Up of a Randomized Trial Among Children at Age 12 Years." *Archives of Pediatric and Adolescent Medicine* 164:412–418.

Klinnert, M. D., J. J. Campos, J.F. Sorce, R.N. Emde, and M. Svejda. 1983. "Social Referencing: Emotional Expressions as Behavior Regulators." In *Emotion: Theory, Research, and Experience*, ed. R. Plutchik and H. Kellerman, vol. 2, *Emotions in Early Development*, 57–86. Orlando Academic.

Knoblock, John. 1994. *Xunzi: A Translation and Study of the Complete Works*, Vol. 3. Stanford: Stanford University Press.

Ko, Dorothy. 1994. *Teachers of the Inner Chambers: Women and Culture in Seventeenth-Century China*. Stanford: Stanford University Press.

——. 2001. *Every Step a Lotus: Shoes for Bound Feet*. Berkeley: University of California Press.

——. 2005. *Cinderella's Sisters: A Revisionist History of Footbinding*. Berkeley: University of California Press.

Kramer, M. S. 1987. "Intrauterine Growth and Gestational Duration Determinants." *Pediatrics* 80:502–511.

Kraut, Richard. 2012. "Aristotle's Ethics." In *The Stanford Encyclopedia of Philosophy* (spring 2012 edition), ed. Edward N. Zalta, sec. 3.1. http://plato.stanford.edu/archives/spr2012/entries /aristotle-ethics.

Kuan, Lisa W., Maria Britto, Joji Decolongon, Pamela J. Schoettker, Harry D. Atherton, and Uma R. Kotagal. 1999. "Health System Factors Contributing to Breastfeeding Success." *Pediatrics* 104:1–7.

Kuhse, Helga. 1997. *Caring: Nurses, Women, and Ethics*. Oxford: Blackwell.

Kupperman, Joel J. 1999. *Learning from Asian Philosophy*. New York: Oxford University Press.

——. 2000. "Feminism as Radical Confucianism: Self and Tradition." In *The Sage and the Second Sex: Confucianism, Ethics, and Gender*, ed. Chenyang Li, 43–56. Chicago: Open Court.

Lau, D. C. 2000. "Theories of Human Nature in Mengzi and Xunzi." Reprinted in *Virtue, Nature, and Moral Agency in the Xunzi*, ed. T. C. Kline III and Philip J. Ivanhoe, 188–219. Indianapolis: Hackett.

Lau, D. C., and Fong Ching Chen, eds. 1992. *A Concordance to the Xiaojing* 孝經逐字索引. Hong Kong: Commercial Press.

——. 1996. *A Concordance to the Xunzi* 荀子逐字索引. Hong Kong: Commercial Press.

——. 2006. *A Concordance to the Lunyu* 論語逐字索引. Hong Kong: Commercial Press.

Lee, Pauline C. 2000. "Li Zhi and John Stuart Mill: A Confucian Feminist Critique of Liberal Feminism." In *The Sage and the Second Sex: Confucianism, Ethics, and Gender*, ed. Chenyang Li, 113–132. Chicago: Open Court.

Lee, Thomas H. C. 2000. *Education in Traditional China: A History*. Leiden: Brill.

Legge, James. 1880. *The Religions of China: Confucianism and Taoism Described and Compared with Christianity*. London: Hodder and Stoughton.

Legge, James, trans. 1885. *The Sacred Books of China: The Texts of Confucianism*. Part 3, *The Li Ki*, 1–10. Oxford: Clarendon.

———, 1970a. *The Works of Mencius*. New York: Dover. Republication of *The Chinese Classics*, vol. 2, Oxford: Clarendon, 1895.

———, 1970b. *The Shijing or Book of Poetry. The Chinese Classics, vol. 4*. Hong Kong: Hong Kong University Press. Reprint.

———, 1971. *Confucius: Confucian Analects, The Great Learning, and The Doctrine of the Mean*. New York: Dover. Republication of *The Chinese Classics*, vol. 1, Oxford: Clarendon, 1893.

———, 2003. "The Book of Rites." In *Images of Women in Chinese Thought and Culture*, ed. Robin R. Wang, 48–60. Indianapolis: Hackett.

Lewis, Mark Edward. 1999. *Writing and Authority in Early China*. Albany: State University of New York Press.

Li, Chenyang. 1994. "The Confucian Concept of Jen and the Feminist Ethics of Care: A Comparative Study." *Hypatia* 9:70–89.

———. 2002. "Revisiting Confucian *Jen* Ethics and Feminist Care Ethics: A Reply to Daniel Star and Lijun Yuan." *Hypatia* 17:130–140.

Li, Ruowei, Sara B. Fein, Jian Chen, and Laurence M. Grummer-Strawn. 2008. "Why Mothers Stop Breastfeeding: Mothers' Self-Reported Reasons for Stopping During the First Year." *Pediatrics* 122 (suppl. 2): s69–s76.

Liu, Xiusheng, and Philip J. Ivanhoe, eds. 2002. *Essays on the Moral Philosophy of Mengzi*. Indianapolis: Hackett.

Locke, John. 1988. *Two Treatises of Government*. Ed. Peter Laslett. Cambridge: Cambridge University Press.

Loewe, Michael. 1974. *Crisis and Conflict in Han China, 104 BC to AD 9*. London: George Allen and Unwin.

Luo, Shirong. 2007. "Relation, Virtue, and Relational Virtue." *Hypatia* 22:92–110.

MacIntyre, Alasdair. 1999. *Dependent Rational Animals: Why Human Beings Need the Virtues*. Chicago: Open Court.

Main, Mary, Nancy Kaplan, and Jude Cassidy. 1985. "Security in Infancy, Childhood, and Adulthood: A Move to the Level of Representation." In *Growing Points of Attachment in Theory and Research*, ed. Inge Bretherton and Everett Waters, 66–104. Chicago: University of Chicago Press.

Mann, Susan. 1997. *Precious Records: Women in China's Long Eighteenth Century*. Stanford: Stanford University Press.

Martin, Anne, Rebecca M. Ryan, and Jeanne Brooks-Gunn. 2007. "The Joint Influence of Mother and Father Parenting on Child Cognitive Outcomes at Age 5." *Early Childhood Research Quarterly* 22:423–439.

———. 2010. "When Fathers' Supportiveness Matters Most: Maternal and Paternal Parenting and Children's School Readiness." *Journal of Family Psychology* 24:145–155.

Mayes, L. C. 1994. "Neurobiology of Prenatal Cocaine Exposure: Effect on Developing Monoamine Systems." *Infant Mental Health Journal* 15:121–133.

Maynard, Rebecca A., Walter Nicholson, and Anu Rangarajan. 1993. *Breaking the Cycle of Poverty: The Effectiveness of Mandatory Services for Welfare-Dependent Teenage Parents*. Princeton: Mathematica Policy Research.

McLanahan, Sara S., and Marcia J. Carlson. 2002. "Welfare Reform, Fertility, and Father Involvement." *Future of Children* 12:147–166.

Millberger, S., J. Biederman, S. V. Faraone, L. Chen, and J. Jones. 1996. "Is Maternal Smoking During Pregnancy a Risk Factor for Attention Deficit Hyperactivity Disorder in Children?" *American Journal of Psychiatry* 153:1138–1142.

Moffit, T. E. 1993. "Adolescence-Limited and Life-Course-Persistent Antisocial Behavior: A Developmental Taxonomy." *Psychological Review* 100:674–701.

Musick, Judith S. 1993. *Young, Poor, and Pregnant.* New Haven: Yale University Press.

Nivison, David S. 1996. *The Ways of Confucianism: Investigations in Chinese Philosophy.* Ed. Bryan W. Van Norden. La Salle: Open Court.

Noddings, Nel. 1984. *Caring: A Feminine Approach to Ethics and Moral Education.* Berkeley: University of California Press.

——. 2002a. *Educating Moral People: A Caring Alternative to Character Education.* New York: Teachers College Press.

——. 2002b. *Starting at Home.* Berkeley: University of California Press.

——. 2003. *Happiness and Education.* New York: Cambridge University Press.

——. 2010a. "Dewey's Philosophy of Education: A Critique from the Perspective of Care Theory." In *The Cambridge Companion to Dewey*, ed. Molly Cochran, 265–287. New York: Cambridge University Press.

——. 2010b. *The Maternal Factor: Two Paths to Morality.* Berkeley: University of California Press.

Nussbaum, Martha C. 1986. *The Fragility of Goodness: Luck and Ethics in Greek Tragedy and Philosophy.* New York: Cambridge University Press.

——. 1994. *The Therapy of Desire: Theory and Practice in Hellenistic Ethics.* Princeton: Princeton University Press.

——. 2010. *Not for Profit: Why Democracy Needs the Humanities.* Princeton: Princeton University Press.

Ogbuanu, Chinelo, Saundra Glover, Janice Probst, Jihong Liu, and James Hussey. 2011. "The Effect of Maternity Leave Length and Time of Return to Work on Breastfeeding." *Pediatrics* 127:e1414–e1427.

Okin, Susan Moller. 1991. *Justice, Gender, and the Family.* New York: Basic.

Olds, David L. 1997. "Tobacco Exposure and Impaired Development: A Review of the Evidence." *Mental Retardation and Developmental Disabilities Research Reviews* 3:257–269.

——. 2002. "Prenatal and Infancy Home Visiting by Nurses: From Randomized Trials to Community Replication." *Prevention Science* 3:153–172.

——. 2006. "The Nurse–Family Partnership: An Evidence-Based Preventive Intervention." *Infant Mental Health Journal* 27:5–25.

——. 2010. "The Nurse–Family Partnership: From Trials to Practice." In *Childhood Programs and Practices in the First Decade of Life: A Human Capital Integration*, ed. Arthur J. Reynolds et al., 49–75. New York: Cambridge University Press.

Olds, David L., Charles R. Henderson Jr., Robert Cole, John Eckenrode, Harriet Kitzman, Dennis Luckey, Lisa Pettitt, Kimberly Sidora, Pamela Morris, and Jane Powers. 1998. "Long-Term Effects of Nurse Home Visitation on Children's Criminal and Antisocial

Behavior: Fifteen-Year Follow-Up of a Randomized Controlled Trial." *Journal of the American Medical Association* 280:1238–1244.

Olds, David L., Charles R. Henderson Jr., and Harriet Kitzman, 1994. "Does Prenatal and Infancy Nurse Home Visitation Have Enduring Effects on Qualities of Parental Caregiving and Child Health at 25 to 50 Months of Life?" *Pediatrics* 93:89–98.

Olds, David L., Charles R. Henderson Jr., and R. Tatelbaum. 1994. "Intellectual Impairment in Children of Women Who Smoke Cigarettes During Pregnancy." *Pediatrics* 93:221–227.

Olds, David L., Peggy Hill, JoAnn Robinson, Nancy Song, and Christina Little. 2000. "Update on Home Visiting for Pregnant Women and Parents of Young Children." *Current Problems in Pediatrics* 30:109–141.

Olds, David L., and H. Kitzman. 1993. "Review of Research on Home Visiting for Pregnant Women and Parents of Young Children." *Future of Children* 3:51–92.

Olds, David L., Harriet J. Kitzman, Robert E. Cole, Carole A. Hanks, K. J. Arcoleo, E. A. Anson, D. W. Luckey, M. D. Knudtson, C. R. Henderson, J. Bondy, and A. J. Stevenson. 2010. "Enduring Effects of Prenatal and Infancy Home Visiting by Nurses on Maternal Life Course and Government Spending: Follow-Up of a Randomized Trial Among Children at Age 12 Years." *Archives of Pediatric and Adolescent Medicine* 164:419–424.

Olds, David L., H. Kitzman, Robert Cole, and JoAnn Robinson. 1997. "Theoretical Foundations of a Program of Home Visitation for Pregnant Women and Parents of Young Children." *Journal of Community Psychology* 25:9–25.

Olds, David L., JoAnn Robinson, Ruth O'Brien, Dennis W. Luckey, Lisa M. Pettitt, Charles R. Henderson, Rosanna K. Ng, Karen L. Sheff, Jon Korfmacher, Susan Hiatt, and Ayelet Talmi. 2002. "Home Visiting by Paraprofessionals and by Nurses: A Randomized, Controlled Trial." *Pediatrics* 110:486–496.

O'Neill, Onora, and William Ruddick. 1979. *Having Children: Philosophical and Legal Reflections on Parenthood.* New York: Oxford University Press.

Overpeck, Mary D., Ruth A. Brenner, Ann C. Trumble, Lara B. Trifeletti, and Heinz W. Berendes. 1998. "Risk Factors for Infant Homicide in the United States." *New England Journal of Medicine* 339:1211–1216.

Parry, Geraint. 2001. "Émile: Learning to Be Men, Women, and Citizens." In *The Cambridge Companion to Rousseau*, ed. Patrick Riley, 247–271. Cambridge: Cambridge University Press.

Peterson, L., and S. Gable. 1998. "Holistic Injury Prevention." In *Handbook of Child Abuse Research and Treatment*, ed. J. R. Lutzker, 291–318. New York: Plenum.

Pine, D. S. 2001. "Affective Neuroscience and the Development of Social Anxiety Disorder." *Psychiatric Clinics of North America* 24:689–705.

——. 2003. "Developmental Psychobiology and Response to Threats: Relevance to Trauma in Children and Adolescents." *Biological Psychiatry* 53:796–808.

Pomeroy, Sarah B. 1999. *Families in Classical and Hellenistic Greece.* New York: Oxford University Press.

——. 2002. *Spartan Women.* New York: Oxford University Press.

Powers, Martin. 1991. *Art and Political Expression in Early China.* New Haven: Yale University Press.

Price, J. L., S. T. Carmichael, and W. C. Drevets. 1996. "Networks Related to the Orbital and Medial Prefrontal Cortex: A Substrate for Emotional Behavior?" *Progress in Brain Research* 107:523–536.

Puett, Michael J. 2001. *The Ambivalence of Creation: Debates Concerning Innovation and Artifice in Early China.* Stanford: Stanford University Press.

——. 2002. *To Become a God: Cosmology, Sacrifice, and Self-Divination in Early China.* Cambridge Mass.: Harvard University Asia Center.

——. 2011. "Sages, the Past, and the Dead." In *Mortality in Traditional Chinese Thought*, ed. Amy Olberding and Philip J. Ivanhoe, 225–248. Albany: State University of New York Press.

Quint, Janet C., Johannes M. Bos, and Denise F. Polit. 1997. *New Chance: Final Report on a Comprehensive Program for Disadvantaged Young Mothers and Their Children.* New York: Manpower Demonstration Research.

Raine, A., P. Brennan, and S. A. Mednick. 1994. "Birth Complications Combined with Early Maternal Rejection at Age 1 Year Predispose to Violent Crime at Age 18 Years." *Archives of General Psychiatry* 51:984–988.

Raphals, Lisa. 1998. *Sharing the Light: Representations of Women and Virtue in Early China.* Albany: State University of New York Press.

——. 2002. "A Woman Who Understood the Rites." In *Confucius and the Analects: New Essays*, ed. Bryan W. Van Norden, 275–302. New York: Oxford University Press.

Rawls, John. 1999. *A Theory of Justice.* Rev. ed. Cambridge, Mass.: Belknap.

——. 2001. *Justice As Fairness: A Restatement.* Ed. Erin Kelly. Cambridge, Mass.: Belknap.

Ray, Rebecca, Janet C. Gornick, and John Schmitt. 2009. "Parental Leave Policies in 21 Countries." Washington, D.C.: Center for Economic and Policy Research.

Reichman, Nancy E. 2005. "Low Birthweight and School Readiness." *Future of Children* 15:91–92.

Renfrew, Mary J., Felicia M. McCormick, Angela Wade, Beverley Quinn, and Therese Dowswell. 2012. "Support for Healthy Breastfeeding Mothers with Healthy Term Babies." *Cochrane Database of Systematic Reviews* 2012, issue 5, article no. CD001141.

Robinson, JoAnn L., and Marcela C. Acevedo. 2001. "Infant Reactivity and Reliance on Mother During Emotion Challenges: Prediction of Cognition and Language Skills in a Low-Income Sample." *Child Development* 72:402–415.

Robinson, JoAnn L., R. N. Emde, and J. Korfmacher. 1997. "Integrating an Emotional Regulation Perspective in a Program of Prenatal and Early Childhood Home Visitation." *Journal of Community Psychology* 25:59–75.

Rosemont, Henry, Jr. 1997. "Classical Confucian and Contemporary Feminist Perspectives on the Self: Some Parallels and Their Implications." In *Culture and Self: Philosophical and Religious Perspectives, East and West*, ed. Douglas Allen, 63–82. Boulder, Colo.: Westview.

Rosenlee, Li-Hsiang Lisa. 2006. *Confucianism and Women.* Albany: State University of New York Press.

Rousseau, Jean-Jacques. 1979. *Émile.* Trans. Allan Bloom. New York: Basic.

Ruddick, Sara. 1980. "Maternal Thinking." *Feminist Studies* 6:342–67.

——. 1995. *Maternal Thinking: Toward A Politics of Peace.* Boston: Beacon.

——. 1997. "The Idea of Fatherhood." In *Feminism and Families*, ed. Hilde Lindemann Nelson, 205–220. New York: Routledge.

——. 1998. "Care as Labor and Relationship." In *Norms and Values: Essays on the Work of Virginia Held*, ed. Joram C. Haber and Mark S. Halfon, 3–26. Lanham, Md.: Rowman and Littlefield.

Ryan, Rebecca M., Anne Martin, and Jeanne Brooks-Gunn. 2006. "Is One Parent Good Enough? Patterns of Mother and Father Parenting and Child Cognitive Outcomes at 24 and 36 Months." *Parenting: Science and Practice* 6:211–228.

Satz, Debra, and Rob Reich, eds. 2009. *Toward a Humanist Justice: The Political Philosophy of Susan Moller Okin*. New York: Oxford University Press.

Sawhill, Isabel. 2012. "20 Years Later, It Turns Out Dan Quayle Was Right About Murphy Brown and Unmarried Moms." *Washington Post*, May 25, 2012.

Saxon, D. W. 1978. "The Behavior of Infants Whose Mothers Smoke in Pregnancy." *Early Human Development* 2:363–369.

Schneewind, J. B. 1994. "Locke's Moral Philosophy." In *The Cambridge Companion to Locke*, ed. Vere Chappell, 199–225. New York: Cambridge University Press.

——. 1997. *The Invention of Autonomy: A History of Modern Moral Philosophy*. Cambridge: Cambridge University Press.

Schochet, Gordon. 1975. *Patriarchalism in Political Thought*. New York: Basic.

Schofield, Malcolm. 2003. "Stoic Ethics." In *The Cambridge Companion to the Stoics*, ed. Brad Inwood, 233–256. New York: Cambridge University Press.

Schore, Allan N. 1994. *Affect Regulation and the Origin of the Self: The Neurobiology of Emotional Development*. Mahwah, N.J.: Erlbaum.

——. 1997. "Early Organization of the Nonlinear Right Brain and Development of a Predisposition to Psychiatric Disorders." *Development and Psychopathology* 9:595–631.

——. 2003a. *Affect Dysregulation and Disorders of the Self*. New York: Norton.

——. 2003b. *Affect Regulation and the Repair of the Self*. New York: Norton.

——. 2012. *The Science of the Art of Psychotherapy*. New York: Norton.

Schwartz, Benjamin I. 1985. *The World of Thought in Ancient China*. Cambridge, Mass.: Belknap.

Schweinhart, Lawrence J. 2010. "The Challenge of the HighScope Perry Preschool Study." In *Childhood Programs and Practices in the First Decade of Life: A Human Capital Integration*, ed. Arthur J. Reynolds, Arthur J. Rolnick, Michelle M. Englund, and Judy A. Temple. 57–167. New York: Cambridge University Press.

Schwitzgebel, Eric. 2007. "Human Nature and Moral Education in Mencius, Xunzi, Hobbes, and Rousseau." *History of Philosophy Quarterly* 24:147–168.

Sellman, Derek. 2011. *What Makes a Good Nurse: Why the Virtues Are Important for Nurses*. London: Jessica Kingsley.

Seneca. 2011. *On Benefits*. Trans. Miriam Griffin and Brad Inwood. Chicago: University of Chicago Press.

Shklar, Judith N. 2001. "Rousseau's Images of Authority." In *The Cambridge Companion to Rousseau*, ed. Patrick Riley, 154–192. Cambridge: Cambridge University Press.

Shore, Rima. 1997. *Rethinking the Brain: New Insights Into Early Development*. Executive Summary. New York: Families and Work Institute.

Shun, Kwong-loi. 1997. *Mencius and Early Chinese Thought*. Stanford: Stanford University Press.

Sim, May. 2007. *Remastering Morals with Aristotle and Confucius*. New York: Cambridge University Press.

Slingerland, Edward G. 2003. *Confucius Analects*. Indianapolis: Hackett.

Sommer, Deborah. 2003. "Ritual and Sacrifice in Early Confucianism: Contacts with the Spirit World." In *Confucian Spirituality I*, ed. Tu Weiming and Mary Evelyn Tucker, 197–219. New York: Crossroad.

Stalnaker, Aaron. 2006. *Overcoming Our Evil*. Washington, D.C.: Georgetown University Press.

Star, Daniel. 2002. "Do Confucians Really Care? A Defense of the Distinctiveness of Care Ethics: A Reply to Chenyang Li." *Hypatia* 17: 77–106.

St. Pierre, Robert G., J. Swartz, B. Gamse, S. Murray, D. Deck, and P. Nickel. 1995. *National Evaluation of Even Start Family Literacy Program: Final Report*. Cambridge: Abt Associates.

Strayer, David L., Frank A. Drews, and William A. Johnston. 2003. "Cell Phone-Induced Failures of Visual Attention During Simulated Driving." *Journal of Experimental Psychology: Applied* 9:23–32.

Streissguth, A. P., P. D. Sampson, H. M. Barr, F. L. Bookstein, and H. C. Olson. 1994. "The Effects of Prenatal Exposure to Alcohol and Tobacco: Contributions From the Seattle Longitudinal Prospective Study and Implications for Public Policy." In *Prenatal Exposure to Toxicants: Developmental Consequences*, ed. H. L. Needleman and D. Bellinger, 148–183. Baltimore: Johns Hopkins University Press.

Swanton, Christine. 2005. *Virtue Ethics: A Pluralistic View*. New York: Oxford University Press.

Tamis-LeMonda, C., and M. H. Bornstein. 1989. "Habituation and Maternal Encouragement of Attention in Infancy as Predictors of Toddler Language, Play, and Representational Competence." *Child Development* 60:738–751.

Thompson, R. 1994. "Emotion Regulation: A Theme in Search of Definition." *Monographs of the Society for Research in Child Development* 59:25–52.

Tiwald, Justin. 2010. "Dai Zhen on Sympathetic Concern." *Journal of Chinese Philosophy* 37:76–89.

Tronto, Joan C. 1993. *Moral Boundaries: A Political Argument for an Ethic of Care*. New York: Routledge.

Van IJzendoorn, M. H. 1995. "Adult Attachment Representations, Parental Responsiveness, and Infant Attachment: A Meta-Analysis on the Predictive Validity of the Adult Attachment Interview." *Psychological Bulletin* 117:387–403.

Van Norden, Bryan W. 2007. *Virtue Ethics and Consequentialism in Early Chinese Philosophy*. New York: Cambridge University Press.

Van Norden, Bryan W., trans. 2008. *Mengzi: With Selections from Traditional Commentaries*. Indianapolis: Hackett.

Wakschlag, Lauren S., Benjamin B. Lahey, Rolf Loeber, Stephanie M. Green, Rachel A. Gordon, and Bennett L. Leventhal. 1997. "Maternal Smoking During Pregnancy and the Risk of Conduct Disorder in Boys." *Archives of General Psychiatry* 54:670–676.

Waldfogel, Jane. 2001. "International Policies Toward Parental Leave and Child Care." *Future of Children* 11:98–111.

Watson, Burton. 2007. *The Analects of Confucius*. New York: Columbia University Press.

Wilms, Sabine. 2005. "The Transmission of Medical Knowledge on 'Nurturing the Fetus' in Early China." *Asian Medicine: Tradition and Modernity* 1:276–314.

Wilson, Stephen Wilson. 2002. "Conformity, Individuality, and the Nature of Virtue." In *Confucius and the Analects: New Essays*, ed. Bryan W. Van Norden, 94–115. New York: Oxford University Press.

Wong, David B. 1989. "Universalism Versus Love with Distinctions: An Ancient Debate Revived." *Journal of Chinese Philosophy* 16:251–272.

Yearley, Lee H. 1990. *Mencius and Aquinas: Theories of Virtue and Conceptions of Courage*. Albany: State University of New York Press.

Yu, Jiyuan. 2007. *The Ethics of Confucius and Aristotle*. New York: Routledge.

Zuckerman, B., and E. R. Brown. 1993. "Maternal Substance Abuse and Infant Development." In *Handbook of Infant Mental Health*, ed. C. Zeanah Jr., 143–158. New York: Guilford.

INDEX

GPSR Authorized Representative: Easy Access System Europe, Mustamäe tee 50, 10621 Tallinn, Estonia, gpsr.requests@easproject.com